Lafayette

Courtesy of The Comte and Comtesse de Chambrun

Lafayette

A Biography by
Peter Buckman

**PADDINGTON
PRESS LTD**
NEW YORK & LONDON

For Jessica and Sasha
who will doubtless learn
as much from history
as we ever did

Library of Congress Cataloging in Publication Data

Buckman, Peter.
    Lafayette : a biography.

    Bibliography : p.
    Includes index.
    1. Lafayette, Marie Joseph Paul Yves Roch Gilbert du
Motier, marquis de, 1757-1834. 2. Statesmen—France—
Biography. I. Title.
DC146.L2B78   944.04'092'4 [B]   76-53319
ISBN 0-448-22060-1

Copyright © 1977 Peter Buckman
All rights reserved
Filmset by Tradespools Ltd., Frome, Somerset
Printed in England by Garden City Press Ltd., London & Letchworth
Designed by Colin Lewis

IN THE UNITED STATES
PADDINGTON PRESS LTD.
Distributed by
GROSSET & DUNLAP

IN THE UNITED KINGDOM
PADDINGTON PRESS LTD.

IN CANADA
Distributed by
RANDOM HOUSE OF CANADA LTD.

IN AUSTRALIA
Distributed by
ANGUS & ROBERTSON PTY. LTD.

Contents

Preface

MY EXCUSE FOR writing another life of Lafayette is that every generation has a new view of revolution. Lafayette, who was born in 1757 and who died in 1834, was involved in three revolutions (one in America and two in France); I felt I was involved in one near-miss (that of 1968), and though it never came to anything, the feeling of amazement remains. I was comforted to discover that history is full of people making the same mistakes as we made. Disappointment (and other distractions) lead many to give up activism – but not Lafayette. The skepticism with which I began my researches changed into admiration for an energy that no disappointment could diminish. Yet he was not so single-minded that he could not be distracted – by beautiful women, for example – or so opinionated as to be the bore many heroes become. He hated routine detail, preferred glory to power, needed constant reassurance, and was still brave enough to attack all those, from Napoleon to the "citizen-king" Louis-Philippe he himself enthroned, whose practice did not match the promise of their rhetoric. He became the hero of the Americans for the part he played in the War of Independence, and twice the hero of France for his leading roles in 1789 and 1830. In between, he was hated, attacked, imprisoned, exiled, ignored, and in opposition to all the rulers of France, through Directory, Consulate, Empire, Restoration, to the last of the Bourbons. Several times he might have taken supreme power, but that he never wanted. He modeled himself on Washington, whom he adopted as his "father," and his experience fighting for American independence convinced him that the cause of liberty would one day triumph everywhere. He was no pessimist.

It is as dangerous to draw lessons from history as to take refuge in it, and I intend to do neither. But the writing of history has changed since the last full-scale biography of Lafayette was published. In particular, we know much more about the crowds which were a feature of the French Revolution and which, if they do nothing else, create heroes like Lafayette, and unmake them again. (Their study has become something of an industry, to which my only objection is that the records, being those of the police, deal with those arrested or killed – and only a small proportion of a crowd consists of suckers or martyrs.) Thanks to the work of scholars like Richard Cobb, now Professor of Modern History at Oxford, we begin to recognize those involved in the French Revolution as ordinary people, with much the same preoccupations and weaknesses as our contemporaries. The motives of that small percentage of activists who made the American Revolution are being constantly re-examined: in short, we are in one of those periods of reappraisal when those we thought of as goodies and baddies turn out to be people as ambitious, enlightened, dedicated, dogmatic, confused, and corruptible as anyone we know. A good climate for biography.

It is a pleasure to thank all those who have helped me to write this book. My gratitude to Edward Lucie-Smith, who first put me onto Lafayette; to René de Chambrun, who talked to me about the cache of unpublished material he discovered, and is still in the process of sorting, and to Mme de Chambrun, who invited me to the Château Lagrange, which she has restored almost to the state it was in when Lafayette lived there; to Richard Cobb, for encouragement despite his antipathy for my subject; to the staff of the London Library, the British Museum Reading Room and the Library of Rhodes House, Oxford; to M. Anglès d'Auriac and the staff of the Library of Clermont-Ferrand, who opened their shelves to me even when the place was officially closed; to the librarian of the Municipal Library of Le Puy; to Mme Peyraube of the Bibliothèque Nationale, who not only allowed me into the sacred enclave known as the Hemicycle, but permitted me to wander among the bookstacks; to Brigitte Marger, former cultural attaché of the French embassy in London; to the concierge of Lafayette's birthplace, the château of Chavaniac, who allowed me an illicit look into the main salon; to my parents, for generous and deeply appreciated support; to John and Barbara Richardson, for their neighborly kindness which enabled me to go off on research trips, and much else besides; to Tina Walker, who typed the manuscript; to Ellen Crampton, for preparing the index; and to Rosemarie, who supported me through the various crises with which writers are afflicted, and whose generous and constructive criticism improved the book out of all recognition. The scholars who have preceded me in the field I acknowledge in the Notes on Sources. For all errors and omissions, I alone accept responsibility.

Part One: An Affluent Society

1
The Rearing of an Aristocrat

REPUTATION CAN BE the most ruinous of legacies, and by the middle of the eighteenth century the Lafayettes were thoroughly impoverished by it. For seven hundred years they had chased after military glory and the end result was that most of them died young on the field of battle. Such a career took its toll in sons as well as cash, but none of them ever thought of changing it. To be descended from great and famous soldiers imposed obligations both of honor and class, and for the eldest sons of the Marquis de Lafayette,* no other profession than that of bearing arms for their king was considered. Indeed, for the nobility of the first rank, the *noblesse de l'épée* to which they belonged, the army was the only career open. National expansion was carried on by force of arms rather than commercial treaty; commissions in the army were kept very much in the families who ran the country. To get a commission you had to be noble, but as in every business, the best jobs went to the best-connected people. The ambitious strove to improve their connections, especially at court, where all favors were distributed; the less ambitious merely served their turn as their fathers had done before them.

The Lafayettes were not particularly ambitious. They had had marshals in the family and had acquired the high rank of marquis, but they were content to carry on tradition rather than enhance it. Lafayette's father Michel was the first to join the estate of Chavaniac* to the title, and he was born in this squat little château in the heart of the Auvergne, an appendage to rather than an eminence in the higgledy-piggledy village whose name it shared. The Auvergne was

---

* The spelling of the family name here adopted, and likewise the name of the family château, is that used by Lafayette in his own published memoirs. Before the revolution, Lafayette was written in two words – La Fayette – but after the abolition of feudal privileges (August 4, 1789), he ran them together as a single, democratic surname, and never went back to the practice.

not a rich region of France, and was a long way from the center of events: to walk around Chavaniac is to be in scenery somehow suited to the lesser and unfashionable gentry who lived in the area. Solid stone houses huddle together against the wind that blows off the mountains and across the wooded plains; the land is hard and yields its resources only grudgingly. The feudal estates, such as that owned by the Lafayettes, scarcely made large profits. In winter, there was so little work that laborers had to trek to the nearest towns to earn enough to feed their starving families.

The Lafayettes had to struggle to keep up appearances, a struggle that can be as wearing as that against sheer poverty. Michel de Lafayette's one concern was to get a commission in a good regiment; to carry on this family tradition, which was all he'd grown up to do, he needed money or influence. The traditional way of procuring both was by arranging a good marriage.

It was explained to Lafayette's father that it was impossible to find "a young woman of good birth, and with a considerable fortune, who would be willing to live in the country." A dowry was a form of investment, and the Lafayettes could offer precious little except the distinction of their title. Michel de Lafayette had to be content with Julie de la Rivière, whom he described as "no beauty, but neither is she ugly": he was happy chiefly because her connections promised a colonelcy in the grenadiers. His mother, a hardened lady who had been married at twelve, would have preferred a cash settlement, but she had little enough with which to bargain.

Michel married, collected his commission and went happily off to maneuvers, leaving his young wife, who had come straight from a convent, to cope under the eye of his mother. There was little to amuse her, and the only companion of her own generation was her husband's unmarried sister. The new marquise saw her husband but rarely, though he must have come home for Christmas in 1756, for by the time he went off again, this time on active service, she was pregnant. Michel de Lafayette hoped to be home for the birth, but he never made it, either because of the demands of the army since the Seven Years' War had begun or because he couldn't afford the journey. His son was born on September 6, 1757, and, with a distinguished covey of godparents from both sides of the family, was christened Marie Joseph Paul Yves Roch Gilbert du Motier de La Fayette.

Michel de Lafayette never saw his son. He enjoyed the war because he could live relatively cheaply, but even then he was bothered about money. The officers were responsible for supplying their troops, and this was particularly expensive in a cavalry regiment such as his. Appearances still had to be kept up and Michel lived gallantly beyond his means – so much so that his mother had to lend him money to buy two expensive horses, which was a severe strain on her tight budget. Michel was properly grateful and tried to show a military ardor by complaining that his superior officers would not engage the enemy. The truth was that the French army was in as poor shape as the French treasury. At the age of twenty-seven Michel was needlessly exposed to English artillery fire, and died during the battle of Minden (August 1, 1759), one of a series of humiliating French defeats. Shortly before his second birthday, his son thus became Marquis de La Fayette, Baron de Vissac, Seigneur de St-Romain, Fix, and other villages around. The new marquis's widowed mother abandoned Chavaniac for her own family in Paris as soon as she decently could, and Lafayette was left in the care of his grandmother and aunt.

The dowager marquise, who knew enough about survival to enjoy a reputation for country wisdom for some distance around, applied to King Louis XV for a pension to bring up her grandson properly. The family of officers killed in His Majesty's service was entitled to something, but that did not always mean they got it. The Lafayette connections were put to work, and the result was an annual pension of 600 *livres**, a modest sum in keeping with their aspirations. It is worth noting that in a few years these financial aspirations became considerably elevated. His grandmother so arranged matters, by judicious use of her funds, that the revenues and feudal rights that went with Lafayette's titles became his alone, and she also saw to it that he became seigneur of Chavaniac. But this was small beer compared to Lafayette's mother's expectations. When she had married Michel she had nothing, but the death of her brother made her – and afterwards her son – heir to her father's substantial estate, which had an income of 120,000 *livres* a year. This was not an uncommon fortune among the smart set in Paris, but in the Auvergne it was a great deal – even if none of it trickled through to help the dowager marquise raise her grandson.

Lafayette grew up surrounded by women who watched the pennies as carefully as they watched him, who worshiped the memory of his dead father and the glorious tradition that was his inheritance. He saw his mother only in the summer, when every fashionable Parisian fled the capital, and what little he knew of her he adored. Neither she nor her mother-in-law showed him much affection; for that he relied on his aunts – Marguerite who was particularly attached to the memory of her brother, and Charlotte

---

* The *livre*, as J. M. Thompson explained in *The French Revolution* (Oxford, 1943), was not a coin but a standard of value, used chiefly for reckoning incomes. The gold *louis*, for example, was worth 24 *livres*; the silver *écu*, 3 *livres*. As to their contemporary value, inflation makes any estimate worthless. A farm-laborer in the 1750s might earn 50 *livres* in a year, a carter 70, a servant under 20. Six hundred *livres* is therefore good for an employer, but no fortune.

who, being widowed and without a place to live, had come back home. She brought with her a daughter who became Lafayette's only playmate. He was four, his cousin a year older.

Lafayette's was a childhood governed by fixed custom. Nobles were allowed to mix only with their peers and this severely restricted the social circle of the inhabitants of the Château de Chavaniac. As a small boy, Lafayette was usually left with his girl cousin in the low, dark rooms of his fortress-like home; whenever he went out the villagers silently took off their hats to him. For the rural nobility, life was a fairly solitary affair, quite unlike the social whirl of the towns. A seigneur had obligations, such as attending weddings, baptisms, and funerals, but Lafayette was too young for that, and doubtless his grandmother or aunts stood in for him. Hunting and fishing, which only those of noble birth were allowed to pursue, were the chief open-air occupations apart from farming – but when a prosperous provincial noble gave a party, it was a mark of honor to be as extravagantly generous as possible. In 1765 in the Dauphiné, just to the east of the Auvergne, a seigneur and his hundred guests managed to eat their way through twelve sheep, one and a half calves, a young boar, a large sturgeon, and a hundred pounds of beef. The peasants of the Auvergne subsisted chiefly on pork. There were said to be more pigs than houses in the region.

Few among the provincial gentry bothered about politics, since to be effective required expensive bribes for those connected with the court. There were large numbers of nobles reduced to penury by trying to keep up appearances, but they did no more than grumble or petition the king for relief. Among the better-off, much time and money was spent in trying to keep up with their neighbors, whether in decorations or in stocking a library, which would at least have to contain leather-bound volumes of Voltaire or Rousseau (both in exile). Entertainment lay in the standard country-house pastimes of charades, cards, games, and music. The only sign of such pleasures in Chavaniac today is Lafayette's old backgammon board.

In the winter, while the villagers shivered and starved, those nobles who could afford it decamped to the nearest town, where at least there was more variety in social life. The Lafayettes had a large mansion in the market town of Brioude, in which they doubtless did all the entertaining necessary to keep up their position and contacts. They also had another château at Vissac, an isolated but picturesque village, to which they might go for a change in the summer. In all, their social life was totally uneventful – which is doubtless why Lafayette's mother stayed away as much as she could.

When he was five years old, Lafayette was put in the charge of a learned Jesuit. The following year, however, as the result of a long factional struggle, the Jesuits were suppressed by the Pope and the young marquis came under the care of the Abbé Fayon. With him he learned how to read and write, in Latin and French, and he also endured hour upon hour of heraldic history. Fayon stayed with his pupil until long after he was married and, although Lafayette was attached to him, he later wrote that his tutor was "full of prejudices and lacking in those qualities which a man who is destined to live in the great world should have." But that was written when he had been a man of the world for over half a century: as a child, his horizons were limited to the skies and hills of the Auvergne, and his dreams of glory, so carefully implanted by his loving aunts, fulfilled only in fantasy.

One such fantasy, conceived when he was around eight years old, was to rid the region of a scourge that everyone dreaded, the "Beast of Gévaudan." The creature killed cattle on the nearby hills, and shocked talk had it eating women, children, and "shepherdesses renowned for their beauty." This discriminating monster was also rumored to put even armed travelers to flight. Over a hundred years later stories of the horror still abounded. They reached the ears of Robert Louis Stevenson, when traversing the Gévaudan with his famous donkey Modestine, and he decided that the beast must have been "the Napoleon Bonaparte of wolves." Lafayette dreamed of meeting the animal on one of his walks, and killing it with his bare hands. Far from setting eyes on it, however, he was mortified to learn that a hunter giving his name as "Lafayette" had reported seeing the beast, but was too frightened to kill it. The young marquis was stung into writing an indignant letter to the journal that carried this slander, but he was prevented from sending it. The animal was later killed by one of the king's own hunters, after a royal reward had been offered. It turned out to be a wolf of no more than average size.

Testimony that Lafayette was an able pupil was given by the Marquis de Bouillé, a kinsman who visited Chavaniac when the boy was ten. Bouillé found him "singularly learned for his age, astonishingly advanced in thought and reasoning, and extraordinary by reason of his thinking, his wisdom, his moderation, his composure, and his discernment. Nevertheless," this encomium, written forty years later when Bouillé had become a bitter enemy of Lafayette, continued, "I discovered in this child a germ of conceit, and even ambition." This would hardly be surprising in a child raised on a diet of dead glories.

When he was eleven, it was decided by his mother and her family that Lafayette should join her in Paris to start his training as an officer and to be groomed as a courtier fit to handle his future wealth. He worshiped his mother with a passion enhanced by distance, but he was upset to leave the family château, his young cousin, and the austere hills, village, and people who owed him allegiance. He had never before left the Auvergne, but it was a question of money and he had no choice in the matter.

Paris would have been a rude surprise to any provincial youth. It was noisy, smelly, and dangerous. It was the changeable arbiter of fashion, much more so than the court at Versailles under the aging King Louis XV. What made it terrifying was the closeness of those contrasts between rich and poor that the spaciousness of the countryside failed to force on the observer. The streets, however elegantly illuminated by six thousand torches, presented extreme hazards – not so much from criminals as from traffic, gutters, and sewage. There were no pavements, and if the pedestrian were not knocked down by the wheels of a carriage, he could be bowled over by the Great Dane that fashion decreed should precede the vehicle (as happened to Jean-Jacques Rousseau in 1776). When it rained, twenty thousand gutters gushed straight down into the streets, turning them into mudbaths whose centers streamed with excrement. Taffeta umbrellas were used by bewigged gallants as shelter while they tiptoed between puddles. If the ears weren't battered by the noise of wheels, the nose was assaulted by the odors, which, apart from sewage, included choking smoke and the reek of blood from animals slaughtered in the very shop-fronts of the butchers. Then there were the cries of those selling water, hats, rabbit skins, fish, or vegetables; and the cries of those publicly executed, broken on the wheel, for minor crimes.

Lafayette, traveling with the Abbé Fayon, noted with surprise that no one took his hat off to him any more. He was taken to live in the Luxembourg Palace, where courtiers who did not have town houses occupied apartments. The de la Rivières, his mother's people, shared an apartment with the Comte and Comtesse de Lusignem, to whom they were related. At last Lafayette came into contact with male members of his family: his great-grandfather, the Comte de la Rivière, and his grandfather, the Marquis de la Rivière (actually the comte's son-in-law), who was reputed to be a miser and spent most of his time on his estates in Brittany. Although Lafayette was proud of the Breton blood in his veins and the lands which provided his fortune, it was to the Auvergne of his childhood that he returned whenever he had the chance.

The gossip of Paris in 1768, when Lafayette arrived, was concerned with the rowdy students of the Sorbonne, the rising price of food, the growing threat to law and order from organized criminal gangs, and the heinous crime of the Comte de Sade. The latter, a gentleman in the service of the Prince de Condé, had offered a job to a woman who had asked for alms, conducted her to his country house with the utmost decorum, and then suddenly locked her up and demanded that she strip. When she refused, he drew his sword, ripped off her

13

clothes, gagged and handcuffed her, and proceeded to make cuts on the fleshiest parts of her body, smoothing in wax – which his defendants claimed was merely an ointment with which he was experimenting. He then left her to meditate on what further outrages he might commit, during which time she escaped and staggered to the nearest village where a doctor called the authorities. De Sade was arrested, but his family negotiated a cash settlement with the injured maiden (who was thirty-two years old), and shut the errant comte up in a château. The king, whose own appetites, while large, were never vicious, confirmed the order immuring de Sade. The middle classes complained that only the influence and privileges of the nobility prevented proper justice being executed on the guilty man. In the very same month as de Sade's first condemnation, seven young men with no influence at all were publicly hanged, and their bodies burnt, for stealing sacred vases from churches.

The destiny of a young and rich noble like Lafayette was fixed by his elders in accordance with etiquette. He would naturally become an officer in the army, and be schooled not only in the military arts but in the social graces that were an indispensable part of noble behavior. Though he was only eleven, a commission in a suitable regiment would soon be arranged for him. There was already talk of marriage and of presentation at court, the expensive but necessary opening to the lush galleries of power. Thereafter he could expect to play the courtier, serve on maneuvers, distinguish himself if there were another war (which all young nobles professed to hope for despite the dismal state of the French treasury) and see his family for a few months each year. He was not expected to worry about money: that, like everything else, was arranged for him. It was a life with all the security of almost total predictability.

The most expensive school in Paris was chosen for him, the Collège du Plessis, next to the Sorbonne and not far from the Luxembourg. Most nobles lived in the college, the richer ones in private apartments where they had their servants and tutors. The fees were some 650 *livres* a year – more than Lafayette's annual pension – and for that he was taught smatterings of theology, law, rhetoric, mathematics, and history. The fees did not include the cost of lighting, heating, furniture, servants, and the services of the wigmaker, which were indispensable, for when the young gentlemen went out to dine they had to wear embroidered coats and swords and have their curls powdered and pomaded. To protect themselves against the weather, or perhaps the insults of urchins, they also wore little hair-bags to cover their pigtails.

Schooling was by rote – repeating what the teacher said without alteration or embellishment – and was conducted in Latin, a subject in which Lafayette excelled. He later claimed that he would have won a prize for Latin composition but for missing out a line in his fair copy, which resulted in every wrong word being counted as a separate mistake.

History was the subject he most enjoyed, and he made a personal hero of Vercingetorix, the Gallic chief who had defended the Auvergne against Caesar. For two out of the four years he spent at the college, Lafayette became deeply religious, so much so that even his confessor told him he envied his devotion. The reason might have been the example of his mother who, though having finished her mourning and been presented at court, had, according to her son, "plunged into religion with all the strength of her character" ever since the death of her husband.

Corporal punishment was the commonest form of discipline for the young nobles, and Lafayette, claiming to have been a leader of his fellows, once tried to organize a revolt on behalf of one unjustly chastised. Lafayette's gang were all ready to fight the authorities, even at sword-point, but the attempt was foiled by being completely ignored. Despite the wealth and influence of their families these noble pupils were quite subdued by their teachers: years later, when his reputation as defender of liberty was well established, Lafayette recalled that nothing displeased him about the school except its spirit of "dependence." He also remembered an essay set by his teacher in rhetoric on "the perfect horse." Lafayette described his ideal as an animal who, when threatened with the whip, threw his rider. Perhaps this was less evidence of precocious libertarian ideas than wishful thinking by a boy whose life was supervised down to the last detail.

When he was thirteen, Lafayette's mother died after a short illness and was followed a few weeks later by her own father. The death of a mother must always be painful, especially at the beginning of adolescence. Doubtless Lafayette was many times reminded of the duties attached to his position, for although an orphan, he was now a very wealthy one. His great-grandfather, the Comte de la Rivière, took charge of his Paris education, and the de Lusignems tried to act as foster-parents. In Chavaniac his grandmother and aunts looked after his interests with the help of a trusted estate-manager. If Lafayette grieved, he showed it only in a certain shyness of manner; if he had lost the somewhat insubstantial support of his mother, the guide-rails of the career that had been planned for him were solid enough. He was not allowed to think too much: that too was arranged for him.

The Comte de la Rivière saw to it that his young great-grandson's desire to wear a uniform was satisfied by a commission in the regiment he had himself commanded, the Black Musketeers. As a member of that company, distinguished chiefly for its rowdiness,

Lafayette had the honor of being reviewed by the king and of riding to Versailles on horseback in full regimental dress. Talk of marriage now became serious. For the benefit of his cousin at Chavaniac, the fourteen-year-old Lafayette sardonically described the "arrangements" being attempted on his behalf, referring to himself in the third person, as though even he doubted his identity. His Auvergnat neighbor La Colombe had tried to arrange a match with a lady some six years older than Lafayette, but it had come to nothing. "There is another offer pending," wrote Lafayette, "but we'll have to come down a peg or two." He went on to describe the haggling – a regiment of cavalry in exchange for a smallish dowry – and how the negotiators seemed to be getting upset with each other. He also showed himself to be a sharp and witty observer of his seniors, presenting his cousin with a digest of court gossip, and writing of a newly fashionable hat whose "contours and compartments" could be described only with the aid of a compass.

His military education was now undertaken in earnest, and he was sent to the Académie de Versailles, the most exclusive military school in France. A former army officer named Margelay was added to his household, which still contained the Abbé Fayon, to teach him practical and military matters. He learned to ride, dance, and drill alongside the Comte d'Artois, the king's grandson. He was rich enough to afford a good stable, and he became a reasonable horseman. But he was awkward and gawky: he usually lost at tennis, and was never any good at dancing.

Versailles, where beady-eyed courtiers already cast covetous glances at Lafayette's income, was dominated by Mme du Barry, Louis XV's last mistress. The king so rarely took decisions himself that his loyal subjects blamed every catastrophe on those surrounding him. The most common and most serious grievance was the rising price of bread and the royal failure to control the monopolists who were making a fortune by keeping prices high. Bread riots were common, and even Paris's ancient Parlement (its magistrature) felt called upon to ask the king to regulate the commerce in corn. Parisians were shattered by the king's furious reaction: all the members of that venerable, and hardly radical, body were exiled, fathers being ordered to retire to villages miles from those to which their sons had been sent, where it was difficult to find food and shelter and dangerous for those of delicate constitution. The Parisians in 1771 felt that these events "came from the distant past" and, though outraged, were sufficiently wary of the arbitrary forces of law and order to keep their feelings to themselves. The king's chancellor hired crowds to "revel" in the streets so that he could tell the monarch how happy his subjects were. Those hoping for the dawn of a new age turned to the Duc d'Orléans, the first prince of the blood royal, who was promptly disgraced by the king when he ventured to criticize the royal policy. Thereafter the young dauphin, and his new bride Marie-Antoinette, were looked to as the hope of France, even though, when their wedding had been celebrated in the capital, several hundred people had been killed in a traffic disaster caused by police negligence (May 1770). While Mme du Barry was cast as villainess by the citizens of the capital, and her influence seen in every banishment and dictatorial edict, and when the king presented her with a carriage worth 60,000 *livres* while so many went hungry, the activities of Marie-Antoinette and the dauphin received praise beyond their deserts.

Lafayette was on vacation at Chavaniac in 1772 when he was told his great-grandfather had arranged a marriage with the Noailles family, one of the most important in France. He was nearly fifteen, his fiancée, Adrienne, daughter of the Duc d'Ayen, was twelve. The marriage had been opposed by the bride-to-be's mother, the Duchesse d'Ayen who, having educated her five surviving daughters herself, and taught them to be tolerant and independent-minded, objected to the youth and orphaned condition of her proposed son-in-law. Being a woman of a greatly pious and reserved nature – in complete contrast to her husband the Duc d'Ayen, who was a witty courtier and a fashionable atheist – she even regarded Lafayette's fortune as a spiritual disadvantage. Her husband, furious at her opposition, refused to stay in their mansion in Paris until she changed her mind. This she finally did, on condition that the marriage be postponed for two years, and the education of both betrothed remain uninterrupted during that time. Reconciled to his wife, the Duc d'Ayen and the Comte de la Rivière drew up a tentative contract of marriage, the details of which were still to be negotiated. Lafayette was reported "quite content" at the proposal, not that there was much he could do. This was a matter of high finance and personal considerations had little part in it. Adrienne de Noailles, the other half of the agreement, was not told of her fate for eighteen months, at her mother's insistence. But she and Lafayette were allowed to meet in between whiles, on drives, walks, and in the Noailles mansion.

When, after prolonged haggling, the financial arrangements of the marriage were agreed – a dowry of 400,000 *livres*, of which only half was ever paid (this sum was twice that received by the Duc d'Ayen on *his* marriage) – Lafayette was absorbed into his new family. He went to live in their Versailles house, seeing his great-grandfather and the de Lusignems in Paris once a fortnight. Shortly afterwards, through the strenuous efforts of the Duc d'Ayen, he was commissioned into the Noailles regiment of cavalry as a second-lieutenant. He continued his studies at the Académie de

Versailles, until on Monday, April 11, 1774, his marriage to Adrienne was celebrated in the Paris mansion of the bride's family. The noble luminaries who witnessed for bride and groom, as well as those attending the reception, were testimony to the prestige of the Noailles, whose sophistication and influence were quite bewildering to the marquis. The old king himself had consented to sign the marriage contract. It was a glamorous match, at least as far as the revenues and power of the partners' families were concerned. Adrienne, aged fourteen, was considered quite pretty; Lafayette, at sixteen, was tall, red-haired, gangly, angular of feature, but quite presentable. The two seemed to like each other, which was as much as anyone could expect in their position.

One of Lafayette's closest friends was the worldly and witty Comte de Ségur, who wrote of these times in terms that are instantly recognizable. His circle of young nobles, to which Lafayette belonged, was bored by the old system and habits of Louis XV, and loudly applauded satirical attacks on them. The lassitude of the aged king, who wielded absolute power (in theory) for sixty years, was mistaken by some for liberalism but, as in the case of the Paris Parlement, any serious attempt to interfere with the royal prerogative was rapidly quashed. The arguments between Jansenists and Molinists, each claiming to represent the true faith, that absorbed the court were ridiculed as irrelevant by the agnostic young. It was a permissive age – a tone set by the monarch, who consorted openly with his mistress Mme du Barry – and this meant that, for those in the charmed circle of the court at least, the rigors of the law could easily be evaded. The Parlements, as guardians of public morality, were constantly banning books they regarded as corrupting, but this only made the public read them more eagerly: to be censored was a necessary accolade for a fashionable author. Diderot, Montesquieu, Voltaire, Rousseau and the Abbé Raynal – the only one of this group Lafayette claimed to have read – all suffered this fate.

Raynal, whom Lafayette's mother had admired, wrote *A Philosophical and Political History of the Institutions and Trade of the Europeans in the Indies*, which was published in Amsterdam in 1770 and which, despite its title, quickly became a bestseller. Even Bonaparte, when an officer at Autun, dedicated some historical essays to its author. Following Diderot and his *Encyclopedia*, the book tried to show how economic concerns dominate nations, and it criticized the greed, intolerance, and corruption that the Europeans brought to the New World. Raynal admired the Quakers of Pennsylvania, which chimed in nicely not only with the passion for all things English that was sweeping aristocratic France, but with the preoccupation with the "noble savage" that Rousseau made so fashionable. America, it seemed, was the home of this fabled creature, where the simple virtues of self-sufficiency were allied to the tolerant democratic values that the English Revolution (of 1688) was supposed to represent. Among the English inhabitants of America who were lionized in France, none was more distinguished than Benjamin Franklin, who first visited Paris in 1767. His wit and intellect, as well as the plain values he was taken to represent, made him the most sought-after dinner guest among the fashionable liberals in the capital, where his inventions were no less respected than his philosophical writings.

If England was admired by the philosophically-minded for the relatively bloodless way in which she had curbed the absolute power of her monarch, and for the liberty that her subjects were supposed to enjoy, it was the "English style" in leisure, dress, gardens, education, and even domestic servants that really caught on in fashionable France. Since the disasters of the Seven Years' War that had ended in 1763 with the defeat of the French by the English and her allies, it was the patriotic duty of the nobility to long for revenge – but meanwhile they imported English gardeners to landscape their châteaux (one banker spent 14 million *livres* on getting his just right), English horses, jockeys, and grooms so as to indulge in the national passion for horse-racing and its attendant betting, English carriages, English dogs, hounds with which to hunt, English card games like "whisk," and English vices like dressing their children in tight clothing and putting them through various tortures to make them "fit." Even the increasing suicide rate in Paris was ascribed to an imitation of English faults without their attendant virtues. As testimony to the international spirit that animated the privileged and civilized members of French society, a writer like Laurence Sterne found himself welcomed and admired by the smart set in both Paris and Versailles even in the middle of the Seven Years' War. France and England were the two major powers and, though traditionally enemies, their frontiers were open to demonstrate their liberality and hospitality. Naturally they were more open to those who attacked their rivals – England had entertained the exiled Voltaire as France did the outlawed John Wilkes – and spies and double agents swarmed around the influential in both capitals. Equally naturally, both powers could be relied upon to give short shrift to those who attacked the common bases on which each system rested, the privileges of royalty, wealth, and title.

The highest ranks in the army, and the most lucrative and influential government posts, were reserved for the nobility. But these things did not come cheap, and the snobbery of wealth came to equal, if not outshine, the snobbery of an ancient title. Life at court, the center of the market-place in jobs, was ruinously expensive because of the cost of bribes and of keeping up appearances. A rare instance of charity among the ladies of the court occurred when the diamonds which fashion decreed should drip from every appendage, were handed round to those who could not afford their own. For the truly grand, to be extravagantly generous was a matter of honor. Paris and the court, indeed, got themselves such a luxurious reputation that gold-digging foreigners swarmed over to seek their fortunes, naturally raising prices for the native gallants. The one consolation for the big spenders was that, if they landed the post they wanted, they could expect a 10 percent to 15 percent return on their investment.

And yet, despite the supposedly pernicious effects of patronage, France boasted the most efficient administrative machinery in Europe. The monarch relied on able and devoted men with a deep understanding of the political art of the possible. He was also surrounded by bird-brained courtiers who pushed pretty women at him in the hope of getting them adopted as the royal mistress (a sure vein of patronage), by politicians of unparalleled venality, by ruthless nobles of the administrative class (*noblesse de la robe*) endlessly ambitious for betterment, by jealous relatives, and by penniless aristocrats who had given their all in his service and who hoped in vain for reward.

Then he had to contend with the ambitious young nobles like Ségur and his friends, who were anxiously waiting to take over from the "old guard." As part of the dauphin's circle, they only had to bide their time until he became king. With the lightest of duties at court or in the garrisons where they fulfilled their military obligations, they devoted themselves to society, to dinner parties and smart talk (scandalizing their elders by their libertarian sentiments), to playing tennis, football, or badminton, billiards, chess, dominoes, backgammon, dice and other gambling games of chance, to dalliance at picnics or dances and to attending masked balls where neither expense nor reputation was spared. They broke the sacred social codes by hobnobbing with their inferiors (mistresses offered one effective way of mingling the classes); they dressed outlandishly; they felt themselves invincible. But of course they never went too far. The public careers for which they prepared themselves were governed by rules they dared not flout: if they wanted to get on, they were going to have to conform, sooner or later.

Lafayette mooned somewhat unhappily around the court at Versailles, where he got himself a reputation for being cold and aloof, simply because of his shyness. He was present when Mme du Barry used a mild bit of slang to express disappointment when her royal consort beat her at cards, and he noted the king's embarrassment at this. Cards (*cavagnol*, a form of lotto, was played for hours on end), eating, and above all hunting were the royal passions; appetites for these seemed to distinguish the Bourbon family. The king's son had actually died from overeating; his daughters, who lived lives of extreme regularity and boredom, relieved themselves only by picking at delicacies and tippling at wine at any given opportunity, day or night, from stores they kept hidden in their chambers. The old king disliked ceremonial and was always on the move. He used to visit his lovers in a house he had bought to hide them from the jealousy of his most celebrated mistress, Mme du Pompadour, but her successor Mme du Barry made him get rid of it: it had acquired a popular reputation as a harem where young virgins were regularly ravished.

Louis XV paid little attention to the wishes either of his subjects or his children. To the latter he never gave advice, nor did he allow them the slightest authority. As for his subjects, he learned regularly of their opinions by having their letters opened by the postmaster-general, but in his last years he got progressively more out of touch with them, and more superstitiously concerned about his own survival. His popularity waned accordingly. When, in 1744, he had been seriously ill at Metz, around six thousand masses for his recovery were recorded and paid for at Notre-Dame. Thirteen years later, after an attempt on his life by Damiens, there were six hundred, and in April 1774, during his last illness, there were only three. He was carried off by smallpox, of which he had, in common with most of his subjects, a morbid terror. Lafayette was at the Trianon Palace, where the king and his mistress were dining when he fell mortally ill. But either the young marquis thought everyone, especially his omniscient father-in-law, would know what had happened, or he was too embarrassed to break the news: his family expressed astonishment, even anger, when it came out that he had witnessed the scene and said nothing.

With the accession of Louis XVI (May 1774), the Duc d'Ayen decided that his son-in-law's career in whose progress he was greatly disappointed, needed another push. He had tried to get Lafayette commissioned as a captain, but had been refused on grounds of the candidate's youth (he was sixteen). A new king, however, might mean that the minister for war would be more open to persuasion. (It is worth noting that a captaincy could be obtained for some 40,000 francs, from which sum the government received a healthy rake-off.) The duc was successful. Lafayette was granted all the honors and privileges of a captain's rank, although he was not to take actual command of his company for two years. The duc then packed him off to Metz, where his regiment was stationed, despite the fact that Adrienne was pregnant.

Adolescents arriving at camp with their commissions first had to learn to drill under a senior officer. Only when they were themselves capable of drilling recruits were they accepted as officers. As a captain, Lafayette's responsibilities would have included recruiting, equipping, and maintaining his troop, as well as replacing them, at his own expense, if they were killed. So much profiteering went on, at the expense of both soldier and the king, that the charge of paying, feeding, and clothing their men had been removed from the captains. Before that happened, it was estimated they could make a profit of 35,000 *livres* in a winter, by falsifying the rolls with non-existent soldiers, claiming false expenses, cheating the soldiers of their food and making them pay for equipment the officers were supposed to supply.

The ordinary soldier in barracks lived a totally regimented life and had to share a bed four-feet wide with two other men. (One of the great reforms carried out under the new king was to reduce the number of sharers to two.) The officer, outside service hours, was free to eat, sleep, and go where he liked; and he spent nearly half the year on holiday. The tedious business of drilling was performed by sergeants, so each noble officer had time on his hands. Some used this to study and write; most used it to dance, brawl, and find girls. A town like Metz offered many distractions: Lafayette wrote to Adrienne telling her of dinners and entertainments and the local beauties, whom he judged "but middling." He reserved his enthusiasm for three ladies of the château of Melet, which at first he had found "dreadfully boring" but which, because of their presence, became "excessively agreeable" – to such an extent that he let two posts go by without writing home.

When he returned from his first tour of duty in Metz, Lafayette decided to be inoculated against smallpox. The disease had already ravaged his mother-in-law, who supported him in his plan and came to look after him and Adrienne in the house they took for the experiment. With child and son-in-law both in a delicate condition, the Duchesse d'Ayen's presence must have been a mixed blessing: since the young couple lived in the Noailles mansion, the chance to be alone, even with a mild dose of smallpox, might have been welcome.

Once recovered, Lafayette escaped the net of his in-laws by paying a visit to Chavaniac, which he had not done since his marriage. Being pregnant, Adrienne could not make the journey, although she had already corresponded with her husband's aunts, and had been commissioned by them to buy the trousseau for the marriage of Lafayette's cousin. Considering that Lafayette's grandmother had been mistress of Chavaniac at twelve, such trust in a fourteen-year-old was not so surprising.

One person thought court life had changed the marquis for the worse: his old tutor the Abbé Fayon, who had remained with him all these years, and who made the journey to the family château with him. "In the course of our drive," wrote Lafayette, "he discovered that I was lacking in prudence and devoid of principles. This provided us with much to argue over. He is of the opinion that I am a good-for-nothing, but that at least I have a good heart." Fayon also attacked his pupil for abandoning the faith and devoutness he had once possessed. But agnosticism or atheism were part of the fashion.

Returning to Paris, Lafayette was a member, by duty rather than inclination, of the trend-setting circle led by the new Queen Marie-Antoinette. The queen loved going to the theater or opera, horse-racing or taking nocturnal walks on the terraces of Versailles (without her husband). According to her mentor, the Austrian ambassador, she never did anything serious, and read "indecent books." She also rejected her mother's advice to wear a corset. She loved jewels, and above all gambling, which she very often did all night. Huge sums changed hands, and when she lost the king paid her debts without a murmur. Lafayette obviously found these marathon sessions very boring, for he acquired an aversion to all forms of gambling which lasted throughout his life.

He did, however, join a wining, dining, and dancing society, the Society of the Wooden Sword, which included the king's brothers, and often the queen, among its revellers. In attempting to keep up with the drinking capacity of his brother-in-law the Vicomte de Noailles, Lafayette had to be carried home, causing much mirth. However, his grave demeanor was just right for him to take the part of the attorney-general in a parody of the proceedings of the Paris Parlement, which the Society of the Wooden Sword put on to amuse themselves. The older courtiers and ministers took strong objection to such frivolity, and to the fact that members of the royal family were consorting with such dangerous radicals. An attempt at censure, however, was foiled by Ségur, who told the king of all they had done, making the monarch laugh so much he proclaimed himself one of their number. Another triumph of the young set was to get the antique costumes of the time of Henri IV adopted as the official dress of the queen's balls. Such fashions were well suited to young people, but their silken cloaks and plumes and gay colors made the older and fatter members of the court look simply ridiculous. Soon the old fashions reasserted themselves, with a great deal of resentment on both sides of the generation gap.

Lafayette was popular partly because he was so generous with his fortune. His generosity, however, failed to work when he laid siege to Aglaë d'Hunolstein, a notorious beauty who was already the mistress of the Duc d'Orléans' son. The lady ignored Lafayette, at least until after he became a popular hero. He tried to work off his frustration by provoking his friend Ségur to fight a duel over her (dueling was illegal but popular). Ségur denied all interest in Mme d'Hunolstein and refused to be drawn. But he found it difficult to suppress his laughter when shortly afterwards the grandees of the Noailles family asked him to use his influence with Lafayette, "to give warmth to his coldness, shake him out of his idleness, and put some ginger into his character."

The Duchesse d'Ayen, thinking it her duty not to shame her husband and sons-in-law by observing her somewhat monastic way of life, devoted herself with dogged zeal to playing the society hostess for the benefit of her family. Adrienne, who had inherited much of her doggedness, threw herself into this new role with equal devotion. Neither she nor her husband was particularly at ease in society, but the family was still determined to make something out of the laggard son-in-law. The Maréchal de Noailles obtained for Lafayette the offer of a position in the household of the Comte de Provence, the king's brother. But the marquis had no wish to be a courtier for ever: it was something at which he was universally admitted to be a failure, and besides, he had been raised on dreams of military distinction. His version of how he escaped (which is the only one extant) has him insulting his intended employer at a masked ball. Whatever actually happened, he was returned to his regiment at Metz and was soon writing letters of eternal devotion to Adrienne, pregnant for the second time (their first child, Henriette, was born in December 1775). But he could not keep coquetry out of his writing:

> We live in a state of confusion and desolation here. The whole garrison is going into mourning, for M. the Maréchal has made a clean sweep of women. They are driven away or shut up. He is their sworn enemy, and they in turn curse him vehemently. . . . Reform is the order of the day. Only legitimate passions are permitted. Legitimate or not, my dear heart, it would, I assure you, be a difficult matter to uproot what I have pledged to you for life.

This may have reassured Adrienne, but probably not much.

Reform was certainly the order of the day, at least in the French army, which was notoriously slack and overburdened with useless officers who cost the king more in salaries than all of the troops. Preparation for a war with England was a permanent feature of French life, a traditional exercise in deterrence and a perpetual hope of revenge. George III was in the throes of dealing with rebellion in his American colonies. For those in Lafayette's circle, whose memories of the defeats of the Seven Years' War were limited to pieties about their wounded or fallen fathers, the moment was ripe for war.

But then the moment was always ripe for war among those whose only career was fighting. Not that the French officers showed disregard for the life of their soldiers: they cost too much to risk in unnecessary battle. However, it was the officers, or the young among them, who were so critical of the caution of their elders. For the poorest among them, the pension that their families could expect if they were killed might be the only alternative to ruin. For those unburdened by such concerns, the rich nobles of Lafayette's acquaintance, dying was merely one other adventure among the many offered along the path to honor. This is not to say that they lacked a sense of self-preservation, but the rigidity of the French social system meant that patriotic sacrifice was expected of the nobility. War was their one and only business, and without it, if they were like Lafayette, they got extremely bored.

The military glory that Lafayette anticipated was suddenly denied him. The young King Louis XVI appointed the Comte de Saint-Germain as minister of war. This was a disturbing choice for the old guard, for Saint-Germain not only lacked the pull and title of the old nobility, he was also known as a reformer. He attacked the worst abuses of the military system, most notably the influence of court favoritism in promoting officers without regard for merit. He reorganized the army into sixteen manageable divisions, all subject to the central authority of his ministry, and he suppressed several superfluous regiments entirely, including Lafayette's old Musketeers. He abolished many of the privileges which, though militarily useless, were dear to the nobles (and a drain on the royal budget), and he insisted that officers spend at least six months with their regiments, rather than letting their juniors run things while they amused themselves in the capital or in their châteaux. He reduced the punishment of deserters, and tightened discipline in everything from modes of address between ranks to the luxuries permitted at officers' tables. (He attempted to limit the number of dishes, which was evaded by piling everything – meat, game, and pastry – onto the same plate.) Ironically, it was a matter of discipline that brought about his fall: he tried to introduce a "modern" form of corporal punishment on Prussian lines, submitting offenders to public beatings on the back with the flat of a saber. For weeks the army and court discussed nothing else, some insisting that this was more humanitarian than the floggings and humiliations inflicted on the guilty, others (including Lafayette some forty years later) that such punishment was "totally alien to the French spirit." The latter won, and the "Rousseau in helmet and boots" was finally dismissed.

Not, however, before Lafayette had been victim of his reforming zeal. One of the targets of Saint-Germain's new broom was the large number of medium-ranking officers who had been promoted, through influence, without having ever seen active service. Lafayette, now eighteen, was a captain who had spent only a few months with his troops, and then only around the garrison town of Metz. Along with countless others, and notwithstanding the protests of his in-laws, he was removed from active service and placed in the reserve on half-pay (June 11, 1776). Barring the outbreak of war, his military career was stymied. There was now no escape from the Noailles; nor did there seem to be any opportunity of living up to the legend which his aunts had so assiduously instilled in him.

2

A Whiff of Revolt

T HE REBELLION OF the English colonists in America was the subject of much fashionable talk among Lafayette's circle. Here was a struggle between the forces of good and evil. Liberty was as widely discussed in Europe as in America, where the same classical and modern writers who adorned the shelves of the French intelligentsia were also available, in translation. Fighting for liberty was not an idea the French applied to themselves; but for the English in America, who had been settled there for two hundred years, the actions of George III's ministers appeared to make resistance not only justifiable, but necessary. The French liberals cheered them on.

The Boston Tea Party, which had taken place in the year before Lafayette's marriage, aroused such passion in Paris that the English game of "whisk" was abandoned in favor of "boston." Conversation was not exclusively about the rebellion, contrary to the memoirs of those such as Ségur who thought of themselves as democrats. One observer, L. S. Mercier, wrote in his *Tableau de Paris* of the "facility with which one passes from one subject to another . . . from criticizing a comedy to discussing the affairs of the Insurgents; how one talks at the same time of fashion and of Boston." Nevertheless, as events on the other side of the Atlantic took a more serious turn and in April, 1775, the first blood of formal war was spilt at Lexington, everyone in Lafayette's set waited to see what the government would do. They hoped for a declaration of war against England; but the king's chief minister, the Comte de Maurepas, had neither the desire nor the funds to commit French forces. Besides, in the same month as Lexington there were food riots near Paris at the rising cost of bread. In May these reached Versailles and the capital itself, and it took a week of massive troop action, hundreds of arrests, synchronized appeals from pulpits, and two public executions, to quell them. But Lafayette's friends were not concerned with domestic troubles or the market in corn. Those who were in the reserve, or who were disgruntled by the reforms in the army, looked for some military adventure in which to distinguish themselves. As serving officers, of course, they were not free to fight under other colors. But if the government should declare war on England and one of the fronts should be America, there would be a legitimate opportunity for seeking glory.

In 1776, the Americans sent Silas Deane to Paris to raise (in diplomatic secrecy) political, financial, and military help for the American war effort. This in itself showed how serious matters were, for the colonists, being English, thought of the Papist powers of Europe as their traditional enemies. But with the home government determined to impose its will by force, and employing German mercenaries, the prestige of the colonists was put into question. More and more the activists among them spread the notion that, though they were small in size and number, they were united by bonds of history and culture in a proud spirit of resistance to oppression, and that they had little to lose and everything to gain from independence. In June 1775 their Congress had unanimously elected Colonel George Washington of Virginia to be their general and commander-in-chief. Later in the year, when it was increasingly obvious that reconciliation with Britain was impossible, a Committee of Secret Correspondence, later known as the Committee for Foreign Affairs, was set up to contact "our friends in Great Britain, Ireland, and other parts of the world." Arthur Lee, an ex-colonial agent, was its agent in London, and Deane, an impressionable merchant, its man in Paris. Originally reluctant to seek foreign alliances, especially among old enemies, the American Congress quickly realized that outside help was essential to victory. And in Paris there were several luminaries willing to give their assistance.

Most notable among Deane's contacts were Caron de Beaumarchais, the romantic and witty author of *The Barber of Seville*, and and Comte de Broglie, the commanding general of Lafayette's old regiment. Lafayette himself first heard of what was happening in America in the summer of 1775, at a dinner Broglie gave for the Duke of Gloucester, George III's estranged brother. He later claimed that "as soon as I knew of this quarrel, my heart was committed to it, and I thought only of joining my colors to it." But that was written after independence had been secured and recognized: at the time, there was no legal way for him to realize such an ambition. The American army was short of trained officers, and Silas Deane sold Congress the idea of accepting French volunteers on two grounds: the first that it would mean more French aid, and the second that the American, or Continental, troops would benefit from seasoned men. But French soldiers – even those in the reserve like Lafayette – could not officially fight under a foreign flag. So unless Lafayette wanted to brave the authorities, he was stuck.

Congress, Deane, and Broglie were all banking on the active intervention of the French government at some time in the near future. Broglie, indeed, kept in touch with the foreign ministry, which was held by the Comte de Vergennes, but he never received official approval for his actions in introducing "volunteers" to Silas Deane. The French felt they could not afford to risk war with England, which is what open support of the Americans would involve. Nor were the English keen to fight once more in Europe when their supply-lines were already stretched across the Atlantic. So even though the English ambassador Lord Stormont knew through his very efficient spy system all about the gun-running and the meetings between Deane and French officers, he was forced to accept Vergennes' assurance that the French government disapproved of all such collaboration and would do its best to put a stop to it.

Broglie was ambitious to be the leading Frenchman on the American front, and he even entertained the idea of being general-issimo of the Continental forces. He furthered these ambitions by sending Deane his most trusted officers, notably "Baron" Johann de Kalb. De Kalb was a Bavarian Protestant who had served under Broglie in two wars. After that he had, on Broglie's recommendation, gone to America to investigate the possibilities of their revolting successfully against Britain. He was a lieutenant-colonel in the French army, and both his rank and knowledge of America made him an attractive catch in Deane's eyes. His recommendation by Broglie and "several others of the first rank" was impressive, and finally, in November 1776, not long after Deane had learned of the Declaration of Independence, a contract was signed whereby de Kalb was to be a major-general in the American army, and was to receive 12,000 *livres*. De Kalb himself was to try faithfully to further the interests of his patron, the Comte de Broglie. For this purpose, and so as to be able to serve in the American army, Broglie wangled for him two years' leave of absence from his French military duties.

Money and the promise of high rank were sufficient to attract many soldiers who hung around the camps and who were prepared to risk official displeasure. Deane was not very discriminating in either his choice of volunteers or his offers of high rank. By the end of the year he complained that he was "well-nigh harassed to death" with applications, and that he could have filled ten ships with officers if he accepted them all. The French government did little to stop these goings-on, though it was always ready to soothe British protests. But neither did it show any signs of actively committing itself to the American cause.

Once the precedent existed, however, once the route to glory in America was opened by people like de Kalb, Lafayette's circle was among those who talked of crossing the ocean. Some of them undoubtedly saw it as an opportunity to escape their debts or a blighted romance; one nobleman who enlisted under republican colors was the Marquis de la Rouërie, who certainly left France because of an unhappy love-affair, and served, in the true chivalric tradition, as "Colonel Armand." Even Lafayette was later rumored to have left because of being spurned by Mme d'Hunolstein, but it is more likely that the gossips who busied themselves with his reputation after it was secure got his reasons confused with Rouërie's.

With all his friends talking of fighting for the "insurgents," Lafayette asked Broglie to introduce him to Silas Deane. Broglie hesitated, and made a speech to the effect that "I saw your uncle die in the Italian campaign, and I was there at the death of your father at Minden. I do not want to contribute to the ruin of the last surviving branch of your family." Nevertheless he finally offered help by making the necessary introductions. Some have seen in this evidence that Lafayette was merely a pawn in Broglie's game to be generalissimo in America. It is true that Lafayette used Broglie's contacts, and it is possible that Broglie thought Lafayette, with all his connections, would be useful to him. But Lafayette had ambitions of his own – for glory and an opportunity to prove himself. And while Broglie's introductions were useful, they hardly constituted a debt Lafayette, always a man of honor, felt bound to repay.

Lafayette and his friends were moved less to fight for "liberty" than for the French interests which they, as the noble warrior class, represented. They saw in the American struggle not a clash of philosophical principles, but a respectable excuse for harassing England. They certainly expected their own government, sooner or later, to back them officially – the foreign minister, Vergennes, was certainly more inclined to risk English wrath for commercial advantage than Maurepas – and they saw "volunteering" as one way of precipitating French commitment. They were not rebels, though their position enabled them to take certain risks.

The simplest explanation for Lafayette's desire to fight in America was that it was an adventure. He was nineteen, and the military career which was all that he had dreamed of was more or less closed to him in France. He needed to earn the respect of those he respected: if their talk was of "liberty," he too could bandy such terms about, but to be commissioned as a high-ranking American officer (as had several men little more deserving than himself) was something tangible.

His closest friends, Noailles and Ségur, resolved to enlist, and he joined them. But they realized that their position as courtiers made a tactful approach necessary. Noailles wrote on behalf of all three to Maurepas, seeking formal permission to go – a mistake in tactics, since permission could hardly be granted without antagonizing the ever-efficient British ambassador. The French officers who were then leaving for America could officially be disowned in answer to Lord Stormont's protests, for few of them bothered to seek official authority. But Lafayette and friends were, through their families, at the center of French political life: their departure would mean official connivance, if not approval.

The Duc d'Ayen, into whose family all three had married, did not approve. The Vicomte de Noailles, the elder of his sons-in-law, was listened to when he solicited the duc's support, but it was not forthcoming. Lafayette's request was curtly and totally rejected. Ségur, who had met a similar response from his own father, withdrew from the scheme. Noailles and Lafayette still believed they could persuade their difficult father-in-law, and they persevered. Through Broglie they met de Kalb, who was busy picking officers to accompany him to America. They told him, untruthfully, that they would get the Duc d'Ayen's approval if both of them were made general officers in the American army. Maybe they thought that high rank would indeed soften the duc. Regardless they were prepared to carry on with their game for a little longer. Noailles, however, soon regretted the wrath he was risking and, like Ségur, withdrew. But both he and Ségur were actually serving officers; Lafayette was not. Moreover, unlike them, he had his own money, or could raise it. He continued to meet de Kalb – even at the Noailles mansion – and that officer never suspected that Lafayette was lying about his father-in-law. The Duc d'Ayen's approval would be a formidable weapon in the American armory. De Kalb promised to introduce Lafayette to Deane, and this he effected in December, 1776.

Deane was authorized by Congress to grant commissions to French officers only in proportion to their length of service. De Kalb had been made a major-general because he was a seasoned veteran. Lafayette had hardly served at all. He had a lot of money and offered to serve without pay. He was also a marquis and of a very ancient family: some Americans might now be republicans, but they had not entirely thrown off the crust of snobbery that lay all over the British Empire. Deane was persuaded that the effect in Europe of Lafayette's departure would be prodigious. Against the undeniable disadvantages of his youth and inexperience was the fact of his being the first court noble to persevere in his desire to fight for the American cause. When his prestigious father-in-law gave his blessing, surely the approval of the French government would quickly follow. Thus dazzled, Deane gave in to Lafayette's insistence that nothing less than the rank of major-general would do. Lafayette was doubtless convinced that he would at last gain the Duc d'Ayen's respect, and thus his permission to go. The contract commissioning the marquis as major-general-elect (Congressional approval would make it final) was signed on December 7th. All that remained was for him to tell his father-in-law. And after that, perhaps, his wife.

3
Escape to Independence

T HE FRENCH GOVERNMENT was prepared to turn a blind eye to
the embarkation of some French soldiers for America in the
expectation of trading advantages from the new nation. However, the military situation there in the autumn of 1776 led them to
greater caution than before. The new British commander, General
Howe, had forced Washington's army to retreat and had occupied
New York City. But although he was in a position to smash the
American forces, Howe made no decisive move. Nor did his
opponent. American losses and inaction greatly eroded faith in
Washington's military leadership. By the winter, matters were
hardly improved: Howe threatened Philadelphia, the rebellious
capital city, and made the Continental Congress prudently retire to
the safety of Baltimore. Nevertheless Washington still managed to
keep an army in the field – encouraged by Tom Paine's exhortations
to the troops, beginning "These are the times that try men's souls" –
and his harassing expeditions across the Delaware led to the victory
at Trenton, and enabled the rebel army to limp into winter quarters
at Morristown, New Jersey.

The situation was nevertheless such that the French foreign
minister, Vergennes, felt it wise to hedge his bets. Secret assistance to
the rebels in the hope of gain was one thing, but to support a losing
cause was quite another. The Duc d'Ayen had been persuaded by
his favorite son-in-law Noailles to try once more to get permission
for him to cross the Atlantic. Indeed, so swayed was the duc that it
was rumored he was thinking of going himself. If Noailles were
allowed, Lafayette humbly considered he had a fair chance of
getting permission too. But as it turned out Noailles was absolutely
forbidden to go, and moreover the foreign ministry started making
things difficult for soldiers to embark. The port authorities at Le
Havre were ordered to stop American volunteers from sailing, and

the police told to arrest "with plenty of publicity" any French soldier who boasted of being ordered to America by the government. All this was a sop to the continuing protests of the English ambassador.

Among the victims of the new policy was the "Baron" de Kalb. This was a great setback to the plans of the Comte de Broglie, whose associates now cast round for other methods to ship de Kalb and companions across the ocean. Franklin had arrived to join Deane in representing American interests and, though not officially received, he added luster to the rebel cause. Soldiers continued to volunteer, and Deane promised them ships, but where and when they would go were unanswered questions. One solution suggested itself to those around Broglie: to commission a ship of their own, rather than wait for the Americans to arrange this. Broglie's secretary put this idea to the wealthy young Lafayette, who immediately agreed. His zeal was commendable, but he still hadn't told his family anything of his plans, and it was they who would sooner or later have to authorize the expenditure for his purchase. (To cover himself, Lafayette wanted his friend and relative the Prince de Poix to go halves with him, but in the end he had to bear the burden alone.)

Lacking both official authorization to proceed and family blessing, Lafayette agreed to ship de Kalb and his chosen fellow-officers at his own expense: this seemed formidable proof of devotion to Deane and, to a lesser extent, Franklin. It required an unusual amount of commitment on Lafayette's part, as well as courage. His meetings with the Americans, despite his attempts, by picking up his contact on carriage-drives and so forth, to conduct them in secrecy were known to the French authorities. Maurepas sent a representative, the Prince de Montbarey, to find out what he was up to. According to Montbarey, Lafayette told all, and promised to give up if Maurepas wished it. But Montbarey was not convinced that the marquis meant what he said, and told his masters so. They were, however, content to let the matter rest: had Lafayette ever before shown a spirit sufficiently mettlesome to disregard the clear wishes of his king, let alone his father-in-law?

But this was the first time Lafayette had been shown attention because of himself, and not because of his family. The Americans, it was true, had commissioned him with due consideration for his usefulness as a contact. But it was to *him* they looked for fulfillment of his promises and, if he was to prove worthy of their trust – and compensate for the conspicuous absence of the Duc d'Ayen's blessing – he could not possibly draw back. He had that kind of shyness which, when circumstances offered, forced him to go to almost excessive lengths to prove his courage. When Broglie's secretary came to him about commissioning a ship, it was the first opportunity he had ever had of taking adult responsibility for an important decision. He dared not refuse. As if to prove it, he added to his coat of arms the Latin motto *Cur non?* : Why not? (His previous motto had been *Vis sat contra fatum* : Determination suffices to combat destiny.)

Still he had not attempted to tell his family of his project. Their suspicions were, however, aroused, especially after the visit of the Prince de Montbarey. A ship called the *Victoire*, worth 112,000 *livres* with its cargo, had been promised for him by the spring of 1777. All in all, if it were discovered how deeply he was involved Lafayette could expect to be in serious trouble, both with the royal ministers, who could imprison or exile him with a royal order (*lettre de cachet*) and with the equally formidable Duc d'Ayen. Prudence was necessary, and to give the impression of being the unchanged Lafayette who did what he was told, the rebel major-general-elect took up an invitation to go to England, which would mean he was constantly under the eye of the Noailles family.

The invitation to visit the French ambassador to England, the Marquis de Noailles, was issued by the Prince de Poix, a dandy of such small stature he was nicknamed "Petit Poix." The prince made a great impression on English society, and even on Horace Walpole. Perhaps Lafayette was a little jealous, for he wrote to his wife, "I very much hope the prince will behave himself well. He declares I am always frightened in case he says something stupid." Nevertheless, he admitted in a letter, "M. de Poix has become a great arbiter of fashion, and determines what hats all the ladies shall wear."

Despite the traditional rivalries between French and English, their upper classes danced to much the same tunes, and Lafayette found every door open to him in London. He was presented to King George III by his uncle-by-marriage, the French ambassador. At the Theater Royal, Drury Lane, when attending a performance of *Israel in Egypt* by the king's favorite composer Handel, Lafayette met General Clinton; they were next to find themselves on opposite sides in North America. He danced at the house of Lord George Germain, the minister responsible for the colonies, and there he met Lord Rawdon, who had been present at Washington's defeat on Long Island. "The pleasures of London move at great speed," he wrote to Adrienne, "and even I, who am not used to leading a secluded life, am astonished at their briskness. But to leave the dining-table at half-past seven and to sup between two and three in the morning seems to me a pernicious habit. Yet there is much to amuse me here. There are many very charming women, and the men are affable and welcoming. When the women can be persuaded to leave their gatherings and the men their clubs, their society is most pleasant."

He still had that coquetry he had shown in the first years of his marriage. "I am impatient to see all the ladies," he wrote to his four-months'-pregnant wife, while assuring her that "Paris is a better place than London." A week later, he was blaming his "evil star" for keeping him in "constant movement" and hence away from his beloved. But while the Prince de Poix dallied with the ladies, we have no actual evidence that Lafayette followed his example. He was, however, a young man away from home, who liked pretty girls, and who had been rejected by a notorious beauty, Mme d'Hunolstein; doubtless Lafayette made the most of his situation.

So trusting, or so devious, were the English authorities that Lafayette was invited to go to Portsmouth and inspect the navy and its arrangements for dealing with the American rebels. The British government could have known of Lafayette's interest in the American cause, through their ever-vigilant ambassador to France. But Lafayette had made no secret of his pro-American sympathies anyway, and this got him an invitation to dine at Lord Shelburne's, who led a Parliamentary faction that supported the demands of the insurgents. Possibly it was there that the friendship began between Lafayette and the Whig M.P. Richard FitzPatrick. If the British government knew of Lafayette's feelings, why did they invite him to Portsmouth? Certainly some Englishmen thought both he and his uncle the ambassador abused the privileges of their position. It is possible that the government planned to make something out of Lafayette's visit, so that if he finally declared himself the perfidious implication of the French with the rebels would be clear to all. But it is most likely that they, like the French government, did not take Lafayette too seriously. Whatever the case, he did not go to Portsmouth. He later claimed that this was on grounds of scruple, that it would have been "an abuse of confidence." But a more pressing reason was the fact that his ship the *Victoire* was ready. Lafayette's presence was urgently needed in Paris.

He had, in the time left between his social engagements, found the courage to write of his plans to his father-in-law. "You will be astonished, my dear Papa, at what I am about to tell you," was how he ingenuously began, and he went on first to express his regrets at not having consulted the duc, and then to say that he had given his word to the Americans, "and you would not have thought well of me had I broken it." Wanting, as ever, the duc's good opinion, he continued, "I have found a unique opportunity to distinguish myself, and to learn my profession: I am a general officer in the army of the United States. My enthusiasm for their cause, and my frankness, have won their confidence."

There followed a reference to the "ship which I have chartered," and a flattering description of:

M.le Baron de Kalb, an officer of the greatest distinction, a brigadier in the king's armies, and a major-general in the U.S. armies, as I am . . . I am overjoyed at having found so excellent an opportunity of doing something and of educating myself. I know full well that I am making enormous sacrifices, and that I will be the one to suffer the most at leaving my family, my friends, and you, my dear Papa, because I love them more than anyone has ever loved. But the voyage is not that long, and people go further every day merely for pleasure. Besides I hope to return more worthy of all who might be kind enough to regret my departure.

He ended with an appeal to "think kindly of me, which is what I greatly desire, and deserve because of my feelings for you and the respect which will last as long as I live."

This letter he took with him on his sudden return to Paris. In his haste to be gone, he even broke a cardinal rule of etiquette and told his uncle that he would not be able to appear once more at court as he was engaged to do. The ambassador was embarrassed, but turned Lafayette's fanciful explanation of the urgency of the call into a case of "diplomatic fever." Lafayette left England but, not daring to go home, stayed in hiding near Paris, posting his long screed to the Duc d'Ayen and putting the finishing touches to his arrangements.

He could well leave without an embarrassing scene with his wife and family, but not without bursting in on his friend Ségur, and later Noailles, to tell them what was afoot. Ségur was full of admiration and not a little jealous; he told Lafayette that he hoped war would soon break out between France and England, after which nothing could stop their reunion. Ségur later wrote that the marquis's family was deeply upset, not only because of the risks he was running in so remote a country, but also because they saw the danger of his spending a large part of his fortune there. But Lafayette did not stop to receive any such warnings. On his way through Paris to Bordeaux, where his ship was waiting, he scribbled a note for Adrienne, and added a postscript to her father. Then he, de Kalb, and the officers who were to accompany them set off before anyone could stop them. They were armed with letters of introduction from Deane to members of Congress, and Lafayette also carried letters to the financier Robert Morris, to Washington, and to John Hancock, the president of the Continental Congress. These letters stressed the importance of the young major-general's wealth and connections. Nothing, naturally, was said about his limited military experience.

Before Lafayette had reached Bordeaux, his father-in-law had opened his letter, and the full force of a Noailles' fury broke in Paris.

Adrienne may have been a little embittered, but she was loyal to the point of saintliness to her husband, and decided that her best course was to keep as quiet as possible. Her mother, somewhat surprisingly, supported her. But her father went straight to Maurepas. What was involved was not simply childish disobedience, but the prestige and diplomacy of the French court itself.

The king's ministers were, however, still in two minds about support for America. On the one hand they could not afford to antagonize either Lord Stormont or, for that matter, the Noailles family. On the other, they did not wish completely to stop the volunteers, who enjoyed the unstinted support of public opinion. The foreign minister, Vergennes, was credited by most people with having created the climate that had led so many to volunteer, but even he was extremely cautious. "Europe is the battlefield on which to fix your eyes," he told the Chevalier de Falquières who had asked his official blessing to cross the Atlantic. "America can only tempt those who have to use any means available to gain any kind of fortune." He was furious at Lafayette for having jeopardized the arrangements for volunteers to proceed to America, against the public protests of the government, but with its tacit support. Seen in this light, Lafayette was acting very irresponsibly. His social position made official reaction inevitable. He could not have been in ignorance of government wishes on this matter. He was, perhaps, being capricious and selfish, but he was also desperate to prove himself, no matter what the cost. Shyness may have been one of his qualities, but prudence never was.

In response to d'Ayen's demands, Maurepas acted to bring Lafayette to heel but not to stop the other officers on the *Victoire*. The king himself said that he was shocked that a man of Lafayette's standing should go to the help of rebels. With monarch and father-in-law opposed to him, drastic measures might be expected against Lafayette. But no order for his imprisonment was issued. All that happened was that orders were sent for him to join his father-in-law and aunt and uncle de Tessé on a long-projected tour of Italy. He might have preferred jail.

In Bordeaux Lafayette and de Kalb discovered that their ship was not ready. They were anxious about what might be done to stop them, and this anxiety led Lafayette to confess to the "Baron" that he had, in fact, set off without the Duc d'Ayen's blessing. De Kalb was astonished and upset. He was a careful and experienced officer who had expended much time and trouble putting this expedition together. As far as possible he had proceeded within legal bounds. Now one of the chief links in the chain had confessed itself weak. Everything was back in the melting-pot once more and there was the added danger of official sanctions. He and the marquis decided to send a messenger of their own to Paris for news. Meanwhile Lafayette pretended all was well by staying with another of his wife's relatives, the Maréchal de Mouchy.

When news arrived from Paris, it was bad. One of Lafayette's friends, the Vicomte de Coigny, reported that Louis XVI and the Duc d'Ayen were both extremely upset and that there was talk of a *lettre de cachet*. Wearily de Kalb advised Lafayette to give up and to sell the *Victoire*. To be imprisoned for volunteering illegally was no small thing. De Kalb must have felt the dangers of his own position, though there was no talk of sanctions against the other officers sailing with the marquis. But Lafayette would have none of it. Perhaps he felt he knew the king well enough not to take this report of his displeasure – and it was, after all, only rumor – too seriously: had not their adolescence passed with similar japes overlooked? And as for the Duc d'Ayen, hadn't the time come to stand up to him, especially as they were separated by some 250 miles of rough roads, and poised for flight?

So Lafayette ordered the *Victoire* to sail out of French waters to Spain, there to await developments. As it was his ship, there was little that de Kalb could do, except lament the fact that his fellow major-general was unable to make up his mind either for outright defiance – which would have meant sailing for America – or submission to authority.

Parisian gossip assumed that Lafayette had set off for the rebel colonies and his action was generally approved. One court lady tartly remarked that if the Duc d'Ayen prevented his son-in-law from carrying out so noble an enterprise, he would have difficulty in marrying off his other daughters. Nevertheless d'Ayen continued to press for the sinner's return. It was not out of tenderness for his pregnant and abandoned daughter, for he intended to whisk Lafayette off to Italy. It was not because he felt Lafayette would actually damage the American cause by jeopardizing Vergennes' careful plans: for those the duc never displayed much enthusiasm. It was most likely that he feared for the good name of the Noailles in London, and if Lafayette joining the rebels did not cause enough embarrassment to them, there was d'Ayen's own position at the center of affairs to consider. Only if the government declared itself officially for the rebels, or if Lafayette covered himself in glory, would it be possible to approve the young man's actions. As neither seemed likely, his return to Marseilles was ordered. In case Lafayette actually reached America, Silas Deane was prevailed upon to write to Washington and Hancock making clear the king's disapproval, and asking them to ensure Lafayette's return. But these letters were never sent, for Lafayette suddenly returned to Bordeaux. While he insisted on going to America, he nevertheless felt that all this fuss must be due to some misunderstanding, and he was determined to clear matters up.

There then followed the most amazing to-ing and fro-ing between Lafayette and the various factions in Paris interested in his plans. He asked permission from the port's commandant to go to Paris and plead his case, but this was refused; his orders were to go to Marseilles and join his father-in-law, and that was that. Lafayette then tried to move Maurepas by writing to him, but all that happened was that his letter was interpreted as a surrender to the wishes of his sovereign and family. As far as Maurepas was concerned, that too was that.

But then the Comte de Broglie took a hand. He had, after his first change of heart over Lafayette's ambitions, been helpful to him, and had a kindly and not altogether disinterested concern in his case. Lafayette had chartered the boat carrying Broglie's trusted lieutenant de Kalb and that alone was worth supporting. Broglie now despatched a messenger of his own, the Vicomte de Mauroy, who was to inform Lafayette that the restraining orders against him were a storm in a teacup designed to reassure both Lord Stormont and the Duc d'Ayen. Mauroy was then to sail with Lafayette to America.

Lafayette was indeed greatly cheered by this news, which was near enough the truth to explain everything. He wrote to Maurepas, taking his silence (for there had been no reply to his last letter) to mean approval. He then left Bordeaux by the Marseilles coach, but got out when they were far enough from the city. Disguising himself as a courier, he galloped towards Spain and the *Victoire*. At one stage his coquetry was nearly his undoing. He was recognized by a postman's daughter he had stopped to talk to on his way to Bordeaux but she responded to his signals to keep silent. They reached Los Pasajes, where the ship was moored, without further incident. Everyone in Paris, except Broglie, believed him to be on his way to Marseilles. The Duc d'Ayen's surprise when he arrived in Marseilles a few days later to pick up his son-in-law can only be imagined.

On Sunday, April 20, 1777, the *Victoire* finally sailed for America. When the news reached Paris, Lafayette became, if not a hero, at least the chief topic of conversation. Franklin wrote to Washington asking him to look after the boy, in financial as well as other matters. He and Deane suggested to the Committee of Foreign Affairs that Lafayette not be placed in too much danger for the sake of his "beautiful young wife." Even Voltaire, who had just returned from exile and was the eagerly sought-after star of every liberal *salon*, saluted Lafayette's name when he was introduced to Adrienne. Only the Duc d'Ayen continued to disapprove, which greatly distressed his daughter. One of his worries was whether his son-in-law would have enough money, and the family sent him five hundred pounds sterling straight away. But even d'Ayen was finally softened by the universal approval Lafayette had aroused and by royal exoneration of any blame that might be attached to the Noailles family through the antics of their relative. Lafayette, terribly seasick, was at least comforted by unofficial connivance at his disobedience. And this, naturally, placed on him the even greater burden of having to distinguish himself in a country of which he was woefully ignorant.

Part Two: Land of Hope and Glory

4

A General in Search of a Division

CROSSING THE ATLANTIC in 1777 was a long, rough, and boring process, one that could take anything from six weeks to over three months. Apart from the elements, there was the British navy to reckon with; any rebel caught by them could expect to spend a long time in prison or experience some other, equally unpleasant, form of servitude. But to Lafayette, whose first weeks at sea were plagued by sea-sickness – which, he told his wife, he cured in his own fashion, without revealing the secret – a skirmish with the navy would at least have relieved the tedium.

After five weeks he wrote to Adrienne:

> I won't give you a diary of my voyage. Here the days follow each other, and, what is worse, seem like each other. Always the sky, always the water, and the same thing the following day. Really, those people who write books about a sea-voyage must be incredible bores: me, I've had contrary winds like anyone else, I've had a very long journey like anyone else, I've suffered storms, I've seen ships – and they were much more interesting to me than to anyone else: yet there you are! I haven't told you anything worth writing about, or that couldn't have been written by anybody.

He was also a little homesick, and anxious for news of the second child his wife was expecting, even though he knew he would have to wait at least three months, and probably more, for replies to his questions: letters too could be intercepted, which made every opportunity for sending them a precious one. Nevertheless Lafayette could not help writing with half an eye on the public he knew he had aroused. Excusing himself for escaping the Italian trip that he had been ordered to take with his father-in-law, he wrote:

You will agree, my love, that the job and life that I am going to have are very different from those reserved for me on that ridiculous journey. As defender of that liberty that I worship, myself more free than anyone, and coming as a friend to offer my services to this most interesting of republics, I am bringing only my sincerity and my goodwill – no ambition, no special interest. In working for my glory, I am working for their good. I hope that, as a favor to me, you will become a good American, which is a sentiment made for virtuous hearts. The fortune of America is closely bound up with the fortune of humanity: she will become the safe and respected refuge of virtue, honesty, tolerance, equality, and of a peaceful liberty.

And he went on to tell her how the journey had changed him, and how he was dividing his time between military and English books, both subjects in which he was rather deficient.

On a long and boring trip even the best-held sentiments can cool, requiring much oratorical huffing to get them blazing again. Not that Lafayette had lost any of his enthusiasm for the adventures he was sure were awaiting him, but he was a long way from the social heights in which he habitually, albeit a little awkwardly, moved, where conversation was shot with words like "liberty" and "equality." He was, not to put too fine a point on it, now among mercenaries, even though for a noble cause: soldiers who had seen battle, who had none too high an opinion of American military skill, and who had accepted money in order to fight England. Lafayette, on the other hand, was to fight, without pay, to prove himself worthy of his ancestry, his country, and his wife's family. Such ambitions required lofty justification, and nearly two months at sea gave him the opportunity to write it all out in his letters. When, after fifty-four days, the last few of which had been passed in expectation of imminent attack, they finally landed on American soil, Lafayette was so grateful that he swore to conquer or die with the American cause. He probably felt readier to face death than another sea voyage.

Hardly had he stumbled, by happy chance, into the hospitable arms of a patriot officer and plantation-owner, Major Huger, and he was writing to Adrienne, "The manners of these people are simple, honest, and worthy in every respect of the country that echoes with the beautiful name of Liberty." The first American city he saw was Charleston (then called Charles Town) in South Carolina, which was the fourth largest in America, and the only one not to suffer an immediate drain of population because of occupation or the threat of it by British forces. In few major cities was there such a glaring distinction between the houses of the wealthy and those of the rest;

soaring rents and scandalous jerry-building had caused as much protest as the zooming price of wood and coal, which was forced up by the monopolists of the city's fuel supply. For Lafayette, however, the reception he was accorded – once its leading citizens realized that he was a marquis and a ship-owner – led him to describe the place to his wife as:

> one of the most beautiful, best built, and most agreeably populated that I have ever seen. American women are very pretty, very simple, and of a charming cleanliness, which prevails here with the greatest fastidiousness, even more than in England. What delights me is that all citizens are brothers. There are no poor in America, nor even what we would call peasants. Every citizen has a decent subsistence, and everyone has the same rights as the most powerful landowner. The inns are very different from those of Europe: the master and mistress sit down at the table with you, preside over a fine meal, and when you leave you do so without haggling. If one doesn't want to go into an inn, one can find country houses where it is enough to be a good American to be treated with the same courtesy that in Europe one would have for a friend.

He had been in the town three days when he made these judgments.

His title and his manners made Lafayette into a social attraction in Charleston, but much though he relished the hospitality lavished on him, he was anxious to get his commission confirmed by the Continental Congress, which had returned from Baltimore to Philadelphia. He had been told that the summer's military campaign had opened, but that nothing much had yet occurred. Nevertheless he wanted to be where the action was, and he made arrangements to sell the *Victoire* and start for Philadelphia. In the meantime he was treated, according to one of his companions, like "a marshal of France or a protector of liberty." To show how much he appreciated this, Lafayette presented the town's General Moultrie with uniforms, arms, and equipment for a hundred men, to mark Moultrie's defense of the fort which bore his name. It was a noble, if ostentatious gesture, and one that caused his financial advisers in Paris no little unease. For Lafayette was never the most prudent manager of his affairs. As it turned out, he found he couldn't even sell his ship, since he was still a minor. But his luck, in which he had great faith, stayed with him, and when the ship was wrecked as she crossed the bar of Charleston's harbor, Lafayette could look forward to collecting on the insurance.

He and his party set out for Philadelphia in great style, in a procession of carriages. But, as he wrote to Adrienne, it did not last.

44

The roads, if any, were rough, the going rougher. The heat was almost insupportable, though Lafayette, after more than two weeks on the road, could say cheerfully, "I have borne the strain of the trip without noticing: it has been extremely long and extremely boring on land, but it was even worse when I was on my miserable ship." Having sent five letters without receiving a reply, he worried about the lack of news from France, and he was completely open about his feelings. "I can't live in such uncertainty," he told his wife. "I've undertaken a task that's really too great for my heart to bear, which wasn't created to suffer so much."

But, in the next line, he was once more able to joke about his misfortunes. He told her how "we are now on horseback, having shattered the vehicles in my usual praiseworthy style, and I hope to write to you in a few days that we arrived on foot." And his high opinion of America had only increased: "the further north I get, the more I like this country and its inhabitants. I've had nothing but courtesy and kindness although many hardly know who I am." Some, indeed, had inflated notions of his standing, and an officer in North Carolina described him as "one of the royal bloods of France recommended by Mr Franklin."

It took Lafayette one long month to travel the eight hundred-odd miles between Charleston and Philadelphia, and one of his companions was sure that no European military campaign could have been worse. But the situation when they finally arrived was little better than their own. The city itself was in danger from British attack. There was even greater danger in the north, since Fort Ticonderoga had fallen, but there was little Washington could do about that. The Continental army had two factors in its favor: its ability to use fighting tactics suitable to the terrain and the aversion of the British General Howe to moving fast, being trained, like his French counterparts, not to risk his expensive fighting machine lightly. But these two advantages had to be set against the appalling situation of the Americans with regard to food and provisions, which might actually compel the men to scatter in order to avoid starvation, and the very low morale among American officers. One of the chief reasons for their dissatisfaction was the pretensions of the French volunteers.

Lafayette, of course, knew nothing of this except the fall of Ticonderoga, which he lightly described as "very annoying, we must try and make up for it." He had formed a low opinion of the Frenchmen he had met in Charleston – most of whom had swarmed in from the French West Indies colonies – but he was patriotic enough to keep quiet about them. Meanwhile, at army headquarters, three American generals – Greene, Sullivan, and Knox – had shown violent resentment at the affected superiority of the Chevalier du

Coudray, a nobleman who had persuaded Silas Deane in Paris to commission him as commander both of artillery and engineers. Franklin had done something to ease this situation by sending over four properly trained French engineers, but Congress was especially touchy about all foreigners. They had already resolved to discourage the granting of commissions to officers unable to speak English, but diplomatic protocol required them to honor at least some of the obligations with which Silas Deane had saddled them. They were outraged at a suggestion from Deane, received the previous winter, that the Comte de Broglie be appointed their generalissimo, and as a result they resolved to have nothing to do with de Kalb, whom Deane had admitted to be Broglie's confidant. The atmosphere was therefore dismal for Lafayette, de Kalb, and the rest who were hoping to have their contracts confirmed.

They presented their letters of recommendation in Philadelphia with great optimism, and were given an appointment first with the financier Robert Morris, who served on the Committee of Secret Correspondence, and then with James Lovell, chairman of the Committee on Foreign Applications. Waiting at the door of Independence Hall, they were treated to an oration by Lovell, in excellent French, in which he informed them how little they were wanted. With that, they were left standing in the street.

Naturally, Lafayette glosses over this miserable disappointment in his memoirs. But he had not braved king and father-in-law, risked life and fortune, and traveled for tedious months across sea and land merely to be given the brush-off. He had spirit enough to request Congress to honor its obligations, as he had honored his. Although every time it did so on behalf of Deane's people a native American officer would have to be disappointed in promotion, Congress soon decided to look more closely at the applications of Lafayette and de Kalb. A French connection like the marquis could not be so brusquely dismissed, and soldiers of de Kalb's experience were still rare in America. Lovell, whose low opinion of Deane led him to wonder if he shouldn't be recalled, came to see Lafayette again, accompanied by another congressman, William Duer, who was more courteous. Duer took the marquis aside, and understood from the ensuing discussion that his motives for serving were to be near Washington (a hero in France as well as in America), to see action, and to "give him an eclat at home, where he expected he would soon return." Duer then got Lafayette to put in writing his willingness to serve free, and to accept a new contract that would avoid making him senior to the generals already appointed. But the crucial point – which Lafayette, with his faulty English, may not have grasped – was that Congress would only grant him an honorary commission. He could enjoy all the privileges of high rank, but he would not have an actual command: that way, Congress hoped, everyone would be happy.

"After my sacrifices, I have the right to demand two favors," he wrote to Congress. "One is to serve at my own expense; the other is to begin my service as a volunteer." Within two hours he had received his major-general's sash, and a letter from Congress that made everything clear. Dated July 31, 1777, it said,

"Whereas the Marquis de Lafayette, out of his great zeal to the cause of liberty, in which the United States are engaged, has left his family and his connexions, and, at his own expence, comes over to offer his service to the United States, without pension or particular allowance, and is anxious to risk his life in our cause. *Resolved*, that his service be accepted, and that, in consideration of his zeal, illustrious family and connexions, he have the rank and commission of major-general in the army of the United States."

The sense of this resolution was to give him the rank he desired, but to leave it to Washington, as commander-in-chief, to decide whether or not he was to get the command that went with it.

Thanks to his persistence, and also to his family name, Lafayette, unlike the officers who had accompanied him, had got what he asked for. Washington himself was briefly in Philadelphia and, at a dinner given by some members of Congress, the new major-general was taken to meet him. "The majesty of his face and figure" at once impressed Lafayette, and he was all but overwhelmed when the commander-in-chief took him aside at the end of the meal, praised his devotion, and invited him to look on headquarters as his home. Washington assured Lafayette that, though it lacked the luxury of the court, doubtless the marquis would find himself able to accept the customs and privations of a republican army. He also invited him to come the following day on a tour of inspection. Although he had more than enough to deal with, Washington found time to devote some routine courtesy to a young nobleman of whose social standing he had heard, and about whose military employment he did not, at this stage, have to worry. For Lafayette, these courtesies were the first he had received from a man of indisputable authority.

While de Kalb and the other officers who had shared Lafayette's dangerous voyage cajoled and petitioned Congress, the young general had his first review of the army in which he now served. He later described their unimpressive appearance: "About eleven thousand men, poorly armed, and worse dressed, offered a singular sight. In a motley state, and often naked, their best garments were hunting shirts, loose-fitting jackets of gray linen much used in

Carolina." He was scathing about their drilling – the one thing that was tested among officers in the French army – and about the way they formed ranks. But this was not the kind of thing he wrote home about: he was wise enough to give a picture of odds heavily stacked against the Americans, but not hopeless.

Washington, too, was conscious of his army's deficiencies. A volunteer army, even one sustained by drafts from time to time, was a difficult thing to discipline, especially when pay, food, and clothing were badly lacking and never supplied in sufficient quantity until the war was some years old. The core of the trained soldiers was the militia, originally raised to protect their colonies from sudden attack. But they rarely volunteered to serve for the extended period that was needed to make a fighting force out of men as deeply concerned about harvesting their crops as beating the enemy. And the democratic principles for which they were ostensibly struggling extended to the relationship between officers and men, at least in the early days, which was another thing of which the commander-in-chief disapproved. He wrote to the president of the Continental Congress late in 1776: "While those men consider and treat him [an officer] as an equal, and, in the character of an officer regard him no more than a broomstick, being mixed together as one common herd, no order nor discipline can prevail."

Even Washington's complaints were not enough to get the payment and supply of the rebel, or Continental, forces placed on an efficient basis. "Whilst we have men, therefore, who in every respect are superior to mercenary troops, that are fighting for *two pence* or *three pence* a day, why cannot we in appearance also be superior to them, when we fight for Life, Liberty, Property, and our Country?" he asked in vain. Continental currency was already badly depreciated, and neither Congress nor the individual states could afford properly to maintain the forces needed for their defense. In these circumstances, it is something of a miracle that Washington kept an army in the field at all.

The condition of his troops was, however, only one of his worries. He was also torn between loyalty to the Congress that had appointed him, and the demands of his officers which Congress seemed frequently to overlook. This dilemma became especially acute over the promotion of the "foreign officers." Congress itself was divided over what to do about the foreigners, as we have seen, but they were faced with a particularly difficult decision when the four trained engineers sent over by Franklin refused to serve under the Chevalier du Coudray. As if their own differences weren't enough, Congress had to shoulder their volunteers' troubles too. Du Coudray had done his bit to stir things up by writing to Congress attacking all Frenchmen serving in America, including Lafayette. Congress tried to heal the divisions among the French by resolving that one of the engineers Franklin had sent, Duportail, should "take rank and command of all engineers previously appointed," as a colonel. Washington was worried about giving such a job to a Frenchman, but Generals Knox, Greene, and Sullivan were even more upset by the knowledge that the insufferable du Coudray would still have seniority over them. The three generals wrote to President John Hancock threatening to resign. The exasperated Congress retaliated by ordering the unfortunate commander-in-chief to tell the three that their letters were regarded as "an attempt to influence its decision," and if they wanted to resign, they were free to do so. Washington nobly did as he was told and administered this rebuke to three of his best officers. A satisfactory compromise was reached only when Congress gave du Coudray a staff, rather than a line, appointment, making him inspector-general of ordnance. Fortunately, as Lafayette put it, du Coudray was later accidentally drowned, thus affording Congress, Washington, and his peeved officers much relief.

Lafayette showed a somewhat different spirit from du Coudray's, one of humility toward the commander-in-chief. When the marquis arrived for his first review, Washington said, "We should be embarrassed to show ourselves in front of an officer who has just left the troops of France." By his own account, Lafayette replied, "It is to learn and not to teach that I am here," and naturally he did not disillusion his general by saying he had been removed from active service in France a year before. But very soon he began asking for the division that went with his rank. An honorary appointment was not enough for him. True, he was given the full honors that went with his grade, and was invited to attend the councils of war held by the commander-in-chief, but he could not accept the role of mere observer. The only way he could prove himself was by having men to command under fire. When writing to Congress, somewhat to their annoyance, in support of the claims of his fellow French officers to the ranks they had been promised, Lafayette made it clear that he expected his division soon. It depended, of course, on Washington. And it was not long before Lafayette added himself to that list of foreigners demanding special consideration of the commander-in-chief.

Washington complained to Franklin of the problems caused by the Frenchmen who "had come over in such crowds, we either must not employ them, or we must do it at the expense of one half of the officers of the army." About Lafayette he wrote to Benjamin Harrison to find out what Congress wanted him to do. "I know no more than a child unborn, and beg to be instructed," he said, asking why he had been "left in the dark with respect to my own conduct toward him?" Harrison instantly replied saying that Congress had emphatically meant Lafayette's commission to be honorary. Showing those signs of strain that the never-ending supplications of the foreign volunteers had wrought, Harrison said of Lafayette, "The other day he surprised everybody by a letter of his, requesting commissions for his officers, and insinuating at the same time that he should expect a command as soon as you should think him fit for one. Depend on it Congress never meant that he should have one, nor will not countenance him in his applications."

So much was clear to everyone, except Lafayette himself. He continued to press his claims, and Washington continued to fend them off. The gentleness with which he did so, blaming Congress rather than the new major-general's qualities, was perhaps due to the letters from Franklin recommending Lafayette. These had again stressed the marquis's family and social connections, and asked that Washington "take occasion to advise him if necessary with a friendly affection." In honoring this request Washington went so far as to ask Lafayette to look on him as a friend and a father. It was irresistible advice to an orphan, and Lafayette took it literally.

The greatest of Washington's problems was his ignorance of what the enemy was going to do. Following the British capture of Fort Ticonderoga, Washington had been convinced that the main British force under General Howe would join up with its victorious northern army under General Burgoyne. When the entire British fleet appeared off Delaware Bay, however, Washington reluctantly concluded that Howe intended to attack Philadelphia. But then the fleet sailed away. Since the British were so effectively masters of the sea, it was hard for spies to discover their intentions. Why hadn't Howe attacked Philadelphia? Did he intend to make the Americans chase him all through New Jersey while he landed at leisure? And why had he abandoned Burgoyne in the north?

Washington decided that Howe wanted to gain control of the American south, and that therefore his destination was Charleston. This was much too far from Philadelphia to make an overland confrontation worthwhile. At a council of war, which Lafayette attended, it was decided to attack Burgoyne in the north. But this involved opening Philadelphia to the risk of attack, and Washington felt he should get Congressional approval. Soon after he received it, intelligence arrived that the British were moving up Chesapeake Bay toward Philadelphia. Despite Washington's astonishment, Howe's strategy was obviously to attack the city from the south. Marching orders were reversed, and the mood of uncertainty dispelled. There was cheering news, too, from the north, where the Americans had had a successful skirmish with Burgoyne's men. Thus encouraged, Washington was urged to march the army through

Philadelphia, on its way to do battle, to impress the patriots and frighten the Tory Loyalists (the supporters of George III).

On August 24, 1777, to the sounds of fifes and drums, the Continental army passed through the city, led by its commander-in-chief, with its youngest major-general at his side. Since they didn't have uniforms, Washington ordered that their clothes be washed, their arms polished, and that each man decorate his hat with a "green sprig, emblem of hope." John Adams found them "extremely well armed, pretty well clothed, and tolerably disciplined." (Lafayette, describing the same scene, wrote that "despite their nudity, they presented an agreeable sight.") Adams continued, "Much remains yet to be done. Our soldiers have not yet quite the air of soldiers. They don't step exactly in time. They don't hold up their heads quite erect, nor turn out their toes exactly as they ought. They don't all of them cock their hats; and such as do, don't all wear them the same way." Such was the state of the army ready to face the drilled and polished might of the mother country.

The British still kept their plans concealed from Washington, who found himself having to defend the rebellion's capital city without adequate intelligence. By Lafayette's twentieth birthday (September 6, 1777), the two armies had taken up their positions. Washington believed that Howe would try to cut off the American forces from Philadelphia, and therefore took up a defensive position on the city side of Brandywine Creek, a stream deep enough to need fording. On the early morning of September 11th, Washington was waiting at Chad's Ford for the fog to clear away. Lafayette was with him. Suddenly the British guns were heard. The Americans answered them, and a cheer went up, which was some comfort to the anxious commander-in-chief as he prowled round the lines hoping he had guessed right.

Soon confusing reports began to come in. Neither side had committed their main forces in an attack when Washington heard of a substantial British column moving upstream. Assuming that this column had left behind comparatively few men holding their first position, Washington decided to strike at these with superior numbers. But as he was about to order his men, and Sullivan's, further up the creek to cross the Brandywine, a new dispatch told him that the moving British column was not where he had thought it was. Confused with conflicting information, Washington decided against attacking. This was just as well, for in the early afternoon, his headquarters received a visit from a very excited farmer, who swore that he had seen the British coming down the Philadelphia side of the Brandywine, and unless Washington moved quickly he would be surrounded.

Washington flatly refused to believe this, and was on the point of setting out to see for himself when reports from Sullivan and others confirmed the story. Sullivan was quickly detailed to direct the fighting on the right, while Washington remained at Chad's Ford. Soon he, Lafayette, and the other officers at headquarters heard the sounds of battle. Washington managed to contain himself, but Lafayette could not: he sought, and obtained, permission to join in the action. Obviously Washington was too preoccupied to remember Franklin's request to keep the marquis out of danger.

The battle went badly for the Americans. Led by Lord Cornwallis, the British advance had outmaneuvered the patriots, and when Lafayette arrived Sullivan's men had been forced to re-form. Being attacked as they did so by a rapid fire of cannon and muskets, the left and right flanks of the American troops gave way, leaving only the center to fight off the enemy. Sullivan's officers had to push, bully, and shout at their men to get them to hold their positions – and that is what Lafayette, in his first battle, found himself doing. So desperate was the situation that he had no time to be scared. He got himself into the forefront of the action; he also got himself shot in the leg. At the same time as he collapsed, so did the line.

Washington, arriving with fresh troops, was too late to save the situation and the force he had left behind at Chad's Ford was also routed. Lafayette tried to rejoin his commander-in-chief, but loss of blood from his wound forced him to wait to have it bandaged. The retreat was so disorderly that he and his aide Gimat had to hurry on in fear of capture. In fact, it took Washington until midnight to get his army in some sort of order.

According to Lafayette's memoirs, every blast of the cannon in the battle of Brandywine could be heard in Philadelphia, where patriots and loyalists silently listened to the outcome in separate groups in every public place. American losses were about 1200, and Lafayette says that English losses were so great that General Howe had to ask for American surgeons to tend his wounded. In fact, it was to tend the *American* wounded left on the field of battle that Howe made the request.

However construed, Brandywine was a defeat for the Americans. Washington reportedly conducted the battle as if in a daze: his indecisiveness, which in victory was hailed as tactical cunning, was here fatal. Worse, he failed to carry out the necessary reconnaissance. Neither he nor his officers appeared to know where the other fords across the creek were. This ignorance of the ground, as well as of the enemy's dispositions, was not only Washington's fault: it was a demonstration of the weakness of the whole American army. Lafayette had not chosen the best time to nail his colors to their mast. And yet, as he later admitted, he never felt so much at peace as when the success of his cause was in greatest doubt.

The marquis was transported by boat to Philadelphia to have his wound seen to. Everyone praised his bravery, and his companions from the *Victoire* were proud of him. But they were bored with hanging around among rebels who, far from showing gratitude for the sacrifices they had made, refused to confirm the commissions they had been promised. They tried to persuade Lafayette, now that he had been blooded, to give up what was obviously a lost cause and return to France with them. He would have none of it. Far from putting him off, his wound had given him a taste for action he would not lightly abandon.

Among the patriots in Philadelphia, Washington's conduct was taken philosophically. Congress prepared to evacuate the city again, which could scarcely be defended against the British. If anyone was to be made a scapegoat, Congress wanted it to be General Sullivan, who was held responsible for the Brandywine defeat through supplying Washington with faulty intelligence. But the commander-in-chief persuaded Congress to let Sullivan remain at his post. There was a severe shortage of experienced men with the rank of major-general.

Lafayette wrote lightly to Adrienne the night after the battle, reassuring her that he had received only "a little wound in the leg, but it's nothing, my dear heart, the ball touched neither bone nor nerve." He added that this news should make her less anxious than before, since he would have to remove himself from all possible danger in order to recuperate. He stayed long enough in Philadelphia to see the defeat of another attempt by Washington to defend the city: this time gales and drenching rain were to blame for failure, soaking both ammunition and men, who were without shelter. They also lacked food and a thousand of them were barefoot. With their army in such a state, the patriots in Philadelphia began to panic, and those who hadn't left now rushed to do so. Lafayette was caught up in the rush and taken to Bristol. From there, in the coach of Henry Laurens, he went to Bethlehem, where the Moravian Brethren fulfilled their pacifist and humanitarian principles by looking after the American wounded and preaching to them against fighting. Lafayette wrote from Bethlehem to his wife, tempering a wryness where his wound was concerned with a lecture on the ultimate victory of the American cause. This was partly to convince himself, fretting after some weeks of tedious convalescence and worried by political and military man-euverings he did not quite understand. But it was also to convince Adrienne and her family that all was not as black as reports might make it seem – especially if these reports came from returning French volunteers more than a little disgruntled at having their services rejected.

Swearing that he didn't know how he came to be wounded, "for

I did not expose myself, really," Lafayette went on to warn his wife against false rumors – such as of his death, or Washington's – and told her of the "ecstasies" into which his doctors fell when they came to treat his leg. He then delivered his "lesson." This was to the effect that, though the Americans had suffered a defeat, their untried soldiers (he forbore to include himself among them) had done well; that though Philadelphia had been taken, it was but a "sad town, open on all sides . . . made famous by being the residence of Congress, I know not why; that is all there is to this famous town which, in parenthesis, we will make them hand back sooner or later."

But then his energy for political instruction ran out, for "if they continue to press you with questions, you will send them packing in terms that the Vicomte de Noailles will inform you, since I do not want to waste time on politics when I write to you." He was as upset about his own "dreadful bad luck" as about the American defeat. He was bored with having to lie around, with nothing to do but read and improve his English, and although there was, as compensation, the daughter of the house in which he was staying, her father kept a close watch on the two, and even showed concern about their friendship. Perhaps this was on philosophical rather than amatory grounds; it is disappointing if the daughter of a pacifist should dally with a general. But more likely her father's fears were groundless: the settlement was communal and open, and offered little chance of privacy.

Most of all Lafayette was desperate for news of home. He still didn't know whether Adrienne had given birth to a son or a daughter, and his doctor worried about his blood-pressure when boats arrived without letters for him. All of his own letters were full of praise for Washington, though in one to his wife he attempted modestly to describe his own popularity, which had grown since his wound, in comparison to the other French officers'. He could not, he told her, understand why they were so hated in America, just as they could not understand why he, alone among the foreigners, was so beloved. This, he went on, was simply because he was a "good man, happy enough to be liked by all the world, foreigner or American. I like them all, I hope to deserve their respect, and we are all mutually most pleased one with another."

The marquis wrote anxiously to Washington hoping to get back into action quickly, and received a cool, if friendly, reply. But his new popularity emboldened him to fire off letters to all and sundry, full of ideas, requests, solicitations, and faulty English. He asked Henry Laurens, who had driven him to Bethlehem, to get a lieutenancy for La Colombe, his childhood friend and son of his neighbor from the Auvergne. He also took on the unenviable role of championing the interests of the French in America.

Even de Kalb, the Comte de Broglie's man, paid tribute to Lafayette's new prestige. Congress had decided to make use of the "baron's" services after all, though de Kalb himself had become increasingly doubtful about the way they were running things. He also had a low opinion of Washington, whom he described as:

the most amiable, kind-hearted and upright of men; but as a general he is too slow, too indolent, and far too weak; besides, he has a tinge of vanity in his composition, and overestimates himself. In my opinion, whatever success he may have will be owing to good luck and to the blunders of his adversaries, rather than to his abilities. I may even say that he does not know how to improve upon the grossest blunders of the enemy. He has not yet overcome his old prejudices against the French.

Despite this, de Kalb had reached the conclusion that to push for his patron Broglie to take Washington's place would be impossible. "It would be regarded as a crying injustice against Washington and an attempt against the country," he wrote. He nevertheless opened negotiations on his own behalf with Congress, and agreed to be commissioned as a major-general. He covered himself with regard to Broglie by promising his patron that he would leave if his decision were disapproved of. But he praised Lafayette's behavior in and out of the line of fire, and complimented his young friend by asking that his commission date from the same day as the marquis's, making them of equal seniority.

Lafayette meanwhile wrote another long letter to Washington, pushing once more for his own division. Not knowing that Washington disapproved of the new appointments, Lafayette praised certain officers who had been promoted by Congress and tried to take advantage of his intimacy with Washington, as "son" and "friend," to put forward his claims. Since Congress were handing out promotions, he wanted advice.

It is not in my character to examine if they have had, if they can have never some obligation to me, I am not usued to tell what I am, I wo'nt make no more any petition to Congress because I can now refuse, but not ask from them, therefore, dear general, I'l conduct myself by your advices. Consider, if you please, that Europe and particularly France is looking upon me. That I want to do something by myself, and justify that love of glory which I left be known to the world in making those sacrifices which have appeared so surprising, some say so foolish.

And in case Washington was confused by the style so as to miss the message, Lafayette went on to say that he had only refused a division at first because of diffidence, but "Now that I am better acquainted no difficulty comes from me." He explained that in France, his rank and title alone would have given him the equivalent of a division, although "I know it is not right. But I would deserve the reproachs of my friends and family if I would leave the advantages of mine to stay in a country where I could not find the occasions of distinguishing myself." *

When Lafayette had completed his convalescence and returned to camp, limping and unable to wear a boot on his left leg, it was as a minor sort of hero. The founders of the new nation seemed unanimous in their praise of his behavior as a patriot and a nobleman. Washington, who as well as having the British to think about was plagued by solicitations for promotion on the one hand, and resignations in disgust on the other, even wrote to Congress asking for further advice about Lafayette. He now seemed more willing to give "the marquis" – as he was beginning to be known – a division, and he too had succumbed to the lure of Lafayette's "illustrious and important connections," who might turn France against America if their young champion returned home empty-handed. As to Lafayette's military fitness for command, Washington described him as "sensible, discreet in his manner, has made great proficiency in our language and from the disposition he discovered at the battle of Brandywine, possesses a large share of bravery and military ardor." He was also, noted the commander-in-chief, a most reliable propagandist for the patriot cause in his letters home.

Lafayette meanwhile was not just sitting around camp waiting for his division. He busied himself with a flood of letters to Henry Laurens (who succeeded John Hancock as president of the Continental Congress) on behalf of every French volunteer who thought to ask his help. Perhaps this was his way of proving to his own compatriots the importance of his American connections. But the leaders of the American cause were not the only recipients of his suggestions. He had schemes of his own to promote, one of which was for an invasion of the British possessions in the East: the Indies, and India herself. On this matter he wrote direct to the Comte de Maurepas. He excused the lack of knowledge and detail in these outpourings of ideas by pleading indulgence for his "incompetence" and "youth." Experience of battle, the respect of the Americans, and above all the friendly interest of Washington, had obviously given Lafayette a new-found confidence. He bubbled over with plans

* This letter was written in Lafayette's English, and is here quoted verbatim. Most of his other letters are taken from his memoirs, where the English was translated into French. Those that appear correctly spelt and punctuated are therefore my re-translations.

(many of which were kept out of his memoirs because they came to nothing). Energy itself would not normally be enough to warrant being given command of a division, but the American army could ill afford to be choosy.

The condition of the soldiers continued to be bad; the commander-in-chief wrote in November that there were four thousand men needing blankets, of whom half had never had one, although some had been in service for a year. Patriotism was not enough to sustain an army without equipment, and the situation was made worse by arrears in pay and the continuing depreciation of the currency issued by Congress. There were times when Washington lost more men through desertion than he gained through enlistment, and as the autumn approached, the militia and many of his best-trained troops returned to civilian life, their periods of service over. The lack of senior officers led to a falling-off of discipline among ambitious colonels, while other officers were disgruntled not only because of their lack of pay but because of the promotion of foreigners over them. These they regarded as the "pets" of influential generals: even in an army supposedly animated by the highest of patriotic principles, jealousy wrought havoc. The fragile edifice of revolutionary solidarity which, with the hindsight of history, seems so polished and smooth, often threatened to disintegrate into a rubble. The friction between officers and men in the army was paralleled by that between the governing élites in the rebel colonies and those citizens demanding more equitable, more efficient, or more democratic government. The economic depressions of the war naturally pressed worst on the poor, who were the least likely to get redress. The colonies themselves were embittered by long-standing rivalries. Even among the leaders of the rebellion there were still many influential men who felt that the fighting was unnecessary and that an attempt should be made to settle with King George. One such appeal was addressed to Washington as late as October 1777. And there were the powerful factions fighting in Congress, which made even the commander-in-chief's position vulnerable. Yet the rebellion persisted.

Lafayette was largely ignorant of all these divisions: the one that interested him was his own. Perhaps people become heroes because their public actions reduce all the complications of the situation to one simple choice: for or against. Lafayette was a brave and very young man (the youngest general in the American army) who was prepared to think well of everybody until he suffered a personal injury. He was titled, generous, his credit was good, and he was also eager to share the hardships of the patriots. He admired, and was well regarded by, the one man whom many regarded as the embodiment of their cause – Washington. He had tremendous warmth and energy, qualities which America, by treating him as an adult, had brought out in him. He preferred action to philosophy and he was obviously not motivated by personal gain. In addition to all these attributes, which go far to explain his personal popularity, he became the symbol of international (or at least French) support for the American cause. This was a role which he embraced with the greatest enthusiasm, and it was his most effective contribution to victory.

Yet despite the mutual admiration of Washington and Lafayette, their relations came under some strain. For Lafayette to hobnob with the Irish-Frenchman Thomas Conway, whom Washington detested, was bad enough. But when the marquis wrote warmly to Washington's chief rival, General Horatio Gates, the commander-in-chief could have easily misconstrued his enthusiasm. True, Gates had led the most considerable success of the war so far, the surrender and capture of the English General Burgoyne with his entire army at Saratoga (October 17, 1777). This made Gates the champion of those who wanted "action" as opposed to the delaying and harassing tactics of Washington, and Lafayette was very keen on "action" himself. But then Conway and Gates plotted against Washington, trying to involve Lafayette. Thanks to the loyalty of others of his officers, Washington was aware of all that was going on. Conway, when found out, tendered his resignation – to which a divided Congress reacted by naming him inspector-general. When that news broke, the officers loyal to the commander-in-chief formally protested to Congress. Lafayette, having realized his mistake, rushed to include his name in the protest. Indeed he hurried to headquarters to reassure the general in person, but Washington was engaged. Lafayette therefore explained himself at length in a letter. He told of his surprise at discovering the bitterness of the faction-fighting in Congress, and of the strength of the Tories (Loyalists), when, in Europe, he had thought that everyone loved liberty and preferred death to slavery. He had believed that at least all good Americans were united, and that Congress had boundless confidence in the commander-in-chief. It was that, he said, that made him certain that America would be independent, if only she did not lose Washington. He went on gently to criticize his friend for not defending himself, and then admitted that Conway had deceived him. He candidly stated that the "Irishman" had dangled before him plans of glory and adventure, by which he had been too easily dazzled. "I am now fixed to your fate and I shall follow it and sustain it as well by my sword as by all means in my power. You will pardon my importunity in favor of the sentiment which dictates it. Youth and friendship make myself perhaps too warm, but I feel the greatest concern at all what happens since some time."

Lafayette did everything possible to model his behavior on that of his "father." Washington in turn at last repaid the marquis's devotion by supporting his plea for a division.

In November 1777, though still not fully recovered, Lafayette had gone, as a volunteer, to accompany General Greene on a reconnaissance party. Near Gloucester, Lafayette's party suddenly came upon a troop of Hessians, mercenaries in the pay of the British. Lafayette attacked, and drove them back toward the British base. It was a small victory, but one of which Lafayette hastened to inform Washington, using praise of the American troops as an excuse for writing. General Greene praised Lafayette's conduct to the commander-in-chief, and this was communicated to Congress, with an anxious note about what might happen if Lafayette were disappointed. "I still feel a refusal will not only induce him to return in disgust," wrote Washington, "but may involve some unfavorable consequences." There were, besides, vacant divisions and the veteran de Kalb, whose commission dated from the same day as the marquis's, had just been given one. If Washington, who after all would have to bear the consequences, could change his tune, so could Congress. On December 1, 1777, it was resolved that "It is highly agreeable to Congress that the Marquis de la Fayette be appointed to the command of a division in the Continental army." At twenty, Lafayette realized his ambition. He not only had the respect of the man he most respected, he was also in a position to bring glory to the family name, the chief reason – so he had been taught – for his presence in the world.

5
A Touch of Glory

LAFAYETTE CHOSE A division of Virginians (from the colony in which Washington was born) which, in a long and confident letter to his father-in-law, the Duc d'Ayen, he described as weak, "even in proportion to the weakness of the army." They were "almost naked, but there is hope of cloth from which I will make uniforms, and recruits from which soldiers must be made at almost the same time. But by bad luck, the one is more difficult than the other, even for cleverer people than me." To show how changed he was, he felt able to tell the duc that "I read, I study, I analyze, I listen, I think, and from all that I try to form an idea which I cram with as much common sense as I can. I will not talk too much for fear of uttering absurdities; I will risk even less for fear of doing them. . . ."

This letter was written just after the third occasion on which Major-General Lafayette came under fire – a small skirmish which he felt scarcely worth a mention. To his father-in-law he used none of the rhetorical flourishes on "liberty" to which he treated his wife; indeed, his letter is almost statesman-like in its moderation, and its hope that France will soon declare herself for the American cause. He had at last received letters from home, telling him of the arrival of his second child – another girl, Anastasie (born July 1, 1777) – and the birth of a son to his brother-in-law. Half humorously and half in genuine disappointment, he wrote, of the house in which they lived, "There is the Rue Saint-Honoré discredited for ever, while the other Noailles mansion has gained a new luster with the birth of Adrien." Yet he also admitted that his anxiety had been too great "to make a distinction of sex."

The problems of command which Lafayette faced were the same, of course, as those of Washington: supplying, training, feeding, and paying his troops. These needs were as important as fighting the

English who had holed up in Philadelphia, hopefully for the winter. Lafayette badgered his friends in Congress on behalf of his division, in vain; he also flooded headquarters with suggestions on uniforms, drill, discipline, and the personal appearance of the Continental soldiers, again without much effect. At the end of the year 1777, the Continental army faced two major problems. For the officers, it was what to do about the "Conway cabal," in which Conway, the man who had so impressed Lafayette and who had been promoted to inspector-general, was again pushing for General Gates to replace Washington. For every fighting man, the problem was the more basic one of how to survive the winter.

The site chosen by Washington for winter quarters was Valley Forge, an exposed and windy hillside eighteen miles northwest of Philadelphia. It had to be near the occupied city, in order to reduce British chances of foraging, but not close enough to be surprised by British troops. The idea of requisitioning quarters in nearby towns and villages was resisted by the local people on the grounds that they were already crowded out by refugees from the capital. The soldiers were thus forced to live in inadequate tents until enough wood could be felled to build huts. There was wood in plenty, and the high ground was a fine defensive position. But there was no food; in the week before Christmas, when the army moved in, the inhospitable hills echoed with the cry "No meat." The commissary had more or less collapsed, leaving the soldiers to face the sleet of winter with nothing to wear, nothing to cover themselves with, and nothing, often literally nothing, to eat. Things reached the point in February, 1778 when there was no meat whatever for over a week. The chant on that occasion was, "No pay, no clothes, no provisions, no rum."

The huts that were eventually built to house the troops were like those of the pioneers, made of logs, with the holes stuffed with moss, clay, or straw. Each one took about two weeks to build, and the officers usually helped. Lafayette was especially anxious to prove himself worthy of his troops' admiration. The roofs let in the wet but often didn't let out the smoke from the fires, with the result that the inhabitants' eyes were always red and sore. Conditions in December 1777 were described by one Elijah Fisher:

We had no tents, not anithing to Cook our Provisions in, and that was Prity Poor, for our beef was very leen and no salt, nor any way to Cook it but to throw it on the Coles and brile it; and the warter we had to Drink and to mix our flower with was out of a brook that run along by the Camps, and so many a dippin and washin it which maid it very Dirty and muddy.

Washington furiously tried to impress upon Congress the

desperateness of the situation. The revolution's representatives at least had roofs over their heads and clothes on their backs, and must have found it hard to believe that the defense of liberty lay with naked men actually dying of exposure. "Unless some great and capital change suddenly takes place . . . this army must inevitably be reduced to one or other of these three things. Starve, dissolve, or disperse, in order to obtain subsistence in the best manner they can," he wrote. On December 31st he described the army as "Our sick naked, our well naked, our unfortunate men in captivity naked!" And he was not a man given to exaggeration. The army could not move without clothes, and only those who had something to cover themselves with could do outside duty. They had to hurry to build huts to shelter their naked comrades before frostbite killed them off, and yet they had to be careful to keep their own garments from giving out. Those without shoes or strips of cloth to bind their feet would have them cut to ribbons by marching on the frozen uneven ground. There was insufficient medical attention: Lafayette noted many feet and legs, blackening from the cold, which had to be amputated. The hospital huts were overcrowded, even with men dying very quickly. It was the middle of January before everyone was in huts, and then they did not always have straw to stop the cold rising from the ground. Washington feared either mutiny or mass desertion on foot, since the few remaining animals were too weak to carry men.

Lafayette, who lived in slightly better conditions than his men, was careful to limit his own rations, and frequently used his own money in attempts to improve the conditions of his solidiers. He was chiefly envious of those generals, such as Washington and Greene, who had their wives at camp. To cheer himself up he wrote a jolly letter to Adrienne. Years later he described the appalling situation, not only in Valley Forge but among the patriots in general – the depreciated currency, the difficulties in raising money and men, the seductions of the English and the influence of their Tory supporters. But even he could not do justice to the horrors of that winter. "The greatest difficulty," he wrote, "was that in order to hide this evil from the enemy, it had to be hidden from the people." And he declared that the Continental officers and men would receive their reward only in the next world.

Yet to the surprise of their officers, an army held together in Valley Forge. From numbering some 17,000 men, the army that survived the winter shrank to 5000. But they were still there when things reached rock bottom. Desertion actually diminished when there were no provisions at all: proof either of indomitable spirit or the knowledge that things were no better elsewhere. Those that stayed benefited from the zealous Prussian drilling of Baron Steuben, who claimed to have been a lieutenant-general under Frederick the Great, and from the close attention of their officers, among whom Lafayette proved himself a strict disciplinarian, making few allowances for the conditions they faced.

Being an American soldier was bad enough when none of the promised pay and provisions materialized. It was worse when local suppliers of food, dairy products, and grain either profiteered (as is common in all wars) or refused to accept the Continental paper currency, which was no more welcome to volunteers for enlistment. Troops who were ragged, ill-fed, and scarcely paid continued to fight until the end of the war and, though conditions marginally improved, the soldiers still had to suffer careless, lazy, or greedy waggoners ruining their precious loads, bureaucratic squabblings over who should provide or ship urgently needed uniforms or provisions, and the reluctance of civilians to give them care or shelter, for fear of being plundered or ill-used. Far from fighting with unanimous resolve, many Americans, while not sympathetic to the king, were equally suspicious of the Congressional bureaucracy, especially when they were taxed, required to provide men and supplies for what appeared to many a greater threat than the Redcoats – a standing army – and paid in a currency which rapidly became worthless. Deserters from the army, instead of being reported to the authorities in a fit of patriotic fervor, were often sheltered by their sympathetic neighbors, and their gaunt and woeful appearance was hardly an inducement to enlist. Enlistment, indeed, was achieved as often through booze and bribery as through enthusiasm for the cause, and if the fighting men suffered privations, their families at home suffered worse, especially as prices rose astronomically. The only remedy for those privates with nothing to go home to was to wait for their pay; when it failed to come, they could only mutiny, since desertion meant the threat of starvation. Officers could at least resign, and thousands of them did. Wealthy men like Lafayette and Washington could sympathize with such people, but it is as difficult to understand another's desperation as it is to share another's toothache. Washington and others, including French observers, were frequently scathing about the "avariciousness" of the common soldier. But they were in little danger of starving to death, or having their meager harvests ruined in their absence.

As time went on, rank became increasingly important in the American army, which had started with the egalitarian spirit of the local militia who elected their own officers. Lafayette was from the beginning extremely sensitive about rank, partly due to his French training and partly his own insecurity. The honors due to rank, common to other armies, were soon introduced into the Continental one, but it did not improve the quality of the officers, many of whom were venal, lax, and deserted under fire. It was charged that many of them resigned when danger approached. A colleague reported a revealing, if semi-serious, remark of Washington's at Valley Forge: "So many resignations of officers that his Excellency expressed fears of being left alone with the soldiers." Lafayette was, without a doubt, one of the more popular officers, and Washington was, by most accounts, adored. The two shared an aristocratic attitude toward their men and were prepared to share their hardships. They were keen on discipline and obviously not in the service for the money; their dedication, perhaps, made their reputations. And even though Washington made no secret of his preference for native-born Americans for sentinels, his personal bodyguard, and officers in general, his lasting and public partiality for Lafayette reassured the young general's troops that their interests would always be well represented to the commander-in-chief.

The military spirit which the officers and gentlemen of the patriotic cause considered so necessary for victory was very irritating to the large numbers of rural volunteers, unused to regular shaving and disciplined behavior, much less powdering their hair and looking "smart" to order. But punishment could be, and very often was, barbarically severe, more to impress the ranks than reform the wrong-doer. Desertion was sometimes punished by death, sometimes by up to one hundred lashes, occasionally administered in two installments, the wounds being rubbed with salt and water between beatings. The lash was most common, but there was also the pillory, running the gauntlet, being degraded, cashiered, drummed out of the army, fined, and imprisoned. Both British and Continental troops accused each other of the hideous maltreatment of prisoners. There was, as already noted, an insufficiency of doctors and hospitals. General Schuyler wrote to Congress in November 1775: "Of all the specifics ever invented there is none so efficacious as a discharge, for as soon as their faces turn homeward nine out of ten are cured." At Valley Forge, the favorite medicine was apparently mutton and grog, when these were to be had. Conditions were so bad at the camp that the men were spared open-air religious services and sermons, which may have afforded them some relief.

Of all the catalogue of woes the American army suffered and survived the most serious from a tactical point of view was the lack of fire-power. The American "rifleman" raised a certain dread among the British troops because of the accuracy of his marksmanship, but guns were not only scarce, they were often antiquated. At one stage Franklin had even suggested that the patriot troops use pikes and bows and arrows. The principal American weapon in the early days of the war was the flintlock, which required at least thirteen separate drill movements to aim, fire and reload. Among the movements were biting off the top of the paper cartridge, priming by shaking powder into the pan, putting the cartridge into the muzzle and shaking more powder into the barrel, extracting the rammer, ramming the cartridge, returning the rammer, shouldering the gun, poising, cocking, aiming, and finally firing. The British and some Americans may have criticized the Continental troops for hiding behind trees or building earthwork defenses where they could, but reloading their guns took so long that the enemy could mow them down with bayonets in between rounds. The open, offensive tactics so beloved by soldiers of the European school would have been suicidal for the Americans. Fortunately, their supplies and equipment improved as the war grew older, especially with help from France.

This, then, was the physical state of the American army at the beginning of 1778. Their emotional state, warmed by their cause, was doubtless much stronger. The British, however, were not as powerful as their position seemed to indicate. Supply lines from England were precarious, and the war effort disorganized. Apart from the task of destroying such military effectiveness as Washington had, General Howe had to divide his army so as to hold on to both Philadelphia and New York. But occupying two large cities was no way to search out and destroy rebel fighters spread widely throughout a predominantly agricultural country. To control the thirteen colonies would have required more troops for a longer period and at a greater cost than England could possibly afford. Moreover, Howe was as reluctant to risk his men as Washington was. Despite the weak condition of the Continentals in Valley Forge, Howe later wrote that it did not "occasion any difficulties so pressing as to justify an attack on that strong position during the severe weather." And the surrender of General Burgoyne with his entire army at Saratoga was an amazing American victory, psychologically as well as militarily. When news of it reached Paris it proved a major turning-point in committing France to the American cause.

The victor of Saratoga, General Horatio Gates, became president of the Board of War. As a rival of Washington, he and the "Conway cabal," which centered on that newly promoted inspector-general, were in a powerful position. Together Gates and Conway planned an invasion of Canada. This British colony, previously under French rule, was, they felt certain, full of disaffected citizens longing to cast off the English yoke. Apart from the financial and strategic importance of the territory, such an invasion was likely to attract the support of the French government to the patriots' struggle. It was with this thought in mind that they turned to Lafayette to command the expedition. Their secondary hope was to detach him from the Washington camp.

For Lafayette, as ambitious as ever for glory, the temptation was irresistible. Washington's careful neutrality on the scheme, however, gave him pause. The commander-in-chief was always obedient to the wishes of Congress, but he avoided actually giving approval to the expedition, confining himself to saying to Lafayette about his command, "I would rather it were yours than anyone else's." Lafayette's suspicions of a plot to wean him from Washington were aroused when he heard that General Conway was to be his second-in-command and that the command itself was to be an independent one. If there was to be a clash between his appetite for honors and his attachment to his "father," there was no doubt in his mind which to sacrifice. He wrote to his friend Henry Laurens, "I am young, I am therefore unexperienced, but every mean in my power, every knowledge in the military way I can have got since the first days of my life, every thing nature could have granted to me, all my exertions, and the last drop of my blood, shall be employed in showing my acknowledgement for such a favor and how I wish to deserve it."

But as for being independent of the commander-in-chief, he said that he hoped the scheme would not be "useless to the success and future glory of our respectable friend – for I dare hope, that Congress will permit me to look upon myself only as a detachment of General Washington's army, and an officer under his immediate command." And in case it was not crystal-clear whose side he was on, Lafayette then protested strongly against the choice of Conway as his number two, and asked for the veteran General McDougall or, if his health were not up to it, General de Kalb.

Setting off northwards from Valley Forge to discuss his command, Lafayette now proved his devotion to Washington in no uncertain way. He spent days in York, where Congress had settled, politicking with President Laurens and the Board of War to ensure that he was still subject to the orders of the commander-in-chief, to neutralize the influence of Conway in the expedition, and to get commissions for several French officers and thus prove himself a patriot on both sides of the Atlantic. To ensure success, he offered the carrot of financing the expedition himself if necessary, and the stick of resigning and returning to France with all the serving French officers if thwarted. With Laurens' support, his demands were granted, though whether the command was or was not finally independent still remained unclear. However, the object of the expedition was somewhat reduced: instead of it being a grand invasion, it now became what Gates called "a mere incursion or ravage." Nevertheless Lafayette was delighted.

Traveling to take up his post through the ice and snow of upper New York, he noted:

the pure morals of the inhabitants, their patriarchal life, their republican spirit. Devoted to their households, the wives delight in them, and get from them every joy. It is to the girls that one speaks of love: their coquetry is as friendly as it is decent. In the marriages of chance that are made in Paris, the fidelity of women is repugnant to nature, reason, one might almost say to the principles of justice. In America one marries one's lover, and it would be like having two at once to break a valid agreement, because both parties know why and how they have committed themselves.

At least his ability to philosophize about pretty girls never left him.

Lafayette arrived in Albany on February 17, 1778, and discovered in full the difficulties of command. He may have escaped the rigors of Valley Forge – though the climate in upper New York State was not exactly mild – but he found himself facing exactly the same problems. Of the 2500 men he had been promised would form his "army," he found less than half, and those mostly "naked." There was nowhere near enough clothing, provisions, ammunition, sledges, or snowshoes. He reckoned it would take two months to get properly prepared, by which time Lake Champlain would have unfrozen, making it necessary to cross into Canada by boat. Officers and men had been unpaid for too long. Not only Conway, who was still attached to the expedition and who had preceded Lafayette to Albany, advised against going on; Generals Schuyler, Lincoln, and Benedict Arnold, all experts in the terrain, agreed with him.

In desperation, Lafayette wrote to Washington. He too felt that it was impossible to proceed with the expedition, and he was miserable about it. His pride was hurt most, for everyone in America and France knew that he had been appointed to the command. Several members of Congress, he claimed, had even asked him to write to his friends saying that he was at the head of an army (to Adrienne, a fortnight or so previously, he had boasted that he was a "general-in-chief"). The public, he said, was expecting great things: how could he answer them? Derision was what he feared most, and he was so anxious for reassurance that he wondered aloud if he shouldn't return to being a simple volunteer – unless Congress found some glorious employment for him to make up for this disaster.

Fortunately he was let down very gently. Washington, despite his own problems, well understood the mild paranoia of disappointed youth, and replied that Lafayette's fears sprang from "an uncommon degree of sensibility" where his reputation was concerned. He pointed out the advantages in having it known that Congress had so much confidence in him that they had awarded him a detached command, and went on to say that "every one will applaud your prudence in renouncing a project in pursuing which you would vainly have attempted physical impossibilities." The marquis, he said, could hardly be held responsible for the elements, and he concluded: "However sensible your ardor for glory may make you feel this disappointment, you may be assured that your character stands as fair as ever it did, and that no new enterprise is necessary to wipe off this imaginary stain."

Congress, too, was well disposed toward Lafayette. Gates had made up his quarrel with Washington, who accepted that he had been the tool of the "cabal," which had ruined its chances by showing itself too soon. Conway was dealt with by being left in charge of the force in New York. At first this news infuriated Lafayette, who blustered and raved at this apparent slight to his own ability. But he was mollified when Congress flattered both his and Washington's sensibilities by resolving that his presence in the main army was urgently necessary, and that he should resume charge of his old division. Congress was now anxious to support the commander-in-chief, whose partiality for Lafayette was well known, and it owed something to its youngest major-general for sending him on what turned out to be a wild goose-chase.

He may have been unable to invade and conquer Canada, but Lafayette was not idle during his weeks in the north. He used his own private credit to relieve his men's most pressing debts. He bought clothing for use in the next campaign. He collected specimens of trees and shrubs to send to his wife's grandfather, the Maréchal de Noailles, and sent several lots in case the first failed to arrive. He became convinced he had uncovered a gigantic Tory plot to foment revolt against the patriot cause, and he showed a somewhat precipitous zeal in ordering the arrest of all suspects. Names had been given by an anonymous informer, but no evidence was found, and the suspects had to be released.

Most impressive of all, he attended a gathering of the Six Nations, the Indian tribes of New York: Mohawks, Oneidas, Senecas, Cayugas, Tuscaroras, and Onondagas. During Burgoyne's northern campaign, the British had bought the support of the Iroqois who, once given the chance of attacking those who had taken their land, did so with great ferocity. Tales of their scalping – an operation which, though painful, was not necessarily fatal and some claim it was a practice taught to the Indians by the invading whites – gave the Indians a fearsome reputation. Congress sought to reassure and treat with them. General Schuyler was appointed to deal with the Six Nations and he invited Lafayette to accompany him. Armed with trinkets, rum, and French *louis* pieces made into medallions, the generals confronted five hundred semi-naked and painted Indians of all ages and sexes, fully adorned with feathers, jewels in their noses, and their ears pierced. Smoking their peace-pipes, the elders discussed matters for several days, and a treaty was concluded, though none of the Americans thought it would last. Lafayette's generosity greatly impressed the tribes, and they adopted him as a "father," giving him the name Kayewla. Nevertheless he felt it prudent to keep them sweet with bribes, and advised the building of forts when they could be afforded.

Lafayette returned to his own "father" at Valley Forge having spent "about twelve thousand dollars more than I should have expended," as he lamented to Laurens. The Americans now faced a political as well as a military assault from the British. Parliament, worried at the course of the war, had propounded two "reconciliation bills," one repealing the most obnoxious acts concerning the colonies – the Prohibitory Act, Massachusetts Government Act, and the duty on tea – the other appointing peace commissioners, who were to offer home rule without independence. Westminster was still undecided whether to crush or conciliate. But matters had advanced too far for compromise, even for Washington, who wrote to Henry Laurens, "The enemy are determined to try us by force, and by fraud. . . . It appears to me that nothing short of independence can possibly do. The injuries we have received from Britain can never be forgotten, and a peace upon other terms would be the source of perpetual feuds and animosities." Congress agreed with him, and so, naturally, did Lafayette. As spring came, new military measures had to be decided upon – though the Continental army still lacked pay, provisions, and adequate foreknowledge of enemy intentions.

Meanwhile, in France, the decision that had been contemplated for so long was now finally made: on February 6, 1778, two treaties were signed by the French government and the American commissioners, who were at last formally received by the king. The Treaty of Amity and Commerce involved French recognition of American independence and an agreement to trade, while the Treaty of Alliance bound both parties to be loyal allies should war occur between France and Britain before American independence. Neither was to make a truce without the other's consent.

A combination of circumstances was responsible for the French commitment to the American cause. There was the news of Saratoga, which proved that the Americans were capable of winning major victories. There were the advantages in trade and territory that had been negotiated, and the chance of attacking British possessions, especially in the West Indies, while the British navy was (hopefully) preoccupied. But French public opinion also played a large part in pushing Vergennes and Maurepas to commit themselves, and for this Lafayette could claim much of the credit. If Washington had become a hero to the French liberal set, as often happens to the leaders of a revolutionary campaign, Lafayette had almost eclipsed him. His battles, his wound, his division, his trials and tribulations, and his intimacy with the great man were the subject of eager gossip in Versailles and Paris, thanks to his letters to his influential friends. His family had become converted to the cause, and American notables such as John Adams were hospitably entertained in, and greatly impressed by, the Noailles mansion. Even his old passion Aglaë d'Hunolstein spoke well of the man she had rejected. That a French nobleman should enjoy such influence and prestige in such a cause stirred patriotic pride and made many of Lafayette's friends jealous. The young noblemen surrounding the king pressed for him to declare himself, using Lafayette as an example of how much could be achieved. When the decision was made, it was as the result of hard bargaining between Vergennes and Franklin, Adams, and Deane. Lafayette played no direct part in what was a strictly political decision. But he was excellent publicity for the cause, and he affected influential opinion. It was enough to be proud of.

6
The Making of a Legend

THE NEWS OF the French-American treaties took nearly three months to reach America. The official announcement was made to the army on May 5, 1778, but Washington had been informed a few days previously. He had, of course, told Lafayette, who startled him by throwing his arms around him and kissing him roundly on both cheeks. There was a *feu de joie* to celebrate, and Lafayette, distinctive in a white scarf, the color of the Bourbons, was honored as his country's representative by being given command of the right wing of the first line. The other French major-general, de Kalb, was given command of the second line. One thing Washington was learning was how to deal with the touchy sensibilities of his dedicated officers, foreign and native.

A salute of thirteen guns, one for each state, followed readings of the treaties and sermons by the army chaplains. Then there was a running fire of muskets from right to left on Lafayette's line, and left to right on de Kalb's. The cheer "Long live the King of France" was followed by "And long live the friendly European powers" – a nice diplomatic touch, since it was hoped that Spain would follow France's example. The final fire and shout was "To the American States," after which every man received a tot of rum. Officers fared somewhat better, being treated to a cold collation in the form of a "profusion of fat meat, strong wine, and other liquors."

Lafayette's celebration of what he had labored for for so long was blighted by news, which arrived at the same time, that his first child, Henriette, and also his nephew Adrien, had died. Never, he wrote to his bereaved wife, had the distance between them seemed so great. Yet he could not, he explained, return immediately, as he would have liked to do. He had had to take part in the celebrations, for not to have done so would have seemed peculiar. And he was needed for the military campaign that was about to open. Both on the diplomatic and the military fronts, he felt that "by serving the cause of humanity and that of America, I have been fighting for the interests of France." The French in America, indeed, had reason to be grateful for the accord between their countries: "French" manners became fashionable, and French teachers set up everywhere. How could Lafayette not stay and enjoy his triumph, now that he was officially lauded in his own country as well as his adopted one?

Washington, as much in the dark as before about British intentions, next dispatched Lafayette on a reconnaissance mission. He gave him about 2200 specially chosen men and very careful instructions. If he discovered for certain that the enemy were planning to evacuate Philadelphia, Lafayette was permitted to harass them from the rear, but this was to be done only with "the greatest prudence." Every mistake, he was reminded, would have the most disastrous consequences. Nor was he allowed to forget that he was in charge of picked men, whose loss would be serious for the army. The marquis was ordered to take every precaution against surprise and not to risk anything without the greatest chance of success. About the only thing he was allowed to choose for himself was the location of posts to occupy.

Lafayette marched to Barren Hill, equidistant from Valley Forge and Philadelphia, being about eleven miles from each. The hill itself was a good defensive position, and he set up pickets and started recruiting spies. Philadelphia itself was celebrating the recall of General Howe and the appointment of Sir Henry Clinton (whom Lafayette had met in London) to take command of the British forces. Amid the jollities, Howe learned of Lafayette's nearness, and apparently, according to Lafayette's memoirs, determined to capture him and make him the chief attraction of his farewell dinner. The British army, therefore, began surrounding Lafayette's force, who might well have been caught if a wakeful American militia captain hadn't seen Redcoats clinking past his window at dawn. Still in his nightshirt, the captain ran toward Barren Hill, and the news was carried to the marquis who happened to be with a young lady who had, he claimed, offered her services to him as a spy.

Doubtless remembering that faulty intelligence had been responsible for the defeat at Brandywine, Lafayette sent men to verify the position. The news was not good: he was indeed almost surrounded. The only light relief was afforded by an encounter between a troop of Indians serving under Lafayette and some Redcoats. Neither having laid eyes on the others before, each ran howling in opposite directions as fast as they could go. But the general, despite the cries of his soldiers that they were cut off, retreated in an orderly fashion along the only road not blocked by the enemy. He took the precaution of sending some men into the surrounding woods with orders to look like the heads of marching columns – and this ruse actually worked.

Washington, meanwhile, could see what was going on from Valley Forge and, when warning guns were fired, mustered the entire army and issued it with ammunition, ready to march to Lafayette's assistance. But his protégé managed to get away in time and, though he had found out nothing about enemy intentions – the object of the expedition – Washington commended his tactics. He wrote to Gouverneur Morris that Lafayette had been caught in a "snare . . . but by his *own dexterity* or the enemy's *want of it*, he disengaged himself in a very soldierlike manner."

It did seem as if the British were going to leave Philadelphia, but they took their time about it. The army fretted at Valley Forge until certain news arrived: on June 18th Clinton had left the city and assembled his men in New Jersey. Washington assumed they were bound for New York, "though they do not appear to be in any hurry." This in itself was worrying, for a long campaign might weaken the already depleted American forces. But there were various roads which the British could take that would make them splendid targets: in all, Washington decided to move with caution and take what chances of attack he could.

Some of the irons Lafayette had thrust into the fire now seemed to redden. His wild scheme for attacking the Indies was endorsed by his relative the Marquis de Bouillé, who was governor of Martinique, but Congress, when apprised of the idea, merely thanked Lafayette for his "zeal and good will." Nothing more was ever done. Then Conway, who had originally been in on the Indies scheme before Lafayette realized his part in the "cabal," returned to plead his own case for promotion. Unfortunately for him, he included a threat of resignation and, despite his protestations, this was taken up. Lafayette nevertheless did his best for Conway, who was, after all, a French officer.

But Lafayette's great enthusiasm was for glorious action, which he agitated for in the army's war councils. In this he was opposed by many of his seniors, and most notably General Charles Lee, a British-born officer who was held to be a great strategist. Lafayette found Lee ugly but witty; their disagreements did not blunt their friendship. In fact few of Washington's officers were satisfied that the right decisions had been taken at the council of June 24, 1778: to avoid a general engagement and merely harass the enemy where possible. Generals Lafayette, Wayne, and Greene all protested to their commander-in-chief, but he would not be moved from the decision. In view of the continuing lack of knowledge about Clinton's army, caution remained essential.

Washington decided that the best person to put in charge of a harassing force would be Lafayette, who had at least been a consistent advocate of offensive tactics. Though Lee was the marquis's senior, he agreed to Washington's personal request to allow the younger man to take command. Only when it was obvious that the task would be an important one did Lee change his mind. The unfortunate commander-in-chief then had one of the perennial pecking-order disputes on his hands. This he resolved by giving to Lafayette the honor of making the first move, after which Lee was to enjoy seniority. Meanwhile reports confirmed that the British were marching toward Monmouth Court House.

Monmouth was some forty miles to the northeast of Philadelphia, on the route to New York where the other main British force awaited Clinton. There was no point in the British staying in Philadelphia if they could not control the surrounding countryside: a joining-together with their northern army might give them the opportunity to smash Washington's army, which was pursuing them. The American general staff was divided on strategy. The decision to pursue and harass the enemy was a weak one, but dictated by the weakness of their forces. It was important, psychologically even more than militarily, to keep the army together; the maintenance of a strong central command was a political principle of the patriot leaders, in the interests of control, unity, and order. Fear of "anarchy" overtaking a weak authority was as prevalent in the New World as the Old, and was another principle Lafayette shared with Washington.

The battle of Monmouth itself (June 28, 1778) was a classic example of the condition of the American command and army in the middle of the revolutionary war. A perspective of its outcome will make the details easier to follow. The American advance force was ordered to attack the British rear, as it marched towards New York. Under General Lee, the Americans got themselves so confused they began retreating without having properly engaged the enemy. Washington took command and made a stand. The Americans pushed the British back a little way, but each side held its ground. During the following night the British left the field and continued on their way. Both sides claimed a victory: the Americans that they had forced a British retreat and inflicted severe damage, the British that they had held off American troops while pursuing their original objective – a march north.

In his anxiety for action, Lafayette pushed his advance force, in blazing heat, so far and so fast that they not only got too far ahead of the main army, but also of the provisions that were sent after them. Other detachments, under Wayne and Hamilton, were badly supplied with food *and* information: they were not sure of the whereabouts of their own army, let alone the enemy's. When Lee finally assumed overall command of the forward forces, with orders to ready themselves for an attack, nothing but the greatest confusion reigned among his fellow-officers and their troops. Washington, trying from a distance to hold things together, again found himself the victim of conflicting intelligence.

Lee himself did not have – or at least did not reveal – a plan of campaign in accordance with Washington's directions. He knew too little about the lie of the land, and about his own subordinates, and he did not bother to familiarize himself with either. He did not have enough reliable aides to relay messages. He confused his troops and the enemy's, showed himself ignorant of the strength of his own men, and caused chaos by shifting around commands. He asked Lafayette to take the place of honor at the head of the crack troops, but then left him exposed and inadequately posted. The British, meanwhile, had time to re-form and attack, and they made the most of the opportunity.

From starting in a strong position to attack the British, Lee discovered in battle that he had to extricate himself from one that was horribly exposed. He ordered the most endangered detachments to retreat to safer ground. Lafayette, in looking for his supporting troops, found himself alone. A garbled message from Lee told him to be prudent, which he interpreted as falling-back to secure a better position. General Wayne, seeing Lafayette retreat, asked him why. Lafayette replied that those were his orders but Wayne, disagreeing, sent to Lee asking for support in an attack. Now Lee ordered Lafayette to take command on the right. Doing so, he again discovered there was no adequate protection. Moreover the enemy were reported to be on the right in strength. Lee ordered a retreat to the left and rear. Though there had been very little fighting, the men were exhausted because of the heat of 96° in the shade. They were dying of sunstroke rather than in battle. Meanwhile, Clinton, the British commander-in-chief, had joined his army to face Lee. Washington was coming up with his army from behind.

The American commander had heard no news from Lee, beyond reports of confusion and difficulties among his troops. Slowly advancing, he came across stragglers who said that Lee's men were falling back. Having heard no fierce fighting, Washington refused to believe it until he ran into a great crowd of staggering Continentals, retreating toward him. Pressing on, he finally met Lee. He questioned him sharply. Lee replied that contradictory intelligence had caused confusion, and that he was in no condition to fight the British. Washington, genuinely angry, replied that he expected his orders to be obeyed, and that if Lee had not believed in the operation he should not have insisted on leading it. Then he continued to the front. The enemy were only a quarter of an hour away.

By luck, he met a man who knew the ground and a place where the heat-shattered troops might rally. His physical presence and assumption of command actually stemmed the flood of retreating soldiers. Leaving Lee in charge of the advance force, he returned to the main army. He might have had to face a general assault by the entire British army – but he did not. The American fire held off the Redcoats. By the late afternoon they had driven the British back some little way; the two armies remained "looking at each other . . . till dark," as Lafayette's friend John Laurens (the son of the president of Congress) put it. Lafayette himself, who earlier had only led his troops in retreat, was ordered to occupy some woods through which the British were expected to pass. He moved back when their attack was dealt with without his help. None of the general officers, except perhaps Wayne, distinguished themselves that day. Washington saved the situation, and in the morning the Americans awoke to find that the British had stolen away, leaving only their badly wounded and unburied dead. The Continentals were themselves too exhausted to pursue.

Washington and Lafayette spent the night sharing a cloak and talking, mainly of Lee. (That officer sought a court-martial to clear his name and was found guilty of disobedience. Sentenced to be suspended for a year, he resigned, and died before the end of the war.) But despite their closeness, Washington did not include the marquis's name in his citation to Congress of the fighting major-generals, nor did he mention Monmouth in the roll-call of Lafayette's glories he sent to Franklin when the marquis ended his first trip to America. Lafayette was of course bitterly disappointed at not having acted more gloriously. Nevertheless he was reassured by having spent that night on the cloak with the undisputed hero of the hour. If he learned nothing else, he was eternally inspired by the "fine carriage on horseback" and the "calm courage" Washington had shown. It became a style he himself adopted. The connection between the two men was stronger than ever. A certain warmth even crept into Washington's normal mortuary style when addressing "the marquis." As far as Lafayette was concerned, Washington could do no wrong, and without his assistance the American cause was lost.

Despite his reputation in America, Lafayette felt that he had not yet sufficiently enhanced the tradition of his ancestors, even though this was a different type of war from theirs, fought not with glittering regiments of hussars and dragoons, but with a citizen army. Lafayette's devotion to France and her military glories remained strong, outweighing his attachment to America and rivaling even his affection for Washington. When, therefore, a French fleet under the Comte d'Estaing arrived, following the ratification of the treaties between the United States and France, Lafayette seized on it as the chance to achieve something heroic. His ambition was to command a force composed of Americans and Frenchmen in a smashing attack on the British. Unfortunately the prosaic details that bedevil all international alliances got in his way.

The presence of the French fleet gave rise to tremendous optimism among the patriots, who regarded the naval superiority of the British as their enemy's most powerful weapon. The Comte d'Estaing, who happened to be a fellow-Auvergnat and a distant relative of Lafayette's, further cheered the Americans by showing a warm admiration for their commander-in-chief. Even while he was having difficulties finding a suitable place to land his scurvy-ridden men, he wrote to Washington saying that "To act in concert with a great man is the first of blessings" – a sentiment Lafayette might himself have dictated. But strains of discord between the new allies soon widened into disenchantment. The American commander in charge of the area where d'Estaing finally landed was General Sullivan, who was, to say the least, undiplomatic. D'Estaing himself was amazed at the American's apparent lack of military preparedness, and disappointed that the mighty forces he had been expecting did not materialize. Under the difficult conditions of conducting a joint expedition against the British garrison on Rhode Island (the actual island in the state of that name), the distant politeness required by etiquette gave way, on Sullivan's part, to outright insult. With Lafayette behaving like a highly-strung fighting-cock, pecking insistently at imagined and real slights to his countrymen, it was all Washington could do to keep the peace. Meanwhile he continued to suffer the endless solicitations, which Lafayette persisted in forwarding, of French volunteers, and the equally endless bickerings about seniority among the native officers. No wonder that he sighed to a congressional friend, "I do most earnestly wish that we had not a single foreigner among us, except the Marquis de La Fayette, who acts upon very different principles from those which govern the rest."

Yet no one was more ardent for the political and military success of the Franco-American alliance than Washington. When the assault on Rhode Island was decided upon, he put Lafayette in charge of the two divisions sent to reinforce Sullivan in the hope of pleasing all sides. Unfortunately he thus ruffled the feelings of General Greene and had to send fresh orders to the marquis dividing the reinforcements between the two men. He did it so flatteringly, however, that both agreed painlessly. Lafayette regarded himself as the liaison officer between the allies. His pleasure at meeting d'Estaing on board ship was reciprocated once the little matter of his being under the official displeasure of his sovereign had been smoothed over. The two French aristocrats discussed at length the plans for attacking Rhode Island. It was only when Lafayette reported back to Sullivan that his prospects of instant glory were dampened. The Americans, his fellow-officers, felt that they did not yet have enough men to make a successful attack. They counseled delay. Lafayette felt that American mettle would appear lacking in the eyes of the French soldiers and sailors. His patriotism began to jar. Even his friend John Laurens wrote to his father that Lafayette's "private views withdrew his attention wholly from the general interest."

The attack was finally fixed for August 9, 1778. French and American troops were to land at the same time. But Sullivan, when he learned that the British had evacuated the northern end of the island, jumped the gun without informing his ally. The French were furious at what they regarded as pettiness over who should be the first to engage, but they nevertheless proceeded according to plan, until the fog lifted and a great British fleet under Admiral Howe made its appearance. D'Estaing prepared to attack, but was prevented by the wind from doing so until the following morning. He left three ships behind, and a promise that he would return to finish the attack on Rhode Island and then rout the British. However a violent storm damaged both fleets, and when the French returned, d'Estaing said that he would have to sail to Boston for repairs. He offered to take the American troops left on the island back to the mainland, but not to continue attacking the British. And he would not change his mind.

It was now the Americans' turn to be furious. In their determination to alter d'Estaing's resolution, they tried to associate Lafayette with their protests. He indignantly refused to be included. Sullivan then compounded this injury by stating, in his orders of August 24th, that "The general cannot help lamenting the sudden and unexpected departure of the French fleet, as he finds it has a tendency to discourage some who placed great dependence on the assistance of it." He went on to hope that "Americans will prove by the event able to procure that by their own arms which their allies refuse them assistance in obtaining."

Lafayette was outraged and went storming off to Sullivan in a mood that soon gave rise to rumors of duels. In deference to his protests, Sullivan withdrew his insinuations the following day in his orders, but the marquis's wound was not so easily healed. He began to lament his attachment to the American cause, which he considered had already dishonored his country. He also found that, for the first time since being commissioned, he was unpopular with his adopted countrymen. This hurt all the more because of the experiences they had shared, and because, paradoxically, they were disappointed in French fighting men. He later boasted of not having given in to the tide of public opinion and of defending French actions contrary to his own interests. But he began to think seriously of returning to France to take part in a war with England. As he wrote to Adrienne a couple of weeks after the event:

Half the Americans say that I'm passionately in love with my country, and the other says that, since the arrival of the French ships, I've gone mad, and that I only drink and eat and sleep following the wind they bring. Between ourselves, they are a little right: I have never had such a strong feeling of national *amour-propre*.

The natural person to turn to for comfort was Washington who was quick to reply in soothing tones. He said that he well understood everything that could wound the delicacy of a man of honor, and he begged Lafayette not to attach too much importance to comments made without reflection. He asked the marquis to use his influence to restore harmony, and he wrote in the same sense to Greene. Sullivan he rebuked, emphasizing the importance of the alliance, and explaining that the French, having a long military tradition, were strict on etiquette, and were ready to take fire where others hardly got heated. His intimacy with Lafayette had certainly taught him that.

Sullivan now asked Lafayette to go to Boston to reassure d'Estaing, and find out what he intended to do. Riding night and day, he found that though the French admiral had been hurt by Sullivan's protests, his dedication to the patriot cause seemed unshaken, as did his veneration for Washington. In Boston John Hancock presented d'Estaing with a copy of the commander-in-chief's portrait, and the admiral proposed to greet it with a royal salute. Though Hancock dissuaded him from this, he still wreathed the portrait in laurel. A happier Lafayette set out to return to Rhode Island, where a battle with the English was imminent. Unfortunately, he missed it: after a bloody action, the patriots held their own, but the presence of the English fleet and the absence of the French one dictated a return to the mainland. There, Lafayette rejoined them, and Sullivan was very pleased with the way he had handled things. So was Congress, who thanked him not only for having sacrificed his personal interests and opportunity for glory by going to Boston, but also for his military zeal. They, no less than Washington, were anxious to keep the French happy.

Lafayette still burned to distinguish himself in action, even more now that his king and his father-in-law smiled on him. He again raised the possibility of attacking the Indies or Canada, and he discussed with d'Estaing whether or not to return to France, especially when rumors reached him of a proposed invasion of England. But if that were not immediately possible, Lafayette wanted the next best thing, which was to join d'Estaing and the French fleet in attacking British possessions, in conjunction with American troops which he felt confident Congress would grant him.

All that paled when his patriotic ire was aroused by a reported insult to his country from the British peace commissioners, who were still hanging around hoping to talk to the patriot leaders – and being persistently ignored by them. The commissioners, he read, had attacked the American alliance with France as a "preposterous connection," and they talked of Lafayette's country as "a power that has ever shown itself an enemy to all civil and religious liberty." Lord Carlisle, the leader of the commissioners, wrote that France's perfidy was too well known to need further proof. Lafayette decided that such an insult could only be avenged in a duel. It was a daft idea, as he later recognized: duels were not uncommon, but one fought over international politics was unheard of. Lafayette took off from his post near Rhode Island, leaving Sullivan hard-pressed for senior officers, and went to Boston to ask d'Estaing's advice. From there he formally asked Sullivan for leave, since after talking to the admiral he was especially anxious to discuss things with Washington in Philadelphia. No word came from Sullivan, so the marquis did what he had done on leaving France, and took silence for consent. His brain buzzing with his plans, all of which he had assumed d'Estaing agreed with (even the duel), he set off for Washington's headquarters.

Washington was gentle with Lafayette, but he made his disapproval of the challenge to Carlisle very clear. He told the heated marquis that the whole notion was antiquated, and harbored only by the French nation (which wasn't entirely true, as his own officers fought "affairs of honor"). He wrote that "however well adapted it might have been to the time in which it existed, in our days it is to be feared that your opponent, sheltering himself behind modern opinion, and under his present public character of commissioner, would turn a virtue of such ancient date into ridicule." Besides, he concluded, these things were often decided by chance, not bravery. But Lafayette would not be put off. The challenge had already been sent, and he felt he could not retract it, even though Washington issued him with "friendly commands" to desist. Carlisle, as Washington had forecast, in fact replied that it was "difficult to make a serious answer" to Lafayette's challenge. The issue, he considered, would be best settled by an encounter between the French and British fleets. The marquis was satisfied that his opponent was "concealing himself behind his dignity." And though some laughed at him in America and England, in France his quixotry only added to his reputation. To prove he could be serious, Lafayette discussed with the commander-in-chief a new plan for the invasion of Canada. Washington had never been enthusiastic about such an expedition, and he had not changed his mind. Lafayette insisted that Canada was of prime importance for the United States, but that they could only take it with French help. Washington became suspicious that Lafayette was being used in a French scheme to take Canada for themselves. He said that he did not feel a Canadian expedition could take place for the moment. Instead, he took up Lafayette's hint that he was thinking of returning to France and fighting for his king, and suggested that his young friend make the trip that very winter. He offered to recommend to Congress that Lafayette retain his American rank while he was away, and also invited Adrienne to visit him when the war was over, if she could be persuaded to leave the "gaieties and splendor of a court, for the rural amusements of an humble cottage" – a quaint way to describe his mansion.

Feeling that he might be more use in Europe, Lafayette adopted his "father's" suggestion. He was not sure whether to resign wholly from the American army in the hope of high employment in the French, or whether to take advantage of Washington's offer to keep his American rank. He consulted the new French envoy to America, Gérard de Rayneval, who advised him that it might look better if he asked for indefinite leave. His friends in Congress, meanwhile, had also told him that they held out little hope of that body agreeing at once to an attack on Canada. He therefore asked them for leave, pleading "patriotic love." He wrote that any time he could be useful to Congress he was ready to answer the call, and Congress instantly appointed a committee to discuss with him how he could best help American interests.

While there were factions in Congress who wished for active French help in the conquest of Canada and who had already approached Gérard de Rayneval on the subject, the majority wanted more tangible aid to prosecute the war in the colonies themselves. (The French envoy, incidentally, with political antennae more sensitive than Lafayette's, thought that there was in Congress a "party of opposition," which included Richard Henry Lee and Samuel Adams, whose aim was to plot against Washington and arrive at a separate peace with England, contrary to the terms of the treaty with France. Since Lee and Adams, along with Gouverneur Morris, served on the committee appointed to liaise with Lafayette, Gérard de Rayneval was immensely suspicious of it.) The Lafayette committee recommended that the marquis carry instructions to Benjamin Franklin, who was to be made American minister plenipotentiary at Versailles. Franklin was to assure Louis XVI of America's gratitude, and to point out ways in which further assistance could be afforded. Lafayette, who was to continue to be an American major-general, was to discuss these ways with Franklin. The marquis was thus honored with the assured trust of Congress – and an active role to play if he wished it.

While waiting to take his leave, Lafayette continued to shower Congress with requests on behalf of French officers serving with the Continentals. Since many of them would be returning with him, they all wanted to go home with as high a rank as possible. Congress was not ungenerous. To mark their particular gratitude to their (by now) most celebrated champion in Europe, Franklin was directed to procure "an elegant sword with proper devices" for presentation to Lafayette. They even wrote to the French king, recommending their major-general "as one whom we know to be wise in counsel, gallant in the field, and patient under the hardships of war." And in the instructions that Lafayette was to carry, there was included a "Plan for reducing the province of Canada," which needed four or five thousand French troops, and on which Franklin was to consult the marquis "on any difficulties which may arise." That his most cherished project was included in his brief, despite the congressional factions for and against it, was an immense tribute to Lafayette and also demonstrated that, whatever he had or had not learned about politics, he had mastered the art of politicking. As if to prove it, he now wrote to Washington, whose disapproval of a Canadian expedition he keenly felt, disclaiming all responsibility for it. Since his need for his "father's" approval took priority over his glorious projects, he said that "the idea was not suggested by me and I acted in the affair a passive part." Even Gérard de Rayneval felt called upon to report to Vergennes that the "prudent, courageous and likeable conduct of M. the Marquis de la Fayette has made him the idol of Congress, the army, and the people of America." And he added that they had a high opinion of the marquis's "military talents."

Congress's final compliment was to offer Lafayette a ship to take him home. Before leaving, he was bound to consult with Washington on the Canadian plan and he also wanted to talk to d'Estaing, whose fleet had been repaired, and who was waiting to set off for the West Indies for the winter. All this running around took its toll of Lafayette who, having "dined, drunk, and worked too much" in Philadelphia, as he later put it, caught a fever. Fortifying himself with wine, tea and rum, he refused to succumb and attended endless parties given in his honor on his way to headquarters. But at Fishkill he was laid low, and thought he was going to die – news which upset the entire army, where he was known as "the soldier's friend." Washington sent his personal doctor to look after him – the second time he had done so, the first being after Brandywine – and according to the memoirs of his protégé, anxiously came to enquire about his progress, going away with "his heart wrung and tears in his eyes."

After some three weeks, however, the fever abated. Washington again came to visit the invalid. In a final discussion of the Canadian venture, he confined himself to saying that he thought there would be difficulties. He did not say that he had written to Congress a long letter outlining his opposition to the project, which he wanted kept from Lafayette. Doubtless this was partly to avoid hurting his friend's feelings, and to escape an emotional outburst that he would have to soothe. But it was also because he felt that an expedition against Canada was "not only too expensive and beyond our abilities, but too complex." In addition, he wrote privately to Henry Laurens expressing his fears of French designs on the territory, and Lafayette's perhaps unwitting part in furthering them. Congress directed that the commander-in-chief write further to Lafayette on the subject, simplifying the plans if necessary. Washington's continued opposition and more congressional deliberation, however, resulted in the whole plan being laid aside. Washington's gentle letter telling Lafayette of this did not reach him before he sailed. It was, however, a letter so filled with affection and good wishes, so flatteringly reassuring, that Lafayette could not be downcast.

The two men made their tender farewells, but when Lafayette arrived in Boston, the *Alliance*, which Congress had designated to take him home, was not ready. So the marquis spent his time continuing his solicitations on behalf of his compatriots – his last letter from Boston to Washington included a request for La Colombe to be made a major – settling some accounts, on behalf of others rather than himself, and penning a letter to the Canadian Indians exhorting them to desert the British. He signed this manifesto "Father Lafayette." He also restored his health by drinking masses of Madeira.

The *Alliance* had difficulty raising a crew, but Lafayette honorably refused to allow a press-gang to work, preferring to use English deserters and volunteer prisoners. Despite being feted by the Bostonians, Lafayette constantly fretted for news from Congress of his projects. Finally he decided he could wait no longer, and the *Alliance* set sail on January 11, 1779, the day before congressional dispatches arrived in Boston.

Apart from suffering grievously from sea-sickness, the homeward voyage of the young general was a good deal more eventful than that which had brought him out a virtual outlaw, callow, and unknown. There was a great storm in which the ship nearly foundered, and then there was the threat of a mutiny, the plot of which was revealed by an American sailor the conspirators mistook for an Irishman. The mutineers were inspired by the hope of reward promised by the British government for any rebel ship brought into a British port, but they were betrayed an hour before they were due to strike. Lafayette tells how he foiled the mutiny by mounting the bridge with his sword in his hand, along with the other officers and passengers. The conspirators were clapped in irons, and the "lucky star" that had watched over Lafayette, waning only occasionally, saw him safely into port at Brest on February 6, 1779.

7
Passing Through

BEING A HERO is as much a matter of publicity as of achievement. In eighteenth-century France, there was no shortage of books, pamphlets, and gazettes, but the chief source of information, then as now, was gossip, and for that Lafayette was a natural subject. Not that there was a shortage of heroes, at least among the intellectual Parisians who were responsible for making fashionable opinion. The times were changeable, increasingly prosperous, and echoed with clashing ideals of progress – conditions in which heroes flourish, to whom the uncertain may, however briefly, cling. In 1778 the hero of those intellectuals who championed the values of reason was Voltaire, while those whose faith lay in the virtues of primitive man adhered to Rousseau. But these opposing luminaries died within three months of each other. The Duc de Chartres, as commander of an apparently successful naval battle against the British Admiral Keppel, was enthusiastically hailed and crowned with laurel in Paris, but when the details of the battle came in, he was accused of not carrying out orders and demoted. That same year Mesmer had arrived in Paris, and occasioned a craze for "animal magnetism," but he was more of a guru than a hero. Heroes serve only a moment, even though their achievements might be eternal; they epitomize a mood, than which nothing changes faster.

Paris in 1779, then, was ripe for Lafayette. He had virtues that were immensely simple to grasp: youth, courage, and money. He had the advantage of, say, the Duc de Chartres in that the field of his achievement was some three thousand miles away and his was a foreign struggle about which rumor was as strong as truth. If the vast majority of Frenchmen couldn't have cared less about America, the glory of their compatriots serving there was a matter of great satisfaction. To the liberal aristocracy who moved between Paris, Versailles, and their châteaux, the War of Independence was not only being fought over a principle that was never far from their mouths, it was also a war of national pride. And Lafayette had actually seen action in the field, which was more than most of his friends had done.

On reaching France he went not to his family in Paris, but to Versailles. Perhaps he thought that the importance of his American mission warranted an immediate interview with Maurepas. Doubtless he looked forward to causing the greatest sensation by his sudden and unannounced appearance. The first place he stopped was at the house of the Prince de Poix, with whom he had traveled to London two years previously. As luck would have it, a ball was in full swing. At 2 A.M. Lafayette made his grand re-entry into French society. That triumph was followed, the next morning, by a long interview with Maurepas. Nothing could have given the marquis more pleasure than being taken so seriously on all sides.

He was, of course, still under the official displeasure of his monarch, and was thus ordered to confine himself to the Noailles mansion in Paris and to see no one but his family. As he was related to practically everybody, that restriction was almost meaningless and a further tribute to his reputation.

The news of his return was broken to his wife by her mother, who had throughout championed Lafayette and shielded Adrienne from the nastier rumors concerning him. Adrienne wrote to Lafayette's aunts at Chavaniac:

> M. de la Fayette has returned to me as modest and as charming as when he went away . . . God has preserved, in the midst of tremendous dangers, the most lovable person in the world. . . . When I reflect on my good fortune in being his wife, I am truly grateful to God. The knowledge that I am very far from being as good and kind as he is makes me sad, but I hope that my affection can make up for my shortcomings.

The rebel had been sentenced to exile and imprisonment – but to exile in Paris and the prison of home, rather than the Bastille, and only for a week at that. Once this was over, he wrote a contrite letter to Louis XVI, pleading that "Love of my country, a fervent desire to see the humiliation of her enemies, a political instinct which the recent treaty would seem to justify, those, Sire, are the reasons which decided the role I played in aiding the American cause." The king, who once before had dismissed charges against Lafayette with a smile, forgave him, set him free, and advised him to avoid frequenting public places where his disobedience might be celebrated. In addition to being consulted by the royal ministers, Lafayette wrote later, he enjoyed "what was much more worthwhile, the embraces of all the ladies. The kisses stopped on the following day, but I kept for a longer time the confidence of the Cabinet." Honored at Versailles, he became the toast of Paris, to the extent that lines in his honor were written into a fashionable play, which delighted the audience no less than himself. And as if to crown his triumph, Aglaé d'Hunolstein, who had rejected him when he was merely an awkward adolescent, now boasted of seeing him often (which was incidentally another blow for the unfortunate Duc de Chartres, who had previously enjoyed the lady's favors).

Parisian etiquette had changed about as little as French society in Lafayette's absence, talk rather than action being the hinge on which everything turned. Mme de La Tour du Pin described the suppers of her childhood, between 1778 and 1784 – suppers that took place at half-past nine (lunch being an informal affair at half-past two or so). There were two kinds of supper party, those that were "open house" and those to which one was invited, which were many and brilliant.

> All the toilettes, all the elegance, everything that the beautiful, fashionable society of Paris could offer in refinement and charm was to be found at these suppers. In those good days, before anyone had begun to think of national representation, a list of supper guests was a most important and carefully considered item. There were so many interests to be cherished, so many people to bring together, so many others to be kept apart! And what a social disaster for a husband to consider himself invited to a house simply because his wife was! A very profound knowledge of convention and current gossip was necessary.

Apart from being a star attraction at such supper parties, Lafayette now regarded himself very much as a politician. Although the importance of his brief from Congress had been somewhat diminished by the final instructions he received, especially as they scrapped the Canadian expedition, he thought of himself as a representative of American interests in France, just as in America he had assumed the mantle of protector of the French. Franklin, of course, headed the American delegation to Versailles that conducted all bargaining, though Lafayette was more up-to-date than he, at least on military matters. But most of all the marquis used his unique position to generate support for the American cause and the ideals it stood for. This did not mean that Lafayette had become a revolutionary, much less a republican. The leaders of the American Revolution were as anxious to defend property, law, and order as any of the French liberal aristocracy. Franklin would hardly have been as popular as he was in Paris if he'd been thought of as a dangerous radical. The chord that found the most sympathetic echo in France was that of patriotism:

for it was as "patriots" (a label attached to winners, as opposed to "rebels," who lose, and "insurgents," who could do either) that the Americans were fighting in defense of their rights. To Lafayette's circle, the values that he and the patriots were struggling for were perfectly compatible with those of an enlightened aristocracy: defense of the nation, liberty (within limits) of the individual, and a gradual equalization of society, to be achieved by educational rather than violent means.

For a certain wind of change had fluttered through French society since the accession of Louis XVI. The king was personally interested in social matters and the plight of the poor, which he hoped to alleviate by charity and reforms in the administration. To this end he had appointed Turgot to be comptroller-general of finances in 1774, the first and only time that a member of that intellectual reform group known as the Physiocrats held high office. The Physiocrats believed that the soil was the only source of true wealth, that nature was superior to man's work, and that thus agriculture was the only fruitful form of labor. A single tax on land was to be the source of the national revenue, while the ideal government would be that of an enlightened despot ruling in accordance with the laws of nature. Turgot interpreted these absolutist ideas to improve the lot of agricultural workers, using the powers of central government, and he tried to abolish the power of the guilds and the labor forced on the peasants known as the *corvée*. He also attempted to reform the tax system and to reduce both expenditure and that immunity from taxation enjoyed by the privileged aristocratic orders. His whole program was thwarted by the vested interests, the higher clergy, and the noble factions at court – the very class to which Lafayette belonged. But that Turgot was appointed to office at all was a sign of the times.

Turgot was opposed to involvement in war, on the theoretical grounds that it was incompatible with prosperity, and on the practical ones that France could not afford it. Lafayette, therefore, was not one of his supporters, any more than he supported Necker, who became director of finance in 1777, and who also opposed French participation in the American struggle. In fact the Physiocrat analysis of the effects of war proved correct, and French entry to the American arena caused an immediate recession, in which the fall in the profits of the small proprietors and tenant farmers was infinitely greater than the fall in prices. The revenues of the great landowners like Lafayette were, however, safeguarded by their unchanged feudal dues. As a rich man finds it hard to understand poverty, so Lafayette only grasped the fierce needs of his peasants when these were thrust upon him. As for those of his own class who were not buttressed by vast revenues, and who were desperate to preserve their precarious position from further erosion, that was something he never understood at all. It was natural that his triumphant reception in Paris should lead him to believe that French involvement in America was universally popular. For most of the country, however, it was probably a matter of vast indifference.

It is curious that there was more genuine internationalism among would-be reformers like Turgot than among those like Lafayette who combined libertarian chat with a blood-curdling patriotism. The ideas of free trade, laissez-faire, and enlightened despotism knew no national boundaries in Europe, any more than did the works of Montesquieu, Voltaire, Rousseau, or Adam Smith. Ideas are, of course, easier to exchange than policies, and Turgot was alone in having the opportunity of testing his principles in practice. Where most thinkers and politicians agreed was on who should conduct the process of reform: themselves and their class. In France as in America there was a desire in governing circles for change that wouldn't threaten stability, that would, in fact, guarantee it. This was hardly what would today be called a revolutionary spirit: modern labels like "élitist," or even "reformist," seem more apt. But the age was absolutist: absolute monarchs governed the states of Europe and only America was embarked on a course of republicanism. Lafayette did not return from his first trip there full of democratic ideas. Rather, he came back fired with a new sense of national honor, that of fighting for a country whose rulers were truly worthy of its citizens. And that was a mood that the court circle around Louis XVI also shared.

It was also, incidentally, a mood fostered by the masonic lodges that were so popular on both sides of the Atlantic. Washington and Franklin were both masons, as were Voltaire, Lafayette, and half the fashionable French aristocracy. Lafayette claimed in 1825 that only after he became a mason did Washington show complete confidence in him, and it is possible that he was initiated in America on his first trip there. In France at least the lodges were no more than select (usually aristocratic) clubs where one could talk of equality. But that members of the nobility of the old regime flocked to take part in leveling rituals centering on a mystical philosophy of brotherhood was further evidence of the new mood – and its élitist tendencies.

In 1780 [wrote Alexis de Tocqueville] there could no longer be any talk of France's being on the downgrade; on the contrary, it seemed that no limit could be set to her advance. And it was now that theories of the perfectability of man and continuous progression came into fashion. Twenty years earlier there had been no hope for the future; in 1780 no anxiety was felt about it. Dazzled by the prospect of a felicity undreamed of hitherto and now within their grasp, people were blind to the very real improvement that had taken place and eager to precipitate events.

Certainly Lafayette was among these eager ones – but his energies were devoted more to the leaders of his adopted country than to the people of his own. For France he wanted a glorious war with England, a wish shared only by his aristocratic colleagues at court and in the army who were, despite the rising wealth and force of the bourgeoisie, consolidating their hold over the government of the country.

At the prompting of Marie-Antoinette, on one of the very rare occasions she found something good to say about him, Lafayette was appointed lieutenant-commander of the king's dragoons, with the rank of *mestre de camp* (the equivalent of colonel). Not that this privilege was accorded gratis: it cost him 80,000 *livres*, an expensive honor, but worthwhile to Lafayette since it took him off the reserve list and placed him in the active service of the French army. He instantly began to try and involve that army – or at least a part of it, hopefully under his own command – in the war in America, even though both Necker, then director of finance, and Vergennes, still foreign minister, felt the need for caution and economy. Lafayette's idea of a conquest of Canada was not seen by these ministers as of great advantage to France, and the idea of a large force setting off to cross the Atlantic was firmly squashed.

Maurepas was reported as saying that Lafayette would have gladly stripped Versailles for the sake of his Americans. Undeterred the marquis plotted an invasion of England from the Irish Sea, to be effected with the ships of the American Captain John Paul Jones. Franklin supported the idea, and the scheme found favor with the French ministers. While Lafayette rushed around getting things organized, public rumor concerning him also began to buzz. It was said he was preparing an expedition to America, and several people volunteered to help. He and Jones, however, were secretly putting together a fleet at Lorient when government support for the proposed invasion collapsed as suddenly as it had arisen. This was doubtless due to the secret plans being prepared for a full-scale invasion of England, now that Spain, also in secret, was preparing to declare war on Britain following the Treaty of Aranjuez (April 1779). This was scarcely a great triumph for French diplomacy, since the treaty compelled France to fight until Gibraltar was returned to Spain (which never happened), and to make no separate peace. Spain did not even promise to recognize the United States, or to fight with them. But one more ally against the English was what France needed.

Without knowing of the new invasion plans, Lafayette was ordered to Saintes to take charge of his regiment. It was a frustrating time, with the officers boiling for war and being kept in ignorance of their government's intentions. Sometimes their bellicosity expressed itself in duels over ladies, but there was no shortage of distractions, in the shape of dances, dinners, games, and festivities, from the routine of maneuvers. Lafayette used the time to write long letters to his American friends, and especially to Washington. Distance, apart from making his heart ever fonder, had made him more statesman-like: in a paragraph about "the great objective, money," Lafayette explained how Necker feared him "like the devil," but that he hoped to persuade the government to make even greater sacrifices for America's sake. He followed this by saying, with lofty objectivity, "For God's sake stop these resounding internal quarrels, tales of which harm the interests and reputation of America more than anything else." He pointed out that there were two "parties" among the Americans in France: Adams and Lee on one side, and Franklin on the other. "These divisions," he said, "upset me so much that I don't go to those gentlemen as much as I would like, for fear of causing arguments and making them break out even more."

In the same letter Lafayette showed a concern for Washington's safety that he admitted was "woman-like." He also told his general that he was hoping to be a father again and in a scribbled postscript he announced that he had just learned he was to be an assistant quarter-master-general to the troops commanded by the Comte de Vaux, who were to take part in the long-awaited invasion of England. This plan was to be implemented with the help of the Spanish fleet, and for weeks it occupied the minds and hopes of the French army. But waiting was not to Lafayette's taste, and soon he was again winging letters full of ideas to the royal ministers. These tried to persuade Maurepas and Vergennes to equip an expeditionary force to assist the Americans – a body Lafayette still hoped to lead. Neither Washington nor the war that had made the marquis a hero were ever long absent from his thoughts. Soon the prospects of invading England dimmed, and finally vanished. Lafayette longed more than ever to cross the Atlantic. In a letter to Vergennes putting forward his claims to command he modestly said he hoped rank would be conferred on him because of his merits as a soldier, not a courtier – which he claimed he was far from being. At least he had the courtier's art of subtlety.

One distraction while awaiting answers to his letters was the presentation, by Franklin's grandson, of the "elegant sword" that Congress had ordered made for Lafayette. With its handle of gold, its allegorical medallions, and its representation of four battles in which Lafayette had taken part (these actually included Monmouth), this gift not only gratified the marquis, but, according to him, the whole French army. Lafayette hoped to carry the sword "into the heart of England" – a hope which was soon deceived, as the French and Spanish fleets had failed to bring the reduction of Britain any nearer by the winter of 1779. But the French and Spanish governments both now felt that the war in America was of prime importance in the struggle against England. A letter from Washington that guaranteed Lafayette a warm welcome back, whether in command of a French corps or an American division, or even when peace should be attained, made the marquis plead more urgently for material French help to be despatched at once across the ocean. As a demonstration of his feeling, when Adrienne at last gave birth to a son on December 24th, Lafayette promptly named him Georges Washington. Once there was no immediate prospect of a glorious invasion of England, Lafayette preferred to take up his old rank among his old friends in a cause committed to victory, rather than soldier in an army where there was more of politics than action, and where he lacked that direct and effective channel to those who directed affairs.

Lafayette's immensely long letters badgering Maurepas and Vergennes finally brought results, and it was decided to send an expeditionary force to America. His reputation and his knowledge of the country made him an obvious choice to send as an officer, but his inexperience of command bothered the French leaders rather more than the Americans. Despite Lafayette's offers to accept any arrangement that would give him, however temporarily, superior rank to his fellow French officers, in order to command the French troops – which he said the Americans *expected* him to do – Maurepas decided to give the command to the veteran Comte de Rochambeau. Lafayette himself was to go ahead and resume his post as an American major-general. He could take credit for the fact that six ships and a corps of 6000 men, more than Lafayette had expected, were to be placed under Washington's supreme command, and that he and his commander-in-chief were to discuss the plan of campaign and remain in contact with the French representative in America, who was now the Chevalier de La Luzerne. The decision was certainly taken by the French ministers independently of Lafayette's pleadings, but his part in its implementation further increased his reputation on both sides of the Atlantic.

In his anxiety to be off, Lafayette, who could never bear attention to detail, especially if it were financial, managed to mess up orders for the shipment of uniforms to America (which never arrived). But he wisely put decisions regarding his own affairs in Adrienne's hands. To the consternation of his financial advisers he ordered them to raise large sums of money, authorizing them to borrow up to 115,000 *livres*. (His first trip had cost him some 140,000 *livres*; by the time independence was won it was estimated he spent nearly three-quarters of a million on the cause.) As financial advisers are not bound by the lofty principles of their clients, Morizot, who acted for Lafayette, promptly began to seek payment from his tenants, doing everything he could to extract his feudal dues. Lafayette himself may have lamented that "Nobility is but an insignificant kind of people for revolutions. They have no notions of equality between men, they want to govern, they have too much to loose." But that was in a letter to Franklin, whom he knew would appreciate such sentiments. He usually knew the right tone to choose to please his audience. As for a revolution in his own affairs, he was not ready for that.

Wearing the blue, white, and gold uniform of an American major-general, Lafayette went to Versailles to take leave of his sovereign. Then he proceeded to Rochefort to embark, writing *en route* the same kind of letters of regret to Adrienne that he had penned on his last trip. Considering the enormous effort he had made to get himself sent to America a second time, this regret might seem artificial. But Lafayette was the kind of man who was sincere about the things of the moment. He was, of course, delighted to be going from France as an officially-certified hero to America, where he would be certain of another rapturous welcome. The contrast between this trip and his last, when he had not only left under official displeasure but had been first received in Philadelphia with more of the same, was manifest. But of course he regretted leaving his wife, his children, his envious friends, and his new circle of admirers. He set off on March 20, 1780, after a storm had blown them back to port a few days previously. The hero was again crippled by sea-sickness. But on April 28th they sailed into Boston harbor, and the welcome they received more than restored his spirits.

8
Once More Unto the Breach

MATTERS HAD NOT much improved, politically or militarily, in Lafayette's absence. Clothing and equipment for the Continental army was still far from sufficient, and the paper money had depreciated to the point when the Board of War itself predicted that "in a very short period, unless some extraordinary event takes place, the present currency will cease to be a medium of commerce." A joint attack on Savannah by French and American troops had failed. D'Estaing had been wounded, and had taken the French fleet to the West Indies, later to return to France himself, a hero of sorts. This defeat left the American south dangerously exposed to the British. Lafayette missed a winter (that of 1779–80) which the army spent in Morristown in conditions every bit as bad as those of Valley Forge; apart from the shortage of food and provisions, there was still a shortage of officers, and that same disintegrating morale that had made Washington despair before. The weather was worse than many could remember. At the end of March, 1780, there was still eight inches of snow on the ground, rendering men as liable to die of cold as of hunger. The army was weak while the enemy seemed stronger, especially in the south, and the economic situation was disastrous. It was, then, with some cheer that Washington received a letter from Lafayette telling him how glad he was to be "again one of your loving soldiers," and hinting at more French aid. Indeed, this was virtually the only pleasant thing to have happened to the commander-in-chief for months.

After leaving Boston, Lafayette wrote to his wife:

My arrival was made known by the men who went in search of a pilot. . . . There was an immense crowd, and I was welcomed with a salute of guns, with the ringing of all the church bells, with a band marching ahead of me, and with cheering from the assembled gathering. It was thus that I was taken to the house that the Council and the Assembly of Representatives of Boston had prepared for me. A deputation from these two bodies received me. I asked to be presented to the two Chambers that were assembled, and tried to remember my English during the hour that I passed there. In the evening a huge crowd gathered in front of my door, where a great bonfire had been built, and the cheering lasted until well after midnight. When I left Boston all the people crowded in front of the house to await my departure. . . . In every place I passed through . . . my arrival and departure were hailed with gunfire. The leading personages rode with me on horseback: in short, the reception granted to me has been beyond anything I could describe.

Do not read to anybody the part of my letter where I talk of my arrival. If, however, my friends press you for details, you have my permission, after swearing them to secrecy, to read what I have said to the small family group which dines every day at the Hôtel de Noailles. . . .

The splendor of such a welcome was far too good to keep a secret.

In his memoirs, Lafayette asserts that Washington received the news of his arrival with tears of joy. Certainly the letter of welcome that the latter wrote was unusually warm and solicitous for his safety. An escort was sent to meet the returning major-general, both as an honor and to ensure he was not captured by Tory outposts; a bed was prepared for him at headquarters, and the commander-in-chief looked forward to embracing him with all the warmth of a devoted friend. Even Congress joined in the chorus. For an emotional youth of twenty-three, the reception must have been overwhelming.

Washington and Lafayette wasted little time in deciding how best to deploy the French fleet when it arrived. An attack on New York, where the British presence was depleted in both men and ships, stood a good chance of success. Lafayette, in his official capacity as liaison officer between the allied forces, hastened to get things organized. But the year that had begun so badly only got worse, and Washington's gloom deepened. In May Charleston fell to the British, leaving the south weak and with no prospect of effective aid until the French navy asserted superiority in American waters. Many patriots deserted to the loyalists, while the shocking condition of the Continental army caused a mutiny in the Connecticut line which was, however, peacefully settled. Both Lafayette and Washington were exceedingly pessimistic, but with the young general such moods never lasted long.

In July the French fleet at last arrived off Newport, Rhode Island. Lafayette forthwith communicated the plans for an attack on New

York, even though Washington had to moderate them "because I never wish to promise more than I have a moral certainty of performing." To Lafayette's intense disappointment, the Comte de Rochambeau, in command of the French force, shared this caution. The fleet had brought, as volunteers in the French force, some of his dearest friends (notably his brother-in-law, the Vicomte de Noailles, and the Chevalier de Chastellux, who was already a distinguished military and literary figure) and Lafayette burned to justify his reputation in front of them. His enthusiasm for glorious action, however, irritated Rochambeau almost beyond endurance, and only a graceful and abject apology by Lafayette, who was unable to bear anyone's hostility, saved the situation. Referring to himself as "old Papa Rochambeau talking to his dear son La Fayette, whom he loves," the comte in return offered the marquis advice "derived from forty years' experience. There are no troops more easily beaten than when they have lost confidence in their commander, and they lose it immediately they have been exposed to danger through private and personal ambition." That was advice Washington might have given, and Lafayette bore the rebuke bravely.

The marquis was given command of a division of picked Americans, which he set about making the best corps of light infantry in the Continental army. At his own cost he provided each regiment with a standard, each officer with a sword, and each man with a red and black feather, and what the troops lacked in clothing they made up for in spirit. Unfortunately, given the desperate condition of the main army, the caution of the French, and the consolidation of the British, Lafayette's division never saw battle. He did however provide himself with a magnificent white horse, which was, much to his embarrassment, presented to him free in the end, so that he looked every inch the modern major-general, even out of action.

Enlistment had provided only a fraction of the troops the individual states had been asked for, and there was not enough food, even in the summer and even taking by impressment from farmers unwilling to accept paper currency. The expected second division of the French fleet, which had so aroused Lafayette's hopes, was blockaded by the English at Brest and could not be expected before the autumn. The lack of supplies meant that an outright attack on New York was out of the question. General Benedict Arnold, who had suffered permanent injury in so distinguishing himself at Saratoga, was ordered by Washington to rally all scattered contingents at the strategic post of West Point, in case of a British advance. In September the southern army, under General Gates, suffered a total and disastrous defeat at Cornwallis's hands at Camden, at which Lafayette's old colleague the "Baron" de Kalb was killed, and which opened up North Carolina to the British. As blow succeeded blow, Lafayette wondered if things would not be improved by Washington being created dictator, which was an idea that floated around without coming to anything. Lafayette's "republican . . . and democratic principles," as he himself wrote to La Luzerne, were against it, except that he believed "Washington's dictatorship necessary to the public welfare."

Washington decided that the time was ripe for a personal meeting with Rochambeau, a meeting the French commander had long asked for. As the commander-in-chief, with Lafayette and other officers, set out for Hartford, in Connecticut, they learned that Admiral Rodney had come with a fleet to strengthen the British ships already guarding New York. Any hope of French naval superiority was, for the moment, out of the question.

The meeting between the French and American officers was cordial, and Washington greatly impressed his allies by his bearing. Lafayette acted as interpreter and secretary. The outcome of the discussion was that the French king should be asked to provide more ships, more men, and above all more money, as a matter of extreme urgency. Everyone expressed themselves pleased with these decisions, though Washington left with the impression that the supreme command he was supposed to hold over the French forces was only "upon a very limited basis."

Washington was anxious, on the return journey, to make sure that the fortifications on the Hudson, and particularly at West Point, were adequate. Arriving at General Benedict Arnold's headquarters, Washington, Lafayette, and the others were surprised to find the general absent. While awaiting his return, Washington inspected the defenses and found them in shocking disrepair. When Arnold still did not show up, they went to the house he was occupying. Washington was then handed some papers, which told him that Major John André, adjutant-general in the British army, had just been arrested carrying some of the most confidential documents concerning West Point's defenses and the plans of the Continental army. Worst was the fact that two of these papers were in Arnold's own handwriting.

A deeply shocked, though outwardly calm, Washington sent men to chase Arnold, but he had made good his escape to the British ship *Vulture*. From there he sent a letter asking that his wife be allowed to go free – a wish that was granted – and exonerating all his fellow-officers. Nevertheless, had his plan succeeded and West Point fallen to the British, the confederation of American states would have been cut in two and the French forces separated from their allies. Arnold might also have captured Washington, Lafayette, and other leading figures, had not his own contact been taken first. Arnold was not the only American officer to feel disgruntled at the conditions and prospects of the Continental army, but he was the only one to have sold himself quite so dramatically.

Lafayette regarded the plot and their somewhat miraculous escape as one of those catastrophes that are necessary to keep up one's interest. He served as one of André's judges and was both upset by and admiring of the spy's conduct when he was hanged. Yet the long periods of inaction which the Continental forces otherwise had to suffer bored him, something which Washington understood and with which he sympathized. As he wrote to Franklin, the marquis "came out flushed with expectations of a decisive campaign and fired with hopes of acquiring fresh laurels, but in both he has been disappointed; for we have been condemned to an inactivity as inconsistent with the situation of our affairs as with the ardor of his temper." Not that the young general was idle. Apart from drilling his light division, and putting his wife down for a hundred guineas on a subscription list got out by the ladies of Philadelphia to aid the soldiers, he also badgered Washington to let him mount an attack on Staten Island. Among the reasons he advanced were that action would please not only the natives but also the French who, he said, were beginning to doubt the American willingness to take risks. (Rochambeau was a living contradiction of such an idea, and all his officers had expressed the highest praise for Washington's tactics and statecraft. But Lafayette was allowed to take liberties.) Finally, said the marquis, even if the expedition did not succeed, the consequences would not be fatal, as the loss of two or three hundred men, of whom half were only enrolled for two months, would hardly be calamitous. To this Washington prudently replied that "we must consult our means rather than our wishes; and not endeavor to better our affairs by attempting things which for want of success may make them worse."

General Greene took over command of the southern army from the defeated General Gates, and Lafayette wondered if he shouldn't go south where the action seemed to be. Washington's war council decided to put the troops into winter quarters in October, and one rather small ray of light in the commander-in-chief's tunnel was provided by a plan of reorganization for the army, based on long-term enlistment. Chastellux and others of Lafayette's friends came to see him before the army disbanded, were well received by Washington, and treated to a review of the army in pouring rain. Chastellux was much impressed by Lafayette's prestige: he reckoned that "private letters from him have often produced more effect on some states than the strongest exhortations of the Congress." The marquis himself said that he was never happier than when he was admitted to the intimate secrets of politics and war at the same time as he was enjoying universal popularity. Chastellux and he were both honored by being elected foreign members of the American Philosophical Society.

Joined by his brother-in-law, Lafayette and friends went to Philadelphia for rest and recreation. Still undecided whether or not to go south, the marquis enjoyed himself. Having aired views on democracy to his wife, he also had developed a philosophy on mistresses.

> If I had a mistress [he had written to Noailles] my feeling for her would be based partly on the discretion or sensibility she displayed in never showing herself to be jealous, and on the freedom I should have to do what I wished, even to the point of neglecting her without her badgering me with demands. A mistress so made would keep me for ever – or at least I think so – if not by the ties of violent passion, then by those of tenderness.

His name was still linked to that of Aglaë d'Hunolstein, and perhaps there was no one in America to meet his requirements.

If 1780 was a bad year for the Americans, 1781 began no better. The soldiers of the Pennsylvania line mutinied, seized arms, and began marching on Philadelphia. Their grievances, as Lafayette and even Washington admitted, were just: the lack of clothing, provisions, and pay in a currency they could trust had driven them beyond endurance. The mutineers made it clear that they would desert to the British if force was sent against them, but when Clinton, the British commander-in-chief, sent emissaries with promises of all they wanted, the mutineers loyally delivered the messengers to their own General Wayne. Congress and the Council of Pennsylvania stepped in and appointed committees to treat with the soldiers. Washington at first disapproved, feeling this might undermine military discipline. But there was nothing he could do, and he waited to see if the mutiny would spread. Lafayette was also employed in peace-making; appreciating his popularity, the committee asked him to use his influence with the mutineers. At some personal risk he approached their camp and was politely received. But when they were joined in their talks by other officers, the soldiers became suspicious, and Lafayette and his colleagues were forced to leave. His report to Washington decided the commander-in-chief to prepare himself to march on the rebels. But he held back, and General Wayne finally reported that terms had been agreed: the men were to receive some pay and some clothes, and those who demanded instant discharge were pacified. Washington felt that this arrangement would have "a very pernicious influence on the whole Army," though he praised the fact that the men did not change sides. Two of Clinton's emissaries were, in fact, hanged.

Both Washington and Lafayette, in their anxiety to minimize the effect of the mutiny, especially in front of the French, drew attention to the fact that the Pennsylvania line was made up of Americans born abroad. But when, in the same month, the New Jersey troops mutinied also, Washington stepped in before any civil authority could further undermine discipline. He sent the American General Robert Howe with a picked detachment with orders "to compel the mutineers to unconditional submission, and I am to desire you will grant no terms while they are with arms in their hands in a state of resistance. . . . If you succeed in compelling the revolted troops to surrender you will instantly execute a few of the most active and incendiary leaders." Howe did exactly that, forcing twelve of the most prominent rebels to act as firing-party for two ringleaders out of the three condemned by summary court-martial. Lafayette, though he played down the mutinies in his letters and memoirs, wholeheartedly approved of Washington's orders. Unfortunately not even draconian measures could compel the states to improve the condition of the army. They could not or would not succor their suffering troops. Almost the only hope was generous aid from France, which John Laurens was dispatched – weighed down with some of Lafayette's longest letters – to procure. In the meantime British activity in the south, where Benedict Arnold, now a British general, had gone with a force to Virginia, required urgent attention.

A storm at the end of January 1781, which damaged English vessels but left the French untouched, led Washington to hope that the French fleet might proceed south, establish superiority in the waters off Virginia, and help to destroy Arnold. The French appeared to encourage such a plan, and Washington decided to send a Continental force south to attack Arnold on land. Since it was to be a joint Franco-American operation, Washington's obvious choice as commander of his detachment was Lafayette, who set off in high spirits for what he thought would be a brief and glorious campaign. Indeed, given the state of Washington's army, its gloom unrelieved even by the news of the ratification of the Articles of Confederation, which promised the formation of a "perpetual union" of the thirteen states, Lafayette may have delighted to get away on his own. The position of the English was strong, but subject to heavy strains. They too suffered from problems of supply, which bickering between their government departments made worse. In England domestic opposition to the war was increasing, chiefly because of increased taxes, and there was international opposition to it in the form of the League of Armed Neutrality, which Catherine the Great of Russia had started to protect the Baltic trade from British interference and which most of Europe had joined. In America itself, lack of native cooperation made it extraordinarily difficult to hold onto territory once the Redcoats had gained it. There were not enough troops for more than one campaign at a time, so that attacking a new target meant abandoning an old one.

The intervention of the French navy had made the problems of the British, especially those of supply, much worse. (Had the French concentrated on destroying the British lines of communication instead of lusting after British possessions in the West Indies, the war might have been over much sooner.) Lafayette was relying on his country's fleet to trap Arnold as he attempted to drive his enemy toward the sea. But his efforts to win a decisive victory were hamstrung by his own supply problems. He certainly chased Arnold, and he managed to do so without unmanageable loss of men or stores. But he lacked the military strength to do more than harass – and worst of all, when he actually got Arnold in what he thought was a bottleneck, the French naval force on which he had been counting proved "less strong than the English." Arnold escaped.

Lafayette's men were all northerners, and hence had a morbid distrust of all things southern. They found the climate, which only doubled Lafayette's appetite, intolerable, and their commander had to fight the Virginian authorities for everything he needed. As Thomas Jefferson, who was governor of Virginia at the time, explained to the marquis, the Americans were a people with mild laws, unused to war and prompt obedience. This enforced the tactics of gradualism on their commanders, for which Washington was famous, and which made Lafayette extremely impatient. But the patriots of the state were none too keen on northerners themselves: even Lafayette's reputation did not prevent them calling for Washington, every inch a good Virginian, to come and take personal command. All in all, Lafayette and his men would have been delighted to have returned north when their campaign to trap Arnold had failed.

But the southern army under General Greene was in grave danger of being overwhelmed by British forces. Lord Cornwallis had learned one thing from the patriots: how to travel light. He put into operation a series of "search and destroy" missions, which proved uncomfortably successful. Worse, if it came to pitched battle Cornwallis's forces were superior to Greene's. The Americans had to be prudent and retreat. If Greene were to be thoroughly beaten, the whole of the south might go British. One skirmish at Guildford Court House, North Carolina, had resulted in an expensive victory for Cornwallis, but his losses were made up, thanks to the superiority of the British navy, by a large force just landed from New York. (By chance they were commanded by Major-General William Phillips who had been in charge of the battery that had killed Lafayette's father at Minden.) Washington considered sending Lafayette to help Greene. To do so was dangerous, in view of the lack of men and equipment, but to take the marquis back into the main army was to admit his inability to do anything to help Greene. Washington could do nothing until more French troops arrived; and it was unanimously decided to order Lafayette, already on his way north, to return to Greene's assistance.

Lafayette was disappointed, chiefly because it appeared that the southern operation was at best a holding one, with more than a fair chance of being defeated. He knew that Washington could not decide between putting his main efforts into defending the south or attacking New York, but he was convinced that he was to be stuck "in exile" while all the excitement went on elsewhere. In fact Washington could do nothing until more French troops arrived; without them the Americans were quite likely to lose the campaign, if not the war. But Lafayette had his own men to think about, and they were no more pleased with their orders than he.

By stern disciplinary methods, which included the hanging or punishment of some deserters, and by his characteristic generosity in getting the ladies of Baltimore to make clothes for his men out of linen he paid for, the marquis succeeded in restoring the spirit of his small army. His own spirit was deeply shaken by the discovery that Washington's estate-manager had cooperated with the British in the hope of safeguarding the commander-in-chief's house and property. Washington, concerned at the bad impression this would give, shared Lafayette's disapproval: the relationship between the two was stronger than ever. But that hardly helped the marquis's military situation. He had an independent command in Virginia (subordinate to Greene's in South Carolina), but so few men that all he could do was to play hide-and-seek with Cornwallis. In so doing he came up against his father's adversary, General Phillips. The two exchanged formal letters on the treatment of prisoners, but Lafayette was not able to avenge his father in person, as Phillips died of a fever during the campaign.

Lafayette was candid about the weakness of his situation – and about his own fears. "I become timid in the same proportion as I become independent," he admitted to Greene. "Had a superior officer been here, I could have proposed half a dozen of schemes." To his brother-in-law Noailles, he excused whatever might happen well in advance, pleading "lack of experience" and "numerical inferiority." In fact he behaved with great prudence, even though vastly outnumbered; but such games were not to his taste.

The situation in Virginia worsened. Cornwallis's troops were joined by Phillips's old division, now commanded by Benedict Arnold. Washington was warned that if Lafayette were defeated, the effect on patriots throughout the south would be disastrous. To avoid such a defeat, Congress endorsed the commander-in-chief's request that reinforcements be sent. Lafayette continued to avoid full-scale battles, for he was well aware that "we cannot afford losing." Cornwallis became so confident of taking him that he was rumored to have boasted that "the boy cannot escape me." But Lafayette proved difficult to pin down, and as Cornwallis withdrew toward the coast, razing stores as he went, Lafayette continued to make the presence of his tiny army felt; so much so that to sympathetic eyes it might have appeared that he was driving his enemy before him. His peculiar sense of honor led him to refuse to talk to Arnold even when military etiquette required it, and he engaged in small and bothersome skirmishes which were claimed as victories by both sides. If Lafayette could continue to avoid capture, and if he could be sufficiently reinforced, all need not be lost.

Then Washington heard from France that a large fleet under Admiral de Grasse was on its way to the West Indies, and a substantial section of it, with six hundred troops, was to detach itself and proceed to Newport. The commander-in-chief decided that the best way to employ this vital reinforcement was in an attack on New York. He imparted this news to Lafayette, but the letter fell into British hands. Washington still felt that New York took precedence over the south, but the idea of a feint entered his calculations. Meanwhile the British commander-in-chief, Clinton, boasted of the news he had captured, and ordered Cornwallis to send back as many troops as he could spare for the defense of New York. Cornwallis too was to play a waiting game. This suited Lafayette. Even after an encounter at Green Spring, in which the marquis was defeated, losing 739 men, Cornwallis continued to march toward the coast, and it certainly looked as though he might be in retreat.

Washington next received the all-important news that Admiral de Grasse would be coming to the Chesapeake, in Virginia, rather than the north, and that he was bringing twenty-nine ships with more than three thousand troops. No further hesitation on the commander-in-chief's part was possible. New York would have to wait; the immediate task, requiring the delicate conjunction of the American and French forces, was to bottle up Cornwallis and his army. Lafayette's task was to try and stop the British general getting into Carolina, until reinforcements should arrive which would tie him down completely. But the marquis was deeply disappointed to learn that he would not be in command of the advance American force that would fight alongside the French. To avoid all quarrels, Washington had awarded the command on strict grounds of seniority. When the troops arrived Lafayette would have to yield his independence to General Benjamin Lincoln.

Cornwallis had intended to take his troops to Charleston, leaving

Virginia entirely, but his orders were to retain a naval base on the Chesapeake which could be used in a future British attack on Philadelphia. He therefore moved into Yorktown, which somewhat puzzled Lafayette. Following orders, he moved close – but not too close – to the enemy. As he wrote to his friend Knox, he retained the greatest respect for his opponent: "Lord Cornwallis's abilities are to me more alarming than his superiority of forces. . . . To speak plain English, I am devilish afraid of him." He even admitted the danger of his situation to Adrienne, although he consoled her by telling her how healthy he was.

The arrival of the French fleet under de Grasse was an immense comfort to Lafayette, and he was deeply flattered when the admiral and the commander of the marines, the Marquis de Saint-Simon, offered to put a large force at his disposal if he would storm Yorktown at once. But a long and difficult campaign of caution had taught Lafayette some prudence and he did not wish to rob his "father" of the triumph for which he had waited for so long. Instead Lafayette started to advance on the town, for now the French had arrived it would have been very costly for Cornwallis to try and get away by land. The British confidently expected to be relieved by sea, but after one skirmish with the French fleet, an English detachment commanded by Admiral Thomas Graves sailed for New York. For the first time in months Lafayette felt that all the frustrations of his Virginian campaign would be assuaged by victory. He promptly came down with a fever. His exertions over the summer had told on him and even his hair had become very thin for a man only twenty-four years old. But the illness could not prevent him galloping off to embrace Washington "with an ardor not easily described," as a bystander put it, when the allied commanders at last arrived in his camp to a salute of drums and the roar of twenty-one guns.

Washington was careful to plan everything that was needed for victory, and he delayed his advance until he was sure of it, even though Cornwallis had begun his fortifications. But suddenly a change of mind by de Grasse nearly upset the whole scheme. Despite agreement to keep his fleet blocking up the York River, the French admiral had been alarmed by news of another British fleet under Robert Digby and proposed sailing into open water, leaving only a few ships in the bay. Washington feared the collapse of his entire plan, and he sent Lafayette, now recovered from his fever, to persuade de Grasse to stay where he was. Meanwhile a council of de Grasse's officers had recommended that the major part of the fleet remain, and the admiral agreed, so that Lafayette's mission became superfluous.

On September 28, 1781, Washington ordered a general advance on Yorktown. They were about twelve miles from the British lines. The French under Rochambeau served on the left, the Americans under Lincoln on the right. As an American general, Lafayette was with the latter. Washington proceeded with his famous caution. He was prepared for attack, but he preferred the classical method of conducting a siege – to dig in and inflict severe damage on the enemy with artillery, when this had been brought up. The lengthy business of "constructing parallels" (the trenches and redoubts which would get the besiegers nearer to their target without exposing them) was slowly carried out. There was so little response from the British that the allies feared a trick. But bombardment had its effect, and the besieging forces crept nearer and nearer. After some two weeks, they were near enough to make an assault possible. The honor of leading four hundred Americans in this attack was given to Lafayette, since a similar French force was also to mount a charge on the British redoubts. So serious did Washington consider this mission that he did a very rare thing: he made a short speech to Lafayette's troops. They were to be firm and brave, he said, since the success of the attack depended on them.

The assault party's orders were to be silent and to use only their bayonets. At seven in the evening of October 12th a shot was heard in the French trenches. The American troops tensed, fearing discovery, then Lafayette's party crept forward. When they reached the British redoubt they came under fire; evidently their attempt at surprise had failed. But they pressed on, using their own guns, and both French and American forces captured their objective. The British did not fight back as tenaciously as had been expected, and though they turned their big guns on the captured posts from the town, soon enough fresh earth had been piled up to make the redoubts safe. Lafayette had gloriously crowned a campaign he had frequently thought lost.

Three days later Cornwallis proposed discussing terms. The allies would consider nothing except total surrender, but Washington did not propose to exact terms that would unnecessarily humiliate his defeated enemy. On October 19, 1781, Yorktown was formally surrendered. The British flags, and those of their German mercenaries, were cased, and their entire army marched out past the French and American troops, who were drawn up with their colors flying and their bands playing English and German music. This was a means of mocking the British who had demanded at the surrender of Charleston that the "rebels" not play "British marches." One tune heard in the lines of the defeated was "The World Turned Upside Down."

The effect of Yorktown was so prodigious that even Lord North, the British prime minister, regarded it as the final blow. Though the war was not over, the backbone of the British effort had been broken. Both sides continued to talk war while they prepared for peace.

Lafayette and Washington tried to persuade de Grasse to help them to take back Charleston from the British, but the French admiral was anxious to get prizes in the West Indies. George III tried to continue the war effort, but parliamentary opposition soon resulted in North's downfall. Peace had been in the air for many months – with Lafayette insisting that a military adventure or two would only improve American bargaining power – but after Yorktown it began to seem seriously possible. Lafayette resurrected his plans for an expedition against Canada, but Washington wanted to assure himself of a larger French military presence for the next campaign, if there was to be one. The marquis therefore proposed returning to France, to raise more aid and enthusiasm for the cause. Convinced as he was that Britain would make one last military effort, he wished to employ himself once more as a soldier-diplomat.

Congress granted this wish, loaded him with compliments, as well as a fulsome letter of recommendation to Louis XVI, and appointed him adviser to their representatives in Europe. They even suggested that the government take over the marquis's debts to the merchants of Baltimore, which had been incurred on behalf of his troops. He was officially lauded wherever he went, and with good reason. He had played a vital part in the greatest victory of the war so far, and he was the figurehead of the allied cooperation that had made that victory possible. He had proved himself in independent command as well as displaying undeniable courage. His reputation at last had real substance. On Christmas Day, 1781, after having penned tender farewells and assurances of his return to Washington, Lafayette, along with his brother-in-law Noailles and other French officers, left America on the *Alliance*. It took him just over three weeks to cross the Atlantic to find that the news of Yorktown, and his part in it, was the talk of all Europe.

Part Three: Hero of Two Worlds

9
Peace with Honor

PARIS WAS IN festive mood when Lafayette arrived home. Formal celebrations over the birth of a son to the king and queen were taking place. Although some jolly market women, carried away by the occasion, offered the marquis branches of laurel when he arrived at the Noailles mansion, none of his family were there. Nothing is worse than having your hopes of a glorious surprise frustrated, but the travel-worn hero resigned himself to wait – perhaps for hours, since his wife and relatives were attending the royal banquet in honor of the new dauphin.

So great, however, was his prestige that news of his arrival reached the royal ears in no time. Marie-Antoinette instantly urged Adrienne to leave and greet her husband, but the marquise had been brought up to know her place, and asked only that the carriages carrying the procession, when they returned, should pass by her door so that her husband could pay his respects to his sovereign. Not even a queen can break rules without peril, but Marie-Antoinette impetuously took Adrienne into her own carriage – to the fury of the court ladies whose precedence was thus flouted – and drove to the Hôtel de Noailles. Hearing the commotion, Lafayette emerged, whereupon Adrienne promptly fainted in his arms, to the applause of the great crowd that had gathered. The queen congratulated the marquis most civilly on his success, and ordered Adrienne to stay with him. As Lafayette wrote shortly afterwards to Washington, this welcome surpassed all his ambitions.

The king too was warm in his greeting to the hero on the following day. He spoke well of Washington also, as he had already done via the Marquis de Ségur, the minister of war and father of Lafayette's great friend. The minister had informed Lafayette that word of his great achievements and military talents in America had reached His Majesty, together with proof of Washington's confidence in him, and that the king had as a result formed an opinion of Lafayette as high as could be desired. In view of this, and as a special and flattering honor, Lafayette was promoted *maréchal-de-camp* (roughly the equivalent of the American major-general), this promotion to date from the surrender of Yorktown, although it was only to be taken up when the war was over. Though the French army was full of such *maréchaux* – there were 742 in 1789, most of whom were unoccupied in peacetime – this promotion infuriated those senior in service to Lafayette, over whose heads he jumped. But the Marquis de Ségur was a popular minister. Apart from reducing the number of soldiers who had to share a bed from three to two, and improving military hospitals and budgets, he had decreed that candidates for commissions had to prove four generations of nobility, unless they had actually risen from the ranks. This of course tightened the hold of the aristocracy over the army, and for that they could forgive the minister much, even jumping-up a "hero" whose "skirmishes," they claimed, had been absurdly exaggerated. Lafayette's command in the king's dragoons was bestowed on his brother-in-law, the Vicomte de Noailles, who had fought under Rochambeau in the last campaign. Ever careless about money, Lafayette sold this commission for 60,000 *livres*, making a loss of 20,000.

Now Lafayette was worshiped in earnest. The old Comte de Maurepas, who had always smiled on the marquis (and occasionally at him), was dead, but Vergennes, the true architect of French policy toward America, told him in a letter that "You may rest assured that your name is held here in veneration." He was asked to dine by the Maréchal de Richelieu, in the company of all the marshals of France. The assembly drank to the health of Washington, and Lafayette was charged with sending him their respects. All the young people of the court sought permission to go to America, to be "little Lafayettes." He was invited to visit Sweden by King Gustavus III. Wherever he went he was followed by crowds anxious "to see a hero." He was the subject of songs, verses, and pamphlets. When he went to a performance of *Iphigénie in Aulide*, the leading actress offered him the laurel crown when she should have been offering it to Achilles. The applause did not die down until the demi-god made a short speech.

And Aglaé d'Hunolstein continued to repay his favors. True, he soon made Adrienne pregnant again, and he had also met, at the house of the recently disgraced but still popular Necker, Mme de Simiane, a beauty with whom his name was soon linked. But it was to Aglaé that he paid most attention, despite the growing disapproval of the lady's family. There is no sign that Adrienne paid much attention to gossip, but if she knew of these goings-on, she kept it to herself; she did admit that so strong was her feeling about her husband that for many months after his return she felt faint whenever he left the room. She was ashamed of so showing her emotions, and she tried to control them. Considering the tribulations she had had to suffer – apart from a number of deaths in her family, little Georges had nearly died while teething – she succeeded well enough.

Lafayette quickly threw himself into the diplomatic role with which he had been charged. Even the great Franklin, plagued by gout and the difficulties of coping both with the French court and his own colleagues, admitted that the marquis pleaded for more aid to America "with greater weight than I could possibly do." But, Lafayette warned Washington, getting money was difficult, and while he thought some would be forthcoming in the end, it wasn't to be counted on. The trouble was a feeling that the Americans weren't making as much effort as they were capable of. The French ministry had little idea of the complex reality of the American political situation, and it was natural that Lafayette and the American envoys should not harp on its weaknesses. The marquis urged Washington to ensure that Congress raised a large and well-equipped army ready for war, not only to attract more aid, but in case of one last British attack, which Lafayette was sure would be made. Yet despite his misgivings, he succeeded in the end in wheedling a loan of six million *livres* from Vergennes, as well as a reinforcement for Rochambeau's army.

Success had changed Lafayette out of all recognition, and he had never been so busy proving it. As a general in a citizen army he had shown himself capable of engineering victory; as a diplomatic "adviser" he now showed himself knowledgeable, statesmanlike, cautious, and firm. The alliance with Spain was troublesome both to America, whose independence the Catholic monarch Charles III refused to recognize, and to France, who had brought Spain into the fight for her own benefit. Although the Americans had won, on the field of battle, the right to be recognized, the discussions around the negotiating tables of Europe attempted to whittle down this victory to suit the interests of the powers. England still hoped that a compromise short of recognizing American independence was possible, though in March 1782 the House of Commons voted that anyone who attempted, or even advised, the use of force to reconquer the colonies was an enemy of the country. This caused the resignation of Lord North, which in turn prepared George III, in the interests of preserving the Constitution, to consider abdication. On reflection he accepted a ministry drawn from the opposition. Spain did not want to see a strong, independent, Protestant America; she was more interested in Gibraltar, which proved impregnable, in the Caribbean, and in extending her influence and possessions upon the American continent. France could not be relied on to intervene on the American side in any dispute with Spain: like her ally she was also keen to

extend her rights and territories. Though she was bound to both
America and Spain by the terms of her treaties with them, her chief
desire was to negotiate an end to an expensive war in a way that
would give her a chance of getting her money back – through increased trade and new colonies acquired in the fighting – without
leaving a strong power on the other side of the Atlantic that could
threaten French interests. Between all these diplomatic reefs Lafayette had to pick his way, and he did it with great finesse.

He achieved this feat by acting as a sort of "referee" (J. M. Thompson's description in his book *The French Revolution*) between the
various conflicting interests. Franklin was the chief negotiator with
the British emissaries, holding out hope of future Anglo-American
cooperation if England were generous, yet refusing any attempt to
divide him from his French ally. Lafayette meanwhile warned
America about the Spanish, and advised Vergennes on the possibilities of a new military campaign. Although he admitted the
American people were "tired of war," he still harped on his old
passion for an attack on Canada. He recommended his friend Ségur,
who was about to cross the Atlantic, to the founders of the new
nation, and also proposed himself as their negotiator in London – an
idea which came to nothing, despite Franklin's support.

As the peace negotiations wore on without much progress
because Spain and Britain still refused to recognize America as independent, Lafayette started to miss the command he had enjoyed in
America. He continued to enjoy, of course, the adulation of Paris –
even the masonic lodge of Saint-Jean d'Écosse du Contrat Social had
awarded him the unprecedented honor of election by acclamation –
and the important consultations which he monitored between the
various ministers and envoys gave him some pleasure. But the
stately dance of diplomacy was not much to his taste, and, he assured
Washington, he was only staying because he felt he was needed. The
hopes of peace rose and fell as face-saving formulae were agreed and
repudiated. The Americans, especially John Jay, became justifiably
suspicious of Vergennes, who was trying to push the interests of
France and Spain before those of America in secret consultation
with the British. Meanwhile the defeat and capture of Admiral de
Grasse by Admiral Rodney in the Antilles had stiffened British
attitudes. Lafayette was told that a Franco-American attack on
Charleston, still in British hands, was now out of the question. To
make amends for this, considering that peace was still some way off,
and in the hope of snatching a few more colonial prizes from Britain,
a joint Franco-Spanish expedition under Admiral d'Estaing was put
together to sail to the West Indies. D'Estaing asked that Lafayette,
with whom he had worked in America, should be in charge of the
land forces, and the marquis joyfully agreed. After assuring him-

self that the U.S. commissioners (Franklin, Jay, and John Adams, who wrote of Lafayette that "he grasps at all, civil, political, and military, and would be the *unum necessarium* in every thing") approved his going, he prepared to join d'Estaing in Cadiz as quartermaster-general.

In September, 1782, Lafayette had turned twenty-five, and had ceased to be a minor. His rich great-grandfather had recently died, improving his fortune and increasing the problems of his financial manager Morizot. He had also, at Adrienne's prompting, shown a sudden concern for the peasants on his estate at Chavaniac, who were still forced by taxes, weather, and lack of tools between the seasons of sowing and reaping to emigrate to more prosperous regions, leaving their families behind. Some seigneurs had found a solution to this by getting schools of weaving started: the sheeps' wool was there, if only the machinery and the teachers could be made available. Lafayette sought government help to set up such a school, but events took his attention elsewhere, and it was left to Adrienne to get things going, with royal aid, in 1785.

On the larger canvas of international diplomacy, the British cabinet at last empowered their emissary to treat with "the commissioners appointed by the colonies, under the title of Thirteen United States." Negotiating privately with the British, the Americans secured the trans-Appalachian West, as well as free access to the Gulf of Mexico, in exchange for giving up the idea of gaining Canada as the fourteenth state. Without the West the much-longed-for American expansion would have been impossible – a crippling limitation which was precisely what France and Spain had wanted. There was still much haggling over the drawing of borders, but the essence of the peace treaty was agreed: the mother country finally let her children go. Even the question of the pro-British loyalists was settled to the satisfaction of the Americans: they would not promise to compensate them for lands seized, but the British, to satisfy their supporters that they had not been betrayed, agreed to a clause stating that Congress would "recommend" the revision of their confiscation laws to the states.

Although this agreement had been privately reached between America and England, it was contingent on peace being declared between England, France, and Spain, who had not so far been kept informed of these latest developments. When Vergennes found out what was going on, he was furious, and it took all of Franklin's and Lafayette's delicacy to calm him down. Soon after this, at the end of 1782, Lafayette joined d'Estaing in Cadiz.

Once again a father (of a daughter, Virginie, born prematurely in September 1782, after which Adrienne was advised to have no more children), he wrote tenderly to his wife, his mistress, to Mme de Simiane, and to his old friend the Prince de Poix about the ladies he met in Spain. His energy was undiminished. He busied himself with his job in organizing the allied armada, but though he was prepared for more fighting he soon learned that, as far as the United States was concerned, the war was over. Nevertheless he hoped to go on and conquer Canada with his great fleet, and had even got permission of the king of Spain – who had, however, reacted to the suggestion that the marquis be made governor of Jamaica (if it was captured) by saying, "Never! He would create a republic there!" But a few weeks after England had come to terms with America, France and Spain also did so, and on January 20, 1783, preliminary treaties were entered into and a general armistice established. Although it took until the following September to settle the details, the Franco-Spanish armada's expedition had to be called off. Lafayette was saddled with the details of disbanding an army, but he still had time to write joyfully to all his American friends. To Washington he recalled the "times that have determined my engaging in the American cause" and, pledging his descendants to be as faithful as himself, he said, "I cannot but envy the happiness of my grand children where they will be about celebrating and worshiping your name." He hoped to see America again as soon as possible.

Perhaps to avoid the feeling of anti-climax, Lafayette now threw himself into new plans and activities. He suggested to Washington, a great slave-owner, that the two of them buy a small property "where we may try the experiment to free the Negroes and use them only as tenants. Such an example as yours might render it a general practice, and if we succeed in America, I will cheerfully devote a part of my time to render the method fashionable in the West Indies. If it be a wild scheme, I had rather be mad this way than to be thought wise in the other task." Although he had never before shown such concern, even when engaged in the Virginia campaign, in France there was a different attitude to enslavement. The Abbé Raynal, whom both he and his revered mother had read, was one of the first opponents of slavery, and certainly fashionable Paris, by the 1780s, shared this opinion, especially since Raynal's work was again proscribed, giving it a new popularity. Turgot, Necker, and even the American envoys, Franklin and Adams, all opposed the exploitation of slaves. Perhaps Lafayette was influenced by them.

Lafayette still wanted to be an envoy of America at the treaty ratifications in London. He expressed this wish in confidence to Washington, hoping that he might be given the commission as a temporary honor. He always wanted to be where the action was, and it would have given him great satisfaction to pay a second visit to London, as an envoy of the nation whose independence he had helped to create. It would have been pleasant, also, to go to England as a victor. But though Washington supported his wish, Congress denied him this pleasure. They doubtless preferred to be represented by someone possessing more gravity.

The confidence that Lafayette had acquired enabled him to express his opinion freely to those in authority, and to expect to be taken seriously. Anything that furthered American interests, or his friends' interpretation of them, was fuel for his energy, which was itself the product of his success and reputation. He wrote about the need for a stronger union between the states "as will forever defy European politics"; and about the gratitude that ought to be shown to the Continental army, without mentioning the sums he had himself expended in the cause. Somewhat uncharacteristically, he acquired an interest in free international trade, doubtless because of the urgent mercantile needs of his adopted country. He proposed easing the restrictions on free trade with America that operated in France, and in this he had the support of Vergennes, who had always preferred butter to guns. In his capacity as diplomat, Lafayette took himself to Madrid and smoothed out the ruffles in Spanish-American relations, skillfully dropping the right words in all the right ears. By the time he left there the American envoy had been formally received, and, Lafayette thought, Spain had agreed to recognize both the United States and her boundaries. In fact these problems took months – in the case of the boundaries, years – to settle. But the marquis's intervention had certainly been successful, and he returned to Paris a satisfied man.

Not everything went smoothly, however; if it had Lafayette would doubtless have been suspicious, or bored. Aglaé d'Hunolstein's reputation for serial promiscuity had caught up with her, and her family and friends, with righteous hypocrisy, bore down on her. Apparently what caused this censure was not the quality of her men, but the quantity. In desperation, she begged Lafayette to break with her, to save both their reputations. He felt unable to make any such decision in the hothouse of Paris society. Luckily, he had an excuse to go to Chavaniac and think things over: his unmarried aunt had died, leaving his aunt Charlotte there alone. Besides, he hadn't seen the place for ten years and Adrienne had never seen it. But Lafayette could not make decisions about his mistress in the presence of his wife. He told Adrienne to expect him to return with his aunt and he set off for the Auvergne alone.

In the peace of his childhood home, he decided to make the break with Aglaé, and, as is natural to men in such a position, he put the responsibility for so doing on her. He told her of his "passion," his "transports," and his "complete surrender," and bemoaned the fact that the decision was forced upon him. He ended, "At least my heart is my own, dear Aglaé: all that you are, all that I owe you, justifies my love and nothing, not even you, can keep me from adoring you." After which the relief of having made the decision allowed him to enjoy his stay to the full. He wrote to his wife of the house being full of guests, and of proceeding with their idea of a school of weaving. His mood also permitted him to be generous to his peasants. The story is told of how his bailiff proudly showed his master the barns full of wheat, and advised him that, prices being high because of the appalling harvest, "this was the time to sell." "No," Lafayette is reported to have replied, "this is the time to give." And grain was distributed to his hungry peasants – who had already been saved from famine, thanks to the previous efforts of Adrienne.

When he returned to Paris, still hailed by crowds wherever he went, the king invested Lafayette with the Order of St Louis, a highly coveted honor (especially as it carried pension rights) bestowed for extraordinary merit or as a mark of special favor. Even more pleasurable, he and his family at last moved into a house of their own, in the Rue de Bourbon. The fruits of maturity were indeed sweet, but also costly, for the furniture alone set the marquis back some 50,000 *livres*. The house became the social center of the "Americans" in Paris: regular Monday suppers, to which the invitation cards were printed in English, saw not only Franklin, the Adamses and the Jays, but those friends and relatives of Lafayette's who had fought for the cause, and indeed anyone who could lay claim to a serious interest in the newly independent nation. As befitted the liberal, civilized internationalism Lafayette had adopted, his doors were open to his one-time enemies: at a gala dinner in October 1783 he entertained William Pitt (the Younger), William Wilberforce, and various other English gentlemen; Benjamin Franklin and his grandson; his brother-in-law and one-time hero the Vicomte de Noailles, and other luminaries from the French liberal circle. Wilberforce approved both of Lafayette's apparently simple domestic arrangements, and the way in which his host avoided card-playing and other courtly diversions (the marquis only indulged at the request of royalty). Lafayette himself was pleased that the dinner went off well; he liked Pitt on this occasion, and still wanted to go to England again, even though his patriotism would not let him forget the injuries France had suffered.

There was no trace now of the shyness that in adolescence had made Lafayette hate society. He was seen and hailed everywhere, and the rupture with Mme d'Hunolstein, who was forced, in the end, to retire to a convent, was quickly healed by a new liaison with Mme de Simiane, a lady of great beauty, and, more important, discretion. His name was also joined to that of the Princesse d'Hénin, and indeed his intimacy with both these ladies continued for many years. But they were also part of Adrienne's circle, and Lafayette often referred to them in letters to his wife. If she resented his infidelities, she certainly did not show it at this time.

Adrienne finally got to Chavaniac for the first time during 1783, on a trip to take her husband's aunt back home. Lafayette meanwhile proclaimed himself eager to return to America, his excuse being that he had promised to do so. He continued to engage in diplomatic activity for his adopted country, and he pursued his interest in freeing trade between France and America, even when those privileged to run the royal monopolies and benefit from the collection of taxes (that class known as the farmers-general) successfully flexed their muscles in defense of their traditional rights. But Vergennes and the new comptroller-general Calonne both knew that if the richest pickings of the burgeoning American trade should go to England, where restrictions were lighter, France's already desperate financial situation would be made even worse. Therefore Lafayette's pleadings in favor of establishing free ports fell on receptive ears and were successful. Trade with the United States was to be accorded preferential treatment. This was a triumph for the marquis who stood to gain nothing personally from these arrangements.

One other activity which kept Lafayette busy among so much else was organizing the French branch of the Society of the Cincinnati. The American army suffered from want in peace no less than in war, and on several occasions mutiny threatened, to be forestalled only by the personal, and highly emotional, intervention of Washington, who longed to return to private life like the Roman Cincinnatus. He accepted the presidency of the Society of the Cincinnati, a club formed by certain American officers desiring "one society of friends" who had shed blood in a common cause. Amid much high-flown language concerning "union," "national honor," and "the future dignity of the American empire" was the provision that membership should be hereditary, and it was this, plus that deep-rooted American fear of anything which smacked of a standing army, that aroused a storm which amazed Washington and the originators of the scheme. Jefferson, Adams, Franklin and Jay were among the Americans who attacked the society as an attempt to set up an "order of chivalry" in the new republic. All this perplexed Lafayette, who had been charged with handing round the society's insignia to those French officers qualified for membership – an extremely delicate task, as everyone wanted to be so honoured once the marquis had got royal permission for serving French officers to accept a foreign decoration. As usual in perplexity, he decided to abide by whatever decision his "father" made, writing in confidence to say that if Washington thought the principle of heredity was a good one, he would abide by it, and if it were considered an affront to democratic institutions, he would vote against it. In fact, Washington adopted the latter course, and the storm abated.

Heroes follow fashion as well as setting it, and Lafayette shared the enthusiasm for ballooning that suddenly flared in Paris. But that was quickly replaced by his becoming a fervent disciple of Mesmer, whose "discovery" of "animal magnetism" became so popular that its founder made his followers sign contracts respecting his rights in the process. Lafayette confessed to Washington that he was counted "one of the most enthusiastic" of Mesmer's pupils, and that he had obtained permission to impart the secret to his general, whom Mesmer admired. There is no evidence that America's first president was converted to mesmerism. Even Lafayette retained a grain of skepticism, for in writing of his new passion he reminded Washington of the time they had talked to someone who claimed to have interviewed the devil, and how they had laughed at such an idea.

Lafayette was now longing to see Washington again, especially since the latter had temporarily retired from public life. The marquis was fed up with having to smooth the hackles of diplomats, and another excuse for leaving was the need to thank in person all those Americans who had showered honors on him in his absence. Yet although Washington had personally invited Adrienne to Mount Vernon, his ancestral home, Lafayette once more decided to make the journey alone. Perhaps he had in America memories and pleasures too personal to share or explain. Perhaps he could not bear to dilute the strength of his relationship with his "father," for sharing one love with another is always hazardous. There was also the simple fact that someone had to look after the children and the family's financial affairs; and no one performed these tasks with more efficiency and less complaint than Adrienne.

Whatever the reason, Lafayette set out on his third trip to America in June 1784, accompanied only by the Chevalier de Caraman. His wife had their seven-year-old daughter Anastasie write the following letter: "Dear Washington, I hope that papa whill come back son here. I am verry sorry for the loss of him, but I am verry glade for you self. I wich you a werry good health and I am whith great respect dear sir your most obedient servent." Adrienne was the subtle one in the family.

Once at sea, her husband showed an optimistic faith in mesmerism as a cure for his perpetual sea-sickness.

I shall fortify myself with magnetism, with sachets of camphor and thorium on the pit of the stomach, and lumps of sugar dipped in either: all new remedies I am going to try which will do me no good whatever. When telling me to fold my arms around the mainmast, Mesmer did not know – and I had forgotten – that it is smeared with tar to a certain height, so that this form of embrace becomes totally impossible unless one is prepared to be covered with the stuff from head to foot.

But to be greeted on his arrival as a living legend, and accorded a reception equalled only by that usually given Washington, made all his suffering worthwhile.

A somewhat uneasy atmosphere prevailed in the United States following the official end of the war and the final departure of British soldiers. Hindsight makes it seem a mere interlude before a strong central government was established under the Constitution, but there were few detailed ideas of what to make of the independence newly won, except to return to normal as quickly as possible. The Articles of Confederation were no guarantee of unity, and the desperate financial condition of the states, the needs and demands of the ex-soldiers of the Continental army, and the traditional rivalries between the old colonies that once more reasserted themselves, threatened to make the "United States" as laughable a collection of territories as any set of quarreling mid-European principalities.

Lafayette was very much aware of this danger. He wanted the best for his adopted country, and the views of those he mixed with left him in no doubt that strong central government was the best, the only way of achieving this. In his speeches and letters on the subject there was a strong vein of paternalism, as was common not only among the liberal French aristocracy but in the writings of the American founding fathers. The Protestant ethic that ruled on the American side of the Atlantic and the Age of Reason that prevailed, in word and sometimes deed, on the other, both demanded change in the name of the greater good of all humanity. But it was up to those at the head of affairs to decide upon the pace and direction of this change: "equality" meant that people were equal before the law, not that the distinctions of education, ownership, or acquired influence were to be laid flatly aside. This is not to say that the War of Independence was merely a cynical maneuver by the property-owning classes to improve their own position: the way the Continental army held together despite the most appalling privation is effective argument against such a view. But those who directed the war effort, and who attempted to secure the peace, were convinced that an "unbridled" democracy would lead to anarchy, which they feared more than anything else. They took it upon themselves to define "the public good" in their own terms, and to direct the public efforts toward achieving it. They, like Lafayette, were members of a privileged class who felt it was their duty not only to serve "the people," but to instruct them in the art of self-government.

Just as Washington did, Lafayette used his enormous prestige to urge upon Americans the need for a strong federal government.

He was very flattering about their achievements, and talked often as if Europe would have to learn to follow America's example – which in 1784 was purely a rhetorical flourish. Wherever he went, guns boomed thirteen salutes (one for each state), official addresses were made, and honors showered upon him. A county in Pennsylvania was named after him – the first of many throughout the nation – and he was made a freeman of New York, a citizen of Maryland, New England, Hartford, Massachusetts, and Virginia, not to mention an honorary Doctor of Law at Harvard. Towns were lit up for him, bands played for hours, gala dinners were given, citizens jostled for a sight, a touch, a dance, the honor of giving him tea. Such adulation could weary even a hero of twenty-seven. Apart from the pleasure of twice seeing Washington, the marquis got tired of the speeches and began to get homesick. There was so little he could *do* in America, since the action was all political not military.

He enjoyed attending a conference designed to bring about peace between the Americans and the Indian tribes of New York state, for as an adopted "father" himself, with the name of Kayewla, he was listened to with devotion and respect. He eclipsed the official American commissioners – but, he wrote to Adrienne, he was "much bored with having to play the part of paterfamilias, which I am constantly compelled to do." He was still doing his best to further Franco-American trade; he sent off a specimen of the plant ginseng to his wife and family; he diligently asked Adrienne about the health of his mistresses and relatives. He also asked to address Congress, and hinted that he would like to be officially considered as a permanent "adviser" to the American envoys in Europe. A special committee of Congress confined itself to showering him with compliments, and by January, 1785, America's favorite foreigner was once more on his way home.

The greatest sadness was the parting from Washington, who wrote of "that love, respect and attachment for you with which the length of years, close connection and your merits have inspired me. I often asked myself, as our carriages distended, whether that was the last sight I ever should have of you? And though I wished to say no, my fears answered yes . . . but I will not repine, I have had my day."

Lafayette waved aside this premonition. Of all that had happened to him on his third trip to America, he had been most impressed by the dignity of Washington's retirement into private life. He knew that if the call to further service came, it would be answered, and he could satisfy himself that he had forcefully and faithfully expressed the opinions of his "father" to his people. To Lafayette, Washington was a model of principled action. He was also a figure with a never-failing sense of the direction in which he wanted things to go – a quality that was by no means easy to imitate.

10
The Old Regime

THE PEACE OF 1783 had restored that prestige to France that she had lost twenty years before, following the Seven Years' War. Apart from taking thirteen colonies away from England, it returned lost territories to France's allies, opened new channels for French trade and agriculture, restored Dunkirk, which had had to suffer the humiliating presence of a British commissioner, and generally helped the nation back to big power status, despite her bankrupt financial position. Since Lafayette was both symbol and instrument of that peace, he continued to be lionized at court and in the country as a whole. Passing through Brittany on his way back from America to Paris, he stopped to attend a meeting of the Provincial Estates, as he had inherited large properties there. The session was interrupted for his benefit, he was greeted with applause, and official tributes paid to him such as he had just enjoyed across the Atlantic. And as soon as he rejoined his family in the capital, his social life immediately started up on the heroic scale at which he had left it the year before.

Some memorialists who survived the Terror wrote in old age of Paris and of France being, in the 1780s, on the "edge of an abyss." A very different picture, however, emerges from the letters and diaries of the time. The years following the great food riots of 1775 were relatively peaceful, since food prices remained stable. That the government was bankrupt, and kept going only by loans, deficit financing, and economic sleight-of-hand was rarely of concern to any but economists. Even Necker's publication of the national budget (in his *Compte Rendu* of 1781) did not fan revolutionary sentiment; cynicism at how the government spent its money could scarcely have increased. Paris, for some, had never glittered so prosperously: old houses were pulled down and new buildings erected, street lamps and sidewalks made walking around less of a hazard, and the boundaries of the city were extended, circled by a new ring of customs posts which brought in some forty percent of the national yield from internal customs duties.

In terms of power the way to the top remained blocked by the aristocracy and those with influence at court, but the capital was thronged with the young and ambitious, to whom it offered an infinity of amusements. Beaumarchais' new satire *The Marriage of Figaro*, with its attack on the privileges of birth, was not only popular with the bourgeoisie; members of the court tried as eagerly to get seats and applaud. Censorship, according to Ségur, was practiced only out of "duty and habit," and as usual it served to increase the sales and stature of the authors condemned. There was vast and rapid progress in agriculture, industry, trade, navigation, philosophy, physics, mechanics and chemistry – and the ballooning triumphs of the brothers Montgolfier (despite frightening the king) made everyone feel that nothing was impossible, especially for Frenchmen. The court was especially brilliant and attractive even to dissident intellectuals, and the royal family – before the affair of the queen's necklace – basked in an unprecedented popularity. Even the other absolutist monarchs of Europe – Frederick the Great of Prussia, Catherine the Great of Russia, Joseph II of Austria – showed themselves influenced by the Enlightenment.

After the end of the American war, English fashions once more reasserted themselves in Paris, because, says Ségur, the French envied the English their climate of political freedom. Clubs for men only became the rage, where members could read, eat, play cards, and talk politics. These were the forerunners of the clubs that played so important a part in the French Revolution, but in the middle of the decade they were merely another haunt for the privileged, like the grand masonic lodges. Mesmer continued to be the guru of the eminently respectable (such as Ségur and Chastellux) as well as of the gullible, contributing to that feeling that there were no boundaries to the expansion of knowledge. Marie-Antoinette, however, remained skeptical about him. The only prophets of doom were those whose job it was to finance public projects, but with Calonne as comptroller-general pleasing all parties by financial wizardry (except the peasants, who seemed inured to suffering), no one was bothered.

To this city of hope and progress, Lafayette returned in 1785 with a young Indian (Ségur had come back with a young Negro) and the orphan son of an American army chaplain, John Caldwell. The Indian, Kayenlaha, was a great success at balls, where he performed native dances practically naked. As to Caldwell, the marquis had undertaken his education, and while a good boarding school was found for him, the fact that he was a Protestant was an enormous difficulty. Lafayette thus encountered the intolerance shown for Protestants, who had no legal standing in France and, as he said to his Protestant "father" Washington, easing their condition became his "present object." For that and the emancipation of the slaves were two of the apparently few causes left now that liberty had been assured across the Atlantic. As a veteran, Lafayette wrote eagerly to Washington of the possibilities of a war in Europe and asked that, if there should be fighting between America and Spain over the latter's American possessions, or in Canada, a command should be reserved for him. Washington, however, replied that he wanted to banish the word war from his letters, after which Lafayette confined himself to reporting on the convolutions of European diplomacy and threw himself into his humanitarian projects.

The cause of the Protestants was one for which, in this enlightened age, there was much sympathy but little action. To take it up publicly was difficult, although Lafayette found covert backing from the naval minister, de Castries, and considered even Vergennes favorably disposed toward reform. Adrienne, though strictly attached to the Catholic Church, backed him to the hilt. She had, however, hired a separate apartment for her six-year-old son and his tutor, M. Frestel, to protect Georges not from her husband's opinions, but from his frenetic way of life.

The largest communities of Protestants were in the south and the center of France, and Lafayette, moving circumspectly, took advantage of a trip to Chavaniac to visit the most eminent. He was careful even to the point of using code in his letters on the subject to Washington. Washington himself urged caution in the matter, saying that an orderly approach was often just as effective as an outright assault, and moreover permitted a safe retreat. In this at least Lafayette agreed, and promised the Protestant leader Rabaut de Saint-Etienne that he would smooth the way at Versailles so that a plea for toleration could be presented to the king. He was reminded of his own popularity and its attractive power by the reception given him in Lyon, through which he passed on his way back to Paris. For him, as for his peers, everything seemed possible.

Although his mansion in the Rue de Bourbon was still a mecca for Americans and their supporters, the restless Lafayette was soon traveling again, this time on a European tour that was to include viewing the maneuvers of Frederick the Great's Prussian army. The trip was ostensibly to improve his military education, and it would also give him the opportunity of explaining and expanding on events in America. His reports to Washington read like the breathless itinerary of the modern tourist: a summer passed in seeing princes and admiring soldiers in Kassel, Brunswick, Berlin, Breslau, Vienna, Prague, Dresden, Potsdam, and Berlin again. He played loto with and talked endlessly to the king of Prussia's brother Prince Henry (who also had a great reputation as a strategist), befriended the king's heir Frederick William, and also Marie-Antoinette's brother Emperor Joseph II of Austria. The Prussian maneuvers were something of an international social event, and Lafayette was a star. He even established cordial relations with his old enemies and fellow guests, Lord Cornwallis and General von Knyphausen (who had commanded the Hessians in the British service in America).

Most of all he admired the almost mythical Frederick the Great, to whom he chatted for hours. He described his royal host as looking like an old and decrepit corporal, covered in snuff, his head bent on his shoulder, and his fingers crippled by gout. But, thought Lafayette, he had marvelous eyes.

He also had something of a malicious sense of humor, for at one of the three-hour dinners which Lafayette attended during his week-long stay, the king placed him next to Cornwallis, and fired at them both questions about America. After listening to Lafayette's answers, the king related the moral story of a young man who, having seen several countries where liberty and equality were the rule, decided to introduce these ideas to his own country and was hanged for his pains. But the general impression that Lafayette made, as the French minister in Berlin reported to Vergennes, was that "he has been able to win universal approval."

Everywhere he heard, to his great pleasure, Washington's name spoken with the utmost respect. There was admiration of the energy and firmness with which America had gained her independence, but some criticism of the lack of power residing in Congress, lack of vigor in government, and lack of union between the states. Strong central government was of course the mainstay of the enlightened absolutists who were Lafayette's hosts, but while he lamented their ignorance of matters American, he agreed with the substance of their criticisms. If his adopted compatriots were not to lose the respect they had built up by force of arms, he urged them, through Washington, to give Congress the power to regulate trade, pay her debts, or at least the interest on them, and establish a well-ordered militia – a program Washington certainly wanted to see adopted. Lafayette assured his old chief that he was writing to all his American friends with the same advice.

Without ever forgetting America's trading interests, which he continued to push with increasing success when back in France, Lafayette had reason to boast of actually doing something about the plight of black slaves. For some 120,000 *livres* he bought a plantation in the French colony of Cayenne where, with the support of the local *intendant* and the naval minister, de Castries, he proposed to practice emancipation. Doubtless the horror shown by his friend Ségur at what went on in the French colonies, which he had seen first-hand on his recent trip to the Americas, influenced Lafayette's decision to make this purchase. It was a project in which Adrienne took the closest interest, and naturally she took charge of the details. One Richeprey was hired to run the plantation along lines laid down by the marquis himself, and although the slaves were not granted their freedom instantly, they were paid wages according to how hard they had worked, their sale was forbidden, their punishment for misdeeds was no harder than that meted out to whites, and they benefited from Adrienne's efforts to teach them "how to know and love God." That Richeprey succumbed to the climate after six months did not stop the grand project, of which Washington warmly approved. The gradualism of the experiment was to his taste: to proceed suddenly from slavery to liberty, Lafayette said later, led only to unbridled licence, which could result in despotism taking hold. A slave should not rejoice in liberty before being gradually enlightened as to the rights it confers, the duties it prescribes, and the limits imposed by reason and justice: these were the opinions Layfayette expressed in old age. They were lessons learned in America, and especially from Washington – who sent him home-cured Virginia hams, lamented that his peach brandy wasn't good enough for the marquis's table, grieved that one of the inconveniences of a democratic government was that the people, "not always seeing and frequently misled, must often feel before they can act right."

Honors continued to be loaded on Lafayette. He was allowed to ride in the king's carriage on a tour of the new harbor at Cherbourg, and was gratified at the monarch's popularity, which had suffered because of rumors of war with Austria – the queen's own country – and the affair of the queen's necklace, which had involved the Cardinal de Rohan being persuaded to buy for Marie-Antoinette an expensive diamond necklace which she knew nothing about and never received. The court and Paris had been so preoccupied with the scandal that little other business got transacted, but the king's reception on his trip to and from Cherbourg seemed to show that, outside the capital, the affection for the sovereign which Lafayette and the aristocracy had always believed in was still as strong as ever.

Lafayette showed a touch of grandeur in buying the seigneurial rights to Langeac, in the Auvergne, for a reputed 188,000 *livres*. Though his enemies accused him of acquiring more lands so as to qualify for a dukedom, both the marquis and his wife were popular in the area, which had suffered from the neglect of its seigneurs in the past. On August 13, 1786, the town gave a great fête in his honor, and in a mock-heroic poem entitled "La Belle Journée" a local inhabitant related the mishaps of the festivities. When the guard of honor arrived at Chavaniac to escort the marquis to Langeac, they discovered he had gone off to have breakfast with a neighbor. They then wore themselves out galloping over there, so overwhelming their sergeant that he was unable to deliver his formal speech. The town notables were kept waiting for two hours at the specially erected *arc de triomphe*, and when they finally got to deliver their address to their new lord, it was drowned by the enthusiasm of the drummers. The wine of honor offered was so rancid it would have turned butter, but Lafayette took it all in good part, even finding the right phrases to utter on a tedious tour of the sights of the town.

Bayonne honored him by making him a citizen in return for getting the city declared a free port – one of many successes in the area of free trade which Lafayette had made his own. His bust by Houdon, commissioned by the Virginians, was accorded an unprecedented place in the Paris Hôtel de Ville (the City Hall), the king having given his permission out of his great regard and friendship for Lafayette. A copy of the head was to be placed next to Washington's in Richmond, Virginia. Artists now came in droves to paint him, and his portrait was actually displayed in several homes. Poets sang his praises or made light fun of his virtues, to such an extent that he perhaps felt impelled to start his own memoirs. The citizens of Nantucket, in gratitude for what he had done for their trade in whale oil, resolved to send him a five-hundred-pound cheese. The king had him frequently to dine and (doubtless unwillingly) play cards. The empress of Russia, Catherine the Great, asked his help with some Indian words for the mighty dictionary she had commissioned, which request he promptly relayed to Washington. She also hinted that the marquis would be welcome to visit Russia, where his friend Ségur was now the French minister. Ever-eager to travel and spread the American gospel, Lafayette, in accepting the empress's invitation, heard that she was to make a royal progress to the Crimea, and asked if he could join her there. This request was granted. But events at home cut short his preparations for the voyage. On December 29, 1786, Louis XVI announced the convocation of the Assembly of Notables for the following spring.

The Notables, as Lafayette explained in a letter to Washington, were the principal men from each "Estate" or order of French society: the First Estate (clergy), the Second (nobility), and the Third (the rest). The king's idea was to submit the state of the nation's finances to this hand-picked body, together with proposals for alleviating the burden on the people and for reforming abuses. The motive, Lafayette wrote, was "at bottom a desire to make money some how or other, in order to put the receipt on a level with the expenses." He thoroughly approved the idea, for it would give him the chance to promote his own program for reform: "popular assemblées in the provinces, the destruction of many schlakles of the trade, and a change in the fate of the protestants." Yet his name was not on the first published list of Notables to be summoned (114 of them). Most people assumed this was due not to Lafayette's supposed radicalism (which was shared by many of those who appeared on the list), but because he had quarreled with the comptroller-general, Calonne, who was responsible for the convocation in the first place. In his memoirs Lafayette denies this rumor, saying that he and Calonne agreed on many things at that time. We do not know the exact reason for Lafayette's exclusion, but a certain amount of fuss followed, the famous Noailles' connections were once more put to work, and, after a bit of juggling, Lafayette's name duly appeared.

The summoning of the Notables was Calonne's attempt to get a measure of national unity in order to carry out plans that were bound to be unpopular; lack of confidence was so great that further loans were almost impossible to raise. Calonne thought that a personally chosen assembly would be easier to deal with than the parlements, or local magistrates (whose members constituted the lower branch of the French nobility and whose duty it was to register royal edicts, making them legally enforceable, and who often took the opportunity – as the old colonial assemblies in America had done – to protest against things they didn't like). Calonne wanted to increase taxes, but he chiefly wanted to make the system more efficient. If all the tax that was supposed to be collected actually got through to the royal exchequer, its position would have been much healthier. He also wanted to tax the noble rich, who had hitherto been virtually exempt, not because he was a great leveler, but because he needed the money and the poor were simply in no position to provide it. Calonne by no means proposed that the First and Second Estates should submit to the back-breaking demands made on the Third: all he wanted was some cash from them to free the king from dependence on the parlements for voting new taxes. If the first two Estates felt that their privileges were being undermined, Calonne offered to allow the amount of tax paid by each individual in a region to be determined by new provincial assemblies. These were to be elected by landowners without distinction of class.

The actual meeting of the Notables was delayed, first by the death of Vergennes, then by the illness of Calonne. It was finally opened by the king, whom many provincial nobles now saw for the first time. Powerful though their respect for the monarchy was, the sight was less than impressive. Louis was small, stout and shambling, and so short-sighted he was unable to recognize people at more than three paces. His sword was always getting in his way, and he never seemed to know what to do with his hat. He was honorable and well intentioned, and his interest in the welfare of his people was second only to his passion for hunting. His indecisiveness was more than compensated for by the unshakeable opinions of his wife who, having made the fortunes of all her favorites, decided to take a hand in the fortunes of France. Louis was unable to resist her advice.

After the king had left, Calonne harangued the assembly about the abuses His Majesty was determined to reform, and outlined his proposals. The Notables – quickly nicknamed the "Not Ables" by those with a taste for English puns – were not impressed. When they separated into their seven panels (*bureaux*), each presided over by a prince of the blood royal, they showed it.

The struggle between the kings of France and the aristocracy was a long one, and although under Louis XVI the nobles held every position of importance (all the bishoprics and all the government ministries: Necker had been the only commoner, and even he was kept out of the cabinet for as long as possible), the nobility had no desire to give the king the means to raise money in the future without consulting them. The mania for imitating England (which in some cases got so out of hand that "English" accents and even what the French thought of as the "English" way of walking were affected) spilled into the political sphere: some nobles wanted to be like their counterparts across the Channel and actually share in the government of the country. The Provincial Estates, of which the most powerful were those of Brittany and Languedoc, where the upper orders ran affairs and even the Third Estate was represented by the privileged, saw no reason why there should be any change in the power over local affairs and taxation which they had built up. The Notables, in sum, wanted to extend their "ancient rights" to include that of consultation over fiscal matters, and to manage local government through provincial assemblies in which they predominated. These were all demands of which Lafayette personally approved.

He was busy, though not outspoken, in the Notables' committee discussions, until the matter of speculation in the royal estates came up. Lafayette, who had never had to deal with the sordid side of money-making, and who was therefore highly principled about it, was not the first to raise this issue. But when it was reported that it had made the king angry enough to demand that those who made charges should write them down and sign them, Lafayette wrote out a speech that did just that. He used the figures put before the assembly to ask for an impartial inquiry, and this provocative request quickly became public. It reportedly angered Calonne enough to make him ask the king to cool Lafayette down by putting him in the Bastille, but nothing had happened by the time of the first recess at Easter. Lafayette needed the break as much as anyone: he was suffering from a chest complaint (perhaps a recurrence of the fever that had hit him when he was exhausted and run-down in America, or perhaps an emotional illness), and gossip tied his name to the unfortunate suicide of the husband of his mistress, Mme de Simiane. Nevertheless he still had high hopes for the assembly when he reported to Washington. He wanted to see strong central government, through representative assemblies, established in France, as in America. While he was delighted by the news that his adopted country had at last got together a convention to discuss a constitution, the rumblings, and outbreaks, of discontent – such as Shay's Rebellion in Massachusetts – seemed to him, as to Washington, serious signs of weakness, and perhaps disintegration.

Calonne had misunderstood the temper of the Notables, and upset them by blandly treating the proposals that resulted from their deliberations as if they were the same as his. They protested and demanded more information on the state of the royal finances so as to be able to arrive at a decision "beneficial to the nation." The royal family had no desire to see their spending subjected to scrutiny, and Calonne was obviously proving unable to deal, either by cajolery or threats, with those he had called together. Marie-Antoinette finally withdrew her support from him, and lent it to Brienne, the archbishop of Toulouse, whom Lafayette also admired. Calonne was therefore dismissed while the Notables were still in recess. Lafayette, in common with many, took the appointment of Brienne to be a sign that reforms would be made, abuses corrected, and government through conciliation established, without the kind of bloody upheaval he had experienced in America.

It was a commonly held view, which Lafayette shared, that the prime cause of the nation's financial troubles was the extravagance of the royal court. This was not blamed on the king, but on the now-unpopular queen and her circle. In fact, the expenses of the court only amounted to six percent of the budget published in 1788, other civil expenses being nineteen percent, the armed forces and diplomacy twenty-six percent, and the servicing of the debt taking over half the entire expenditure. Nevertheless Lafayette and others called for economies, which made him popular with the country at large, but not at court. More important was his call for a "national assembly," which went a little further than the suggestion that had been made for the summoning of the Estates-General, the ancient body that was supposed to have the authority to vote new taxes. This antique institution had not been convened since 1614, one hundred and seventy-three years previously. The Notables referred to it as part of their campaign to strengthen their hand against the king's by appealing to scarcely remembered rights and traditions. Lafayette's way of saying things – in his use of the term "national assembly" – may have been different, but he was asking no more than his peers. The American motto of "no taxation without representation" was adopted by many who had no wish to see "liberty" inscribed on their banners.

Brienne, who now headed the royal government, was unable to persuade the Notables to grant new taxes, and the assembly was dissolved on May 25, 1787, the king having promised to look into their various proposals for reform. Full of hope that toleration would be extended to Protestants, that provincial assemblies would be called, and that a new order would begin, Lafayette advised the young dauphin's tutor that the prince "would do well to begin his history of France with the year 1787." But to raise money Brienne had to take the course Calonne had wanted to avoid and face the parlements. They were not in receptive mood.

The Paris Parlement agreed to the creation of the provincial assemblies, to the commuting of the *corvée* (the duty of maintaining the roads that fell to the peasants), and to establishing free trade in grain throughout the kingdom. But when Brienne tried to get them to register a change in the "twentieth" tax (which was equivalent to a five percent tax on income), they refused, stating that only the Estates-General had the right to vote new taxes. When the king held a formal session (*lit de justice*) to force the measures through, the Parlement pronounced it null and void. As a result the magistrates were exiled. But Brienne then retreated, and the Paris Parlement – which was, after all, acting in the same spirit as the Notables had, and which enjoyed the solidarity of its sister bodies throughout the country – was reinstated. It obstinately proceeded to register the restoration of the old "twentieth" tax. The price for granting the king some much-needed cash became the promise to summon the Estates-General, a body which, it was assumed, would be firmly under the control of the upper orders.

In reporting as usual to Washington, Lafayette felt sure that what he called a general assembly of the nation could not come about immediately, but he was delighted by public reception of the idea, and convinced that the promised provincial assemblies would assume a great importance. Washington himself had meanwhile agreed to preside over the American Constitutional Convention, which pleased the marquis, for he was still concerned that America's reputation was declining. He thanked Washington for a gift of hams, reported that some ducks that had been sent had died *en route*, and asked for some mocking-birds. He touched briefly on the constantly threatening European situation. In Holland the bourgeois Patriot party was challenging the authority of their ruler the Stadtholder. Prussia and the English appeared ready to intervene on behalf of the ruler, and France was likely to be involved, as the Patriot party had made alliance with them and had given them support during the American war. In fact there was serious danger of a European war, which in other circumstances would have given Lafayette much pleasure. But he had been ill and he was preoccupied, for the king had named him a member of the Auvergne provincial assembly. Obviously his reputation outweighed the "great enemies" he claimed to have made at court because of his speeches to the Notables.

With the enthusiastic support of his fellow-delegates, Lafayette campaigned, both in the Auvergne assembly and throughout the province, on behalf of the ancient rights that had once served to protect the region from royal interference. The cry of "inalienable rights" may have sounded truly American in his ears, but to his peers it referred to an old order in which the only "rights of the individual" belonged to the privileged. As part of Lafayette's campaign he undertook a triumphal tour of the area, on which he was rapturously received. Crowds accompanied by drums and dignitaries turned out for him, streets were lit up in his honor, endless speeches made and, more pleasurable, endless balls given. The Comte d'Espinchal, a fellow Auvergnat who was sourly critical of everything the marquis did, accused him of announcing his arrival in advance to those towns he knew would receive him well. It is doubtful that Lafayette was so organized, and his popularity was undeniable.

When he returned to Paris the European situation, especially in Holland, appeared far more threatening than the domestic one. As the Prussians took offensive measures a war loomed steadily nearer, one in which France was honor-bound to take part, through her ties with the Dutch Patriots. Now that his provincial campaign was over, and he was feeling buoyed up by the reception he had been given, Lafayette was ready once more to distinguish himself abroad. As it happened, one of the French agents in Holland was the Chevalier de Ternant, who had served under Lafayette in America and who was now a colonel in the Patriot (or Republican) army. France had promised aid to the Patriots, but Lafayette went one step further: he hoped, through the influence and connections of his old subordinate de Ternant, to be offered the command of the entire Republican forces, and he somewhat prematurely made his preparations. But the Patriots dashed his hopes by choosing someone else – the Rhinegrave de Salm – to command them. Their first campaigns resulted in heavy defeat, and the disappointed Lafayette was severely critical of de Salm's incompetence and indecisiveness. But he also poured scorn on the French ministry of war for not honoring their obligations: lack of cash finally doomed them to inaction. Lafayette was forced to adopt a diplomatic attitude, and he wrote to Washington, successfully concealing his frustrations, advising him to keep America neutral because of the cost, and because it would help France (who could do little else) to insist on peace.

In the course of the long letter which included this advice,

Lafayette took the opportunity to give Washington the benefit of his political views, which were, of course, a reflection of Washington's own. For America he wanted a strong and solid union that would not depart from democratic principles, "for any thing that is monarchical or of the aristocratical kind is big with evils." But he worried about the bad effects of a relaxed democracy. He hoped that "enlightened, experienced, and virtuous senators" would find the right balance so that the people could enjoy their natural rights in equality, while the government, with powers that were to be frequently renewed, would be able to "act with vigor."

If he thought that such a program might work in France, he showed a sober understanding of the limitations of its existing system. He rightly considered that ideas of liberty had spread fast since the American revolution, and that "combustible materials have been kindled by the Assembly of Notables." He reported the unpopularity of the government and the queen, who dared not go to Paris, and he hoped for the acceptance of the notion that the king could only tax the nation with its consent, expressed through an assembly. But progress depended less on "the people" who, if they were slaves, were not inclined to admit it out of a "becoming sense of honor," than on the fact that "powerful people will put bars in the wheels." As far as that was concerned, no one was readier with his spoke than Lafayette himself.

This he demonstrated once more in the Auvergne provincial assembly, where he led and formulated the protests over the amount demanded from the province for the "twentieth" tax. Although full of assurances of loyalty, their address complained that the raise asked for was unjust and exorbitant. At the same time, Brienne as comptroller-general was trying to get a five-year loan from the Paris Parlement, in return for which the Estates-General would be called in 1792. It was decided to present this proposal in the form of a "royal session," during which views could be stated but no vote taken. Given only a day's notice, the Duc d'Orléans (the king's cousin) stood up to speak for the opposition. The king ordered his decree registered; d'Orléans claimed this was illegal. "That makes no difference!" cried the flustered king. "It is legal because I wish it!" When he left, the Parlement reacted by declaring the registration null, upon which d'Orléans and two leading members of the Parlement were exiled from Paris. But the process of polarization between the king and his antagonistic nobles was not confined to Paris. Even in the Auvergne the provincial assembly continued to protest, despite reforms promised by the crown, and despite obvious signs of royal displeasure. As Lafayette pointed out, popular protest had forced the monarch to retreat on several occasions. There was no reason to stop now.

11
The French Washington

T
HE PARIS PARLEMENT began 1788 by condemning the exile of
two of its members and demanding individual liberty as a
"natural right." The Americans had at least set a fashion for
putting demands in the form of declarations. Lafayette started the
year by writing to Washington and criticizing the draft Constitution
of the United States. This he had discussed with Jefferson, now a
close friend and American minister in Paris. Their criticism was
based on two points: the lack of a declaration of rights, and the considerable powers granted to the president. Nevertheless Lafayette
showed his sense of priorities by insisting that Washington stand for
president. In his hands all would be well, and the desired reforms and
changes could take place in an orderly manner.

His own philanthropy had meanwhile borne fruit, for that same
month French Protestants were granted civil rights. And he did not
neglect another cause dear to his heart: in the spring he joined the
Society of the Friends of the Blacks, founded by Brissot and Clavière.
At the same time he was associated with societies with similar aims
in England and America. He never did things by halves.

The European situation again worsened, but the shifting loyalties
of the various states made war avoidable. Lafayette had asked to serve
under his father-in-law, the Duc d'Ayen, during the spring maneuvers, but he was too ill, with a resumption of his chest complaint,
to take part. He complained to Washington that he had become sick
because "the people . . . have been so dull," and that in general they
had no inclination to go to extremes. To die for liberty, he explained,
was not a motto adopted on his side of the Atlantic; what he hoped
for was "a kind of passive discontent or non-obedience" which might
foil the government's plans.

For the government had suddenly taken the offensive, to the
resentment and astonishment of people like Lafayette who had

hoped for orderly reform. Two leaders of the Paris Parlement, which had condemned the whole system of arbitrary government, were arrested and, in a move reminiscent of Louis XV, the power of registering royal edicts was transferred to a new Plenary Court, whose members were to be royal officials and princes. Other powers enjoyed by the parlements were also superseded, and it was widely felt that an attack was to be made on provincial autonomy.

Despite Lafayette's opinion of "the people," their reaction was anything but dull. In Paris, where the previous year there had been an outburst of anti-royalist sentiments by crowds of young people, popular feeling was restrained only by the presence of troops, who prevented a crowd burning down the Law Courts. But in Toulouse the implementation of the new decree was made impossible by riots; in Grenoble, as the exiled Parlement was leaving, crowds pelted the soldiers with tiles; in Dauphiné the nobles and commons joined forces against the crown. The government moved new regiments into the villages near Paris, fearing further riots. And the nobles of Brittany, after their Parlement had been exiled, denounced anyone who served in the new courts – a resolution Lafayette, with his Breton possessions, proudly signed.

The Breton nobles actually wanted the return of their old Provincial Estates. Their control over it was greater than in the new provincial assembly, where double representation had been granted to the Third Estate (on the lines of the ancient Estates of Languedoc) and where voting was by head rather than by order. Although all members were appointed or co-opted, and came chiefly from the privileged classes, the nobles were as unhappy with a possible challenge from below as they were with the challenge from the crown. Other provinces followed suit and demanded the return of the old institutions, of which the Estates-General was of course one. Brienne once more retreated. On July 5, 1788, he promised to summon that venerable body, and all historians and archivists were requested to look into the forms which had been followed and to report to the ministry. Although Brienne hoped to appease the nobility by recalling an institution so ancient it had assumed almost mythical significance, he fell foul both of those who resented the delay (which was deliberate) that all the researching would cause, and those who were suspicious of any appeal to the Third Estate. The Breton nobles, with Lafayette supporting them, continued to press their own petition, and denounced the king's advisers for misleading him. The king reacted severely: twelve of the signatories, including La Rouërie who had been with Lafayette in America, were put (briefly) in the Bastille, and four of the courtiers associated with the protest were deprived of their civil or military posts. Lafayette was one of these, and although his military rank remained the same, he lost his active command in his father-in-law's army. It worried him not at all. To the queen's reported inquiry as to why he should associate himself with Breton troublemakers, he replied that he was Breton in the same way as she was Austrian, through his mother's family. Neither his activities nor his popularity diminished, though Adrienne's worries increased.

Lafayette's hopes for effective civil disobedience were fulfilled in August when the date for the Estates-General was finally set at May 1, 1789, the new Plenary Court was suspended, and Brienne resigned. Necker, whom Lafayette had doubtless forgiven for his opposition to French involvement in America – since he had met Mme de Simiane at his house – was recalled by the king. All this was celebrated by crowds in Paris – but the celebrations turned into fierce rioting, caused chiefly by the rising price of bread. Demonstrators were fired upon and some killed. The occupations of those arrested for taking part show that this was no "rabble," but that there was a high proportion of wage-earners, apprentices, and craftsmen in their ranks, whose opposition to the government was anything but ephemeral. Yet it was the "revolt of the nobles" that had resulted in the king surrendering his absolute power to raise taxes, and Lafayette, like Washington in 1775, felt himself in good and safe company as a protester. The keynote of their revolt was the loyal and restrained appeal to the king's "benevolence" in respecting the "rights" of his subjects. Precisely what these "rights" were, and who should share in them, was the next subject of struggle. Lafayette bemoaned the inflationary policies of the government, but he felt that no one should rock the boat by making new demands now that the Estates-General was promised. Because he was a hero, even if not at court, his views carried weight. But when the reinstated Paris Parlement resolved that the Estates-General should be composed of the three separate orders, with equal numbers of deputies and each order having a single vote, as in 1614 – thus giving the two upper orders superiority over the Third Estate – rocking the boat became a necessity, at least for the unprivileged.

Lafayette remained a strict constitutionalist, in keeping with what he had learned in America and the views of his own order. He believed in gradualism, and that no challenge should be made to the law until the proper legal channels were exhausted. Hence his condemnation of revolts against the American government which had established itself by taking up arms only when all other forms of protest had proved futile. And hence his view on the burning issue of representation in the Estates-General, that the old precedents should be followed so that the assembly could meet as quickly as possible. The right place to discuss reforms, he felt, was in the meetings of the Estates-General – a view with which his peers concurred, for when Necker, hoping to avoid further trouble, reconvened the Notables to advise on the summoning of the Estates-General, they held out for the forms of 1614, just as the Paris Parlement had done. Lafayette was impatient with all this debating, which he felt was only delaying matters. That the Third Estate could be outvoted at every turn did not appear to worry him: he believed that his noble colleagues could be persuaded to vote for a constitution that would guarantee the rights of all Frenchmen, in a spirit of patriotic dedication such as had sustained his comrades across the Atlantic. If he appeared to be facing both ways, he wrote to Mme de Simiane that "my heart is pure, my spirit free, my character objective; my conscience and the confidence of the public are my two supports: I would lose the second, for the other is enough for me."

Necker, however, was not so confident that the country would peacefully accept the restrictions of forms dating back 175 years. A new and equivocal decision of the Paris Parlement on the representation issue enabled him to persuade the king to ignore the Notables' advice and grant double representation to the Third Estate. Whether they voted by head or by order still remained to be decided. Necker's hope seemed to be that the assembly would, in the last resort, vote by head on financial matters only and that all three orders would then quarrel over other reforms, leaving the king in the strong position of arbiter. (With the Third Estate equaling the other two combined, a vote abolishing the tax exemptions of the privileged could be expected.) The government would thus receive the money it so badly needed, assuming it could be collected, and all the other hornets raised by the calling of the Estates-General would, Necker hoped, die of boredom in the endless wrangling that would certainly ensue.

The summoning of the Estates-General caused as much excitement and optimism as had the coronation of Louis XVI after sixty years of his "well-beloved" grandfather. Doubtless there was as much cynicism and apathy as usually attends elections, but for those who took part in the choosing of delegates – on the whole, the articulate and educated members of society – the process offered important opportunities for participating in government. Necker's announcement of the doubling of the representation of the Third Estate was rapturously received, except by some members of the privileged orders. Precedent could, in fact, be cited for and against doubling: the important issue was the one Necker had left unresolved, whether to vote by head or by order. Some members of the Third Estate assumed voting by head had already been won, a view that brought them into bitter conflict with the privileged. In Brittany this broke into actual fighting; the nobles recruited toughs who clashed with law students, and lost, whereupon the proud Breton aristocrats refused to elect deputies to the Estates-General, and went unrepresented there.

In the Auvergne, and specifically at Riom, to whose nobility Lafayette presented himself as a candidate for delegate, similar views to those of the Breton nobles were held, although no gangs were recruited to fight for them. Despite having joined a constitutional ginger group in Paris called the Society of the Thirty and including Mirabeau, the Abbé Sieyès, La Rochefoucauld, Condorcet, du Port, Talleyrand, and the Vicomte de Noailles, Lafayette still argued that precedent should be observed, and that the three estates should, in the first instance, vote by order. In this he felt he was only playing by the rules and exercising that moderation that Washington had advised – and which had incidentally brought the marquis a tribute from King Stanislaus-Augustus Poniatowski of Poland. Yet despite this moderation, and despite his orthodox views on voting, he found the campaign at Riom – his first for elective office – a hard one.

To Mme de Simiane, to whom he entrusted his political problems, he wrote of the bitterness between the orders, the cantons, and the individuals of the region. If he were prepared to compromise, he told her, he would have been elected unanimously, whereas if he didn't, he wouldn't stand a chance. Perhaps Mme de Simiane made him especially defensive about the purity of his motives and actions, as the tone of his letters to her implies. He assured her that his reply to the advice to compromise had been that he desired "to convince and not to flatter." He told her of his chance of fame with the Third Estate, whom he could have represented even as a noble, but he reckoned it was more important to leaven the ranks of the aristocracy, to whom he "preached moderation at the risk of displeasing them. It may well be that instead of a nomination, I will come away with only a mass of quarrels and a pile of good opinions. But I shall do my duty and be moderate, although between ourselves their oppression revolts me and their personalities make me furious."

Whether he was referring in this to the Second (noble) or Third Estate is unclear; maybe the whole business of electoral politics revolted him. In the event, he was elected a delegate with only a small majority, and he accepted a mandate binding him to oppose voting by head in the Estates-General. Doubtless the Riom nobles mistrusted Lafayette, not as a radical, but as an aristocrat of a very different style from their own. They lived in a poor province, and looked to the Estates-General to strengthen their own declining position. Lafayette had enormous wealth and vast estates in more prosperous regions. He was also much-traveled and enjoyed an international reputation: all in all, a far from typical Auvergnat. Naturally there was suspicion that he would not adequately represent the interests of his order, even though he was bound by his mandate.

The Estates-General was due to meet in May, but Lafayette was in Paris in April, partly to be in the center of affairs, and partly to take part in the Paris elections, which as a noble landowner there he was also entitled to do. The same month Washington had, with great reluctance, accepted the presidency of the United States, to which he had been unanimously elected. Instead of having his "father" to hand for consultation, Lafayette had to make do with two very different American "advisers": Jefferson, the American minister to France, and Gouverneur Morris, in Paris on business, who was a waspish observer with so great a taste for things aristocratic that he even feared the marquis was "too republican for the genius of his country." Perhaps Lafayette teased him or, more likely, became more radical when talking to his adopted countrymen. Certainly he was no "republican" in the sense of championing an elected rather than a hereditary executive for France. He was at this stage something of a "fellow-traveler" of the American system, admiring it at a distance but feeling that too much of its own republican spirit was wrong for France. He referred to the times as "the American era," but, like Washington, believed that despite the equality of man important distinctions between them existed. Both he and Washington, in fact, venerated the idea of a monarchy that was truly constitutional, answerable to its subjects. Lafayette's ideal was a legislature on American lines that was binding in most respects on the existing French executive, the hereditary monarchy. From this ideal he rarely deviated.

Nor was it, in the spring of 1789, an ideal different from that of the rest of France. From the lists of grievances (*cahiers*) that were drawn up at the same time as the election of delegates, it is obvious that all three orders were against absolute royal power, and all wanted a constitution that would give the ability to make new laws and vote new taxes to an Estates-General that met regularly. Nobody questioned the royal right to approve, or initiate, legislation, nor did anyone seek to limit the king's freedom of choice in ministers or his absolute power as commander-in-chief. All three estates even agreed that the burden of taxation should fall more fairly on all those able to pay. But after that agreement stopped. The Second (noble) Estate wanted to see its privileges enforced and extended; the Third proclaimed its desire for an equal share in government and equal rights before the law.

The Abbé Sieyès wrote the most famous summing-up of their position in his pamphlet *What is the Third Estate?* The answer to that question was: Everything. What has it been up to now? Nothing. What does it demand? To be something. He went further than the thought of those optimistic months when he said, "who would dare to deny that the Third Estate has within itself all that is necessary to constitute a nation?" But contemporary feeling was not far behind him.

Paris itself was not exactly a haven of grateful calm on the eve of the Estates-General. For a start it had a different electoral system from the rest of the country, which resulted in a full quarter of its citizens being denied the vote, as opposed to a sixth in the rest of the nation. The excuse given by the government was the sheer size of the capital's population, but in fact they were afraid of the influence of its vociferous commoners. Nevertheless the Paris Third Estate showed its spirit early. It rejected, in its primary assemblies, the presiding officers chosen by the municipality, and chose instead 407 electors (being officially entitled to 147). These then picked their delegates in their own good time, so much so that they were a fortnight late for the opening of the Estates-General. But the electors did not disband after they had done their choosing. They remained as a constituted authority ready to act in the name of the city; in under two months, they simply took over.

The franchise aside, Paris, having suffered one of the worst winters in living memory, was also hard hit by the ever-rising price of bread. Bread took up as much as three-quarters of the wage-earner's budget at a time when prices were rising three times as fast as wages. In the provinces bread prices were even higher than those of the capital because the government feared the Parisian's wrath more than anyone's and sold them imported grain at a "subsidized" price. Even this did not stop the fierce rioting of late April that broke around the person of a wall-paper manufacturer called Réveillon, who made a speech in his electoral assembly regretting the rising prices and the fact that artisans could no longer make ends meet on fifteen *sous* daily. He was in fact a reasonable and successful employer, who paid his artisans above the going rate, but his remarks were misunderstood and aroused the wage-earners of the district (the Faubourg Saint-Antoine) to spontaneous demonstrations of protest which escalated into riots. Réveillon's house (and that of a similarly indiscreet or unfortunate manufacturer, Henriot) was sacked, and many, perhaps hundreds, of people killed by troops. While there were *agents provocateurs* anxious to foment trouble – some paid by the Duc d'Orléans to further his own popularity, some working for the government to give it an excuse to crack down – the Réveillon riots again involved wage-earners anxious about their survival at an inflationary time. They were a demonstration of the temper of the Parisian working people, and as such they worried the royal authorities (who were savage in their sentencing of the guilty) no less than the bourgeoisie, many of whom came to gawk and tut at the damage to property.

On May 5, 1789, after three days of official welcomes and masses, the Estates-General opened amid the expensive glitter of Versailles (the king being too fond of his hunting to go to Paris). The first meeting was in the Salle des Menus Plaisirs du Roi, a vast hall to which the Third Estate were called three hours ahead of the opening, for their places to be assigned to them according the rules of 1614. Even then they were put well to the back, and this slight, as well as the expense and inconvenience of lodging in Versailles, added to their irritation. (The rich or favored had their own places; Lafayette stayed with his in-laws.) The difference between their ordinary, formal clothes, the glitter of the First Estate of clergy, and the costumes in the style of Henri VI that custom prescribed for the nobles disturbed rather than overawed the representatives of "the people." After hours of hanging around they received the king's short speech, full of paternalistic sentiment, dutifully. Necker, however, the darling of reform, was a great disappointment. His speech was so long he had to rely on a powerfully voiced assistant to finish it for him, and even then it was "the speech you would expect from a banker's clerk of some ability," according to the critical British observer Arthur Young. Worst of all, it contained little that the deputies wanted to hear. Necker proposed to deal with the government's deficit by raising further loans, not by giving control over taxation to the Estates-General. He still would not commit himself on the voting issue, and apparently hoped that the Third would leave the Second and First Estates to surrender their tax privileges voluntarily (as they had hinted they might). He stressed that power flowed from the king to his people, not vice versa, and that what the king chose to do would depend on the good behavior of the deputies – who were then supposed to separate and verify the credentials of their members, order by order.

The Third Estate did no such thing. They were not yet prepared for outright defiance of the law, and, knowing each other's temper as little as they knew the king's, proceeded with caution. They simply asked that all three orders verify their credentials in common, on the grounds that, although the law stated this should be done by order, it was important that each Estate should know that the others were legally composed. They took the title "Commons" for themselves, to the great indignation of some nobles. And while they were waiting for answers to their demands, they did nothing that could give the impression that they were legally constituted: they didn't draw up rules, or keep minutes, or appoint any officers except a "dean" to direct debates. After June 3rd this was Jean-Sylvain Bailly, a distinguished astronomer who the previous year, aged fifty-two, had suddenly got married and given up science in favor of city politics. The "debates" over which he presided in these early days were more like public meetings, but at least the Commons got to know each other and, under the nervous strain of waiting for official reaction, began to push each other further along the road to protest – just as the members of the American Continental Congress had done.

The Second Estate, meanwhile, proceeded to verify its credentials in the prescribed manner, sending home the odd delegate, appointing officers, grumbling at the "Commons," and in the process boring Lafayette stiff. Under Jefferson's influence, he was working on a draft of a declaration of rights which he hoped would be approved by the Estates-General and by the king. The second draft of this declaration, while proclaiming that nature had made men "free and equal," recognized distinctions among them "based on general utility" (a phrase Lafayette doubtless owed to the advice of the English philosopher Jeremy Bentham). Among men's "inalienable rights" were "liberty of opinion," "care for his honor and life, the right of property, the power to dispose of his person, his industry, all his faculties, the communication of his thoughts by all available means, the pursuit of well-being, and resistance to oppression." Jeffersons's hand is clearly in evidence here: these careful phrases represent an attempt to capture some of the liberal ideas of the day, and to make them respectable by giving them the patina of immemorial nature. These notions had been on the lips of the fashionable for so long that they had passed into the general vocabulary: Lafayette had every hope of producing a declaration that would be acceptable to everyone.

But the debate on whether to vote by head or by order still raged. Arthur Young wrote that "Not a word of any thing else is talked of." The artisans were undoubtedly more interested in the still-rising price of bread, and the wrangles in Versailles doubtless confirmed their worst suspicions. But Young moved among the nobility and bourgeoisie; he noted especially the "incredible" flood of pamphlets: "Every hour produces something new. . . . Nineteen-twentieths of these productions are in favor of liberty, and commonly violent against the clergy and nobility."

Still no one knew what to do, not the king nor any of his Estates. The monarch was pushed to take a firm stand by Marie-Antoinette, brought up as she was in a strong tradition of discipline, but it was not his way to do anything decisively, and besides, his son the dauphin had just died (June 4th). The nobles were divided, and they had no program, or leaders, or ideas other than those of rolling back the clock as far as they dared. The clergy were even more divided, since the majority of them were ordinary parish priests, who were gradually inclining toward joining the Commons. And the Third were still extremely uncertain: the pamphlets then pouring out may have excited the people of Paris, but they hardly impinged on the precarious dignity of Versailles. The Commons had Bailly, and Sieyès, and they had the oratorical thunder of Mirabeau, though few trusted him. The temper of the times was optimism and excitement inflammably combined with uncertainty, especially over the use of force. Would the king use his troops to enforce his will, once it was known what his will was? Would the privileged orders use force against the representatives of the people? Would the "mobs" of Paris attempt to hold the government to ransom? No one knew: everyone expected something to happen. And in the middle of June, after six weeks of nothing, it did.

Following the lead of the Abbé Sieyès, the Third Estate proceeded to invite the First and Second to unite with it. If they refused, a roll call of all deputies, regardless of order, would be held, and those not appearing would be considered defaulters. This motion was accompanied by a humble address to the king stating their reasons for so acting. Some parish priests appeared with the Commons, but not one single noble. Lafayette was bound by his mandate and stayed away. The Commons next declared themselves the National Assembly, for the title Estates-General implied division by order. Finally they authorized the collection of existing taxes, so long as they were in session. This was, of course, a direct challenge to the crown, and it was not taken unanimously. Nevertheless it was designed to force the king to act – a ploy, perhaps, to show the Commons' strength, which could be abandoned if other reforms proceeded satisfactorily.

The nobles panicked and demanded that the king act to bring the Third Estate to heel. Necker thought reforms were now inevitable, and proposed that to fiscal equality be added the accessibility of all Frenchmen to public office, and vote by head in the Estates-General. A divided royal council, after the intervention of the queen and the king's brothers, rejected this. The king then ordered a "royal session" in which he would declare his intentions. To prepare this session, the meeting-place of the Third Estate was closed. When they arrived on June 20th they found it guarded by soldiers. They proceeded, in a state of great indignation and excitement, and attended by a no less expectant crowd, to the empty royal tennis-court. There they swore the famous oath that, wherever its members were, there was the National Assembly, and that they would continue meeting wherever circumstances dictated, until the constitution of the realm had been set up. Only one deputy signified his opposition, but a few stayed prudently away. Jacques-Louis David was later commissioned to immortalize the scene in oils.

Lafayette was extremely upset by the way things were going. He had been for the reforms proposed by Necker, and he wrote out the whole history of his dedication to liberty for Mme de Simiane's benefit. He was obviously uncertain about the Third Estate and the reactions of his own order, and he was pinning his hopes on his declaration which would, he prophesied, "become the catechism of France." He was keenly aware of the ambiguity of his position, and while he felt he "ought to be charmed by that which advances the revolution," he was intent on "working out everything which prevents it reaching the point at which I want us to stop."

At the promised "royal session," the king dissolved the mandates binding their holders (such as Lafayette) to oppose voting by head, so as to get the money he needed voted through the Assembly. He also annulled the decisions taken by the Third Estate. Each of the three orders was still to verify its own credentials, but disputes could be resolved by all three in common, with the king as arbitrator. The orders were to meet in common to discuss affairs "of general interest," but the rights of the privileged were excluded from these discussions. He then offered his own program of reform, or rather that of the "court party" led by the queen. The Estates were offered the right to grant taxes and loans, except in an emergency, and they were allowed to decide on the allocation of funds for certain public services, including court expenses. Equality of tax burdens was to be granted as soon as the privileged orders voted for it, but private property, together with its rights, privileges, and titles, was to be retained intact (even though its abolition had not been demanded). Internal customs were to be abolished, and provincial assemblies – with double representation for the Third Estate and with voting by head – were to extend the powers of local government. Among other matters the Estates were permitted to discuss were the liberty of the individual, freedom of the press, changes in various taxes and reforms in the administration of matters previously considered the exclusive domain of the crown. The king personally concluded this session, in which he offered to become a constitutional monarch if the traditional social order were preserved, by saying, "If you abandon me in this great enterprise I shall work alone for the welfare of my people. I shall regard myself alone as their real representative." He then ordered them to separate, and to convene in their separate orders on the following day to begin their discussions.

The nobility marched out, and most of the clergy. But when the royal chamberlain came back to the hall to remind those remaining of the royal orders, Bailly replied, in the spirit of the Tennis Court Oath, that "the nation assembled cannot be given orders." To which Mirabeau added, "We shall not leave except at the point of a bayonet," and Sieyès, "You are today what you were yesterday." They were not ready to question the hereditary monarchy, but they were prepared to call the king's bluff.

The king retreated and allowed them to remain. The Commons

declared that "the person of every deputy is inviolable," and the next day a large number of the clergy joined them, soon to be followed by liberal nobles (excluding Lafayette who still had scruples about his mandate). Despite the queen's reported call for the use of troops, the king, for the sake of peace and quiet, then ordered the first two Estates to join with the Third. Lafayette, along with the Riom deputies, formally protested at this move, as he was bound by his mandate to do, but on June 27th the three orders were officially united as the National Assembly. Two weeks later they renamed themselves the National Constituent Assembly, whose job was to formulate the Constitution. It was a victory for the forces and hopes of reform in all classes, and one that was joyously celebrated.

All was not, however, sweetness and light. Many of the nobles practiced non-cooperation by abstaining from attending or debating; some still insisted their mandates forbade them to sit in a united assembly – which on July 8th annulled the mandates. The king then allowed those nobles affected to seek fresh powers from their electors, a decision which gave Lafayette even further anxiety. As he lamented to Mme de Simiane, he didn't know whether to go back to Riom, resign and offer himself to the Third Estate (if someone would step down for him), or to stay and take part in the important discussions that were about to begin. He couldn't bear to miss anything, and he certainly didn't see himself as a mere Auvergnat representative, when he had "contributed to the liberty of another world."

The members of the Third Estate grew increasingly suspicious of their colleagues in the Second, even though many of the latter – including Lafayette – boasted of being on the court's proscribed list. But more alarming to the Third was the massing of royal troops in Paris and Versailles. Following the Réveillon riots in the capital, the 407 bourgeois electors, who on June 25th set themselves up as an unofficial city government, called for the formation of a militia electing its own officers. This was to protect them against two evils: attacks on property by those without it, and attacks on their newly won rights and privileges by the royal forces – either the troops or the guards under royal control in the city whose job it was to preserve law and order. Although the Assembly itself did not yet dare to go so far as to create an independent militia, such was the ferment caused by the ever-increasing number of soldiers, naturally exaggerated by rumor, that Mirabeau moved that the king be asked to withdraw them. Lafayette, making his maiden speech to the Assembly, seconded him, and the motion was passed. Lafayette suspected that the Duc d'Orléans, whose own pretensions to the throne Mirabeau was at that time pushing, was behind many of the Paris disturbances, and he frostily brushed off any suggestion that d'Orléans and he, each with their own popular following, join forces. He was, amid all these alarms, preoccupied with his declaration of rights. A preliminary report of the Assembly's constitutional committee called for such a declaration as a preamble and statement of the principles on which the Constitution was to be based. On July 11th Lafayette presented his draft. It was, he said years later, his "profession of faith, fruit of my past, pledge of my future," as well as being "at the same time a manifesto and an ultimatum." He was immensely proud that it was the first of its kind in Europe.

His speech began by reminding the delegates that "for a nation to love liberty, it is enough that she understands it; for her to be free, it is enough that she wishes it." He considered his declaration to be a draft, and only a preliminary to a proper Constitution agreed by the Assembly and the king. He modestly finished his introduction by saying that such a declaration of rights should only state truthfully and precisely "what all the world knows, what all the world feels."

The actual declaration began, as we have seen, with the equality of man, the necessary distinctions between them, and man's inalienable rights. The only limits on the exercise of these rights were those which assured their enjoyment by other members of society. No one could be made to submit to a law that had not been passed by him or his representatives, for all sovereignty resided in the nation. The only goal of government was the common good, which required the separation of the legislative, executive, and judicial powers, in which the free representation of citizens must be assured. Laws were to be clear, precise and uniform for all; subsidies or taxes were to be freely agreed to and proportionately allotted. Finally, "since the introduction of abuses, and the right of succeeding generations, requires the revision of every human institution, it should be possible for the nation to have, in certain cases, an extraordinary convocation of deputies, whose sole object would be to examine, and correct if necessary, the faults in the Constitution."

It is interesting that in the three drafts that Lafayette went through, his final one notably omitted freedom of religion as one of the rights of man, presumably to avoid offending the clergy. But as an apostle of toleration, Lafayette could certainly point to safeguards in his declaration that guaranteed freedom of opinion. A more significant change concerned the ability to revise the form of government. His first draft had called for meetings "at fixed though distant intervals" of conventions to examine faults in the Constitution; his second left out the bit about fixed intervals and substituted a call for revision to be carried out by "constitutional means which assure in certain instances an extraordinary convention of representatives." His final draft watered this down further, though the principle remained; it was nevertheless a far cry from the American Declaration of

Indépendence, which enshrined the "Right of the People to alter or abolish" any form of government "destructive" of the ends for which it was, by consent, set up. Like all fellow-travelers Lafayette was naturally anxious to avoid the havoc of revolution in his own country – and he could genuinely persuade himself that it was both unnecessary and undesirable. Indeed, that was the opinion of most of France in July 1789, as indicated by the rapturous reception accorded to Lafayette's speech, both inside and outside the Constituent Assembly. That body referred his proposals to its committees, and the Declaration of the Rights of Man and the Citizen that finally passed the Assembly on August 27th owed much to Lafayette's initiative.

But as soon as Lafayette had made his presentation, the whole subject became, for the moment, academic: the king delivered his long-expected counter-blow. That same day, July 11th, Necker was dismissed, and the military cordon around Paris was tightened. The news reached the capital the following morning, which was a Sunday. Despite his minimal achievements, Necker was seen as the one hope of peaceful change; now he was gone, the city was in danger, and the Assembly apparently powerless. A genuine panic arose that the troops would massacre all dissident citizens. The cry "To arms!", which Camille Desmoulins claimed to have been the first to utter to a large audience, was eagerly taken up. To do something – anything – was reassuring, and armed self-defense was the most reassuring of all. Busts of Necker and the Duc d'Orléans were seized from Curtius's waxworks in the Palais-Royal, and paraded through the streets. Spectators were forced to cheer the Third Estate. There were scuffles with soldiers, which only made matters worse, especially as they were German mercenaries. Gunsmiths were looted. Then the French guards, whose job it was to keep order, left their barracks, fully armed, and declared for the people. Rising prices, perhaps the use of mercenaries, the fact that the king never wooed his army the way other rulers did, and the simple truth, demonstrated in the previous few weeks, that limited revolt was respectable, made this crucial move possible. True, some of the direction of this agitation could be ascribed to the Duc d'Orléans, who had been one of the first to join the Third Estate at Versailles. Nevertheless it was panic at the king's measures that first led to action in Paris.

To the Paris electors, representing the bourgeoisie, the royal troops were only one of the threats facing them. Just as serious would be an armed "rabble" of "vagabonds" and "brigands" – an army of unemployed who could even be used by the court party to strike terror into the hearts of innocent citizens, a terror which had already come to the provinces. When it becomes generally recognized by the active and influential sectors of society that the accepted rules of behavior have been suspended, or can be flouted with impunity, the first reaction of those with anything to lose is panic. So on Monday, July 13th, the electors took steps to bring the situation under control. They set up a standing committee in the City Hall to administer the capital, and every one of the sixty electoral districts was to contribute two (soon afterwards eight) hundred men of good standing, to form the basis of a citizen's militia. Their uniform was to be the red and blue colors of the city of Paris. In most districts, property and residential qualifications for service were imposed, and all unemployed and vagrants rigorously disbarred. Such potential troublemakers were to be disarmed forthwith. Paris was taking no chances.

Under the control of the electors, the search for arms and powder was organized and extended. The raid on the Bastille, in fact, had as its purpose the seizure of the powder that was known to have been sent there from the royal arsenal, not the release of its prisoners (who turned out to be only seven in number). Meanwhile the Assembly in Versailles, united by the crisis and cut off from reliable sources of news in Paris by the royal soldiers, heard rumors of what was happening while debating their own answer to the king. Terrible stories of fighting, looting, shooting, and raping began to circulate, and a deputation was sent to the king to ask for the withdrawal of his soldiers, in return for which they would send a deputation to Paris to calm the people. Lafayette was to be a member of it, as he reported in a 3 A.M. note designed to reassure his mistress about his safety.

But the king stood firm, leaving the Assembly in even greater uncertainty and fear of being arrested themselves. While the streets of Paris rang with cries of "Cheap bread! Arm the people! Open the prisons!," which frightened the bourgeois citizens more than the loyal troops, the Assembly, encouraged by a speech from Lafayette blaming the present crisis on the king's new ministers, affirmed its confidence in Necker, called again for the withdrawal of the troops, held the government responsible for what was happening, and once more declared its own inviolability. Further, to avoid the threat of being caught off guard, they resolved to sit in permanent session. Their president, the old archbishop of Vienne, was not up to this, so it was decided to appoint a vice-president. By a majority of 122, Lafayette was elected. He still felt himself to be unable to vote because of his Riom mandate, but he accepted the honor. From then on, he decided that force of circumstances freed him to do what was necessary.

He spent a sleepless night (July 13th–14th) on a bench in the Assembly. At 6 A.M. he scribbled a note to Mme de Simiane that the news from Paris was that all was quiet and the bourgeoisie armed. At 9, the Assembly tried to resume its debate on the Constitution. The king was apparently still holding firm, promising little to another delegation that the Assembly had sent. Then two members of the standing committee of Paris electors arrived with a report of the outbursts in the capital. The Assembly again asked the king to withdraw his troops, and he again refused, though this time he promised to "support the zeal of good citizens" by taking control of the newly formed militia. Still blaming the evil influences surrounding the crown rather than the person of the monarch, the Assembly told the Paris electors they would renew their efforts to restore order on the following day. The king retired to bed, having written in his journal the word "nothing." He meant that he had again been prevented from killing something in his favorite sport.

The news of the fall of the Bastille, and the parading of two bloody heads on pikes through the streets of Paris – to a frenzied reception that, perhaps surprisingly, sickened many used to seeing public executions without displaying emotion – reached the Assembly in the early hours of the 15th. It now seemed to them obvious that if action were not taken at once, Paris would be beyond their control. The Duc de Liancourt reportedly awoke the king with the news. "Is it a revolt?" asked the bewildered monarch. "No, Sire, it is a revolution," was the most famous version of the reply. Louis resolved to do something before the Assembly could come to him again. He arrived informally at their debating chamber and told them he was ordering the withdrawal of his troops. He asked them to let Paris know of his decision, and he requested their help in restoring calm. He still would not commit himself to dismiss his ministers, but the mood of the Assembly when he left was that of triumph. In the afternoon forty carriages bearing deputies set out to tell Paris the good news. At their head, in his official capacity as vice-president, was Lafayette.

In the great hall of the Hôtel de Ville, seated not far from his own bust that had been donated by the citizens of Virginia, Lafayette congratulated the electors on their victory, and reported that "The king was deceived, but is so no longer." He now hoped, he said, to return to His Majesty with the guarantee of peace and order which he so desired. Then he read the king's statement to the Assembly, which was punctuated by cries of "Long live the king!" and "Long live the nation!" His official position, and his own reputation, gave Lafayette undisputed authority. After more speeches, he was about to leave when he was asked if he would take charge of the citizen's militia. The question of who was best fitted to command this force had come up that morning, and the president of the electors had pointed to Lafayette's bust, to widespread approval. Now cries of

"Make Lafayette commander-general" were heard on every side. In one of his most emotional gestures, he drew his sword and raised it high. He accepted. By acclamation also, Bailly was "elected" mayor of Paris – a new title for an all-powerful city.

By his thirty-third year Lafayette was one of the best-known mouthpieces for liberal ideas in the western world. Although the ideas may not have been his own, they carried the enormous weight of his authority. He was still rich, though less so than when he had nailed his colors to the American mast, and he managed to appear sure of himself to all but some of his intimates. He stood, above all, for moderation, for a constitutional monarchy with constitutional guarantees of law and order. Now he was appointed to "rule in Paris," as he described it – to restore law and order to a turbulent city with the smell of victory in its nostrils, fear in its wallet, and revolution in its vocabulary. (Such was the resounding rhetoric of the time.) In such a task, moderation is usually the first quality to be swept away, but on July 15, 1789, Lafayette had every confidence in victory. Upon him the hopes of all moderates rested.

Part Four: The Revolution in France

12
Ruler of Paris

Arevolution creates a new order, or several. Lafayette's task was to dominate them all. He reported to his mistress, Mme de Simiane:

> The people can only be moderated by me ... Forty thousand souls gather, the excitement reaches fever pitch, I appear, and one word from me disperses them. I have already saved the lives of six persons who were about to be hanged in various parts of the city, but these furious, intoxicated people will not always listen to me. At this very moment of writing, eighty thousand people are surrounding the City Hall and saying they are being betrayed, that the troops will not withdraw, that the king must come to Paris. They will not agree to anything unless I sign it personally. When I am not here their heads are turned ... I rule in Paris over an enraged people manipulated by appalling plotters; on the other hand, they have suffered a thousand injustices of which they have good reason to complain.

To rule in Paris was not an enviable job. Lafayette's enormous popularity, and the flattering way in which he was made commandant-general by acclamation – which he insisted be formalized by the votes of each section of the city – gave him a good start. And those who elected him were chiefly the bourgeois citizens, who had a lot to lose if "anarchy" prevailed. What they wanted was what the Americans had asked for before 1776: an affirmation from the king of their right to run their own affairs.

But they were only one class among many, and none too solid at that. What is liberating about revolutionary situations to some, and frightening to many, is the energies that are released. Nowhere are these more obvious and more unpredictable than in crowds, which feed on their own successes. Crowds are prone to fear and panic, but they are also capable of incredible bravery. They only consist, after all, of individuals each with their personal ambitions and responsibilities; few of these would perform on their own the acts a crowd encourages, such as facing, unarmed, the guns of disciplined soldiers, or lynching, untried, a single representative of a hated system. Lafayette was both excited and revolted by the crowds that were so much a feature of the revolution. What excited him was the challenge of persuading and controlling what was at times a citizen army; what revolted him was the violence they used against individuals.

The first problem was to establish some form of officially recognized order, not only to protect property but to give the new authorities in the capital a look of legitimacy. No one would take the electors seriously – or Lafayette for that matter – if they could not control those who claimed to support them. More important was that these supporters needed leadership they could respect, for without it their fragile confidence would collapse, and further "excesses" would result. In this situation Lafayette knew what his role was. It was to show the world that the assumption of collective authority by the electors – which was far more significant than the fall of the Bastille – was the act of responsible men. And responsible men, in Lafayette's eyes, respected law and order.

As it happened his view was shared by the great majority of activists. Even before he took command of the militia, "patriot patrols" had been set up to search for unauthorized arms, stop looting, and generally take on the role of police. Gouverneur Morris strongly objected to being asked "a number of foolish questions" every time his carriage was stopped at barricades, but his inconvenience was little compared to that caused by the paying off of old scores: the patrols had to deal, for example, with many cases of people maliciously denouncing their enemies as "royal spies."

Yet only two days after the fall of the Bastille, most of the barricades had been lifted, the shops had reopened, bread appeared – accompanied by long but peaceful lines of customers – and letters were once more being delivered. The enormous tensions generated by the uncertainty of the situation led some to lynch those supected of "starving and exploiting" the people, but on the whole the mood was one of excited optimism, at least among those who had seized the initiative and assumed the leadership of events. There was no reason to think Paris was out of their control: rivals they had, but none yet strong enough to challenge their authority successfully. Lafayette and the electors believed that the only people who would oppose their measures were those who would oppose any form of authority: the unemployed, "foreign agitators" and such, and those who were paid to stir up trouble. Their chief concern, and that of the Assembly, was what the royal government would do, and what their own next move would be in response to it.

On July 16th Lafayette began his new duties by proposing to a meeting of the electors at the City Hall that the voluntary armed militias that had been formed in Paris (and other cities) be properly organized. To this end, he suggested that each district send a representative to him at the City Hall, to discuss the rules and regulations that should govern the citizen forces. He also proposed that these be given the title of national guard, with each city adding its name, as in "the national guard of Paris," and that the internal defense of each city be entrusted to these guards, with the capital setting the example for all. This was enthusiastically agreed, and Lafayette forthwith began issuing the necessary orders. In case there was any doubt as to who controlled the city, when the king paid a ceremonial visit to Paris on the following day, Lafayette, on a white horse, which soon became as famous as he was, made sure that the vast crowds were superbly marshaled and organized. The king was either numbed or overawed by it all; only when he was getting into his carriage to leave did he tell Lafayette that he had been meaning to confirm him in his post of commandant-general. For the marquis this gesture legitimized his role in the revolution.

Lafayette also claimed credit for having invented the tricolor, the red, while, and blue cockade which was presented to the king when he came to the city, and which he stuck in his hat to shouts of "God save the king." Certainly the events of July 1789 were a godsend to the makers of colored ribbon. Before the formation of the militia everyone who wanted to be taken for a patriot wore a green cockade, the color of the Third Estate. The militia adopted the red and blue colors of the city of Paris – but these were also the colors of the Duc d'Orléans, whose ambitious designs on the throne Lafayette had no desire to encourage. Whether for that reason, or to symbolize his fidelity to the monarchy, the commandant-general added white, the color of the royal house of Bourbon, to the red and the blue, and presented the result to his guards. It would, he promised them, "make its way around the world."

The business of organizing the guard must have reminded Lafayette of his dealings with the voluntary militia in America: to begin with they were full of enthusiasm, but their mood was fickle. The first national guard of Paris consisted of six divisions of sixty battalions, each one containing six volunteer companies and one paid company. Remnants of the old peace-keeping forces of the city, a group of police on horses, and one hundred and forty cannon completed the organization. There was no shortage of volunteers among the middle classes, but Lafayette's guard (for it was essentially his creation) was by no means universally popular. Of course any police force runs foul of those who, for their own purposes or in the name of the revolution, want no interference in their activities. When the old order declines, the gap is filled by a variety of claimants for leadership, any one of which is usually as dedicatedly hostile to all the others as it was to the old regime itself. Lafayette's guard was deliberately a safe, bourgeois organization; naturally it ran into opposition from the other classes, as well as from those of its peers who found its zeal obnoxious. And of course it could count on the hostility of all those who saw in it merely the law-and order brigades of the old regime in new ribbons.

Lafayette was well aware he had landed himself with a lot of problems, and by making his first priority the organization, along military lines, of his peace-keeping force, he at least had his experience to guide him. He wrote, much later, of the confusion that reigned at the time, but even the calm of recollection does not disguise the chaos. There was an enormous population armed with a mysterious variety of weapons, swelled by soldiers who had deserted the royal lines for those of the patriots, and several hundred Swiss and French guards roaming around without officers. The city was starved, perhaps deliberately, of provisions and the means for obtaining them; the authority and apparatus of the old regime were destroyed and despised. *Agents provocateurs* from the old order, the aristocrats, and the Orléanists were all hard at work, and there was the disturbing presence of more than thirty thousand "foreigners or unemployed." There was no military or civil organization, no national laws or judicial forms to guide and contain the people, except for an armed mass in each district constantly engaged in debate and discussion. There were the electors in the City Hall, and the "leaders of the moment" (himself and Bailly), "charged with looking after everything, who were liked and respected, but whose faces were unknown to the vast majority, which could only be persuaded to obey by the gaining of its confidence."

A mere week after having assumed command of the guard, Lafayette told Gouverneur Morris that he

> had the utmost power his heart could wish, and is grown tired of it; that he has commanded absolutely an hundred thousand men; has marched his sovereign about the streets as he pleased, prescribed the degree of applause which he should receive, and could have detained him prisoner had he thought proper. He wishes therefore, as soon as possible, to return to private life. In this last expression, [Morris gravely notes] he deceives himself or wishes to deceive me, or both, perhaps. But in fact he is the lover of freedom from ambition, of which there are

two kinds: one born of pride, the other of vanity, and his partakes most of the latter.

Morris much preferred the life of the salon to that of the streets where the revolution was taking place, but he was nothing if not a shrewd, though sarcastic, observer of his peers. Certainly when Lafayette chose to make a test of his following out of the murder of the ex-intendant of Paris, Berthier, and his father-in-law Foulon, neither pride nor vanity were absent from his motives. These murders, which took place on July 22nd, sickened most literate observers, including Morris and the more earthy Restif de la Bretonne. A week is a long time in revolutionary politics: the fall of the Bastille had already acquired mythical significance. At a stage when the revolution seemed to be bogged down in the endless debates that were taking place in every section – debates which were a splendid school of democracy, but which, if they did not soon produce some resolutions, would begin to pall and become the preserve of dogmatists – the only drama, the only achievements in fact, seemed to be the severing of heads without benefit of due process.

Foulon had been appointed a minister by the king after Necker was dismissed; on that score alone he was identified as an enemy of the patriots. He was also a financier, suspected of hoarding grain, and he was believed to have said that if Paris was hungry the people could eat hay.

Rumor had it that Foulon so feared for his life after the fall of the Bastille that he retired to his estates and had his own death announced. While his servants dressed in black, he tried to flee to Belgium, but he was given away. He was sent to the capital to be tried for crimes against the state, in a hay cart, his shirt stuffed with dry grass. That he was old and ill weighed little with those who believed him guilty. His condition, after all, had not stopped him accepting the king's commission to govern.

Foulon was taken to the City Hall through an immense and threatening crowd which was quietened only by the arrival of Lafayette. (He noted that at this time of "seething crowds" who were certain of nothing, when "everything was excitement or distrust," the only means of control was personal dominance, "the only influence which each individual dared or knew how to exert.") Lafayette made a long speech defending the process of law he had pledged to uphold, "the law without which there is no liberty, the law without whose help I would have contributed nothing to the revolution in the new world, and without which I could contribute nothing to the revolution which is preparing itself here." This, he said, was not to defend Foulon, whom he was not qualified to judge as he had on several occasions attacked his actions, but the proper forms had to be observed, and he ordered Foulon to be taken to the prison of Abbaye Saint-Germain.

Those in the vast hall who had heard him were prepared to carry out his wishes, but they were howled down by those at the back. Foulon then tried to address the crowd, saying something to the effect that he was "in the midst of my fellow-citizens" and that he "feared nothing," but this only made things worse. For hours the debate continued: Lafayette made continual pleas for the law to be obeyed, while voices from the ever-growing throng insisted that Foulon had already been judged by his actions, that they were being betrayed, that something must be done, that people were coming to take the prisoner away. As the tumult grew and people pressed closer and closer around the prisoner, Lafayette bellowed one more time for him to be taken to prison. There was some applause, in which Foulon, doubtless scared witless, unhappily joined. Somebody screamed, "There, you see, they're all in agreement!" and with that Foulon was dragged out of the room, across the square, and strung up on a lamp-post. Lafayette could do nothing, so great was the crowd, members of which went on to sever the head and parade it through the streets, leaving the body in the mud.

Foulon's son-in-law Berthier, who had been arrested in Compiègne when trying to flee, was also being brought to the Paris City Hall that day. As intendant, or steward, of Paris, and a supporter of the royal court, he was suspected of having starved the capital for his own benefit. The sides of the coach bringing him to judgment were knocked out so that everyone could have a good look. It was reported that he was shown the severed head of his father-in-law, its mouth stuffed with straw. It was early evening, and very hot, when they arrived at the City Hall, where Lafayette tried to provide a detachment of his scarcely organized guards to act as escort. The marquis was out of uniform at this time; popular hero though he may have been, he was not widely recognized, and when he tried to address the crowd, it was easy for some to persuade the rest that this was not the commandant-general speaking. Mayor Bailly arrived and tried to order Berthier to be taken to prison; the prisoner was only inside the City Hall for a few minutes before being dragged out again, looking half-dead, by the guards. Then a group pushed the guards aside, and Berthier was carried along in the crowd to the lamp-post. There, according to Restif de la Bretonne, Berthier put up a fight. Trying to support his weight by grabbing at the rope, he had both his arm and the noose slashed; hauled up a second time, the rope broke; finally, he was finished off at the bottom of the lamp-post, his head subsequently joining Foulon's as a trophy. Within three days the price of bread fell, which was instantly attributed to the lynching. And the Bastille, a great tourist

153

attraction, was ordered to be demolished. Crowd action appeared to have some effect.

Lafayette, furious and hurt that his orders were ignored, forthwith offered his resignation. Perhaps he was in earnest when he told Morris he wanted to return to private life: it would certainly have pleased his wife who feared for his safety every day. His opponents saw in his resignation a ploy to consolidate his power, and it is true that there were few contenders for his job. He was fairly certain of getting it back on his own terms. But he always preferred glory to routine power, and his resignation proceeded more from dejection and disgust than some sinister motive. "The people," he wrote formally to Bailly and the sixty districts of the capital, "have not listened to my opinions, and that day when the confidence which they promised me is missing, is the day on which, as I said well in advance, I should leave a post in which I can no longer be useful." He understood the emotions and frustrations of the crowd, but he could not excuse their illegal violence. He felt, with some justification, that if, in an uncertain time, people decided that there was no power capable of controlling events, they inclined to panic, and worse. They would then turn to demagogues rather than the legal authorities, an act which, Lafayette was sure, would lead to anarchy or dictatorship.

The reaction to his resignation by the electors, and by the various sections of the city, was one of consternation. Insisting that the safety of Paris lay in his hands, they urged him to remain. The district of St-Merri addressed him as "the object of the admiration of all France, and even the universe," and described his post as having been bestowed by "public opinion, which is never wrong." It went on to call for unanimous affirmation of his command, and the suppression of all disorder, which cry was taken up on all sides (those who couldn't support it prudently keeping quiet). Deputations besieged his house, and, as he wrote to Mme de Simiane:

> they throw themselves on their knees in tears, and promise to obey me in everything. What can I do? I am in despair. Terrible lies are said about me; the population is led by an invisible hand. Yesterday I had to offer the hope that I would stay in order to guarantee the peace for the night. I cannot abandon those citizens who put all their confidence in me, and if I stay, I'm in the terrible position of seeing the evil without remedying it.

But he did stay, and Paris became a little calmer. Bailly and the district leaders began the reorganization of the administration; Lafayette began in earnest the organization of the guard, making it clear as he did so that the military power was to be regarded as subservient to the civil. He was not short of advice, as contemporary pamphlets show. These were the early days of the revolution, when everyone felt entitled to have their say, in a situation so fluid anyone might be listened to.

Organization, of course, altered the spontaneous nature of the revolution, which began to take on the more familiar features of bureaucratic zeal and officiousness. The election of the guards' officers – itself an innovation – aroused both exitement and disturbance, while the citizens of the Jacobins St-Honoré district complained at "outrageous manipulation." More than that, the epaulet which Lafayette had designed for paid soldiers was considered "a lasting outrage . . . provoking internal strife" among those who had got "over-excited" by ambition. Some citizens, at least, considered that the old powers of wealth and position had lost none of their strength, and that the new regime might be worse than the old, by arming "brother against brother, and citizen against citizen." Certainly Lafayette and the electors wanted only men they could trust in the guard, for they constituted a considerable armed body, a possible danger despite their oaths of loyalty. But those who volunteered – supplying their own uniforms designed by their general, but being equipped at the city's expense with arms and equipment – not infrequently let their patriotic zeal run away with them. Many citizens who tried to go about their normal business got fed up being ordered around by those who were supposed to be their comrades.

An anonymous pamphlet objected to the expense, the noise of drums in the streets, and the permanent state of military preparedness (which included daily drilling for all volunteers). Already, it seems, people were allowed to pay someone to take their place which, said the pamphlet, is fine for those who can afford it, but useless to the small merchant who can neither afford the substitute nor the time wasted in training. And there were the horror-stories about those who were away or ill when they should have been on guard-duty, of the entire neighborhood being aroused in the middle of the night by a detachment of fusiliers in full battle order, set on dragging their man from his bed to do his duty, come what may. Lafayette's position was that, in this time of crisis, rules must be obeyed; that complaints would be investigated, but that they were inevitable when a volunteer army had to be formed from scratch in the shortest possible time. This position is perfectly understandable from his point of view, but it looked different to the ordinary Parisian who was for ever being stopped and questioned about a parcel he may have been carrying, to the citizen still lacking food to whom the expense of the guards' uniforms may have appeared superfluous, and to the wife and family of the small trader who patriotically volunteered, and whose business then suffered from his absence.

The zeal of the volunteer guards was in large measure due to the "great fear" that took hold of the countryside and spread to the towns of France in late July, 1789. The fear was that bands of "brigands" were about to overrun all private property, doing all the things that brigands are rumored to do in such circumstances. Although the brigands were entirely mythical, the fact was that bands of landless peasants had risen and burnt châteaux in places where their grievances went unheeded and their spokesmen were out-voted by the bourgeoisie. They had seen the "revolution," and for them it hadn't worked. The Assembly at Versailles heard of the uprising just as they were beginning to debate the Declaration of Rights: they instantly denounced disorder and the non-payment of taxes and called out the troops. In some country towns retribution was savage. In Paris, where nothing had actually happened, the bourgeoisie rallied even more enthusiastically to the guard, who promptly disarmed all the unemployed who might be considered subversive.

On August 4th in the Assembly, following a proposal by La-fayette's brother-in-law the Vicomte de Noailles, landowners, clerics, magistrates, and even local dignitaries all volunteered to surrender their rights and privileges. By this astonishing and dramatic action, feudalism was abolished in France. Tax privileges and ex-emptions were swept away, and taxation was declared equal for all from January 1, 1789. Serfdom was abolished, and feudal rights could be extinguished by purchase. Seigneurial rights were ended, civil and military posts opened to everyone, justice was to be adminis-tered free and the sale of legal posts stopped. Tithes ceased, and church pluralism was prohibited. Mme de La Tour du Pin claimed that her family and countless others were thus ruined by a stroke of the pen. The legislation was certainly revolutionary: that the king endorsed it, thus receiving on the way the title "Restorer of French Liberty," was a sign of the times; that the First and Second Estates accepted it showed that for the majority of them the hardship could not have been unbearable. Not everyone who might have benefited cared. Arthur Young was in the Auvergne at the time, and he was furious that no one was interested enough to discuss the changes. In other parts of France the effect was immediate, but in Paris it made little difference, especially to those convinced that privilege still ruled. Lafayette publicly rebuked a nobleman who tried to use his titles to advantage; he dropped his own and began writing his surname as one word. But nothing he could do could make him immune from attack from one quarter or another.

With the presses suddenly free, everyone was putting out papers and pamphlets, many of them attacking the new administrators. The electors soon banned anonymous sheets, and also news-vendors who added to the general panic by yelling out scare headlines that had no facts to back them up. But there were still printers cautious about their new freedom: the journalist Jean-Paul Marat, with his strange and sallow appearance, his inflammatory but always readable opinions, had difficulty finding himself a publisher. But he did the rounds, and soon his paper *The Friend of the People* was in business. It began by denouncing the bourgeois administrators of Paris as enemies of the revolution, and it singled out Bailly and Lafayette for special and bitter attack. Lafayette minded, as he made clear in his memoirs and to his mistress. Perhaps it was pride or vanity, but he was only thirty-two, with sole responsibility for immense decisions, and he was hurt by crude attacks made in the name of "the people" he claimed to serve. To his credit, he did little to silence his critics, beyond the degree of harassment usual to zealous police forces. And he had his defenders, so sycophantic his opponents accused him of paying for them.

Work, of course, occupied all his energy and thoughts, and he had more than his share of the problems affecting the capital. His signature was needed for anything from passports to orders for grain – and it was not infrequently forged, which did little for his reputation. So much business had to pass through his hands that he was virtually besieged, without even time to attend to his family. Gouverneur Morris, wanting to discuss something with Lafayette, was asked to dinner, but found the invitation "idle, if I am rightly informed, because he generally has a crowd and is but few minutes at home." And then there were the outbreaks of disorder which the general, with good reason, believed himself alone capable of calming without bloodshed. Such an occasion arose in Montmartre, where several thousand workers revolted at having to forfeit two days' wages through being forbidden to work on a feast day. Lafayette dismissed the incident in his memoirs by saying he "harangued them severely, and threatened to arrest the mutineers," after which all was orderly. But a pamphlet paints a fuller picture of his methods, which were a combination of persuasion and threat that was obviously effective. Arriving on his white horse with a dozen cavaliers around him, he first looked for a place with enough room for the people to gather and listen to him. Then he assured his audience, whom he addressed as "my children," that the city cared for them all, but that as it could not afford to compensate everybody for their loss of earnings, those who had come from villages to work in Paris should return to them, with the city's help. (This was part of a major effort to cut the number of those dependent on the capital, which was treated to the sight of long marches of workers returning to the land.) Lafayette next went on to adjure the natives of the quarter not to gamble, since games for money distracted them from work and caused quarrels. Then he asked them not to go to the City Hall in a body to present their demands, but to appoint a "small number of wise representatives." If they did this, he would do all he could to further their requests; if not, he would do his utmost to see they were refused. He warned them not to listen to agitators in their midst, and he assured them he was not in the least frightened of revolts: he had come on the orders of the commune, and he headed a force of 30,000 well-armed men. He would not hesitate to use force to quell disorder, regardless of the cost. Misfortune, he concluded, awaited anyone who troubled public order.

This speech was received in silence but, the pamphlet maintains, its finish was greatly applauded. Two hundred workers left the following day, and more followed. Yet the area was still turbulent. Five days later Lafayette returned, obviously in tougher mood, and made a similar speech, promising help for those who deserved it and punishment for those who made trouble. This time, cries of "Long live M. de Lafayette" were heard on all sides. Many observers, however, including Gouverneur Morris, still doubted Lafayette's ability to control events. "If the clouds which now lower should be dissipated without a storm," wrote Morris, "he will be infinitely indebted to fortune; but if it happens otherwise, the world must pardon much on the score of intention. He means ill to no one, but he has the *besoin de briller* [need to shine]. He is very much below the business he has undertaken, and if the sea runs high he will be unable to hold the helm." It is always tempting for a biographer to believe a contemporary witness who can write in epigrams, and the evidence is much on Morris's side. Lafayette could keep order, but who knew for how long the volunteer guards would remain so zealously loyal? The legislative business of the revolution seemed to be proceeding, but how long would the unity of the Assembly last? And who knew when the enemies of the revolution – the royal troops, the plotting aristocrats, the agitators of all colors – would make their move?

As a matter of fact, the first serious splits in the unity of the Assembly occurred over the question of the royal veto. No one presumed that the executive power would reside other than in the king, acting with his ministers on the English model, but the question was what kind of power the king should have to reject the decisions of the legislative body, in whom resided that hallowed precept, the sovereignty of the people. Mirabeau, the Assembly's best speaker, maintained that it was better to trust a single king with an army behind him than six hundred deputies to put decisions into effect, while Sieyès argued that it was the Assembly who represented the will of the nation, and that the job of the executive was merely to carry out that will, not to thwart it. Lafayette, basing his position entirely on the only model he knew and trusted, that of America, told Mme de Simiane (who had demanded to know his opinion) that he didn't consider the veto question all that important. He opted for the suspensive veto, which would give the king the right to delay legislation for two sessions, or six years. But while he agreed that an absolute veto might be too much to the crown's advantage, he thought that there were several things to be said in its favor, and maintained that he wouldn't be broken-hearted if it passed. Nevertheless he preferred the suspensive version, because it was the one more likely to pass the Assembly without being too divisive or holding matters up. Years later he wrote that he supported the suspensive veto because it had the double advantage of moderating the legislature and giving time to sound public opinion. (In fact, given the speed with which events were moving, a six-year delay on legislation was equivalent to an absolute veto. And it could be operated at the whim of a monarch hardly renowned for his consistency and firm principles.) But Lafayette was much more interested in the question of whether the new legislature should have one chamber or two. Again faithful to his American mentors, he supported the idea of an elective senate also armed with a suspensive veto. Public opinion, however, had seized on the royal veto question, and though not everyone understood what it meant, that did not stop them feeling passionate about it.

Furious meetings against the veto were held in the grounds of the Palais-Royal, part of which consisted of shops and cafés, part of which was owned by the Duc d'Orléans. To understand how a royal duke could be behind demonstrations effective enough to trouble both the Assembly at Versailles and Lafayette in Paris, we have to take account of the Palais-Royal itself as much as of its most ambitious occupant. The buildings are of the right height, the covered galleries of the right width, the lawns and fountains so perfectly juxtaposed, that anyone entering is struck first by the magnificence of the place, then by its proportions, which are so balanced as to welcome the presence of people, rather than dwarfing them. It is no small thing to start a demonstration in a place where the very architecture inspires confidence, and the fact that its patron reputedly opened his purse to the demonstrators would naturally have made them sympathetic to his cause.

Meetings were held, and threats made against the Assembly, such as that of the Marquis de Saint-Huruge, who tried to lead a march on Versailles. Delegations of respectable citizens armed with petitions besieged the legislators with demands that the veto be dropped. They were not well received. The real issue was bread, but the veto became a convenient stick with which to beat an Assembly still debating the rights of man while people went hungry. By the end of August Lafayette had become so exasperated with the demonstrations that he had some of the Palais-Royal's most popular meeting-places raided and shut.

Lafayette was determined to show his loyalty to the king, to the Assembly, and to the commune of Paris, and he was prepared to use martial law to enforce this loyalty on any who questioned it. But he feared most of all that the Assembly would forfeit popular respect by getting bogged down in debate, especially over the veto, and he determined to try and arrange a way out of the apparent impasse. Every time he did something in public, however, he was suspected – by his enemies, who hastened to publish their suspicions – of advancing his own position at the expense of the people's. Even when he had gone formally, with Bailly and a detachment of the guard, to present the city's respects to the king on his name-day, Lafayette was accused of trying to exert undue influence on court and Assembly. (Mme de La Tour du Pin reported that when Lafayette came forward the queen's color rose and that she appeared to be "under the stress of some very strong emotion": her lack of graciousness toward the whole delegation angered many.) All he had wanted to do, he complained to an anonymous correspondent, was to be loyal to both. His two watchwords, he maintained, were simply "impartiality, tranquillity." But playing the referee as passions rose higher was becoming harder for him.

That he still had political influence he showed by arranging a secret meeting to thrash out a solution to the veto problem that would be acceptable to both king and Assembly. As meeting place he chose Jefferson's house, who, as American minister in Paris, became seriously concerned at the thought of becoming involved in French domestic affairs. However, he could not very well refuse his old friend, even though he knew that the presence of Lafayette's carriage outside would guarantee that the French foreign ministry would be aware of what was going on. He sat, a silent witness, from four in the afternoon till ten at night while Lafayette and seven of the Assembly's most influential deputies strove to arrive at a united front. Lafayette opened the discussion by deploring the divisions among their ranks, and promising his influence, as head of the national guard, to get whatever they decided carried out. He proclaimed himself in favor of a bicameral legislature and a suspensive veto, but he was prepared to compromise. When the meeting finally broke up, Jefferson was under the impression that unanimity had in fact been achieved – in favor of a single-chamber legislature and suspensive veto. But rifts continued to appear among the ranks of Lafayette's friends in the Assembly – sometimes called the

"American" party, sometimes the "Patriots" – and the veto question still agitated the people of the capital. Even the court wondered if Lafayette would be able to contain the Parisians, and the Marquis de La Tour du Pin was commissioned to write, as an old friend, warning him of royal displeasure if things got out of hand and sounding out his feelings. Lafayette replied with protestations of loyalty, but begged the king to do all he could to keep on the right side of the citizens of his capital. (Rumors were strong that Louis had considered fleeing to Metz, only being dissuaded by the remark, "and what shall we do when we get there?") The Assembly finally decided for a suspensive veto (and against a bicameral legislature) on September 11th.

Rumor and the shortage of bread in Paris were the chief threats to the order Lafayette was charged with maintaining. It was especially easy to believe the king capable of anything, for that monarch, unprepared for and uncomprehending about what was happening, while being buffeted with differing advice from his wife, his brothers and his ministers, scarcely knew his own mind. He delayed publishing his approval of the Assembly's resolutions, and in the meanwhile he took the step of ordering the Flanders regiment from Douai to Versailles. The explanation for this was given as the urgent need to protect the king from attack by the Parisians, thus implying Lafayette either couldn't control them or was inciting them to be disloyal. In normal times the usual mistrust of the capital felt by the provinces, coupled with an appeal to protect the person of the monarch, would have assured the king of support for his summoning of troops. But these were not normal times, and while the Assembly did not exactly command an ecstatic following, neither did the king. Paris was setting the national pace in organizing under new management – and when news of the Flanders regiment's orders became known, the Parisians indulged in an orgy of rumor, all based on the conviction that an aristocratic plot was in the making, either to capture the king, or to mount an attack on the revolution and its leaders, or both.

Reports of plots against the monarch, the Assembly, the city, and against him personally, came flooding into Lafayette, and he could not afford to take them lightly. At one point, the royal minister for foreign affairs, Montmorin, came to see him, warned him of the Orléanist designs on the throne, and suggested the possibility of Lafayette taking the ancient and honorific post, vacant for some hundred and fifty years, of constable of the kingdom, or that of lieutenant-general. The offer was made because Montmorin, an old friend of Lafayette's and one of the more moderate of the royal advisers, wanted the general to affirm his support for the crown. But Lafayette was indignant that his loyalty should be questioned. Why should he stagger under the sword of the kingdom when he was only with difficulty controlling the capital? Why should he accept royal office, with all its attendant restrictions, when he had a more or less free hand in Paris, although that hand was in constant danger of being forced? He refused with dignity – as he refused an offer enthusiastically made by all the guards of France to be national commandant-general, and refused the salary voted by the commune, saying he had enough money, that he would ask them if he needed it, but meanwhile they could give it to those who had suffered in the revolution. In these refusals he was following an ancient noble tradition, that of demonstrating that he wanted neither power nor reward, that he was merely doing his duty. His popularity was accordingly enhanced (even Marat complimented him on his sacrifice) and the commune insisted on reserving a sum for his expenses (which were considerable, especially his entertaining bill), whether he wanted it or not. Nevertheless his financial manager tried to convince him that "our revolution is costing you more than that of America."

But plots, rumors, and bread riots were only three of the things occupying Lafayette's mind. In all the confusion, when most people thought only of getting from one day to the next – not out of selfishness or short sight, but because this was still a revolution against dogma and the old orthodoxies; there were so many ideas, expressed in so many journals and pamphlets, that the luxury of choice was almost an embarrassment – in all this, Lafayette had the simple advantage of knowing in which direction he wanted the revolution to go. Basing his aspiration, naturally, on his American experience, he proclaimed to anyone who would listen that he wanted a constitution that would guarantee an hereditary executive (the king) responsible to an elective legislature (like the Assembly). For this ideal he was prepared to lay down his life. Meanwhile he did all he could to bring his ideal into being. The trouble was that the cornerstone of his belief was his confidence in the king. Such confidence was in short supply in the Assembly and elsewhere, and getting shorter. Lafayette didn't exactly have blind faith in his monarch, but he felt sure either that reason would prevail, or that the monarchy, as but one leg of the tripod consisting of king, Constitution, and people, could be jiggled into position as the others could. The disadvantage, though, of knowing what you want when all else is confusion is that you find it hard to believe others don't, won't, or can't share your vision. And this tends to make you somewhat short tempered.

Lafayette urged the king, through Montmorin and others, to put all ideas of fleeing, whether to Metz or elsewhere, right out of his mind. If the king felt he needed protection, he said, let him come to

Paris, where the city's national guard would guarantee his safety. Meanwhile, he busied himself with the continuing organization of the guard, an endless task further complicated, so he complained, by those inescapable trappings of democracy – committee decisions. He spent his remaining time on a pet project he had of reforming the criminal code. Lafayette felt that his fellow-citizens were far removed from the state of mind and development in which the ancient code had been conceived, and he was also revolted by the "barbarity" of some of the sentencing, which still included being condemned to serve in the galleys. This "barbarity" had the wrong sort of deterrent effect on patriotic citizens: they deterred the guardians of law and order from making arrests, for who would want to condemn a fellow being to such a sentence for a misdemeanor? And it made the new France look somewhat ridiculous in the eyes of the "civilized" world (which is to say America). Having made representations about these matters in the old Assembly of Notables, Lafayette took the matter up again, this time before the new Paris government, the Assembly of Representatives that had replaced the old. (Elections and changes of title took place at a bewildering rate at this period, during which the bourgeoisie consolidated their power. The more artisan districts complained of manipulation.) Somewhat to the annoyance of Bailly, who felt Lafayette was meddling in affairs that did not concern him, the general persuaded the Paris representatives to get the royal chancellor to suspend sentences on all those convicted for taking part in disturbances in the capital, until the Assembly had done something about a new criminal code. The chancellor granted this suspension, and Bailly complained that the prisons were filling up while nothing was done under the old procedure and nothing could be done about the new.

Another personal triumph for the general was the solemn blessing, in Notre-Dame, of the new standards of the Paris national guard. The trickiest problem was to organize the proceedings in such a way as to avoid offending the touchy sensibilities of each section of the guard. Lafayette made all the arrangements, and managed to avoid hurting anybody. All the bickering he had experienced as a foreign major-general in Washington's army had obviously taught him much.

These triumphs notwithstanding, the mood in Paris, if an entire city can share a mood, grew increasingly impatient. Everyone felt the shortage of bread, which meant that angry groups of people gathered daily at the bakeries. In the central and artisan areas those in line could buy the newspapers that were the best form of education, gossip, and attack – and the juiciest bits were doubtless passed on by those who could read to those who could not. The flurry of activity worked up by the municipal authorities and in the guard doubtless convinced most Parisians that, for better or worse, the affairs of the city were being taken in hand. But what could the city do against the plotting that centered on the king, plotting that was held responsible for everything from the shortage of bread to the lack of progress in cementing the achievements of the revolution?

The city could utter assurances – which failed to fill the bakeries – and it could crack a few heads, which calmed no one. The frustrations felt by everyone from Lafayette to the domestic servants, who angrily demonstrated at being thrown out of work by the emigration from France of their noble employers, were aggravated when news reached Paris of the arrival in Versailles of the Flanders regiment. When the markets had to be patrolled by members of the guard, when fights broke out at the bakeries, when some demanded the king come to Paris to alleviate the sufferings of his people and some called for "a second revolutionary upheaval," when, in addition to all of that, young bucks in the capital began to sport the black cockade of the Hapsburgs (the queen's family) critical excitement welled up and overflowed into street action.

The rumor was that, at a banquet given to honor the Flanders regiment (who had ostensibly come solely to defend the court), the royal family had been toasted, rather than the nation; that in the drunken aftermath, the tricolor had been trampled, and replaced by the black cockade; and that on October 4th some ladies of the court had tried to distribute white cockades, the colors of the Bourbons, to those whose loyalties should have been to the red, white, and blue. It was even said the national guard of Versailles had been chased from the palace by the royalist troops.

The truth, according to Mme de La Tour du Pin, who was there, was a little different, but not much. The banquet itself, given by the royal bodyguard, was held in the theater of Versailles, a magnificent and windowless hall lit by hundreds of candles. When she arrived, Mme de La Tour du Pin's husband, whose father was minister of war, whispered that things were getting a bit heated, and rash things being said. Suddenly the king, the queen, and the four-year-old dauphin appeared – "an imprudent step which produced a very bad effect." There were shouts of "Long live the king," but Mme de La Tour du Pin heard no others. The dauphin was paraded round the room, the queen embraced him, and the royal family left. So, soon afterwards, did Mme de La Tour du Pin. She heard later that evening that some ladies, including the Duchesse de Maille ("a heedless chit of nineteen") had distributed white ribbons from their hats to some of the officers. So much for the story of the white cockades.

Rumors of bread riots in Paris on October 4th reached Versailles, but these were so frequent, and caused so little alarm, that on the 5th the king went hunting. In Paris, the shops that were usually open on that day, a Monday, remained closed, a situation which alone would have aroused ordinary citizens. By about ten in the morning on the 5th, a huge crowd had gathered around the City Hall, and troops were everywhere. The crowd had two distinct elements, each having begun by demonstrating for different causes. One, consisting of workers from the Faubourg Saint-Antoine, had been demonstrating about a workmate arrested on some charge during the demolition of the Bastille: they wanted him freed. The other, consisting chiefly of women – those closest to the bread shortage, for it was they who had to wait, fight, and listen to rumors about speculation in corn – demanded that Bailly and Lafayette do something: arm the populace, march to Versailles to bring the king to Paris.

These two elements had coalesced in front of the City Hall. The workers' demonstration was led and controlled by Stanislas Maillard, who had assumed this role in the Faubourg Saint-Antoine itself (where the Bastille was situated). The women had also started in Saint-Antoine, and the markets nearby, apparently following the lead of a small girl beating a drum and shouting against the lack of bread. From this beginning, the women, of all classes from fish-wives to smartly dressed bourgeoises, had the tocsin, or alarmbell, sounded, and began collecting, sometimes forcibly, supporters for their demonstration. By the time they were joined by Stanislas Maillard and his men, the cry had become to go "to Versailles to fetch the baker and the baker's wife" – the king and queen. Maillard allowed himself to be persuaded, whether to avoid bloodshed or for political reasons, to lead a march to Versailles. One witness said the demonstrators had only sticks and pikes; another, axes, bars, and guns. They marched, anyway, some six or seven thousand of them, through the Tuileries, and stopped in the Place Louis XV. Near the Champs-Elysées Maillard claimed that he persuaded the women to proceed without arms. One observer reported seeing an ancient cannon being drawn by two horses, on the shaft of which sat a pretty girl shouting "To Versailles." When some guards whistled at her, she pointed between her legs and shouted "For the grenadier who does his duty!" They cheered her to the echo.

To march to Versailles, a distance of some twelve miles, in the rain, was in the old tradition of a loyal populace asking their "father" the king to put things right. The Assembly was also there, for those who had faith in that. A crowd with a single, simple objective is difficult to dissuade and easy to anger, the more so when, in a male-dominated society, the crowd consists chiefly of women (some observers claimed that there were a large number of men in female attire). The mass advancing on Versailles was not a drunken rabble, although the weather made many glad of wine. It contained all types of people, but certainly most of them had homes to look after: these were consumers enraged by shortages and rising prices. Paris was the largest city in the French empire; if the king could only see how his citizens there suffered, the reasoning went, he would do something for them. Once this idea had taken hold it was unstoppable. Most seemed to feel animated by the highest patriotic motives; far from uttering violence against the crown, they threatened only those who tried to stop them. These included Lafayette.

He regarded the whole exercise as an illegal attempt to force the hand of king and Assembly. (He later blamed "factious elements" for arousing the demonstration, while the court saw in the affair the hand of the Duc d'Orléans.) The general's strategy during the day of October 5th was to try and disperse the people with oratory and the guards, thus treating it as a "normal" outburst. But the crowd was too cross – and had not the cry "To Versailles" been taken up, the City Hall itself might well have been endangered. Once the crowd had left the city center, Lafayette first wanted to leave it severely alone. Members of the guard came to plead to be allowed to accompany the people to Versailles; Lafayette sternly refused. Possibly he thought the demonstration would fizzle out. Certainly he did not wish to become involved in an attack on two of the institutions, the crown and the Assembly, for which he had proclaimed his readiness to lay down his life.

But his guards did not see it like that. Though we know little about their social composition, they seemed to be mainly householders, journeymen, professional people – the bourgeoisie, both upper and lower ends of it. So were most of the crowd marching to Versailles. The guard identified with them and their objective. At one stage, Lafayette relates, a deputation of grenadiers burst into a meeting he was attending and said, "General, the king is deceiving us and you like the others: we must depose him. His son will be king, you will be regent, and everything will be all right." Lafayette merely concluded that the "idea of a regency had been suggested to them without a name attached" (by the Orléanistes, of course), and that they had "naturally" taken it to apply to their general. But most people were critical of Lafayette when there were all these people marching toward their king and the commandant-general refused either to stop them or to allow his guards to join them. He obviously thought his example of staying put would have more effect than it did. Yet the march continued.

In the various versions of these events written later and published in his memoirs (all of which are credible when compared with contemporary accounts), Lafayette stresses the patriotic desire of the national guard to avenge the insults to their colors and their comrades reported to have taken place during the Versailles banquet for the Flanders regiment. Doubtless some did feel this desire, but the main issue in the demonstration was bread. Lafayette points out that the Assembly had interfered in the question of the supply of grain by creating a food committee, which led some of the crowd to besiege the Assembly as soon as they arrived with demands for action. Lafayette, who thought supply was the business of the executive (the crown), thus blamed the Assembly for what happened, as much as he blamed the court for allowing the tricolor to be insulted and the Orléanists for fomenting unrest. But when it was obvious that the march was going all the way to Versailles, and growing bigger and more excited all the time, Lafayette was forced to allow his guards to join it, in the hope of controlling it. Yet his guards, in his view, would not join a mere bread riot, of the kind that they had to deal with every day. They could be animated only by the highest of patriotic motives – avenging the insult to the revolution's colors: this was the gloss Lafayette put on an event which got somewhat out of his control.

In the early evening, Lafayette, having asked for and obtained orders from the City Hall, finally set off for Versailles with his men. He was in a strange position, for the force on which he relied – the guard – wished to associate itself with a demonstration directed at the very bodies whose safety he was supposed to guarantee. He related, uncharacteristically, how he was applauded on leaving by "the crowd of well-dressed persons" in the Tuileries, who shared his disgust at those who had first provoked these disorders. He was a monarchist, and a member of the Assembly: what would the king and his fellow-deputies feel about his arrival? Would he be able to control his guard, let alone the crowd, in front of them?

Gouverneur Morris, for one, thought he was lost:

> Lafayette has marched by compulsion, guarded by his own troops, who suspect and threaten him. Dreadful situation! Obliged to do what he abhors, or suffer an ignominious death, with the certainty that the sacrifice of his life will not prevent the mischief. I go to supper. Much discourse about what is to happen at Versailles, and we agree that our Parisians will be beaten and we consider it as fortunate that they are gone. I venture the assurance that from this day forward the French army will return to its sovereign, presuming, always, that the Régiment de Flandre will, as it said, do its duty this night.

Lafayette was hardly a prisoner of his own troops. Indeed, by the time they were halfway to Versailles, he was sufficiently in command to order his men to be ready to "push aside everything that got in their way." He was referring to the possibility of the

Flanders regiment coming at them – but he was also determined to protect both Assembly and king from attack from any quarter. He wanted to show that he, at least, was acting with proper authority: this authority included not only his orders from the Paris City Hall, but his own conception of his duty.

Meanwhile the march, tired, wet, and hungry, had reached Versailles. Some went straight to the Assembly, where Maillard spoke for them. He demanded bread for the capital and the punishment of those who had insulted the tricolor. The deputies were soothing. They had problems of their own: already they had asked that the king sanction both the Declaration of Rights and the articles of the Constitution that had been passed, and Louis had only prevaricated. The Assembly was once more debating what to do when the march arrived. The deputies resolved to take some of the women to the court to add their voices to the Assembly's demands. The château meanwhile was in a ferment. It was quite as prey to rumor as was Paris. According to Mme de La Tour du Pin, the courtiers prepared themselves for battle. They feared "massacre"; both the Versailles national guard and the Flanders regiment were drawn up ready to fight off the demonstrators. The king had been hunting. He only returned, at full gallop, at 3 P.M., whereupon he shut himself in his apartments with his advisers. As night fell, it became obvious that the Versailles national guard would take the side of the Paris guard. The king meanwhile refused to allow the Flanders regiment to fire on women demonstrators; the troops returned to barracks. This left the defense of the monarch in the hands of the royal bodyguard, of whose position the national guard were somewhat jealous. Some of the king's advisers begged him to flee. At one stage the royal carriages were ordered to be ready to take him to Rambouillet. But the queen did not like the idea of a night flight, and Louis kept repeating, "I do not want to compromise anyone." No one around him apparently considered the crowd outside would try and stop him leaving. Meanwhile the Assembly continued to press for him to sanction their decrees. And the people shouted for bread.

At last Louis made the decision neither to fight nor to flee, but to agree to the Assembly's demands. He handed its president a paper which said, "I accept without qualification the articles of the Constitution and the Declaration of Rights presented to me by the National Assembly." A scared and unusually silent court waited to see what would happen, ignorant of what was going on outside, and fearful most of all of attack by "the mob." No wonder that when Lafayette's arrival was announced, it was greeted with relief, although some, of course, suspected him of being involved with the demonstrators and saw in his delayed departure from Paris a plot to create a crisis for the monarchy. (Lafayette himself saw plots everywhere.)

At the head of an enormous column, Lafayette determined to do everything with the utmost correctness. He sent ahead to the royal château to announce the disposition of his troops, and to explain his orders from the capital. The king sent back word that he looked forward to the general's arrival "with pleasure, and that he had just accepted *his* [Lafayette's] declaration of rights" – an obvious piece of flattery. The column advanced, ignoring a few gunshots which Lafayette coolly dismissed as mere provocation. Near to where the Assembly was meeting, he halted his men, harangued them about their duty, and then made them renew the civic oath they had all taken on enrollment: the oath of loyalty to "the nation, the law, and the king." Satisfied that the solemnity of the ceremony would impress them to follow his orders – which were to defend the person and property of the crown, not join in attacking it – the general then went to "offer his respects" to the president of the Assembly before seeking orders from the king.

Neither the Assembly nor the court knew quite what to expect from Lafayette, any more than did the demonstrators who had preceded him, and who were still milling about the Assembly and château. Had he come to impose a law on them at gun-point? Had he come merely to restore order? Were his vast forces to awe the king and deputies, or the people? Were they controlling him, or he them? Was the whole thing an elaborate prelude to a military dictatorship? Whose side was he on, if not his own?

The way he was treated, in view of the uncertainty about his intentions, was nervously flattering. The king had complimented him, and now so did the president of the Assembly. The civilians who had accompanied his guards fell in behind them – a further compliment to his control of the march. But whatever he said he was suspected of subterfuge. The climate in Versailles was, admittedly, one of distrust on all sides. The people distrusted the Assembly, the king, and Lafayette; the Assembly distrusted the people, the king, and Lafayette; the king didn't know who to trust. When neither the executive nor the legislative branches of government are trusted, the climate often favors a leader who pledges to restore the rule of law, and indeed order. Lafayette's actions, so strict in their observance of the law, might have been interpreted as a bid for leadership. For those who wished to see them, all the signs of an impending military coup were there: a general on a white horse leading a vast army through the streets, so well-disciplined only a roll of their drums could be heard, and moreover a general who had pledged his troops to the old virtues of obedience and respect for property.

But the simple fact was Lafayette had no such ambitions. Power as such did not interest him. His great model Washington had a certain contempt for politicians. But when it was thrust-upon him, he did his duty. Lafayette was likewise prepared to do this. No more, and certainly no less.

The Assembly received his assurances of devotion with relief. The king had submitted to them; now Lafayette proclaimed his submission to their will. All that remained to make them entirely happy was that the Parisians who were milling about the place would go away, and let them have some sleep (it was now past midnight). But no one could sleep easily before knowing what the king was going to do. There was still the possibility of his fighting back with the Flanders regiment and the royal bodyguard; even Lafayette proceeded with great caution against just such an occurrence.

Accompanied only by two representatives of the City of Paris who had traveled with him, Lafayette presented himself at the gate of the royal château. The place was full of Swiss guards, whose captain expressed surprise when Lafayette insisted he would enter alone with his two companions. "I always feel confident when surrounded by the brave regiment of Swiss guards," said Lafayette gracefully, whereupon the gate was opened and, despite the protests of those of his own guard who had escorted him, and who feared for his life, the general, dirty, and so tired he could scarcely stand, went to see his king. As he passed through the ante-room, his memoirs tell us, someone said, "Here comes Cromwell." "Sir," replied Lafayette, "Cromwell would not have entered alone."

Mme de La Tour du Pin, who was waiting in an ante-room with the rest of the court, reported that Lafayette's "exact words" to Louis XVI were, "Sire, I thought it better to come here and die at the feet of Your Majesty than to die uselessly on the Place de Grève" (the square in front of the Paris City Hall). A sentence can of course get jumbled out of all recognition in a very short space of time and a very small number of mouths. The Paris representatives who were with Lafayette reported that he told the king that they had come to show their love for the king's person, that they were prepared to shed their last drop of blood to ensure his safety, that the armed force outside was there in obedience to the will of the people, and that they had taken an oath to observe the strictest discipline. Whatever the exact words spoken at this emotional meeting, no one was in doubt that Lafayette, and the representatives of the capital, pledged their total loyalty to the king. That must have afforded the courtiers who believed it some relief.

The king then asked what the Parisians wanted. Lafayette replied that the national guard wanted the sole honor of safeguarding the royal person (in other words, replacing the royal bodyguard), that the people wanted bread during the coming winter, and that every-one wanted the king to take up residence in the capital, at the Tuileries. He added the hope that a court system would soon be provided to hasten the trial of prisoners.

The Paris national guard contained a large number of the old French guards, who had previously been the royal bodyguard. La-fayette's inclusion of them in the Paris guard had caused much criticism, especially from those who saw in this yet another example of the "old ways" prevailing over the new. But Lafayette was no believer in novelty for the sake of it: the French guards had been absorbed, and for the king to have them as his bodyguard, albeit in their tricolors, was merely to restore them to their old duty. That demand was therefore granted. The king had already ordered his ministers to discuss with the appropriate officials the problems of supplying Paris, so that meant agreement over another important request of the demonstrators. On the matter of the king taking up residence in Paris, there was talk but no conclusion. Nevertheless Lafayette and the two Paris representatives left well satisfied. Mme de La Tour du Pin says that the guard there and then replaced the Swiss as the royal bodyguard, but this was not entirely true. The long march began to break up, some members of it sleeping in the Assembly chamber, some around the château, some in the town. Lafayette still had to issue his orders for the guarding of Versailles (now that he had taken responsibility for it); he still had to find places for his men to sleep; he still had to ensure calm. He performed these tasks despite his exhaustion, and when he retired to the Noailles' family mansion at Versailles in the early hours of the morning, it was in the knowledge that peace appeared to reign, with the chief aims of the demonstration achieved and his own honor satisfied.

But at dawn the alarm was given. Some of the demonstrators of the previous day had found their way into the château – by a secret door, it was said by those who suspected treason – and they swarmed up the staircase that led to the royal apartments. One of them fell, apparently fatally wounded, in the courtyard; believing him shot, the intruders attacked the royal bodyguards nearest to them – who were not, presumably, national guardsmen – and killed one of them. Then they continued toward the chambers of the king and queen, overpowering all resistance on their way. A Swiss guard found time to warn the queen before himself being killed; she fled, half-dressed, to the king's room. The rest of the Swiss guards – there were few on duty, since confidence had been placed in Lafayette's defense of the château – obeyed the royal order not to fire, and defended them-selves as well as they were able.

Lafayette, having been woken with the news, immediately

started running toward the château, and then grabbed the first available horse. He was sure of his guards: those who had invaded the château must be "brigands," and they had obviously got in through an entrance not guarded by men under his orders. It was plain that the royal bodyguard had become the chief object of the crowd's anger; doubtless rumors of "massacre" had been widely spread, and those milling about, already excited by the irruption to the holy of holies, were intent on lynching as many bodyguards as they could get hold of, in revenge for their fallen colleagues. Lafayette passed the heads of two such victims stuck on poles. Hearing of further planned lynchings of the bodyguards, he rushed to order those held to be released. The bodyguards were given into the care of national guardsmen, but Lafayette remained surrounded by a furious crowd, one of whom shouted for him to be put to death. Adopting a "commanding tone" (his own words), Lafayette ordered the heckler to be seized. He was dragged towards the general, his head bouncing on the cobbles. Lafayette once again reminded the guards of their duty and the oath of loyalty they had sworn. His appeal and his authority worked. The crowd outside grew a little calmer, and when he reached the inside of the château, he found it more or less under the control of his own national guardsmen. He praised their conduct, and again reminded them of their sworn loyalty to the king. Meanwhile the rest of his forces arrived. Versailles came under his control

A curious crowd waited for something to happen. When the king appeared on a balcony, they cheered him frenziedly. Yet Louis still did not know what to do. The rules of etiquette still being in force, Lafayette had to obtain formal permission to enter the royal inner chamber. He was convinced that the king should yield to the shouts of "To Paris!" that were coming from the crowd, but having delivered this opinion, the general respectfully stayed aloof from the royal discussion of the matter. If it was to be his job to guarantee the royal safety and if he was also to ensure the peaceful working of the Assembly, Lafayette was more confident of seeing to these things in Paris than in Versailles. That, and the demands of the crowd outside, decided the king to agree. Stepping out once more onto the balcony, with Lafayette standing between him and the queen, and flanked by his children and his restored chief minister Necker, Louis promised to go to the capital with his family. "Long live the king!" rang out on all sides. Mme de La Tour du Pin, in a genuine state of fear and trembling, "the cries of people being murdered" ringing in her ears, heard the news while sheltering at the home of Lafayette's mistress, Mme de Simiane. The world of Versailles was a small one: Lafayette, perhaps, had prevented it from collapsing into civil war.

The general followed the king's speech by berating the crowd for being misled by plotters and enemies of liberty. Whether or not many heard him, his presence and his assumption of leadership resulted in another ovation. The tension had been relieved by the king's promise to go to Paris. Anybody instrumental in bringing that about was of course enthusiastically received.

The king then asked Lafayette to see to the welfare of his bodyguard. Obviously confident of his mastery of the crowd, the general went out again onto the balcony with a bodyguard, embraced him, and presented him with his own tricolor cockade. When it came to the dramatic gesture, Lafayette was often inspired. "Long live the bodyguard!" shouted the crowd, and the general, having urged them to disperse, went in. But the people stayed where they were and, boredom being fatal to good order, soon began to shout again. Inside, Lafayette asked the queen what she intended doing. "I know what fate awaits me," she replied (according to Lafayette's memoirs), "but my duty is to die at the feet of the king and in the arms of my children." "Then, Madame, come with me," said the general, ready once more to face the crowd. "What?" said the queen. "Alone on the balcony? Did you not see the gestures they were making?" "Yes," replied the confident Lafayette, "let us go." And he went out with her to brave the populace barely contained by guardsmen ranged round three sides of the courtyard. So great was the clamor, he could not make himself heard. He decided on a "risky but conclusive" gesture: he kissed the queen's hand. Moved, or perhaps bemused, by this chivalrous symbol, the crowd enthusiastically shouted "Long live the general! Long live the queen!"

Nevertheless they were still anxious to get going on the road to the capital – one very good reason being that the volunteer guardsmen had all lost a day's wages by accompanying Lafayette to Versailles. The cries of "To Paris!" didn't stop, and finally the general, the king, and the queen made a last appearance on the balcony and promised to leave around noon. Lafayette immediately began issuing orders; activity chased away the crowd's boredom; and members of the royal family, even the queen herself, thanked the general for what he had done. He, of course, could not afford to relax, despite having gone virtually without sleep. The safety of all was in his hands, and he alone was in charge of all arrangements. These included signing passports for members of the royal family and the court, which were required on the orders of the City of Paris for anyone intending to live in the capital. To a man tired, not only physically, but of the obstructions and insults he had suffered from the courtiers, the authority he now had over them must have afforded him some ironic pleasure. It was, he pointed out, their fault, not his, if the conduct of the royal ministers toward the people and the revolution had been such as to make their ministerial signatures more of a danger than a guarantee of safe conduct.

Nevertheless Lafayette was embarrassed by his position. He was, for the moment, sole master of the three forces – king, Assembly, and people. Each of the three was jealous and suspicious of the others. It was up to Lafayette to avoid friction, to get them – all sixty thousand of them – to Paris in good order, and to look after them when they arrived. If he could manage to prevent them from turning on each other, there was still a strong chance they would all turn on him.

His embarrassment was greatest where the royal family was concerned. At the head of his guards, he was getting used to controlling the people, whether by persuasion or bullying: he'd had some ten weeks' practice at it. His respect for the Assembly had been somewhat diminished by their regrettable tendency to ignore his advice and fall to faction-fighting, which was to his military mind the worst of all sins at a time of national emergency. But, for Lafayette, the king was the one unchangeable factor in the whole revolution, for whose hereditary executive power all respect was due. It was respect for the office rather than the person: Louis and Lafayette had known each other since their adolescence, and if Louis never quite understood what was happening, Lafayette at least understood his sovereign's weaknesses. Yet Lafayette pledged his life-blood to defend the king's safety, because he believed that the good government of France depended on it. He believed in an American-style democracy with a king at its head, because that was what the traditions of France demanded, and moreover it was what her people wanted – a view that was absolutely justified at this time, when a "republican" was merely someone who believed in constitutional government. That the king was not someone who could be trusted, and who was at the mercy of "bad" advisers, did not alter, in Lafayette's view, the cardinal need to preserve his person, his office, and a substantial part of his prerogatives. As a matter of fact, the invasion of Versailles by the people of Paris had, he said, made him more royalist. He regarded the invaders as having been misled by "factions" whose chief in this case was the Duc d'Orléans. Two days after the march Lafayette threatened d'Orléans that he would get to the throne only "over his dead body." But chiefly the general saw himself, as he had before, in the role of referee: the king had broken the rules by allowing the tricolor to be insulted, and the people by attacking the royal bodyguard and threatening the royal person. Lafayette could comfort himself, as he rode beside the royal carriage and fretted at the delays caused by the enormous crowd, that he was doing his duty. But he was embarrassed at having to be part of the spectacle of the king being taken to Paris by his people, as he was embarrassed at having the king so much in his power. The crown should have been above such things: it was not only Lafayette's tragedy that it wasn't.

The procession reached Paris by nightfall on October 6th. The guards led the way, their bayonets stuck through chunks of bread miraculously obtained from Versailles. Then came a procession of deputies, followed by the royal coach carrying the king, the queen and the dauphin, surrounded by a crush of women, which also enveloped Lafayette. Finally there were the courtiers and the rest, in carts or carriages if they were lucky, on foot if not. Everyone was wet and tired. The mood was both ominous and triumphant. The rain continued to fall.

In Versailles, reported Mme de La Tour du Pin, the only sound to be heard was "the fastening of doors and shutters which had not been closed since the time of Louis XIV." Lafayette, the "ruler of Paris," had brought king (who, true to family form, managed to eat an enormous supper) and Assembly to the capital under his personal guarantee. He was undoubtedly the hero of the moment. But even that was not a safe position.

13
Law and Order

ONCE THE ROYAL family had been settled in the Tuileries, and the Assembly in the royal riding school, everyone complimented Lafayette. Mirabeau praised his "industry and vigilance" in a typically extravagant eulogy; a Monsieur Kornmann published a letter humorously complaining at the way Lafayette was adored by the women of the capital: "I'm very fond of our general," he wrote, "but I wish our wives would love him a bit less." By a happy coincidence, the grain from the harvest began to arrive in Paris at the same time as the king, so even the bread shortage was "miraculously" relieved.

But the royal family soon began to complain to Lafayette about being cooped up in their gloomy apartments (the reason was that no one trusted them not to flee if they left the city, even to go hunting), and the once-united Assembly found itself divided into a Left and a Right by the geography of its new meeting-place: these divisions soon assumed their modern political importance. The people of Paris, with the revolution unfolding in their midst, had their own ideas, all different, of how matters should proceed. The city was governed by committees which, however democratic, were slow to reach decisions and increasingly monopolized by men with political ambitions. Newspapers and pamphlets continued to pour out daily: one result was that reports of the doings of the Assembly reached a wider, and a more critical, audience; another was an increase in attacks on those in control.

About the direction of the revolution, no one was certain. The time when everyone had their say, and was listened to, was already passing. Now what everyone said began to fall into increasingly familiar categories, and these were used or abused by those ambitious for power. Spontaneity is tiring; those who wanted action increasingly followed others' leads. Clubs, originally part of the mania for

English fashions, mushroomed as guardians each of their own political ideas; although the debates in them were endless, the results were usually predictable. This is not to say that the fizz had gone out of the revolution. (The Constitution, although still in the making, had had its first principles sanctioned by the king.) But it was at that stage when it appeared its foundations had been laid and all that remained was to build up the rest. Most people, however, are bored by details, except those that affect them personally. Details are the peculiar concern of politicians (a large number of whom, in the Assembly, were lawyers). At this stage, therefore, the revolution was taken over by them. Tricks like packing the public gallery with supporters (which Mirabeau was probably the first to use); financing a newspaper to put across their views (which didn't cost much); taking over or founding a club; spreading libels about their opponents: this was the business of the moment. That faction-fighting which Lafayette deplored replaced the dramatic unity of the July days, and it was especially fierce among the Left. Why the Left always disintegrates when the emergency is past, while the Right maintains (or appears to) its united front, is one of the mysteries of history. Perhaps it is to do with the energy required: the Left is usually the party of change, the Right the party of consolidation, and change is always more exhausting.

Lafayette saw himself as in the Center, which of course invites attack from all sides. He believed that the main aims of the revolution had been achieved: anyone who didn't share this belief was an agitator. He was inundated with work, scarcely having any private life with either family or mistress. Indeed, one of the remarkable things about the man is the way his public and his private lives appeared to be one. Even when he writes to his mistresses, it is usually of politics; like Washington, his dedication makes him seem a somewhat marble presence, a person to respect but scarcely to love. Yet people did love him, notably his saintly wife Adrienne, whom he was too busy to appreciate until later. Washington loved him in a paternal way, Aglaé d'Hunolstein and Mme de Simiane appeared to do so in a more carnal manner.

Although little can be found about his personal life in his own memoirs, certain deductions can be made from his friends, and especially his women-friends. Mme de Simiane, whom he certainly saw a lot of at this time, judging by his letters, was reputedly beautiful, and she was certainly intelligent and articulate. She was also childless. Adrienne was plain, devout, quiet, surrounded by children (her own if not her sisters'), and above all capable. She ran family and domestic affairs extremely well, but the strain of constant entertaining hardly left her time or energy to scintillate. She had also been married for over fifteen years. Lafayette was proud of her, but because she performed her chores uncomplainingly, he took her very much for granted. Moreover she rarely, if ever, disagreed with him, whereas Mme de Simiane constantly attacked him for his "liberal" attitudes. Lafayette was obviously more inspired by the smell of danger in his relationships: all the women with whom he was intimate held strong views usually opposed to his own, and he spent as much energy (so far as we can tell from his published letters) persuading them of the consistency of his own principles as he did in wooing them. He appeared anxious to put himself in the right light where they were concerned, rather than trying to win them round to his way of thinking. Though he was consistent in his principles, he needed encouragement. Certainly he needed always to be thought well of by his intimates.

As far as his private life was concerned, this appeared to lead him toward people whose strength and fluency he could admire, and who in turn would admire his energy and devotion. In his public life, his need of approval may explain the curious fact that, despite the exalted positions he occupied, he was never ambitious for the responsibilities of power. Indeed, he preferred being in principled opposition. Maybe this was because he could never concentrate on one thing for too long; maybe because, as with his women, he preferred the smell of danger to the odor of security. Whatever the case, he was never an initiator in public affairs; when called, he did his duty, but as the servant of the principles in which he believed, not as their master. This reticence, this preference for opposition, coupled with the sense of humor expressed in letters to his mistresses, makes him far more human than his public life allowed him to appear.

Such was his prestige in the autumn of 1789 that Lafayette appeared to be the maker of governments, if not kings. He took part in long, secret discussions about forming a new ministry, which went on for months and in the end came to nothing. The talks included several meetings with Mirabeau, also abortive. The two never got on well: Mirabeau was extrovert, flamboyant, a brilliant extempore orator, and so much in debt he was always ready to sell his abilities, if not his principles. Lafayette was personally shy, a stilted speaker who always had to prepare his addresses, flamboyant only in a military sense (for glory rather than fashion), and rich enough to be shocked by venality. He regretted, in his memoirs, treating Mirabeau with "a wounding disdain," but that was written long after the latter's death. The two men met frequently during this period; neither trusted, or influenced, the other. If there were plans among royalist circles to bring into being a moderate government based on the Assembly's most powerful speaker and the military commander of the capital, they were in vain. No scheme which relied on the two of them could have held together for long.

Lafayette regarded the successful arrival of the king and Assembly in Paris as a triumph over factionalism, and he took the opportunity to have a showdown with the Duc d'Orléans (who was also one of Mirabeau's patrons). The two men had once, when the duc was only heir to the title, been rivals for the affections of Aglaé d'Hunolstein; now the stakes – the affections of the people of Paris – were even higher. Prince and general met at the house of Mme de Coigny, d'Orléans' mistress (whom Lafayette described as "a woman of great spirit"), and after a discussion later characterized by Mirabeau as "very imperious on one side, and very resigned on the other," d'Orléans agreed to Lafayette's demand that he leave the country. A royal mission to London was invented as cover, but then d'Orléans kept changing his mind. At their third meeting, he said that "his enemies were inventing the story that [Lafayette] had evidence against him." "It is more like my enemies to say so," retorted the general. "If I could produce evidence, I would have already had you arrested." And he went on to say that he was looking everywhere for such evidence. D'Orléans then really did leave for England with his retinue. Lafayette's friends numbered this among his greatest triumphs, while his enemies referred to it as one more high-handed action against the "friends of the people." The general himself was not bothered. He was even confident enough of the loyalties of the guard, and his supporters in Paris, to turn down for the second time royal offers of high office, such as constable of France, generalissimo, or marshal. Gouverneur Morris thought him too elated by power, but Lafayette preferred being his own master. Indeed, in a memoir on the political future, delivered to the king at his personal request, the general firmly maintained that "the end of the revolution," the acceptance of the Constitution, should be marked by his own "complete abandonment of any political involvement." Morris again thought he was deceiving himself about retiring.

Although one source of "factionalism," the Orléanists, appeared to be extinguished, others sprang up in its place. There were those, like Lafayette's old friend and fellow-deputy Mounier, who felt that the events of October 5th and 6th had resulted in the domination of Paris over both king and Assembly. They became "federalists," returning to their native provinces to risk civil war (as Lafayette saw it) in defense of their freedoms. And there was still a shortage of bread, despite the new harvest. Lafayette joked with Mme de Simiane "it seems hard to give up a supper with you to put down a revolt," but he was determined, now that the deputies and the court – whose safety he had guaranteed – were watching his every movement, to act with great firmness. As it happened, most of Paris supported him.

One particular trial of strength began when a baker of the Notre-Dame district ran out of bread. The women surrounding his shop accused him of reserving his loaves for the members of the Assembly; they broke in and found a small number. The guard arrived to take him to the City Hall for his own safety, but he was snatched from them and lynched. This lynching was widely condemned. Lafayette and Bailly went so far as to declare martial law, the sign of which became a red flag flying from the City Hall. Under the new criminal procedure which Lafayette had long demanded and which had at last been sanctioned, two of those arrested by the guard were given a rapid trial and instantly executed. A court martial disciplined the members of the guard who had been found derelict in their duty. The king and queen promised to be godparents to the unborn child of the baker's widow, and gave her a pension. Everyone except Marat professed themselves shocked at the murder, and supported the strong measures created to prevent further "outrages."

To his strongly royalist relative the Marquis de Bouillé, who had attacked both him and the revolution, Lafayette wrote, "today we fear the same evils – anarchy, civil discord, the dissolution of public authority; we want the same benefits – the re-establishment of credit, the strengthening of constitutional liberty, the return of order and a strong dose of executive power." In the true liberal tradition, Lafayette wanted all parties to unite in the name of the nation, and establish an order that would command universal loyalty. He was surely right in thinking that most people were fed up with the "disorder" that constantly interrupted daily life, but he was wrong in thinking that it could be cured simply by a firm dose of "order," or that the enthusiasm of those who now supported martial law would last for very long. There were still shortages of bread (which were, however, less severe than before), and a growing number of people who felt, with some justification, that despite all the self-congratulation of the Paris authorities and the majority in the Assembly, the revolution had so far changed little. More important, the very freedoms it was supposed to champion were being suppressed in the name of "order." None of these important grievances would vanish because Lafayette, or "General Goldilocks," as one hostile pamphlet described him, "charged round the capital on a white horse." Nevertheless, he knew his duty, and all Paris saw him doing it.

Lafayette wrote to Washington in January 1790:

How often have I missed your wise counsel and your friendly support! . . . . While what existed has been destroyed, a new political edifice is being built; without being perfect, it is enough to guarantee liberty. Thus prepared, the nation will be in a state to elect, in two years, a convention that will be able to correct the faults of the Constitution. . . . The result will be, I hope, a happy one for my country and for all humanity. One can see the germs of liberty in the other nations of Europe: I encourage their development by every means in my power.

(He had recently spoken out for liberty in Corsica, whose citizens were then granted the same rights as other Frenchmen.)

The Constitution was almost done: all that remained was to see its provisions carried out. As far as Lafayette was concerned, this was again a question of "order": it was his job to foil all plots, disarm all conspirators, put down all insurrections, and generally attack "counter-revolution" wherever it interfered with the steady march of constitutional progress. But despite the hopes of bourgeois citizens that the revolution was in fact over, they were still subject to periodic nervousness caused by the activities of the "enemies of the revolution." One scare pamphlet picturesquely described a "Mighty Conspiracy against M. de Lafayette and the Nation that was planned for Saturday, 16 January 1790": this one was supposedly engineered by the aristocrats sheltering on the French borders, and involved infiltrating into Paris no less than thirty-three regiments of cavalry (hidden in empty barrels), plus a considerable quantity of artillery (hidden in apple-carts), as well as a fleet of fifty ships, which were to arrive in the capital via a specially built underground channel, constructed by some two thousand priests, under the direction of Paris's top clerics. Their object was to massacre the guard, Necker, Bailly, and Lafayette, and to take the king to Metz or elsewhere. Following the monarch's safe removal, his brother Artois was to enter France with the whole of the Sardinian army, while the veteran Maréchal de Broglie was to march from Luxembourg to Montmartre, at the head of 900,000 Cossacks and Tartars. Scare stories of Russians entering the capitals of "free" Europe are older than one thinks.

That particular plot was reportedly foiled by a defector who revealed all to Lafayette, who was then supposed to have rallied his men with the cumbrous line, "If I die in defense of my country, take up my blood-stained shirt: it will serve as a red flag to the sixty districts, while martial law is proclaimed in order to break up the gatherings of aristocrats." But while that conspiracy may have been entirely imaginary, the affair centering on the Marquis de Favras was not so lightly dismissed. Favras was charged, beside two other aristocrats, with plotting to overthrow Bailly and Lafayette – a charge which was, under the new criminal procedures, a crime against the nation. The head of this plot was supposed to be Monsieur, another of the king's brothers who was to be declared regent while the king was spirited abroad. Monsieur naturally denied the charge, but it was a sign of the times that he took the trouble to go on to the City Hall to do so. The two accused with Favras were acquitted on the grounds that they were merely carrying out orders. Favras however, was found guilty, and became the first noble to be publicly hanged.

Lafayette, though he thought the sentence just, was greatly upset by it. He admired Favras for dying nobly, and though he was by no means a snob, he was put off by the noisy attendance of the public, who insisted on witnessing the execution. But what may most have given him pause was the enviable simplicity of Favras's position compared to the complications of his own. Favras had died in the course of what he regarded as his duty, and Lafayette greatly respected duty. Favras believed that the new order was the mortal enemy of his king; Lafayette frequently declared himself loyal to both monarch and revolution, and was as frequently attacked by both for his pains. He had recently proclaimed, in defense of the new order, that "insurrection" was "a sacred right" and "the most holy of duties" against "despotism" and "oppression." He hated being misinterpreted, yet here was Favras exercising his own "right of insurrection" in a patently counter-revolutionary way. Who knew how many others would twist the meaning of what Lafayette had intended to be a simple call for eternal vigilance in defense of liberty?

Perhaps Lafayette's chief problem was his ability to respect others' principles when he chose to. A moderate, if that much-abused term retains any meaning, he lacked that peculiar blindness that affects those totally committed to radical change at all costs, a blindness that leads them to crush their opponents in the name of the "freedoms" they alone interpret. Lafayette was certainly an establishment man, willing to break the heads of rioters and to see lynchers hanged, following due process of law. But it upset him most when those who insisted on breaking the rules he regarded as established were people he thought of as reasonable. Their unreason shook his confidence in the future, in the triumph of liberty and the perfectability of man.

For comfort Lafayette turned to Mme de Simiane. "I need to be calmed by your friendship, for I am bored by men almost as much as Mme de Tessé," he wrote to her at the time of the Favras affair, and, a little later, "I have work to do, but I remain in hope that, either on the way to supper or when going home, you will pay a little visit to my door." He went on to talk of the politickings of the clubs before ending, "I will come to see you tomorrow and shall be very happy." The troubles he had convincing the king and queen of his fidelity, while trying to get them to act in a politic manner toward the

Assembly and the commune of Paris, wore him down, as he complained to his mistress:

> You've often preached to me of deference towards the king and queen, but it doesn't matter because such deference is part of my character, since their misfortune [he presumably meant their having to come and live in Paris]. But believe me that they would be better served by a hard man, as would the public good. They are big children who only swallow the medicine that is good for them when one threatens them with bogeymen. Don't think that I am being flippant about governing: we [he doubtless referred to the court and himself] are agreed on all that I shall do on that score. Good-bye until tomorrow at eight. I am delighted by your sentiments, but I feel that for the next six months I shall owe excuses to whoever has the misfortune to love me. Speak of me to all those living and inanimate beings that remind you of those marvelous days I long to see return.

And a little later he poured out his troubles to her – or the troubles of France which he considered his own. She had good reason, he said, to have sympathized with him for having to deal with a council as devious as that of the king. The court was full of mistrust and "aristocratic sentiment," while the ministers uttered tirades and looked after each other's interests, letting the executive power decline. The Assembly was divided into twelve or fifteen parties, and Lafayette himself had to deal with Orléanists, conspirators, unruly patriots, disaffected members of the parlements (which the Assembly had suppressed), counter-revolutionaries, the state of the nation's finances, arguments between the civil and the military powers in Paris, an army uncertain of its future, trouble with plans for the judiciary, thirty thousand workers starving, Necker's notions for the future, Mirabeau and his party with their aristocratic libels. But with all of that he found time to follow Mme de Simiane's orders and attend Easter service with the queen, who appeared pleased by the gesture. He was still deeply involved in plans for a new ministry, but none of his clandestine consultations appeared to offer solutions to the problems that faced the administration. "I think I should occupy myself with the Constitution and with order, independently of the intrigue of the clubs," he told her.

He was a founder-member of the expensive and exclusive Club of 1789, whose other subscribers included Bailly, Mirabeau, Sieyès, and Talleyrand, and which met, ironically, in a sumptuous apartment above the arcades of the Palais-Royal. Any club that contained all those various and warring talents was not one which could hope to enjoy the kind of influence that the Jacobin Club, through the single-mindedness of its commitment, was beginning to wield. Nevertheless, thanks to Mme de Simiane, Lafayette enjoyed at least some moments of calm amid all the troubles he felt personally responsible for solving.

The pamphlet war continued unabated, those who caricatured Lafayette as "General Goldilocks" being attacked by his supporters, who were in turn accused of being paid by the general. The Duc d'Orléans determined to return to Paris from London, despite Lafayette's best efforts to prevent him, and the pros and cons of each side were hotly aired in yet more pamphlets. Lafayette himself, in between trying to prevent lynchings and disturbances, found more time to attend the debates of the Assembly now that it was under his wing. Despite its cumbersome procedure, its "party" divisions, and its time-consuming habit of receiving deputations which often marched through the chamber to receive a presidential embrace, the Assembly had passed some remarkable legislation. With Lafayette's support it had abolished titles and the trappings of nobility altogether: the snobbish Gouverneur Morris complained that he would "have to learn new names for one-half of my acquaintance." It removed from the king the right to declare war and peace – a move to which Lafayette was opposed, on the grounds that the separation of powers, that mystic principle he had learned in America, would thus be endangered. It passed a civil constitution for the clergy which reorganized the church and made its offices elective. And, having passed a decree prohibiting deputies from accepting ministerial posts, it accepted a motion from Lafayette that nobody could hold a command in the national guard in more than one department. The general was sincere in his desire to show that the military power was subordinate to the civil – and he also had no wish to accept an offer to be commandant-general of all the national guards of France. He had enough trouble just dealing with Paris.

He wrote to Washington in the spring of 1790, a happy letter coinciding, perhaps, both with the season and the pleasure afforded him by Mme de Simiane. "Our revolution pursues its course as well as can be expected in a nation which, having received all its liberties at once, is still subject to confusing them with licence," he said. He then gave a frank résumé of the troubles faced by the new order, but concluded optimistically that everything would come right in the end. He sent his "beloved general" not only a picture of the Bastille, but its principal key (he also had one in his own possession, which is still among his things at Lagrange, his last home). Washington replied in encouraging and grateful phrases, encouraging about the state of America as well as the future of France, and emphasized again his own repugnance for high political office. The correspondence that took place between the American president and Gouverneur Morris, a little earlier in the year, showed that Washington actually thought France was in bad shape, a view which Morris of course shared. But neither of them wanted to disappoint Lafayette by telling him so (not even Morris, who was more willing to be frank). Washington certainly treated his protégé like an indulgent parent, praising him for his efforts and withholding criticism for fear of causing a fit of gloom.

One way of counteracting the gloom and disarray that Morris wrote of was by mounting a mighty demonstration of national unity. Circuses are always considered an excellent diversion for an excited populace, especially if bread is in short supply. Marches and displays of military might are much cheaper than war, which is the traditional method of pulling the nation together (and which was suggested by Morris as the way to solve France's economic problems as well as her social ones). It was, in fact, Lafayette who came up with the idea of turning the first anniversary of the fall of the Bastille into a festival of federation, and it grew out of the mushrooming affiliations of provincial formations of the national guard to that of Paris. What started as a celebration of the unity of the volunteer militia became an ambitious demonstration of the law and order of the new regime. The provinces were to demonstrate their alliance as one nation (rather like the confederation of American states), the guard were to swear their loyalty to the civil power, and the king was to take an oath of fidelity to the Constitution (which still wasn't finished). The priorities Lafayette had in mind show in the terms of the original oath, which contained injunctions to "protect in particular private property, the free circulation of food, the collection of taxes, and to remain joined to all the French by the indissoluble ties of brotherhood."

Lafayette was put in charge of all arrangements, and he was also to swear the oath in the name of all guardsmen and soldiers. The oath was to be taken in the Champ de Mars, a mighty space that had to be cleared, equipped with triumphal arches and an "altar of the fatherland," as well as with seats for dignitaries and stands for over 300,000 spectators. When it seemed as if the work might not be completed by July 14th, volunteers crammed the place, and the most hardened cynics appeared amazed at their dedication. Singing the "Ça ira," whose chorus ("It will come") promised the dawn of liberty and the destruction of tyranny, men and women from all classes toiled side by side in a sea of mud, the labor, according to one of the official pamphlets describing the occasion, transforming ordinary humans into saints who never argued or stole each other's goods, and who worked until they dropped. Lafayette, of course, came to put in a few hours' spade-work, but he must have been hampered by crowds of admirers who surrounded him and insisted on shaking his hand.

The deputations from the provinces began to arrive well before the event: the early ones, doubtless amazed by their first sight of the capital, were received with great enthusiasm, but the novelty wore off, and the Parisians soon abandoned themselves to the usual complaints of the metropolitan besieged by tourists: where were they all to sleep? who was to feed them? why were prices shooting up? was this a festival for decent citizens or for thieves, vagabonds, and prostitutes? The commune kept putting out declarations designed to reassure everyone, and strict police measures were announced to control traffic, pickpockets, and the like. But no one believed they would work.

On July 12th, Lafayette, at the head of a deputation from all the guards of France, addressed the Assembly. He demanded that they give the nation a Constitution, "which would grant it that repose that cannot exist without a firm and complete organization of government." In reply, the president defined the function of the guards as keeping "a permanent watch over the safety of people and goods, that is, to give every citizen that security without which there is no happiness, to protect everywhere the free circulation of food, thus preventing inequality of prices . . . and finally to assure the collection of public taxes, thus maintaining the national treasure . . ."

The following day the king reviewed the guards' deputies, under Lafayette's command, in the pouring rain. On the great day itself, July 14th, the weather was also appalling: a cold wind, and heavy showers five of which were so notable between 7 A.M. and noon that they were christened by the egalitarian wits "an aristocratic storm in five acts." But it had not deterred people from spending all night at the Champ de Mars, dancing and fighting mock battles around fires. The only trouble that occurred among this genial crowd was when they discovered that some city officials had given their friends and neighbors tickets to the covered parts of the stands. In a revolution it is still useful to know the right people.

The provincial guardsmen and soldiers assembled at 6 A.M. Many of them were wet and hungry: sympathetic citizens rained gifts of bread, meat, wine, and eau-de-vie down on them from their windows, so that some at least must have arrived at the stadium in proper celebratory mood. It was half-past three in the afternoon before everyone from the king downward was in place and the ceremony could begin, with a mass celebrated by the bishop of Autun, Talleyrand. When he had finished, in a "hushed and religious silence" appropriate to what can only be described as this religification of the revolution, Lafayette mounted the altar of the fatherland, and took the oath of fidelity to "nation, law, and king." Fifty thousand guards and soldiers shouted in one voice "I so swear," which might almost have drowned the constant roar of cannon and guns, the rolling of more than three hundred drums, and the ringing of church bells throughout France.

Lafayette was followed by the president of the Assembly, and after that the king, who spoiled matters a little by allowing the weather to deter him from taking his oath at the altar, in full view of his subjects. Instead he took it from the covered stand where he was sitting, so that few saw him. Lafayette was asked if he couldn't persuade the king to take it again, at the altar, to which he is supposed to have replied, "My children, an oath is not an aria; one can't simply give an encore." The jolly mood of the crowd was not, however, dissipated, and the ceremonies continued until 6 P.M., when the dignitaries returned to the center of the city for a formal dinner, and the guards had a spread laid out for them in the park surrounding the Champ de Mars (which must have been somewhat damp). Three hundred and fifty thousand people, according to the official estimate, then celebrated in the Champ de Mars – which was renamed the Champ de la Fédération – and returned, happy and in good order, to a city whose splendid illuminations had unfortunately been put out by the rain. The only mishaps occurred among the soldiers firing off ceremonial salutes: one gunner was careless enough to get himself killed.

The day was also celebrated by the Society for the Revolution in London, and by students at the University of Cambridge. In Paris, where shopkeepers and hoteliers never take these things lightly, the jollifications went on for a week.

A parade of unity, however impressive, is still only a show, and while Lafayette set great store by the swearing of solemn oaths, for others the perfectly genuine euphoria aroused by the moving ceremonies of July 14, 1790, quickly evaporated. Lafayette had now been in power for a year, and the attacks on him increased. One powerful source was the Jacobin Club, which might well have helped finance pamphlets from the anonymous hands of "A good citizen," which accused the general of anything from enriching his aides to paying an army of spies, from suppressing the freedom of the press to wining and dining "the capitalists" – who were certainly often at his table, and who were the mainstay of his hopes for a businesslike government. Lafayette did zealously enforce orders against "seditious writings": his argument was that "freedom" did not mean freedom to spread lies, that those writers "whose sole object is to nourish the support of the people for liberty and the Constitution, to instruct them in their duties and enlighten them as to their rights" deserved the "recognition of the entire nation," but that "those writers whose only fault is their desire to write" should be ignored, for "the absurdity of their politics and principles is the strongest weapon one could use against them." But he never personally initiated proceedings against those who attacked him, and he was in many respects more tolerant than his critics.

His pride and joy, the national guard of Paris, also came under pamphlet attack, anonymously but with some force. It was criticized for being a military force, bound by army discipline, blind obedience, and orders delivered in secret, instead of merely being "citizens guarding one another." "A citizen should not be like a soldier," one pamphlet maintained. "He is not the blind executor of his general's will, but the enlightened minister of law. He should never ignore the reason for an action, the order he is to carry out, or the power from which that order comes." And since "publicity is the safeguard of the people," why should orders be kept so secret when they should be known to everyone? "I don't believe that our enemies are multiplying as we are so often told. There are discontented people, not enemies. War is preached at us, when we need peace. . . . It is not men that are wicked, but laws that are bad." And to end this telling attack on the strong dose of order Lafayette was intent on administering to the people of Paris, the writer concluded, "We need zeal, patriotism, and honesty, not moustaches and bonnets" – sentiments with which even Lafayette might agree.

But it is too easy to caricature him merely as a sort of crude policeman. Seen from his point of view, every one of the revolution's achievements, which he applauded, presented him with a series of crises with which he had to cope. He had pledged himself to respect the Constitution, the completion of which depended on the Assembly, whose debates he had no time to influence and whose party divisions he deplored. The revolution was given shape and form by the politicians, and he had proclaimed himself their servant and guardian, not their master. He tried to ensure their decisions were carried out in tranquillity, but the people, when they felt ignored by the politicians, insisted on noisily expressing their feelings. Lafayette's position was curious, and at times most uncomfortable: he was like a bolster used to keep a passionate but as yet unmarried couple apart. As long as he appeared their only safeguard against counter-revolution, both sides, the Assembly and the people, tolerated him; in their virtuous moments they even extolled him. But when they desperately wanted to get at each other, he was only in the way.

There was another reason why his position was difficult: he was an *elected* general who depended on the good will of those he was trying to keep in order. He had, it is true, an enormous reputation, but because he had *contributed* to great events rather than creating them, his fame was the more easily tarnished. He also lacked the patriarchal self-sufficiency possessed by someone of Washington's stature. In the end Lafayette lacked real power, partly because of his personality, and partly because of the nature of the role in which he had cast himself – the referee, the general who could be dismissed by his troops, the armed civil servant rather than the legislator. It is understandable why, dealing with the revolution in the streets daily, he remembers the battles rather than the peace. He was a soldier, like his ancestors before him, and it is to be expected that a soldier's memoirs should have an air of embattled glory about them.

In the year between the first and second anniversaries of the fall of the Bastille, Lafayette progressed from being the living symbol of national unity, the very watchdog of the revolution (for moderate men, at least), to being the villain of the people of Paris and principal enemy of the royal court. He himself saw this as the sad but natural consequence of simply doing his duty, which is no excuse. But it is fair to say that his actions over this period were entirely consistent with what he had done before. Perhaps that was his trouble: everyone else move on, leaving him as guardian of nothing but obsolete values. He was the only one to stand by his own promises, and they became irrelevant.

The soldiers of Nancy put the promises of the revolution to the test in the summer of 1790. A decree of the Assembly authorized regiments to settle their financial accounts and pay their soldiers their due, but the officers of the king's regiment at Nancy refused to do this. According to a pamphlet sympathetic to the troops, the officers even hired brigands to scatter the committee elected by the soldiers to organize settlement. When they demanded what they were owed, their commander wrote to the minister of war, La Tour du Pin, claiming that the men were in revolt, that they had pillaged the regimental cash, and that they were insisting on naming their own officers (a principle Lafayette supported, but only for the national guard). As it happened the Nancy soldiers had been among the first, in July 1789, to assure the nation that they would disobey orders to fire on the people. But the Assembly, following the demands of La Tour du Pin, decreed that troops in the royal service were to act solely as instruments without a will or their own, and that the "rebels" were to be crushed with all the rigor of the old regime. That Nancy was not far from the French frontier, and that paid soldiers were more dangerous than volunteer militiamen, had much to do with their decision.

The Marquis de Bouillé, Lafayette's elderly relative, was put in charge of suppressing the "mutiny." He called out the local guard and marched in "loyal" troops. After a bloody encounter in which many of Bouillé's guardsmen and even more mutineers were killed, the result was a crushing victory for the Assembly's forces.

The Nancy affair was one of those trials of the revolutionary temper of the new regime such as Washington faced during the mutiny of the Pennsylvania Line. Can justice be allowed to interfere with security? Must soldiers put discipline above principle; if not, must they be taught discipline at bayonet-point? Washington and Lafayette thought so, and Lafayette strongly endorsed not only the Assembly's stand, but Bouillé's ruthless actions. He wrote him a series of cordial letters, which claimed that their disagreement on principles did not interfere with their agreement on the harsh but exemplary practice necessary to preserve unity (when Bouillé came to write his own memoirs he was not so kind to Lafayette). But the Assembly's action, and Lafayette's support of it, was bitterly attacked in Paris and elsewhere. It was said that the mutineers had been tricked, deliberately provoked, lied to, and obstructed; that the whole thing was one of those exercises in which somebody had to be made an example of to discourage others. Lafayette, it was recalled, had voted for the suppression of a similar "revolt" that had taken place, on a smaller scale, in Marseilles. He replied to his critics by ordering the national guard in Paris to celebrate, on the Champ de la Fédération, a funeral service in memory of "their brothers killed at Nancy in defense of the law" (September 20, 1790). To the accompaniment of muted trumpets, and with standards wreathed in crêpe, Lafayette harangued the guard, as well as deputations from the Paris commune, headed by Bailly, and from the Assembly, on the glory of having avoided civil war, and of having shed their blood to defend the Constitution. (There was no mention of the mutineers' "sacred right of insurrection.") The contrast with the July celebrations on the same spot must have struck Lafayette forcibly. The guard and their cannon subsequently had to be called out to put down demonstrations against the administration. The Nancy affair even contributed to the resignation of the king's ministers: although their failure to cure inflation was the chief cause, the "massacre of patriots" at Nancy lived long as one of the chief indictments of the authorities.

The growing strain between Lafayette and the people of Paris was no less than the strain between Lafayette and the court. This was greatly aggravated by the "Day of the Daggers" (February 28, 1791), a day that started badly for the general. Some demonstrators attempted to demolish an old prison at Vincennes, and the detachment of guards sent to restore order, under the command of the brewer Santerre, was unhappy at having to arrest friends and neighbors for doing something which, in the case of the Bastille, had been hailed as an achievement deserving of the highest honor. But times had changed, and the new order was intent on preserving property, whatever its merits. Lafayette sent an aide with orders to be firm; the guards protested. They nearly manhandled him, but he was saved by the intervention of Santerre. When Lafayette himself charge up on his horse, he worked himself into a fine rage. He threatened to run through with his sword any guardsman who deserted his post, and when they submissively formed ranks he ordered them to arrest the "rioters." When order had been restored, and sixty prisoners taken, Lafayette then turned on Santerre and accused him of firing on his aide. Santerre indignantly denied it, saying that on the contrary he had risked his own life to save that of his fellow-officer, but Lafayette, sticking by his staff, high-handedly professed not to believe him. This upset Santerre's men even further. Then the general determined on a further show of force, ordered the guard to fix bayonets, and decided, despite advice to the contrary, to take the prisoners through their own Faubourg. The effect on the district of seeing their neighbors being frog-marched through the streets in the middle of a strong military column of cavalry and cannon was hardly to endear Lafayette to the spectators. They demonstrated their feelings by turning up in their hundreds to support Santerre at the trial which took place later.

Lafayette returned to the center of the city in an extremely bad mood, only to hear rumors of the royal apartments being filled with armed supporters of the king. What had apparently happened was that the national guardsmen on duty at the palace, perhaps out of boredom, perhaps to show just who was boss, stopped a few of the aristocrats who were leaving the royal apartments, took away their arms, and roughed them up a little. Those who got back inside alarmed all those around the king, while rumors and counter-rumors ran riot outside. Some royalists, hearing that an armed crowd of Parisians was marching on the palace, came rushing to the defense of the monarch; some citizens assumed that another attempt to spirit the king away from them was about to take place. The poor king pleaded for the greatest moderation, and asked all those present to deposit their arms with him and to leave quietly. Most of them tried to do so, and had to run a gauntlet of blows and insults from the guardsmen and citizens assembled.

Lafayette arrived at a quarter to eleven at night, by which time the palace was calm. He showed his temper by complaining "loudly and haughtily" that there were many in the château who should not have been there, and that the agreement that had been made between the king and commune as to the nature and number of those permitted to visit His Majesty had been breached. When an unfortunate gentleman of the bedchamber said this was not so, Lafayette turned on him. How could the guards on duty, he said, be expected to recognize people he contemptuously called "that type"? If they were good citizens, why hadn't they enrolled in the national guard (which Lafayette obviously regarded as the party badge of the patriot)? When the courtier ventured to reply that many of those present came from families whom Lafayette knew personally, he reportedly said, "It is precisely because I know them that I have no confidence in them, and will not allow them here." Those present were then roughly dismissed, and their arms, daggers and pistols, were ordered to be taken away. (In fact their arms later disappeared, perhaps as souvenirs, perhaps to be sold by those who got their hands on them.) Many of those arrested remained in jail for some days without being charged, and were then released for lack of evidence. "Agitators" of the lower orders weren't the only ones to suffer from the occasionally rough temper of revolutionary justice. And the worst opinions of "the people" held by aristocrats could only have been confirmed when the royal apartments and royalist clubs were surrounded by jeering crowds who occasionally daubed their entrances with excrement.

It was rare for Lafayette to lose his temper, and it was a sign of his frayed nerves that he twice that day resorted to bluster and bullying. Obviously it was the crack in the solidarity of the guard that upset him, the evidence that his personal popularity was not eternal. Certainly day after day of dealing with crises of that nature took their toll, and given his need of admiration, Lafayette was likely to over-react when he felt his dignity to be at stake. On the "Day of the Daggers" his over-reaction paid off, though at a great price to his popularity; his next major attempt to awe a crowd into doing his bidding did not work at all.

The civil constitution of the clergy that had been passed by the Assembly the previous year (July 1790) included the provision that every priest should swear an oath of loyalty to the nation and the Constitution – the same oath that Lafayette had sworn on behalf of all the national guards at the Champ de Mars. Hundreds of priests and all the bishops except four refused, on the grounds that their loyalties were to a higher power. In the spring of 1791 the Pope supported their refusal by condemning the whole of the civil constitution. Nevertheless there was no shortage of priests prepared to take the oath – and certainly no shortage of those who wanted to be "constitutional" bishops. But although those who refused to swear loyalty – known as non-juring priests – were not supposed to have care of souls, their spiritual authority to celebrate mass could not be stripped from them. Religious toleration was one of the provisions of the Declaration of Rights, and it was one Lafayette strongly supported. When Adrienne, who clung to the old ways, sought out non-juring priests to hear mass from them, Lafayette did nothing to prevent her despite the adverse publicity this caused him. When she was conspicuously absent from their table at a dinner in honor of the constitutional bishop of Paris, he understood. And when the king expressed the wish to go to St-Cloud to celebrate Easter

Monday, 1791, with a non-juring priest, Lafayette did his utmost to see that his wish was granted.

The king was acting perfectly within his rights, although this was hardly likely to endear him to his subjects. On Easter Sunday he had mass said by a non-juring priest in the Tuileries chapel, and despite the attendance of both Lafayette and Bailly, the general had to harangue the guards before they agreed to perform their ceremonial duties. The following day everyone knew the royal family wanted to go to St-Cloud. When they got into their carriage, which was provided with a strong detachment of cavalry, an enormous crowd gathered and prevented them from leaving. Those surrounding the king were insulted and attacked, which upset the monarch no less than the jeers made at the queen. Bailly arrived, then Lafayette. But this time the guards refused to listen to him. According to one account they would not accept the distribution of arms to restore order, and when their general spoke of proclaiming martial law, they insulted him. Worse, when he threatened to resign, they jeered and whistled.

For two hours Lafayette tried to persuade his guards to obey. He failed ignominiously, and the royal family were forced to get out of their carriage and return to the Tuileries, where they effectively became prisoners. Their fate only made the queen plot harder to escape, and she, as the royal ministers well knew, could persuade the king to do anything. Lafayette, exhausted and shattered, blamed the "stupidities" of the court and his old standby, the "factions." He still defended the king's right to go, and urged him to demand the Assembly's support, to prove he was "a free man." The king balked at this. The fact remained that the national guard of Paris had rejected, in front of their sovereign, the orders of their general. Lafayette therefore resigned. He nevertheless found time to scribble a note to Mme de Simiane, which ended "My day has been very distressing and a little dangerous. I can at least end it pleasantly by talking of my love for you."

One person who was delighted by Lafayette's resignation was his wife, who feared constantly for his safety, and now hoped he would return quietly to private life, as he had so often said he would. Lafayette himself, maintaining that the reason he had resigned was that the king refused to persist in exercising his rights, abandoned his house to hide from those who might urge him to stay. Adrienne was left to receive "loyal" deputations of the guard, who arrived with flags and drums beating, frightening everyone in the district. Certainly his decision caused uproar and demonstrations in his favor, mostly from the battalions of the national guard. While the new regime was by no means as popular as it had been, no one had any alternative to propose that would command majority support.

Lafayette's opponents saw in his resignation a move to carry him further, on a wave of public support, along the road to military dictatorship. But in fact this was the last thing he wanted. He had several times been offered posts that would have set him on the road to such power and had always refused. It was not his style at all. I think he was tired of trying to persuade everybody to act according to the rules – and that he was personally humiliated, in front of his king and the people of Paris, by the refusal of the guard to obey him. On top of that the king refused to take the one course that would have given Lafayette a second chance to pit his strength against "the factions": had Louis gone to the Assembly and demanded his rights, they could scarcely have denied him, and the general could doubtless have arranged for an overwhelming military force to guarantee the royal passage. But the king had no taste for confrontation, which left Lafayette in an exposed position. In his eyes, resignation was the only honorable course. But why, if he was – as he so often complained – the subject of attack from all sides, was there instantly a loud clamor for his return?

The clamor was led by Mayor Bailly and the administration of the commune of Paris, who were totally reliant on the guard not only for their own safety, but to see their decrees carried out. Lafayette was the creator of the guard, and there was no one to challenge his reputation or authority. Moreover they had all worked together for nearly two years, and since politics is a club like any other, they naturally preferred someone they knew.

Information on the composition of the guard itself is almost impossible to obtain, for few of the lists of their occupations have survived. We do know that Lafayette and the commune were anxious to recruit the bourgeois citizens to its ranks, those with a vested interest in maintaining order; and we know from complaining pamphlets that the militia elections were subject to all the abuses of the old regime, and that the privileges of wealth and influence remained relatively unscathed. Perhaps we may assume from this that those in charge of the battalions of the guard at this time shared the same sentiments as the administrators of the capital. And we must not ignore the sentimental attachment soldiers have for their commanding officer, when his reputation adds luster to theirs – and especially when he has left them.

Then there is the apathy of the rest of Paris. Those sections of the city who had come to see the guard merely as the old law-and-order boys in new uniforms could not have cared much who commanded them. Those who had listened to the rhetoric of the revolution and compared it to the reality had little faith, by now, in king, Assembly, or commune, let alone the commandant-general. But for them there was no organization, except perhaps the Jacobin Club, that presented a possible alternative to the present regime. They were not yet made part of the political process: soon they would be used, and exploited, by the Jacobins and others, but now they were excluded, kept down, and hence indifferent. Lafayette was as bad or as good as any other for them. And his power was only that of a super-policeman. Now police chiefs may sound pretty dreadful but, except in cases of military coups, they serve the politicians. To those in Paris, and the rest of France, who were always at the wrong end of the system, who always had somebody else's law and order pushed on them, it didn't matter what uniform the bully-boys wore, or what their chief said and did: it was all the same.

If, then, those who begged Lafayette to reconsider, who besieged his house all night, if they represented the bourgeoisie, the perennial administrators, they were successful. He did stay, on condition that the national guard swear to uphold the law. They did more: they resolved to punish and expel from the guard those who had "outraged the royal family." Lafayette thanked them from the bottom of "a heart whose first need, after that of serving the people, is to be loved, and which is astonished at the importance that one has been good enough to attach to an individual, in a free country where the only thing that matters is the law." When he returned to his office in the City Hall, a huge crowd waited with music and flowers. He couldn't enter before some 1500 women and 500 guards had personally kissed him. The only cloud on his horizon appeared to be a row with Mme de Simiane about his beliefs, for he wrote (in May) an anguished letter proclaiming devotion to the revolution "to the last breath; but all its charms are poisoned by the effect it produces on those dearest to my heart." Nevertheless, as he wrote to Washington, despite all his troubles, "we go forward." He spoke of strengthening and disciplining the army, of suppressing "licence" in favor of "liberty." A few weeks earlier he had written to his "father" that he hoped to take up "the quiet life of a simple citizen" within four months. He was sure that, despite the "factions," despite the threat from the émigrés (departed nobles) to invade France with foreign troops, the Assembly would finish the Constitution and give way to a new legislative body. Once the king sanctioned the document cementing the revolution, Lafayette felt his work would be over. Law and order would be enshrined in statute, doing away with the need for him to beat it into people's heads. Everything that he felt the revolution to be about – the Declaration of Rights, sanctity of property, religious toleration, separation of powers: the American system, in other words, with the king at its head – would be achieved. But Lafayette had too much faith in written documents and sworn oaths of loyalty, and not enough understanding of the trickery of men. The person who deceived him most cruelly was the one who commanded most of his loyalty: Louis XVI, king of the French.

14
Against Paris

THE CREDIBILITY OF the new regime was breaking down. Rumors of plots and counter-plots, rumors that were as dangerous, and certainly as infectious, as smallpox, rumors that had enough truth in them to make people believe them, steadily undermined the ability of the authorities to show they could cope.

To some, of course, these alarms were a welcome diversion from everyday boredom. To the politicians in the Assembly and the clubs, instead of being a warning sign of their growing irrelevance, the alarms sent them scurrying to wrap themselves in the protective muffler of endless debate – except the Jacobins, who began to preach more violent opposition to the administration. To Lafayette, the alarms were something to be borne stoically.

The alarms centered on the king, or rather the queen and her circle. It was said that a royalist rising was being planned in which all good patriots were to be massacred; that the troops of the foreign monarchies were going to invade the country and crush the revolutionary regime; that the queen wanted to flee; that the king might be unwillingly abducted. And all these stories were more or less true. The queen was planning flight, and the king went along with her. Indeed, there seemed to be no other possibility open. They could count on military aid from the royal courts of Europe, as well as from their own *émigrés* (aristocrats who had left France to fight the régime from outside). If their flight were successful, the royal family did contemplate an invasion of France, headed by foreign soldiers. And if that worked, given the expected state of chaos and turmoil their escape would cause, the court could revenge itself on all its enemies at once. First on the royal list was, of course, Lafayette.

Lafayette's popularity had been strengthened by the withdrawal of his resignation under public pressure. Of those on whose good opinion he relied, the one who cared most was Adrienne, who continued to worry about his safety. In fact he was looking forward to the completion of the Constitution, which would enable him to retire. Once the renewed enthusiasm for his leadership had worn off, it was back to the same old grind of dealing with the outbursts of a volatile and vociferous people. He was bored with that.

He was also in the impossible position of being personally responsible for the safety and welfare of both king and Assembly, neither of whom exactly showed unbounded gratitude. Lafayette had pledged his loyalty a dozen times, and to allay the fears of the Parisians that something would happen to the king, he had even given his personal guarantee that the royal family would stay safely in the Tuileries. The king had also given his word to stay put, and Lafayette was almost embarrassed by the precautions he was forced to take to keep the family under surveillance. He was careful to grant them all that they wanted, within reason, for he did not want it to appear that the king was a prisoner. That would have been a denial of the very principle of liberty. Louis had also written to the courts of Europe assuring them that he was free, and that he had freely assented to those parts of the Constitution that had been passed by the Assembly. Lafayette just wanted the Constitution completed so that there could be a return to ordered government. If everyone had played the parts he wanted them to play, it is quite possible that the revolution would indeed have ended with the Constitution's acceptance. Napoleon himself is reported to have said, "If I had been in Lafayette's place, the king would still be sitting on his throne."

Lafayette's view was that it was essential to maintain confidence in the king, the very cornerstone of government. It wasn't a question of absolute confidence, for he had seen too much of the court, and suffered the queen's hostility for too long, for that. But the whole of French tradition, and the feeling of the majority of the French people, was for the monarchy and the king appeared willing to cooperate in becoming a constitutional monarch. What alternative was there?

On the night of June 20, 1791, the general attended the king's retiring to bed (*coucher*), a ceremonial occasion played according to the traditional rules of etiquette. The ceremony passed off normally, and Lafayette went home satisfied that the daily ration of rumor was as usual false. He was woken early the following morning by a member of the Assembly with news that the royal family had fled in the night, to the amazement even of the king's personal valet who had slept undisturbed. The people of Paris, when they recovered from the shock of seeing what they forever gossiped about actually come true, were furious. Signs bearing the royal arms were blacked out, and there was open talk of a republic. More serious, there were justifiable fears of foreign invasion, or of bloody faction-fighting if the royalists moved against the regime.

Lafayette himself was horrified and humiliated. Had he not given his word that the king would not flee? No one had certain news; no one even knew what could be done. Can the king be arrested, constitutionally speaking? Lafayette went to Bailly and the president of the Assembly and formally asked whether they considered an arrest necessary for public safety, as the only way to avoid civil war. They left him in no doubt of the necessity, for there was, in fact, no other choice. "Well," replied the general, "I shall take the responsibility for so doing myself." And he forthwith wrote notes to all members of the national guard, and all citizens, to do their duty. He took this decision personally, because there was no time to delay while the Assembly got into session, because he was the only person in Paris with an armed force under his personal command, and because his own honor was at stake. But the wording of his note shows that even in this crisis he could not let it be believed that the sovereign would betray his own people. "The enemies of the fatherland have taken away the king and his family" was how he explained it – and it was this formula, later adopted by the Assembly, that saved the monarchy for France, temporarily.

Lafayette could not have believed this formula entirely, for papers were soon found, intended for publication had the flight been successful, in which Louis condemned the Constitution to which he had so recently assented, complained at being a prisoner, and concluded that, in such circumstances, "It is natural that the king should have sought to put himself in a place of safety." But a belief in "plots" on which everything can be blamed is necessary for an uncertain people, for it absolves them from personal responsibility, and draws them together in defense against some unknown and evil "them." It was certainly a belief that Lafayette had long entertained.

National guardsmen were sent all over the country to find the royal family; the borders were sealed; the capital waited in a state of enormous anxiety. Lafayette was surrounded by a jumpy and hostile crowd when he went to the City Hall. He managed to joke with them that "each citizen will gain twenty sous by the suppression of the civil list," but it was really his appearance of calm, and the fact that he remained in their midst without escort, that appeased them. To those who described the flight as a disaster, he wondered what name they would give "to a counter-revolution that would deprive them all of their liberty?" At the same time the Assembly rallied round him, in answer to criticism of his actions: they sent a deputation to ask him to attend their debates, offering to escort him out of concern for his safety. He agreed to attend, but scorned the escort, "never having been so safe, as the streets are full of people."

In front of the Assembly, Lafayette again insisted that agents of the counter-revolution had abducted the king, and again he took personal responsibility for the family's arrest. This was no light matter. If it were a question of rescue, nobody knew what forces of royalist troops might be arrayed against them. And if the king were unwilling to come, if he stood on his rights and privileges, was Lafayette the man to deny him?

The Assembly itself proceeded with honor and firmness, according to Lafayette. The commissioner of the civil list appeared before them with the manifesto that the king had left for publication. He was asked how he had got it, and replied that the king had left it hidden with a letter addressed to him. A deputy asked where the letter was, at which, by Lafayette's account, the whole assembly said, "No, no, it's a confidential letter, and we haven't the right to see it." They then summoned the royal ministers before them and ordered them to continue their functions under the orders of the Assembly. The seal of state, which Louis had foolishly left behind, was placed before the president, who handed it to the minister of justice, its usual custodian. The minister of foreign affairs, Montmorin, a personal friend of the king's, who had, possibly in ignorance of its true purpose, issued the monarch with a false passport in the name of the Baron de Korf for his flight, had a special guard attached to his person, for his own safety. The king's pathetic manifesto, reneging on all his promises, was read. The Assembly issued a proclamation calling for public confidence. The national guard zealously set about maintaining order in the streets: if there were separatist movements in some sections they were suppressed as much by the mood of "togetherness in this crisis" as by force. The Assembly then proceeded with the normal day's business, as if nothing extraordinary had happened. Perhaps that was the most telling sign of where the real political power lay at that moment.

Everything, meanwhile, was going wrong for the king and his family. They were traveling in a big, four-horsed coach, a *berline*, painted brown and yellow, the colors of the Duc de Condé. They were accompanied by a smaller coach carrying two maids, and various accomplices rode with them. They were hardly an inconspicuous sight as they moved slowly through France on the year's longest day, toward Thonelle, a good six hours from the frontier. Bouillé, the relative to whom Lafayette had sent such cordial letters following his suppression of the Nancy uprising, was waiting at Thonelle with royal troops. The king was disguised as a valet, the queen as a governess, the king's aunt as a nursery-maid. Why they thought domestics traveling in so grand a coach would not cause suspicion is a mystery, but there had to be some way of camouflaging the unmistakable Bourbon features.

Once they reached Bouillé and his forces, the king planned to dismiss the Assembly and restore the church to its property. This would have knocked away the political and financial props on which the revolution rested. The royal family would then wait and see what happened, and if nothing did, they would march, at the head of an Austrian army, on Paris – which they assumed would be in no state to resist. Especially if, as they fervently hoped, Lafayette would have fallen as scapegoat for their escape.

There were delays. At Chalons, where they changed horses, they were recognized, but the mayor didn't have the courage to stop them, and only reported their passage six hours later. The advance troops that were supposed to meet them, after having waited only one and a half hours, were ordered to withdraw by their commander, the Duc de Choiseul, who also sent word ahead to Bouillé that the royal party would not arrive that night. When they arrived at Sainte-Menehould, the detachment of dragoons that was supposed to be their escort had unsaddled. Another body of royal troops had arrived the same day without telling the municipality. Alarmed at all these troop movements, the town ordered out the local national guard. While the royal horses were being changed, the postmaster recognized the king from his portrait on the *assignat* (paper currency) with which he was paid for the fresh horses. He did not stop the *berline*, but he stopped the escort following it, and himself rode after the royal fugitives. He was on the road to Clermont with one colleague when he met men who had heard the coach's drivers being ordered to Varennes. By taking a cross-country route, they arrived in the town at a quarter past eleven at night, just ahead of the king. With the help of a local publican, they blocked the bridge at the foot of the hill and armed themselves to arrest their sovereign.

The royal family was stopped, their passports demanded. They allowed themselves to be taken to a room over a grocery, where Louis admitted who he was to a local judge who had been woken to identify him. There were loyal troops within a few hundred yards, but Louis, who dreaded violence and had been traveling for twenty-four hours in great anxiety, refused to issue any orders until, as he expected, Bouillé should turn up. But Bouillé did not arrive. In the early hours of the morning his troops, who could have mounted a successful attack on Varennes, were drinking with the local guard. When Bouillé finally appeared, the royal coach was already on its way back to Paris, accompanied by two deputies sent by the Assembly.

Paris heard nothing for two days, and hourly expected to be attacked by royalist troops. The Jacobin Club got very heated: Lafayette was worried that "anarchists" such as Robespierre and Danton (whom he alleged took money from the court, in a vain attempt by the royal family to buy his silence) would propose "inflammatory motions." Danton actually demanded Lafayette's head, since the general had promised the king's person on it, but the

Left in the Assembly rallied round the flag of moderation. All the generals in Paris swore an oath of loyalty to the nation, followed by Lafayette and representatives of the national guard. Any outbursts of "extremism" were widely condemned and quickly dealt with.

Then came the report that the king had been arrested and was on his way back to the capital. The tension lifted slightly, except that no one quite knew what to do with the prisoner. The extremists of both Left and Right would have been delighted had the king escaped; everyone else, including Lafayette, was embarrassed. The first task was to ensure the security of the royal personages. Both Assembly and the commandant-general, united by this crisis, considered themselves so tricked they had to take the most stringent precautions. Thousands of troops lined the return route, and there were strict orders against outbursts of any sort. The Paris crowd was huge, quiet in the heat of the day, and all wore hats or ribbons as a sign of disrespect for the monarch. The double row of guards held their rifles upside-down, the usual sign of mourning. When the royal carriage finally appeared, there were no cries or insults, only an "ominous hum." When the queen caught sight of Lafayette, presumably to relieve her feelings, she screamed, "Monsieur de Lafayette, save the bodyguards!" But the crowd was not bent on violence. Its mood was alarmingly funereal. The royal family arrived without incident at the Tuileries.

Lafayette presented himself to the king "with pity and respect." "Your Majesty knows my devotion to the crown," he said, "but if it separates itself from the cause of the people, I shall remain on the side of the people." The king replied, "True, you followed your principles: it's a matter of party. Anyway, here I am." He went on to say that he had thought himself hemmed in by a crowd of people of Lafayette's persuasion, whose opinions were not shared by the people of France; but that his journey had proved him wrong, and that public opinion agreed with Lafayette's. "Has Your Majesty any orders to give me?" asked the general. "It seems to me," said the king, laughing, "that I am more at your orders than you are at mine."

Lafayette then read him the Assembly's decree. The king would henceforth be under guard responsible to Lafayette himself, while the dauphin and the queen would have special guards of their own. There was to be an inquiry and interrogation at which the king and queen were to give evidence. The king's sanction of the Assembly's decrees was for the moment suspended.

The king listened to all this without fuss, but the queen became impatient. What appeared to disturb her most was that the boxes containing their personal papers and effects, which were still in the *berline*, might be rifled. She insisted that Lafayette take charge of the keys, and she put them on his hat (which he, of course, had respectfully removed). He replied with dignity that no one would touch the boxes. "Well," said the queen, "I shall find people less delicate than you!" The boxes nevertheless remained untouched. Lafayette's embarrassment at being thought of as a spy on the actions of the royal family was only increased when the king's valet reported to the general that his master had given him some newly written letters. Yet, as always happens to the well-meaning, his royal charges took advantage of him: when he asked the king for a list of those who would be allowed into the royal apartments without challenge, he was presented with an enormous number of names, including many renowned for their anti-revolutionary sentiments. Nevertheless he carried out his distasteful task of guarding the fugitives, his attitude being that "when a harsh measure was capable of two interpretations, he always took the one that was more humane."

Lafayette insisted that the unfortunate monarch had been misled, that he had recognized his mistake and had freely returned to the bosom of his people. The general was at some pains to point out that the king was not a prisoner: the close watch kept on him was supposedly to forestall another kidnapping by his enemies. By this explanation Lafayette and the Assembly allowed themselves to think that, when the king finally sanctioned their Constitution, this would be a meaningful act freely made by the legitimate executive power. They were of course fooling themselves, but they could think of no other way to resolve the constitutional problem. Lafayette, besides, was committed to the hereditary monarchy, and he said he could think of no other king than Louis. The choice was not wide: the Duc d'Orléans was his sworn enemy, the dauphin was so young there would have to be a regent, and the king's brothers had emigrated. The only practical alternative was a presidential republic, and only "extremists," in Lafayette's eyes, wanted that. No, the formula they had been working on since 1789, a constitutional monarchy, could not be allowed to go to waste after so many tribulations. Lafayette pledged himself once more to see it carried out, come what may.

If the king's flight was like a nightmare come true, it was important, once he had been brought back, to make everything seem normal again. The Assembly and the Paris administration had taken the lead with great boldness during the crisis, but the sudden relaxation of tension, as well as their need to keep the initiative, made them hyper-sensitive to criticism from the people of the capital. Some clubs, such as the Cordeliers and the Jacobins, passed motions calling for a republic, which the Jacobin Robespierre conveniently described as "every form of government under which men can enjoy freedom and a fatherland. One may be as free under a king as under a Senate," he prudently continued, staying well within the law, and he concluded that France was "neither a monarchy nor a republic," but both. But these motions were academic: despite the fiction that the king had been abducted, public opinion believed firmly that he was guilty. Whatever he said, and whatever was said by his defenders in the administration, the chief executive no longer enjoyed the trust of his subjects. This did not make them thirst for his head. What it did was to render suspect any system of government in which he played the leading part – including the Constitution that had been so long in the making.

The Assembly nevertheless could not bring itself to start all over again. There were all the articles of the Constitution, each one the result of months of drafting and debate by a body rich in lawyers and, in the two years of its existence, sufficiently bureaucratized to dread upheaval. There was the national guard, apparently ready to suppress, in the name of the revolution, any moves against the unity of the nation, whether in the cities or the provinces. And there was the king, in no position to refuse to do the Assembly's bidding. What better way was there to crown their labors than by finishing the Constitution and declaring the king inviolable, so that, whatever crimes he or his accomplices might commit as personalities – and in future fleeing the country would be considered an abdication of the throne – the crown was safe, and the weighty principle of the separation of powers might at last be put into practice?

Doubtless the main feeling in the Assembly was relief that they had found a way, through Lafayette's formula, to maintain their Constitution intact while keeping the king in their power. Many of them felt the time had come to call a halt to the revolution before public order deteriorated further. The deputies agreed that while, under the principle of royal inviolability, the crown could do no wrong, Louis himself had certainly sinned. But the vast majority of them felt it would be dangerous to depose him. Apart from all that work going for nothing, there was the very real danger of a reprisal attack by the armies of foreign monarchs. And the equally real danger of "anarchy" among their own people. But that was what the guard was there to prevent.

The Parisian bourgeoisie, which made up the ranks of the national guard, were happy with a compromise that would return things to normal. They preferred to turn on those below them rather than those above: there was talk of "teaching the workers a lesson," for apart from everything else much nervous tension had been engendered by the growing number of unemployed in Paris. The public workshops for those out of work, maintained by the commune, were readily believed to provide fodder for counter-revolutionaries; because they were "trouble-centers" the closure of many by the administration (in the summer of· 1791) was widely supported – except by those thrown on the streets and those in work who were prepared to show solidarity. This was at a time when there was a lot of agitation over minimum wage-rates: so alarmed was the Assembly that in June it passed the Loi Le Chapelier, which forbade working men to combine in any way whatever, to petition or to strike, a law which remained on the statute-books through French republics, empires and monarchies until 1884.

The struggle of the artisans, the cause of the unemployed, and the doctrines of republicanism were all taken up by the left-wing clubs, especially the Cordeliers. It is easy to exaggerate the influence of these clubs, because the rhetoric of opposition is usually more interesting than the platitudes of power. There is no denying that Lafayette and the Paris commune regarded them as a fairly serious threat to public order. Equally, there is no denying that they provided the principal voices against the Assembly's declaration of royal inviolability in face of the king's personal guilt. Petitions were supported by street agitation and these increased the fears of bourgeois citizens.

The second anniversary of the fall of the Bastille – and the first of the Fête de la Fédération – was celebrated by a march and a mass. Obviously the authorities had circuses high on their list of popular diversions that month, for, only three days before, the remains of Voltaire had been carried with great pomp and circumstance to join those of Mirabeau (who had died the previous April) in the Panthéon. On July 15th the Assembly declared its renewed confidence in Louis as chief executive. The Cordeliers called, in a petition, for a referendum on the future of the king, which the Assembly refused to accept. Another petition on the same lines was rejected as having been presented too late, for the decrees reinstating the suspended royal powers had been passed. This left the Cordeliers with little to do but demonstrate in protest. Yet they moved cautiously. They agreed to cooperate with the Jacobins in drafting a petition for circulation at the former Champ de Mars on Saturday, July 16th.

This petition called for Louis to abdicate, and for the Assembly to "provide for his replacement by such means as the constitution may allow." Even this moderation – after what Marat and others had been screaming in their papers – was too much for the lawyer Robespierre, and under his influence the Jacobins withdrew their sponsorship of the petition, leaving the risk to the Cordeliers. On Sunday, July 17th, they drafted a fresh petition which wanted a new constituent body to try the king as a criminal, and to "organize a new executive power." This was, perhaps, stronger than the previous day's version, which had not attracted many signatures.

The day had, however, started with a lynching at the Champ de Mars. Two men were found hiding under the altar of the fatherland, and although they claimed they were only there for a good view up the skirts of the ladies who would come to sign the petition, they were hanged. When word of this reached the City Hall, they over-reacted and hung out the red flag of martial law. That martial law had been declared remained unknown for some hours to the crowd in the Champ de Mars, which was a fair way from the center. Their demonstration was gathering strength, and some six thousand people signed the petition. Considering that it was illegal to petition against decrees passed by the Assembly, their signatures may just have been witness to their frustration: protest demonstrations are usually more of a safety-valve than an effective political weapon.

In the evening, some twelve hours after the lynching which had caused the declaration of martial law, when the crowd was drifting home, Lafayette arrived at the Champ de Mars, accompanied by guards on foot and horseback, cannon, and the red flag. He ordered the peaceful crowd to disperse. Some people on the edge threw stones. There were cries of "Down with the red flag." Lafayette claims a gun which failed to go off was fired at him, that the man guilty was brought to him, then released. Certainly more stones were thrown. The guard fired into the air to clear the area. Stones continued to fly, and the guards, or at least the bourgeois volunteers among them rather than paid detachments, apparently could take it no longer. They fired into the crowd, and killed perhaps fifty people. This became known as the Massacre of the Champ de Mars.

At home Adrienne de Lafayette was desperately worried, for her husband's sake. Suddenly her own house was surrounded by people, claiming – if the account of her daughter Virginie, who was eight at the time, is to be believed – to want to cut off her head and parade it before her husband. Virginie tells us that Adrienne cried with joy because this meant that the "brigands" had left the Champ de Mars and that her husband was presumably safe. Her own household was now terrified, the more so when a few people climbed the wall and invaded their garden.

A couple of hundred people were arrested following the demonstration, charged with criticizing the guard – one of them claimed the guard had "fired on the workers as if they were poultry" – or with insulting the commandant-general. If the majority of those who had actually signed the petition were semi-literate, most of those arrested were wage-earners, shopkeepers, craftsmen, or small property-owners: working people in the main, but on their way up – those whom an insecure bourgeoisie might resent most.

Indeed the bourgeoisie rejoiced at the "victory." Gouverneur Morris spoke for many when he wrote, "This affair will, I think, lay the foundation of tranquillity, although perhaps a more serious affair is necessary to restrain this abominable populace." The red flag of martial law flew for three weeks, during which papers in opposition to the administration were suppressed, many of their editors proscribed, and Marat, among others, taken to prison. Bailly and the Assembly were infuriatingly smug about the "massacre." It was the first time unarmed citizens in a large demonstration had been killed by their brethren in the capital. The minister of justice urged prosecution of those arrested to save "the state and the Constitution from the attacks mounted on it by a mob of rebels, whose only objects were murder, pillage, disorder, and anarchy, which they called liberty." Those were terms Lafayette would have approved. Even the queen wrote of her "pleasure" at the "courage" shown in upholding the monarchy.

What the affair did to Lafayette was to destroy his credibility in the eyes of that generation of working people. He himself agreed with Bailly that it had been necessary to fire on "the rebels" in order to "safeguard the law." But it is always easy for the authorities to invent a pretext for disallowing a protest demonstration: in this case, they used the lynching and the fact that it was "unconstitutional" to petition against the decrees of the Assembly. But there was no excuse for allowing the guard to fire on a crowd that could have easily been dispersed without bloodshed – a crowd that was in the process of leaving the Champ de Mars anyway, the sort of gathering that the guard were used to handling every day. Theirs was by no means the kind of threat to "order" that "the rebels of Nancy" had been, for the latter had been armed soldiers in a garrison town. The worst sin of the crowd in the Champ de Mars was that they were protesting against the constitutional arrangements made by the Assembly with regard to the king, whom many, now that the shock of his flight had worn off, regarded as a traitor. The way the Assembly hurried through their decisions, cutting off all forms of protest was, to those outside the legislative process, an outrage. This is not to talk in terms of a "mass movement" against the elected representatives of the nation, but of the furious reaction of several thousand Parisians. Nevertheless the over-reaction on the part of the city authorities seemed to have a class air about it. Lafayette, perhaps, had saved the Constitution for its authors and their supporters – but at the price of the support, or at least the indifference, of those who were allowed no stake in the new order. This is what enabled the Jacobins and their friends to count on and organize working people's support in sufficient strength to overturn the bourgeois administration. And it nearly destroyed Lafayette.

The Assembly rushed through the remainder of the Constitution. They tried to ensure that their labors could not be altered for a long time ahead, and they so fixed the franchise that only owners of property could vote for deputies, bishops, judges, and top administrators. On September 14, 1791, the king accepted the Constitution and swore loyalty to it. On the 18th his acceptance was proclaimed from the City Hall, and public celebrations took place at Notre-Dame and the Champ de Mars, while there was a balloon ascent – festooned in tricolor ribbon – on the Champs-Elysées.

Lafayette next proposed in the Assembly that an amnesty be granted to all those arrested for offenses connected with the revolution. This included those arrested after the "massacre" of the Champ de Mars and also, as he himself noted, "many truly guilty enemies of the revolution." But it also released a large number of people arrested on obscure charges and many victims of party revenge. The Assembly enthusiastically endorsed Lafayette's motion, and on September 30th it met for the last time. In Lafayette's view it had failed to profit from the example of the United States, especially in not adopting a bi-cameral legislature. He also thought it had erred with regard to the church, the judiciary, and in passing a self-denying ordinance which meant that those who had, over the protests of some Parisians, pushed the Constitution into being would not have the responsibility of carrying out its provisions. On the other hand it had destroyed feudalism, the titles and most of the privileges of the nobility; it had passed the Declaration of Rights; and it had shifted the balance of power from those whose only claim to rule was their title to those prepared to submit themselves to election (albeit by their peers). These were without question redoubtable achievements. The chief fault of the Assembly – a natural one in the circumstances – was to regard its work as the end of the revolution.

In keeping with his promises to himself, his family, and the people of Paris, Lafayette resigned his post as commandant-general of the Paris national guard and determined to return to his native province in the Auvergne. His job was finished, for the Constitution was not only accepted by the king but by all sections of the kingdom. As he told the guard in his farewell speech, "The days of the revolution have given way to a regular organization, to that of liberty, and the prosperity which it guarantees." He praised the guard for their vigilance, and warned them to take care for the future. He went through all the freedoms that it was their duty to preserve, and he concluded his speech – an impeccable example of liberal rhetoric – with the injunction to "live free or to die!" The guard voted him a sword forged from the bolts of the Bastille, the municipality a medal and marble statue of Washington. He made a triumphal exit from the capital, a triumph which continued all the way home. As he wrote to Mme de Simiane he was "forced to stop everywhere, to walk through towns and villages on foot, to receive enough civic crowns to fill the coach." Clermont was lit up for him, and he was accompanied from the town by the local national guard.

On the way he and Adrienne stayed with her sister Pauline de

Montagu, who, being forbidden by her father-in-law to receive Lafayette – whom he hated for his "radical principles" – had to take temporary residence in a small roadside inn. The Constitution had not brought peace to every family. Pauline wrote from the inn to her father the Duc d'Ayen that Lafayette intended to live in the greatest simplicity. "Not one single secretary has he brought with him to the country. He will install his library and his furniture. Books, Swiss cows, Spanish sheep, and a Maltese donkey will be his sole preoccupations. Those in which he has been involved over the last twenty-seven months have properly exhausted him."

Gouverneur Morris noted, in his tart way, that Lafayette's "sun seems to be set, unless he should put himself at the head of the republican party, who at present are much opposed to him. All this results from feebleness of character and the spirit of intrigue which bring forward the courtier, but ruin the statesman. I am very sorry for him, because I believe he meant well." A few months later Lafayette complained to Washington about Morris's aristocratical and counter-revolutionary principles, when the latter was designated U.S. minister to France. Yet it might have seemed to many that Lafayette's sun had indeed set. His name was put forward as successor to Bailly as mayor of Paris, but, though he did not himself canvass, he was badly beaten in the election by Jérôme Pétion. Instead, he professed himself delighted with the simple country life. His sixty-two-year-old aunt, who had brought him up, was still living at Chavaniac, and Adrienne's mother also joined them. Adrienne, for once, had a few weeks of absolute contentment, with the people who meant most to her – her mother, her husband, and her children – all in attendance.

The ripples of the revolution reached even their rustic retreat. The old clergy who had refused to take the civic oath of loyalty to the Constitution threatened eternal damnation to those who subscribed to the doctrines of liberty so dear to Lafayette – yet he saw to their welfare, in the name of religious toleration. "I cannot tell you with what delight I bow before a village mayor," he wrote to Mme de Simiane, joking about his devotion to equality. There was calm enough to enable him to put on some weight.

He imported an English agricultural expert to teach him better methods of farming, which naturally astonished the locals; and he hired a fashionable and expensive architect, Vaudoyer, to redo the château, which doubtless upset his aunt. But if he was going to stick by his promise and remain in retirement it was only fitting that he should leave his mark on the birthplace he had scarcely visited since leaving France for America. The result of Vandoyer's work is garish and out of scale with what was a modest country château. In fact Lafayette hardly stayed long enough to notice. He had not yet acquired the thick skin nor the inner reserves to bear self-imposed retirement, especially when his reputation came under fierce attack in the Paris papers. Well might he write to his mistress: "Those who believe I've come here to make a revolution are great fools. I get as much pleasure and possibly self-esteem in complete rest as I did from fifteen years of action which, always in the same cause and crowned by success, now leaves me with nothing but the role of a laborer." But that was two days after he'd arrived. Once his batteries were recharged, he longed for another role to play, if only that of seeing fair play between the warring elements of the constitutional power. He was, after all, only thirty-four years old.

One way in which the new Assembly and royal government could deal with the discontent and divisiveness that its predecessors had tried, and failed, to suppress, was to unite the nation around a common threat: that of war. Certainly the threat existed. There were the *émigrés* gathered at Coblentz declaring their aim to restore the king and the church. There was the Declaration of Pillnitz by the Austrian emperor Leopold and the king of Prussia (August 1791), which threatened intervention in ambiguous terms, but which could easily be interpreted as a war-like gesture. It was decided to mobilize three armies, just in case: to show the new government was resolute, to deter the *émigrés* and their backers from marching on their brethren, to demonstrate that a democratic nation was just as capable of defending itself as an authoritarian one, and to take the mind of the French people off the tiresome problems of rising prices, bureaucratic bigotry, and religious schism.

Two of the armies were given to old soldiers, Rochambeau (who had commanded the French force in America) and Luckner, both made marshals of France for the occasion. The third was given to Lafayette (who later claimed he could have been made a marshal if he'd wanted, but that he declined). The king was reported to have objected to his nomination, to which the minister of war replied, "If Your Majesty does not name him today, public opinion will force you to do so tomorrow." This was not entirely true. The Parisian electors had already shown how they felt about him by rejecting him as mayor, and the supporters of the program of law and order known as "Fayettism" were under attack. On the one hand there were those who wanted new faces to run the new order, and on the other those who sought to gain the political influence from which the Constitution had excluded them. The nomination of Lafayette to command the aptly-named Army of the Center (December 1791) immediately attracted hostile comment from the Left – and there was precious little enthusiasm from elsewhere to counterbalance it. Lafayette, eagerly rushing to the capital to be back in the saddle, at once found himself criticized by both Jacobins and royal court merely for paying his respects to the king. The court said he was bullying them, the Jacobins that he was playing the courtier. Only the Assembly and the national guard, which saw him on his way to his headquarters at Metz in fine style, showed him respect.

Back in the town where he had been garrisoned as a raw recruit, Lafayette found his army "patriotic" but in a deplorable state (as he reported to Washington). He forthwith put rigorous disciplinary measures into effect and the Jacobins in Paris took exception to that too. Every move that Lafayette made to consolidate his position was interpreted by his opponents as the possible prelude to a military coup. The political divisions which he had always attacked had grown so menacing that collision was inevitable. Even he got enmeshed in them, by trying to intrigue with the royal ministers in order to strengthen his hand against the "factions." This was the normal type of political maneuver favored by generals who recognize the politicians as their masters, even if it somewhat dented Lafayette's claim to be completely above party. He could not allow himself to be attacked in the capital without ensuring he had powerful supporters: that was all his intrigue amounted to. When, by a change of ministers, those with whom he had established an understanding were replaced, all he could do was to write letters, or rather lectures, to the Assembly recalling them to the glorious principles of 1789. The trouble was that faith in those principles had been eroded by the behavior of the king and the first National Assembly. Those associated with them were tainted with their brush.

War-fever enveloped the capital. The king wanted war, for he believed it would make the people rally around him. The queen supported it, because she hoped that the French armies would be defeated and her Austrian relatives would come to her rescue. The new Assembly, under the domination of the Girondins, wanted war to gain the popularity usually associated with firm decisions in an uncertain time. It was also because their theorists, notably Mme Roland, believed that the corruption that had overtaken the revolution would thus be purified. She meant political corruption, the fall from the peaks of idealism to the plateaux of compromise. But, as was natural in the spring of the revolution, Paris enjoyed an air of what many observers called "decadence"; sex shows, scurrilous books, and a great relaxation in dress abounded. Unfortunately, this soon gave way to a hypocritical intolerance.

The only people to oppose the war were the Jacobins, of whom Robespierre was the leading orator. They showed their contempt for the generals, and for Lafayette in particular, by staging in Paris a demonstration for the surviving rebel soldiers of Nancy, who had been released from their servitude in the galleys under the terms of the armistice Lafayette himself had proposed. There were the usual junketings around the Champ de Mars while Lafayette, in Metz, fumed in vain. When, one month later, the war fever actually broke out into hostilities (April 20, 1792), Lafayette was more worried by the "factions" than by the enemy.

The war began badly, and a further change of ministers did little to repair matters. The "Austrian committee" that was supposed to surround the queen was rightly suspected of working from within to destroy the Constitution and aid the nation's enemies. Wariness toward the court increased. The Assembly voted to disband the royal bodyguard because of its "unpatriotic spirit." Soon after, it proposed that the national guard, who were to arrive to celebrate the Fête de la Fédération on July 14th, should be given training for several months in Paris. This would have meant an armed republican force in the capital, and the king, who had already vetoed a decree against priests who refused to take the civic oath, and a decree directed against émigré landowners (the most notable of whom were his own brothers), used his veto a third time. This brought on another ministerial crisis, and those who were finally appointed to portfolios were court men all. They were also men of no ability. The Jacobins and their allies saw this as a major opportunity and prepared to call on force. The court hoped to be able to use force – their own or that of their foreign friends – to strengthen their position. The Girondins in the Assembly were in turmoil, while the administration of Paris was finally being challenged by more radical elements who, denied a part in the political management of their affairs, also prepared for force, in which they were assisted by the Jacobins.

Far from uniting the country, then, the war revealed exactly the weaknesses its sponsors had hoped it would hide. Though the threat of foreign invasion existed, the fact that France had declared war first, and was not immediately faced with defending her strategic centers, may have encouraged the administration's critics. There was no strong executive power taking decisions on behalf of the nation: the king himself was under heavy suspicion of treachery, and his ministers had the confidence of no one. The commune of Paris itself next forfeited the allegiance of its radical sections, by refusing permission for a demonstration to mark the anniversary of the Tennis Court Oath, on June 20th. The demonstrators wanted to present a petition to the king and the Assembly, and to arrive wearing their 1789 uniforms, including weapons. The commune urged the section leaders to obey the law against armed petitions; they replied they could not answer for their men.

The demonstration took place, despite Mayor Pétion, who looked the other way. It burst into the Assembly, and denounced the king for having dismissed the Girondin ministers over the use of his veto. The right of "resistance to oppression" as proclaimed by Lafayette and guaranteed by the Constitution was mentioned. Then the demonstrators flowed on toward the Tuileries, where they trampled down the railings, and found their way into the palace itself. They had with them some pieces of artillery, but their most powerful weapon was their numbers. The king was standing behind a table, with a few unarmed guards, and a polite smile on his lips. He listened to a speech about his veto, and he replied that he would do his duty according to the Constitution. He was offered a red bonnet, which he perched on top of his wig. He was handed a bottle of wine, with which he drank the health of the nation. The crowd applauded with shouts of "Long live the king! Long live the nation!" The king and his family allowed themselves to be goggled at by their subjects for some six hours.

Lafayette was outraged by the invasion of the Tuileries. It was bad enough that the national guard had merely stood by, but that armed bands should have insulted the king was too much. The fact that the king had behaved well proved, to Lafayette, that the whole thing was a Jacobin plot, with the connivance of the Girondins whose ministers had been dismissed. That Jacobins and Girondins had quarreled over the war issue meant nothing to him. He had sent a letter to the Assembly attacking the clubs (meaning the Jacobins and Cordeliers), and it had gone unheeded. Lafayette decided once more that the country was in greater danger from within than without. Fortified by addresses from all sections of his army protesting the attack on the king and swearing their loyalty to the Constitution, he determined to go to Paris and make one last attempt to rally opinion around the crown and the authorities, and to destroy the Jacobins. The loyal addresses he received may be a little suspicious: when a massed choir sings so in tune a little orchestration may be taken for granted. But other sections of the country also protested in formal terms, and in Paris a petition of 20,000 was collected against the insult to the throne. Lafayette and his army were certainly not alone.

It is a curious thing for a serving general to leave his army in a state of readiness and appear before the legislators to appeal to their patriotism. Though he made every preparation in case the enemy should attack, and concerted his plans with his colleague Maréchal Luckner, Lafayette was acting impulsively, even foolishly. History looks kindly on impulse and folly when they lead to success. When they serve only an appeal to "the old values," they are usually regarded as the preliminary to a *coup d'état*. And that, in fact, was what Lafayette was thinking of. He regarded it as his duty to prevent the Jacobins subverting the Constitution which had been freely created by the elected representatives of the sovereign people, and freely – in his view – sanctioned by the king. What he failed, or refused, to recognize was that the Constitution depended on those who made it work, and that the king particularly wanted it to fail.

The Assembly listened with respect but with some surprise when Lafayette arrived and made his plea. He asked that those responsible for the invasion of the Tuileries be punished, that "a sect which invades the national sovereignty, tyrannizes the citizens, and whose public debates leave no doubt of the atrociousness of those who direct it" be destroyed, and that measures be taken to defend the constitutional authorities – notably the king and the Assembly itself – against attack. The president replied simply that the Assembly had sworn to maintain the Constitution, and accorded Lafayette the honors of the sitting (a presidential hug and a complimentary speech). Then the general had to listen to a series of rhetorical attacks. Things were worse than he expected. He left to pay his respects to the king, and tried to get permission to rally the national guard whom the king was to review the following day. But Mayor Pétion canceled the review – and was soon afterwards himself suspended for his failure to stop the invasion of the Tuileries. The king upheld the suspension, but far from being the touch of firmness Lafayette had demanded, it only gave Pétion a popularity he scarcely deserved. The Assembly, besides, revoked the suspension.

Seeing that there was nothing he could do in the capital, a furious and miserable Lafayette returned to his army. Violent protests were made against his action, and against the Assembly for having received him. His effigy was burned at the Palais-Royal. On his way back, however, he received sufficient proof of support to confirm him in his by now unshakeable view that every evil was directly attributable to the Jacobins. They so preyed on his mind, in fact, that their destruction became a personal crusade. It was from this that his plans for a coup were made: not for a takeover of government, but for the removal of the king from Paris, where the Jacobins obviously held him in thrall, and a rallying of support for the Constitution throughout the country, against a legislature no longer free to carry out the wishes of the people. Lafayette wanted Louis to reaffirm his own loyalty to the revolution, and to promise to lead the soldiers of France in person against the country's enemies.

But the king wouldn't play; Marie-Antoinette, when the project was conveyed to her, remarked that it would be "too boring to owe [Lafayette] their lives twice over." And although the Girondins drew back from the outright attack on the monarchy that Lafayette was dreading – and still managed to retain their popular support – the Jacobins pressed on. They received a great fillip through the Duke of Brunswick's manifesto of August 1, 1792, which threatened a terrible punishment on any who attacked the royal family. Paris was to be destroyed if the king and queen were not at once released, and any town to which they were taken would suffer a similar fate. Naturally this declaration, which may well have been drafted by the court itself, or at least its pig-headed and double-dealing "Austrian committee," had the instant effect of rallying all patriots against the crown. In a letter to Jefferson, Gouverneur Morris wrote, "In the present state of things, it seems evident that if the king be not destroyed he must soon become absolute." The sentence before that read, "I verily believe that if M. de Lafayette were to appear just now in Paris unattended by his army he would be torn to pieces." This was perhaps because of the story put about that Lafayette had gone to Luckner (who was summoned to Paris to represent the army at the Fête de la Fédération, to Lafayette's great chagrin) and proposed that they combine forces and march on Paris to deliver it from the Jacobins. The story was denied both by Lafayette and, later, by Luckner. Nevertheless to a city in the kind of turmoil Paris was in, such a rumor was readily believed.

On August 3rd a petition was presented to the Assembly by Mayor Pétion on behalf of forty-seven of the forty-eight sections of Paris. This called for the *déchéance* (forfeiture, lapse, downfall) of the throne and the summoning of a national convention – the same demands as Robespierre made on behalf of the Jacobins. The Girondin majority, hopeful of compromise, asked the Assembly merely for the king's suspension. That they were prepared to go even that far showed the temper of the capital, full of federal representatives, armed national guards of whose loyalty no one was certain any more, and subject to violent demonstrations around the theme "The Nation is in Danger!" The petition was referred to the Assembly's Committee of Twelve, to be debated a week later. The commune of Paris, under Pétion, was playing a double game: claiming to be able to prevent trouble while desperately trying to appear more radical than its sections, so as to retain control over them. On August 8th the Assembly refused, after acrimonious debate, to indict Lafayette for his conduct in leaving his army. It was held he had committed no crime, though it was proposed to make it illegal for serving officers to desert their posts without express permission. Lafayette had two-thirds of the Assembly on his side – but the Assembly itself, along with the administrators of the capital, had now lost the confidence of the Paris sections. That the Jacobins exploited this to take control is undeniable, but the carefully planned events of August 10th, which saw both the fall of the monarchy and that of the commune, were not merely a Jacobin plot. There was too much feeling, distrust of the administration, and desperate elements combining to make a new revolution for that.

On the night of August 9th, three groups sat up without sleep. There was the royal family, expecting attack and putting the finishing touches to their defense; the Paris commune under Pétion, deliberating the defense of the royal palace, which was their responsibility, but more concerned about their own fate; and the Paris sections, twenty-eight of which acted to "save the state" by taking over the City Hall, suspending the commune that was sitting there and assuming power under the name of the "insurrectional commune." The same thing had happened before the fall of the Bastille.

At about seven on the morning of the 10th, when the first armed men advanced on the Tuileries, the king allowed himself to be persuaded to seek refuge, with his family, in the Assembly. His palace was guarded by 900 Swiss, a couple of hundred Knights of St Louis, and two thousand national guardsmen, although these later went over to the other side. Facing the royal soldiers were columns of thousands of federal troops (including the Marseillais) and national guards. The king left before battle was joined; his abhorrence of bloodshed led him to order the Swiss to lay down their arms while under attack. As a result two-thirds of them were killed.

The Assembly, still with its Girondin majority, tried to maintain that it was in control of events. It declared the king was suspended from his functions, as it had done after Varennes, and suggested various places, such as the Luxembourg Palace, where he might be kept under guard. But the insurrectional commune was not having any of that. The royal family were imprisoned in a narrow tower in the Temple – and still the Assembly maintained the fiction of government under the old Constitution. They were as anxious as anyone to prevent a Jacobin takeover. They failed.

All Lafayette's fears had come true, but he would not give in. The new commune had claimed the "sacred right of insurrection against oppression." So would he. The dire warnings he had uttered the year before against civil war he now forgot. He also forgot the most important lesson of his time as commandant-general: that whoever controls the capital controls the revolution. Certainly the Constitution had been violated, despite the Assembly's maintaining the contrary. But this was the king's fault as much as anybody's – although there were few alternatives left for him to take.

Lafayette had an army, and he felt he could count on feeling outside the capital to defend the monarchy. He denies, in his memoirs, ever planning to march on Paris, and there is no reason to disbelieve him. Perhaps he could not have led soldiers against the national guard he had created. First, he decided, he would have to set an example of fidelity to the Constitution. Spurning peace overtures from an Assembly he now regarded as unable to act freely, he attempted to raise the standard of revolt in the Ardennes, where his army was stationed. He did this in the most orthodox way, by writing to the administrators of the department saying that, as the Constitution has been violated, he wished to swear allegiance to the nearest loyal civic power, to which the military was always subject. His idea was now to form "a sort of congress of united departments," presumably on the lines of the old American Continental Congress. He hoped that all anti-Jacobins, in the Assembly and throughout France, would join him. The Ardennes people were sympathetic, but there were not enough "patriots" willing to do what Lafayette regarded as their duty.

Meanwhile the Assembly, which for better or worse was the only government the country had, was perturbed by the possibilities of civil war (the shortage of weapons made them order the issue of eleven-foot pikes for interior defense) no less than by the rumblings on its frontiers. It sent commissioners to report. When those destined for Lafayette's army reached Sedan, they were arrested by the municipal authorities, partly as a gesture against the Assembly which, they said, no longer represented the people, and partly as hostages for the Ardennes department's support of Lafayette. Lafayette maintained the arrests were carried out on the initiative of the Sedan authorities, and that, when he knew the game was up, he left behind a letter claiming responsibility in order to protect the mayor. The mayor later claimed he acted on Lafayette's orders, with an army at his gates. Either way, Lafayette did what he always did in times of crisis: he made everyone swear another civic oath of loyalty.

His hopes that bold action might arouse the Parisians to arm themselves against the Jacobins, and presumably to free the king, proved quite vain. Every other army and every other department in France accepted the events of August 10th: it was he who appeared to be the "rebel." He realized the futility of continuing, and the risks to which he was submitting his followers. On August 19th the Assembly proscribed him, which involved the seizure of his property, trial, and probably death. He could not fight further, and to stay was pointless. After taking every precaution to ensure that his army was in a state of preparedness in case of enemy attack, Lafayette, with a score of officers similarly proscribed, crossed the French border near Roche-fort. The general refused to consider himself an *émigré*, which might imply he was ready to take up arms against his own people. He hoped that he would be allowed to proceed to a neutral country, probably England, where his family might join him. From there, if things in France got so bad there was no hope of her "regaining her freedom" he wanted to become "*only* an American again," and cross to that land of liberty to tell Washington and all his friends how "France, despite me, had been stained with crimes, riddled with plots, and destroyed by ignorance and corruption."

Part Five: Leader of the Opposition

15
Prison

THE PROSCRIBED AND fugitive general, accompanied by his little troupe, crossed the border as it grew dark on August 19, 1792. They did not know whether they would run into French troops or those of the enemy coalition. From their own countrymen they risked arrest; from their enemies they hoped for free passage to Holland, the nearest neutral country. Bureaux de Pusy, a long-time colleague of Lafayette and a captain of engineers in his army, was sent to reconnoiter. Discovering that Rochefort, the town they reached first, was held by the Austrians, he asked for permission to pass through, explaining that the group had been forced to leave France but had no wish to take up arms against their compatriots, as *émigrés* usually did. Permission was granted, and the officers asked to advance and be recognized. Once Lafayette's features were discovered, however, the situation changed. The local commander sent Bureaux de Pusy and an Austrian officer to Namur, to see if his own general, Moitelle, would sign a passport for the fugitives. But when Moitelle realized that one of France's leading generals had fallen into his hands, he couldn't believe his luck. "Lafayette! Lafayette!" he kept repeating, and sent couriers rushing to tell his emperor while putting the group under strong guard. The fugitives, meanwhile, signed a declaration insisting they were not to be considered as enemy soldiers and demanding the right of free passage. It was perhaps naïve of Lafayette to expect that the coalition forces, whom he had so often denounced as the enemies of liberty, would allow him to pass through their lines. For this naïveté he paid dearly. It is difficult, however, to see what else he could have done: to have stayed at his post after having had the Assembly's commissioners arrested was tantamount to suicide.

Lafayette behaved from the start in a totally uncompromising manner. He waved his dignity like a flag in his enemies' faces, and in every communication that he was able, legally or illegally, to get out, he lectured posterity on the virtues of his principles. Given his position this is unsurprising. At the age of thirty-five he had now sacrificed his post, his position, and quite possibly his family. His pride was all he had left. It was a matter of survival. When surrounded by enemies and in a hopeless position he could either be broken or attempt to appear unbreakable. Lafayette was determined to be the latter. Everything he said or did would justify him for eternity.

To Prince Charles of Lorraine, who arrived to interrogate him about the state of affairs in France, Lafayette coldly replied that he did not imagine anyone would allow themselves to ask questions which it would not be proper for him to answer. When he was asked for the "treasure" the Austrians supposed he had brought with him, he laughed and answered, "All that I can understand from your request is that if your prince had been in my place, he would have stolen the army's cash." And when, a fortnight after their arrest, those of the group who had been members of the old constituent Assembly – Alexandre Lameth (an old opponent, now also proscribed), César de Latour-Maubourg, Bureaux de Pusy, and Lafayette himself – were separated from the rest and escorted to Luxembourg, the general left his long-time aide-de-camp, Louis Romeuf, a testament of his political faith to be published if he should be killed. This declared his anticipation of death at the hands of those whom he had so long attacked, but insisted that he found this preferable to dying at the hands of his misled compatriots. It ended on a ringing note: "The aristocracy and despotism are in their death-throes. My blood, crying vengence, will provide new defenders for liberty." Soon after this, the four prisoners were conducted to the fortress of Wesel, in Westphalia.

Lafayette, who had explained his position to Adrienne from Rochefort, dared not write further to his wife or family in France, for fear of compromising them. He sent what news he could, written with a toothpick on such paper as he could get hold of, to the Princesse d'Hénin, another of his close lady-friends, who was living safely in England. Not only did she keep Adrienne informed of her husband's welfare, as well as she as able, but also Mme de Simiane, for whom Lafayette continued to show concern. The tone of his letters to d'Hénin, a lady of magnificent figure and bearing, whose beauty was marred only by the scars of smallpox, is at least as warm as those to de Simiane, which is to say they are political documents with tender sentiments of affection tacked on. They were meant for publication, or for being passed around, and were hence less than intimate. Since he rarely unbent to anyone in the letters published in his memoirs – and the unpublished ones have not yet been properly sorted – it is likely that the Princesse d'Hénin was also his mistress.

Their names were not linked by gossip in the same way as were his and Mme de Simiane's, but d'Hénin was enormously useful to him during this period, and doubtless Lafayette showed a proper gratitude.

While in Wesel the king of Prussia – whom Lafayette had last met as heir-apparent to Frederick the Great, and whom he now regarded as the chief architect of the coalition against France – proposed to ease Lafayette's confinement if he would reveal what the French military plans were. The general replied that "the king was extremely impertinent to mention his [Lafayette's] name in connection with such an idea." It was hardly surprising that the coalition decided that "Lafayette's existence was incompatible with the safety of the governments of Europe," a declaration the general naturally regarded as flattering. The prisoners were separated and kept under extremely close guard, being forbidden any news of the outside world, even of their families. Lafayette's principles, however, continued to sustain him.

Handed by the Austrians to the Prussians, Lafayette and his companions were next taken to the fortress of Magdebourg, where the privations to which he was subjected began to tell on his health. He was forbidden to take fresh air, even if he should be dying, on the express order of the king; he suffered from trouble with his stomach and nerves, as well as sleeplessness and fever. His cell was five and a half paces long and three paces wide. It was situated in a wet wall of the fortress, and reached only through a series of four doors whose clanking bolts and chains had to be undone every time the prisoners needed anything. He was watched constantly, and allowed only the company of his servant, a native of Chavaniac, during the day. "My health deteriorates daily," he wrote to the Princesse d'Hénin. "My physical constitution has almost as much need of freedom as my moral constitution, but I am set on living, and my friends can count on my gathering all the feelings which will help me to preserve myself although, given my situation and afflictions, I don't know how long they will last." The cell was decorated with jolly couplets rhyming "*souffrir*" (to suffer) with "*mourir*" (to die); the only distraction was an occasional execution. Alexandre Lameth became so ill they were forced to allow him air. After that the authorities relented sufficiently to permit each of the prisoners an hour's exercise each day.

They did manage to pick up some fragments of news: the successes of the French armies, the activities of Lafayette's old enemy the Duc d'Orléans in voting for the death of the king, and the execution of the unhappy Louis XVI, which for Lafayette meant the end of the laws of humanity. He learned little of his family, whom he still hoped would join him; he had been in prison seven months without hearing from them, which made his condition even worse. One ray of light was a deposit of ten thousand florins by the United States – the first of several American advances. This enabled him to pay for bedding, furniture, heat, light and books, but left him little to eat well on, since his jailers exploited him mercilessly. He hoped nevertheless that his American friends were more concerned about his liberty than his nourishment.

It is said that those who survive best in prison are sustained by the belief that their cause will triumph over their jailers'. Certainly Lafayette believed it. But national and international events, in which he had played so prominent a part, moved as if he had never been there. Paris, having smashed to pieces the bust of him that stood in the City Hall, had outgrown his patriarchal version of law and order: under the stresses of war, treachery, inflation, and the bitter faction-fighting between Girondins and Jacobins, panic was beginning to lead to terror. Lafayette's family were arrested in the Auvergne as part of a campaign against former nobles and enemies of the revolution. Adrienne throughout remained cool to the point of haughtiness. She desired to be allowed to join her husband, to be true to his principles, and to clear his debts. Around Chavaniac she was known and respected, and this enabled her to survive. She found time to write to the king of Prussia – rejecting as too humble a draft prepared for her by Gouverneur Morris – soliciting her husband's release, but she also saw to the family finances, including the welfare of the blacks on the Cayenne estate which had now been sequestered by the state. She was always the one to take care of important details, an ability Lafayette did not fully appreciate in her. Panic of the kind that was spreading throughout France, the natural panic of a people unable to control events and uncertain of whom to trust, made concentration on everyday survival a priority. The lofty appeals to principle that Lafayette favored, and which, from his prison cell, he continued to expound, had an emptier ring than ever in a France scared stiff of its own bogeys.

Lafayette could not believe he would die. By all the rules of war he could not be executed; the most his jailers could hope for was to wear him down to shadow. This, of course, he was determined to resist, but there were times when the strain showed. As far as his family was concerned, no news was almost good news: when, after eight whole months of hearing nothing, he learned that they were alive and well, his chief concern was to let them know, via his channels of communication, that he too was battling on. He was told that the Americans were making efforts to get him released, and this had the effect of making him double his efforts to appear the man of principle, come what may. Nevertheless he was not so inhuman as to bore his women-friends sick with rhetoric. He demanded of them whole-hearted devotion to the cause of getting him released, writing to the Princesse d'Hénin that "any way of getting out that will not compromise my principles or my freedom" would be acceptable. But he ended the letter with great tenderness:

Good-bye, my dear princess, the proofs of your friendship do not astonish me, for I have long known whom I loved so much. When will I be allowed to see you? Never has my heart had so much need of those who are left to it, and of those tender feelings that fill it so well. I have lost some mighty chances of glory and fortune: the greatest loss it that the injustice of the people, without lessening my devotion to their cause, has destroyed for me that delicious feeling of the smile of the crowd.

And in a possible reference to Mme de Simiane, who was now also a prisoner in France, he said he was sure that "the test of misfortune" might be too strong for ordinary friendships, but that if he ever got out, he would have learned discretion, and would avoid being too curious.

The difficulties of writing surreptitious letters with a toothpick and soot on scraps of paper torn from books were only part of the bothersome aspects of prison – and they did not prevent him from writing at very great length. His secret letters were smuggled out at great risk by bribing his custodians: the cash the Americans had put at his disposal was at least useful there. In one letter he was allowed to send openly to Adrienne, under the supervision of the authorities, he complained at his "unfortunate talent for reading fast." This meant that the few books he was permitted, mostly classical works in Latin, English, or French, did not last him long. His ignorance of German led him to start learning its grammar, but he did not persevere. To those who spoke only German, such as the doctor who sometimes visited him, he tried talking in Latin, but not everyone was up to his standard. One book that cheered him – a surprising one for him to have got hold of – was the memoirs of a man who had actually escaped from Magdebourg. Naturally this immediately filled his head with hopeful plans for getting out himself.

In January 1794 he was transferred to the prison of Neisse, in what is now Poland. He was still a prisoner of the Prussians, but he hoped that the friendship shown for him by King Stanislaus-Augustus Poniatowski, from the days when Lafayette had been a liberal member of the Assembly of Notables, might result in an attempt to get him released. Unfortunately Poniatowski had troubles of his own, which soon forced him to abdicate. A resolution asking for Lafayette's release was moved in the United States Congress by R. G. Harper, but such was the desire of the Americans to stay uninvolved in the European war that it was voted down. In the English House of Commons, General FitzPatrick, an opposition member of Parliament who had once fought the "rebels" in America, and who had met Lafayette there and in London, proposed a motion that the government intercede on the imprisoned man's behalf, but it was Edmund Burke who swayed them against passing it (on political, not personal, grounds). England had by now joined in the war against France: FitzPatrick's motion could be no more than a gesture, designed perhaps as much to embarrass Pitt as to save Lafayette.

In May, 1794, the Prussians handed him back to the Austrians. Lafayette reckoned it was because they had been embarrassed by the publicity over his detention, small though this had been. He was finally shut up, with Latour-Maubourg and Bureaux de Pusy, in the fortress of Olmütz. His friends, especially those in exile in England, continued to work on his behalf, but a European war was no time to push, through diplomatic channels, for the release of an intransigently principled prisoner who was proscribed in his own country. In France, the government by committee which had been the first fruit of the revolution reached its apogee under the Jacobins. Robespierre, a year younger than Lafayette, was a bureaucrat with little sense of balance: even the Terror over which he presided was mechanically methodical rather than a massacre through blood-lust. The curious thing is that, in office, the Jacobins stood for many of the ideas Lafayette had championed, above all order and virtue. But Lafayette despised their methods, and one cardinal difference between him and Robespierre was that the general was always capable of seeing another's point of view when he wanted to.

If hubris had ever been a characteristic of the Lafayettes – and many would have said it was – they were now suffering its consequences. Adrienne was moved from house-arrest at Chavaniac to prisons in Paris, one of which was the Collège du Plessis, where her husband had been a schoolboy. The Terror, that massive public purge which threatened to drown the real achievements of the revolution in blood, took, with mechanical efficiency, on the same day and on the same scaffold, Adrienne's grandmother, her mother, and her sister. She herself daily expected execution, and in her agony of mind welcomed it. The historian can view the statistics of the Terror in a perspective that might make it bearable, but it is impossible to remain unmoved by the deaths of individuals. Those who had stood with Lafayette, those who had attacked him, from Right and Left, his defenders, proscribers, and successors in public office, were all "shortened by a head," a jolly phrase that masks the spectacle of public execution. Those who waited in prison knew there was no defense: some found consolation in religion, others tried to kill themselves. Dr Guillotin's contraption was a triumph of technology, a civilized machine which was quick, supposedly painless, and which saved the expense of a fresh axe and the agony of a missed cut. It was egalitarian also, for beheading used to be a privilege reserved for the nobly born. But the guillotine could not staunch the founts of blood gushing from severed necks; there was no way, then, of killing someone in a way that was not messy.

Adrienne was saved by the fall of Robespierre. Lafayette himself was undoubtedly preserved by being a prisoner abroad, not that his condition there was enviable. His first prison cell had been alive with rats and vermin; twenty months' captivity had robbed him of his health, his weight, and much of his hair. The time at Neisse, under the Prussians, had been the best, for he was permitted the company of his fellow-prisoners Maubourg and Pusy. When he was handed back to the Austrians – which the emperor later told Adrienne was the king of Prussia's doing, while the king blamed the emperor; both said the matter was out of their hands – Lafayette's treatment was made infinitely worse by the psychological strains of isolation. His belongings were taken away, leaving him with only a watch, garter-buckles, and a change of shirt and collar. Any book that contained the word "liberty" was confiscated, and he was told that from now on he would see only the four walls of his cell, that he would receive no news of anything or anybody. It was forbidden for even his jailers to pronounce his name: he was to be known only by a number. He was to hear nothing of his family, nor even of his two colleagues imprisoned with him. As it was considered this might drive him to despair, knives, forks, and anything which might help him to commit suicide, were removed. Lafayette replied that he was not going to be so considerate as to kill himself.

Olmütz itself was an old Jesuit seminary, converted into a massive prison. It was surrounded by stagnant and pestilential water, covered in mosquitoes and fogs. The river nearby served to take away the sewage of the village; it wound its stinking way right past the prisoners' windows. The buildings in which they were imprisoned excluded fresh air, which was freezing in winter and burning in summer, except at midday. As Latour-Maubourg described things, it was like living at the center of a funnel: the outer walls were six-feet thick, and the dividing walls four, "all built with that solidity which distinguishes religious works the world over."

As is the way with prisoners of war, they found extraordinary methods of communication, in which other Olmütz prisoners generously cooperated. Lafayette's secretary, Félix Pontonnier, who was sixteen when arrested with him, invented a special code to talk to Latour-Maubourg's servant: it involved singing, whistling, and facial grimaces. It was the only way Lafayette knew his colleagues were still alive.

When Félix was caught, his windows were bolted and he was put on bread and water for three months.

After a while, Lafayette became sufficiently ill for the doctor, who at least could talk Latin passably well, to recommend his need for fresh air. This need had to be urged three times before it was granted; the first two requests met with the response "his condition is not yet bad enough." Finally, he was allowed out every other day in the afternoon, accompanied by one of his jailers. Wearing a round hat and a plain overcoat, he was taken in a carriage away from the unhealthy air of the prison, and permitted to walk for a while, which privilege he regarded as the only way to cure, or at least regulate, the troubles he was having with his chest. He was lucky: Latour-Maubourg and Pusy were not allowed out at all. His carriage was of course accompanied by an armed escort.

The privilege of being taken outside the mighty walls of Olmütz was the basis of Lafayette's one serious attempt at escape. The organization of this attempt was undertaken by Dr. Justus Erich Bollmann, a young doctor from Hanover who had met Lafayette's friend Mme de Stael in Paris and who helped get some of her proscribed companions to London. There he met the Princesse d'Hénin and the whole of her French refugee circle. Perhaps it was d'Hénin who persuaded Bollmann to undertake a rescue mission on Lafayette's behalf; certainly money for it was forthcoming from Thomas Pinckney, the U.S. ambassador to Great Britain, and from Angelica Church, daughter of Lafayette's old American comrade-in-arms General Schuyler and sister-in-law of his dear friend Alexander Hamilton. Bollmann had a taste for adventure, and he was sent to try and intercede with King Frederick William of Prussia – who refused to see him. Since Lafayette's whereabouts were an official secret, and since he had not yet smuggled a letter out of Olmütz, none of his friends knew he had been handed over to the Austrians. But by perserverance and a great deal of luck Bollmann chanced upon Olmütz, impressed and befriended the fortress's doctor, and got him to smuggle into the prisoner whose name he was not supposed to pronounce a book with a message in lemon juice. Lafayette, using the same channel, replied, his spirits soaring, and communications were established.

On a visit to Vienna Bollmann met John Jay, then American chief justice on a diplomatic mission, and Francis Huger, the young son of the first American Lafayette stumbled on when he landed near Charleston in 1777. Whether Huger's was a personal crusade to liberate his father's famous guest, or whether he was briefed by the American government to undertake a secret mission of release, more formal methods being too difficult, is pure speculation. Despite Washington's personal concern – which he had not yet demonstrated in an effective manner – the American public was not particularly aroused by Lafayette's plight. That came later; meanwhile, everyone had troubles of their own.

Bollmann and Huger concerted plans and informed Lafayette of their ideas for escape. One of these was to smuggle in a file, but to saw through the bars and walls of his cell, while weak and under constant surveillance, might have taken literally years and no more was heard of that. Lafayette smuggled out, via his doctor, a message written on the margins of a novel in what he called Chinese ink, which was soot and water. He was full of questions, and said he was "defending my own constitution as steadily, but actually with as little success, as the constitution of the nation." He at least had kept his sense of humor. Fearing that Bollmann, who was obviously keeping a close watch on the prison, had mistaken him for another prisoner, Lafayette described his coat and hat and the walks he took. But in a further note scribbled in lemon juice, he said that any ordinary methods of escape were out of the question, and that the only hope of success was a plan improvised on the spur of the moment. He said that Latour-Maubourg and Pusy were in agreement, and that they had not sought permission to go on walks so that Lafayette would have a better chance of using this method of escape. This was obviously during the period when Félix Pontonnier's singing-and-whistling code was in operation.

So it was to be a waiting game. While the main details are in the memoirs, we have to piece together the rest. We do not know if Lafayette knew Bollmann by sight, or if he was aware that young Huger – whom he could not have seen for years – was with him. He must have watched and waited for something to happen every other day, when he was taken out. He had never been a patient man, and after endless months in prison the thought of escape was enough to make anyone feverish.

Some plan must, however, have been concerted between Lafayette and his rescuers, for on the day the attempt was made everything happened by design. Bollmann and Huger, each on horseback, waited, hidden, off the road that Lafayette's carriage always took. Lafayette asked his escort of soldiers to do something for him in the village; any suspicions they might have had were allayed by his giving them money to drink with in a village bar. Lafayette then got out of his carriage with his jailer, to take his walk in the normal way. This jailer, a corporal whom Lafayette had described as "cowardly," was armed only with a saber. Lafayette asked if he could examine the weapon. The guard, not unnaturally, became a little suspicious, and Lafayette tried to seize the saber. A struggle ensued, in which Lafayette ricked his back. Worse, and more painful, the guard proved less cowardly than expected, and bit off a small piece of the general's finger. Bollmann and Huger now rode up with a pistol, in an attempt to intimidate the corporal, who ran off to get help.

The idea was that Lafayette would get up behind one of his rescuers, and they would make for the Silesian borders. The corporal, however, managed to raise the escort of soldiers very quickly from their drinking, and Huger, who spoke no German and would therefore not have been as useful a companion as Bollmann, nobly decided to sacrifice himself so that Lafayette would make better speed. Muddy and bleeding, Lafayette scrambled onto Huger's horse, and Bollmann, already mounted, yelled, "Go to Hoff," in both English and French. He then galloped ahead and was soon out of sight. Lafayette, confused, thought he had said, "Get off," which he interrupted as "Get a move on." He had never heard of Hoff, which was a small village where Bollmann had arranged for fresh horses to be waiting. With the soldiers already in pursuit, he rode straight ahead. Bollmann had disappeared, and Lafayette never took the turning that would have brought them together.

Lost, unarmed, in considerable pain, liable to cause attention by the state he was in, Lafayette now worried about the fate of his rescuers. Not knowing what else to do, he turned back, but the sight and noise of the escort that was chasing him made him turn again and continue the flight. He had, however, lost time, blood, and Bollmann: unless he could find the last very quickly, he knew the attempt would fail. When he reached the village of Sternberg, about twenty miles from Olmütz, he was exhausted and dispirited. He was recognized and arrested. Huger was already in custody. Bollmann was arrested a week later on Prussian territory and was handed over to the Austrians for trial.

Lafayette was brought back to Olmütz the day after his capture, and it goes without saying that an even more rigorous regime was imposed on him. He was threatened with chains, but he still had sufficient spirit to protest. "Your emperor did not order this," he later remembered saying. "Watch out for doing more than you are ordered, and displeasing him by exceeding your orders through misplaced zeal." This impressed the officer enough to leave off chaining his prisoner, but Lafayette was no longer allowed out of his cell. He became ill with fever, and alarmed even his jailers. But they did not relent: he was left alone, without light, for fourteen hours a day, and if his condition had become so critical as to need emergency treatment, he would have died, since the keys to his cell were now kept at the other end of the village. He was reduced to two shirts, and not allowed another even when both of those were soaked with sweat from his fever. The doctor who came to see his chewed-off finger was not allowed to say a single word to him.

In addition to these physical privations, he was subjected to a refined form of mental torture. He was of course forbidden all news of the outside world, and when he asked about his fellow-prisoners, the jeering reply was "How do you know they are here?" Félix's code had been stopped, and security throughout the prison was tightened, making everyone suffer. Lafayette was told that his would-be rescuers had been caught, and he was assured they would be hanged in front of his very windows, with the prison's commanding officer performing as executioner. This caused him agonies of guilt. In fact Huger and Bollmann were sentenced to six months' hard labor. This sentence was considered too light by the Austrian court, and a new trial was ordered, but a kindly magistrate considered that the six months they had spent in chains in Olmütz was sufficient punishment. They were released and already out of Austria when the order for a new trial arrived. For the suspiciously-minded, the lightness of the sentence – considering the importance of the prisoner – is another small piece of evidence that the whole thing may have been a put-up job to make things worse for Lafayette. But certainty is impossible.

Months went by, and although Lafayette's condition was worse than it had ever been, he still managed to survive. One of the nastiest of his privations was being denied all news of his wife and children. Latour-Maubourg received a letter which told him Adrienne was still alive, but when he asked to be allowed to tell this to Lafayette, he was expressly forbidden to do so. After that, any letters addressed to him that contained Adrienne's name were held back. But the ingenious Félix had found a way to keep up his code of communication, and Lafayette managed sometimes to talk through his window to the prisoner in the next cell. By this means he learned, at the end of the summer, that Adrienne and his children were still living. A letter which referred to her under another name had got through to Maubourg.

Living she was, but only just. Her release from prison following the end of the Terror was delayed, and it was partly due to pressure from friends, and partly to the efforts of James Monroe, who had replaced the unpopular Gouverneur Morris as American minister, that she was freed, after a period of detention lasting some twenty-eight months. For seven whole months she had lived in daily expectation of execution. At the end of January 1795, she was reunited with her children. The loss of her mother, grandmother, and sister haunted her. Her father was living in Switzerland with his mistress; some of her family survived in exile. Of her husband, she knew only that he was incarcerated at Olmütz. To join him there now became her only wish. Her two daughters elected to accompany her; her son Georges Washington Lafayette was sent to America, accompanied by his old tutor M. Frestel, to be put under the care of the family patron, Washington himself. Adrienne paid a visit to Chavaniac to see that Lafayette's aunt was all right. Then she waited to see the outcome of a proposal to restore the estates of those who had been killed during the Terror. The proposal was passed, in the circular way revolutions have, and Adrienne found herself once more in charge of reorganizing the family fortunes. Her mother's properties in Brie, near Paris, were confirmed as hers and her sisters'; with the help of Monroe, again, and the proceeds from the sale of her sister Rosalie de Grammont's diamonds, Chavaniac too was restored to the Lafayettes. These matters settled, as well as the debts incurred while she was in prison, she provided herself with a passport to leave France with her daughters.

To say that Adrienne de Lafayette was extraordinary is a considerable understatement. She was proud, religious, stubbornly independent, immovable when her mind was made up, and devoted not only to her husband's principles but to his person, despite knowing all his weaknesses. These included his infidelities. André Maurois, who was allowed to look through some of the mass of still-unsorted and unpublished material recently discovered at Lagrange, the château that Adrienne inherited from her mother and where she died, came across a letter she wrote on her journey to Olmütz. We do not know if it reached Lafayette – in fact, that is doubtful – but it was kept out of the memoirs edited by his son.

> I am persuaded that you have not always been fair [*juste*] towards me, but I hope to convince you that, in everything that I've done, there is no single detail of my conduct that you would not have approved, as if you had dictated it yourself. You will judge how important it was for me to have this certainty deep in my heart at a time when we were buried beneath the horrors that have kept us apart for so long.

No wonder that Lafayette only began really to appreciate his wife when she suddenly appeared without warning in his cell. She was very like him in many ways: plain but strong-featured, incapable of tact though able to turn a courtier's phrase, dogged in the cause of duty. The chief difference between them was that he was concerned only with principle, while she took care of all details. This is the woman who was proud enough to end a letter, "I consent to owe you this favor," when she was requesting her freedom from Brissot, a powerful Girondin deputy, founder of the Society of the Friends of the Blacks, who had used Lafayette's contacts on a trip to America. And when she sent her son to Washington, whom she had never met, she wrote: "Although I did not receive the consolation of making my pleas heard and of obtaining from you the kind of service I believed proper to deliver his father from the hands of our enemies, because your views were different from mine, my confidence has not altered. . . ." She also scornfully refused to do what many wives of *émigrés* or proscribed persons did, and go through a form of divorce to safeguard her family's property. And she boldly signed herself as "wife of Lafayette." She was regarded even by her surviving sisters with awe for her strength of character. And it was, in fact, Adrienne who, by joining her husband in prison, not only made him aware of her qualities, but also made the public aware of the injustices of his imprisonment.

Adrienne determined to go to Vienna and make a personal plea to the young emperor. She passed through Altona, near Hamburg, where her skeptical and prudent aunt Mme de Tessé had purchased a farm and was keeping not only herself but a whole clutch of relatives and fugitives. Everyone told Adrienne she was mad to think of joining Lafayette, but no one managed to sway her. To join her husband was the most difficult of the choices facing her and that, perhaps, was why she chose it. She had failed to share the martyrdom of her mother, grandmother, and sister: this was one way of compensating. Her suffering had marked her face and health, but reinforced her determination. She impressed everyone, even the true *émigrés* who regarded Lafayette as a traitor. She shared with her husband the ability to forgive enemies who were pleasant to her.

She got to Vienna – an achievement in itself considering that France and Austria were at war – and through family connections she saw the emperor. He granted her request to join her husband, while telling her that the whole matter of his imprisonment was "very complicated" and "didn't depend on himself alone." He assured Adrienne that Lafayette was being well treated, that her presence would be an added pleasure, and that she could write to him (the emperor) direct if she needed to. So little did she know of her husband's condition that there was no reason to disbelieve the emperor; even her own awful experiences did not shake her faith. She went next to see Baron von Thugut, the emperor's most influential minister, and mentioned her surprise that the ministers of the coalition should attach so much importance to a single individual. "Too much importance?" he said to her several times, in a tone that implied their strong feelings about their prisoner.

The administrative obstacles to this self-sacrificing pilgrimage being overcome, Adrienne and the young Anastasie and Virginie hastened to Olmütz, where they arrived on October 15, 1795. It was a year since the escape attempt, and in the interval Lafayette knew only that his wife was alive. That, of course, was not even certain: the Terror of which he heard rumors might have taken her at any time. Wife and daughters were escorted through doors that were locked immediately behind them. They passed along endless corridors and came to the two heavily bolted doors of Lafayette's cell. The prisoner had been given no warning of their arrival. He had been in solitary confinement for twelve months; he was terribly thin and his face terribly altered. His wife too was changed. The emotion of their meeting was too great to describe. The pain each saw in the other's face made them hesitate to ask questions, and the authorities interrupted to search them, taking away three forks the women had brought with them. Only when night fell, and Anastasie and Virginie were locked in a separate cell, only when they were alone together, could Lafayette ask and Adrienne tell of what had happened.

Lafayette's condition was in fact better than it had been a year before, following the escape attempt. Adrienne's presence improved his morale, if not his physique. She showed her mettle by forthwith writing to complain about their treatment. All her demands were refused; the promises the emperor had made were meaningless. Lafayette at least had got used to eating without a fork: as he told a guard who asked him about it, it was something he used to do among the Iroquois Indians. But the fact that his wife and young children had to suffer his privations began to arouse indignation outside. Adrienne and Latour-Maubourg, using the secret channels that involved enormous risk for everyone concerned, smuggled out details of their confinement: Adrienne to Mme de Tessé, Latour-Maubourg to a French journalist living in England called Masclet. Masclet was, like the prisoners, an enthusiastic constitutionalist who was proscribed and who had intended to go to America. He stayed in London, however, and used his talents to publicize the cause of "The Prisoners of Olmütz" in the *Morning Chronicle*, using the pseudonym "Eleuthère," from the Greek for "free man." Papers on the Continent carried the stories, and as is often the case, publicity succeeded in rousing protest where the close channels of refugee diplomacy had failed.

The cause was dramatic because of the conditions inside the prison, and the fact that the captives were not guilty of any crime except holding opinions that were radical only outside France. Masclet and Adrienne described how Lafayette, Latour-Maubourg, and Pusy had been isolated, and how all had terribly aged. The double doors to their cells were only opened at 8.00 for breakfast, 11.30 for lunch, 2.00 P.M. to take away the lunch things, and half an hour before nightfall for supper. Lafayette's daughters were locked away a quarter of an hour after the arrival of supper, which forced them either to forego the meal or rush their way through it. As the days got shorter they got less and less time with their parents: they had perhaps five or six hours with them before being led, the one blushing

230

to the roots of her hair, the other sometimes looking proud, sometimes comic (according to her mother), under an archway of crossed
swords to their own cell. The first winter they were allowed to stay
until eight at night, giving them almost twelve hours together, but
this was changed because, as Latour-Maubourg commented, it made
them too happy.

Their cells were never unlocked without a full guard being
assembled in the corridor; to add to their discomfort of always
being watched, the punishment-yard was right next to them, and the
cries of the beaten were loud in their ears. As to heating, this was only
done when it became necessary to heat the guardroom. A fire was
lit at 5 A.M. and at 4 P.M.; if in the interval it smoked or went out, no
one bothered to look after it. For lighting, they were given tiny
lamps at supper, but these had to be snuffed at 9 P.M. For the rest of the
time they were mostly in the dark.

Mealtimes were among the worst moments of the day. This was
chiefly because whatever they ate – paid for out of Adrienne's
resources or Lafayette's remaining American credit – aroused the
envy of their guards, fifteen of whom were permanently on duty,
on double pay. Two of this platoon were specially charged with
reporting on everything the prisoners said or did. The guards were
forbidden to reply to questions, and reported any attempt to communicate with other prisoners. The meals that made them jealous
included a breakfast of chocolate or milky coffee, the one indis-
tinguishable from the other. All the meals were made in a filthy
kitchen which the soldiers wandered in and out of, smoking all the
while; everything the prisoners ate stank of tobacco, and often had
strands of the stuff included. The butter was rancid and the cook tried,
and failed, to disguise the badness of the food by excessive use of
spices. Lunch was served in earthenware bowls all of the same size and
shape, and had to be eaten with a tin spoon, since knives and forks
were forbidden in case of suicide attempts. They were supposed to
have wine and water served in bottles, but these were replaced by
jars full of foul red wine and dirty water, out of which they had to
drink directly, glasses also being denied them. After the jars were
taken away they were left in the corridor, where they collected dirt,
insects, and more tobacco from the soldiers who also swigged from
them, or even used them to wash with. According to Latour-
Maubourg, the jars were only cleaned twice a month, by being wiped
around with a wisp of straw.

Their clothes were in a worse state than they were. When Lafayette
needed breeches, for his old ones were in rags, the prison had made him
an enormous pair of trousers and a jacket of thick serge – cloth being
too dear – without bothering to take his measurements. They were
so badly made he couldn't put them on, and Adrienne had to exercise

all her ingenuity to get some cloth to make her husband some wearable clothes. Anastasie made him some slippers out of material from an old dress. When Latour-Maubourg's shoes had been cobbled so often there was no room for more stitching, he had to lie on his bed until new shoes were made.

At least Lafayette's daughters bore up under these barbaric conditions. Anastasie was eighteen, and Virginie was thirteen. Despite being deprived of air and exercise, which gave Virginie a stoop, the two girls – who shared a single straw mattress in their tiny cell – never complained once. Anastasie took dictation from her father and from her mother, when Adrienne was too ill to write, and wrote notes with toothpick and Chinese ink in the margins of books. The girls made fun of their guards by drawing tiny, satirical pictures of them; they employed to the full the illegal opportunities even the most secure prison affords to vary their regimen.

Adrienne's health suffered badly. Her limbs swelled and her skin erupted with rashes. She was refused a chair; when she asked if she could go to Vienna for a week to consult a doctor, she was told, after infinite delays, that if she left Olmütz she could never return. She chose to stay. Still preoccupied with the deaths of her mother, grandmother and sister, she began to write her mother's life in the margins of a book by Buffon. To write with a toothpick is hard; to do so with deformed and swollen fingers almost impossible. Anastasie took over when the task became absolutely unbearable. Yet Adrienne did not fail in her maternal duties: she gave lessons to young Virginie and read to her. She could not allow her to write, for the margins of books were too precious to waste on practice.

One could say that the Lafayettes ought to have been grateful to be alive. They were. One could say that they were lucky to be together, fortunate in avoiding the horrendous convulsions then shaking France. Perhaps. But it was no light thing to be shut up in a small, stinking cell, preserving pride and principles only at great personal risk, watching a wife who had voluntarily given up freedom grow steadily more ill, perhaps incurably, and hoping that all the sacrifices made for the cause would result in pressure to secure release from those in a position to exert it. Fallen heroes can rely on nobody. Lafayette was a political prisoner, held without trial. His way of standing on his dignity and refusing to compromise could be immensely tedious. But his tenacity, his consistency, and his endurance compel admiration, even awe, and Adrienne's devotion even more so.

The advent of the Directory in France, the whiff of grapeshot with which Bonaparte saved it, and the latter's Italian victories altered the European political climate. Lafayette learned of these things not only through their underground channels of communication, but by the subtle changes in the attitudes of his jailers, wrought by French military successes. He dictated to Adrienne another defense of his principles that was smuggled out as part of the campaign for release. He now felt there was a government in France which might exert itself in his favor. This, at least, was better than relying on friends who had not so much proved false as ineffective. He was, after all, still very much a French citizen; he regarded the new government as nearer to his own principles than its predecessors; he thought it time to claim some credit for the achievements of the revolution, not only in his own name, but in the name of all those who had died during the Terror, the dead whose living representative he felt himself to be.

He was not, he said, the ardent royalist his enemies made him out to be. The Constitution of 1791 that he had defended was more republican than any since. He claimed to be in no position to judge if the country were not still so restless, "so deprived of public spirit and servants of the first rank," that it might be necessary to put the highest post in the land out of reach of "plotters." But it would be as stupid to re-establish constitutional royalty as it had been cowardly to put in its place the aristocracy of the Jacobins and the arbitrary kingship of its leaders. There was no reason for him to come back and fight the abolition of royalty, which had been bought at a price a hundred times greater than it was worth. On the principles of the Declaration of Rights, however, he remained inflexible, even if he were "alone in the universe." He felt himself to be first of all a man of universal liberty rather than a man of a particular country, and believed "the revolution rather than his own birth gave him his real title of French citizen." Anyone who accused him of mere pride was unjust: he "asked nothing of any country or any person."

By this declaration Lafayette proclaimed himself a friend of the new order, or at least not an enemy: he had a right to expect that they would respond. Public pressure on the French government for his release increased, and while few made Lafayette into a martyr, it was widely felt that, as a founder of the revolution that had once more swung round to moderation and bourgeois compromise, he did not deserve to languish in an Austrian jail. Washington wrote a private letter to the emperor. He had not even tried to communicate with his "adopted son" from June 10, 1792, to October 8, 1797 – on which date he assured Lafayette that the reason for his long silence was not that his affections had in any way diminished, but because of the difficulties of his position as president of the United States, a nation which was still determinedly neutral. Lafayette was understanding and grateful, Adrienne less so. In England, FitzPatrick and Charles James Fox renewed their attacks on Pitt for permitting an ally of England to commit such atrocities on an innocent man and his family. Nevertheless it was victory in the field that was the most effective weapon in the campaign to get the Lafayettes released. General Bonaparte's victories threatened Vienna itself. When peace negotiations began in April 1797, at Leoben, Bonaparte was in an immensely strong position. By this time, the pressure of publicity made the Directory ask him to secure the prisoners' release.

The request for the freedom of the Lafayettes, Latour-Maubourg, and Bureaux de Pusy was formally delivered by the French plenipotentiaries, Generals Bonaparte and Clarke. The Austrians sent the Marquis de Chasteler to get the prisoners to agree never to set foot in the dominions of His Imperial Majesty. After a few jokes, among which Lafayette asserted that he never wanted to see Austria again, not even if the emperor should invite him personally, Lafayette made one of his statements of principle. He refused to recognize that the Austrian government had any rights whatsoever over him: he owed duty to the sovereign French people, and them alone. A chill came over the discussions, for de Chasteler had to have a yes-or-no answer. The Austrian behaved amiably, according to Adrienne, but Lafayette stood ever more firmly on his rights, even though this would prolong his imprisonment.

In a written declaration, Lafayette repeated his principle that, although he had no desire to revisit Austria, he could not agree to a condition which his duty to his country might one day force him to break. His fellow-prisoners, after a touching reunion with each other, penned similar statements. The Viennese court was so enraged that, as far as they were concerned, the Lafayettes and their friends could rot for the rest of their lives. Even Louis Romeuf, Lafayette's old aide-de-camp who was sent by Bonaparte to pursue the negotiations, regretted this hardening of attitudes. It took him weeks to get to see the Baron de Thugut, the emperor's chief minister, and when he did he was treated to a violent and rude outburst against Lafayette and all he stood for. Nevertheless the Austrians realized that Lafayette also represented a matter of principle for the French victors. It was agreed that if the American consul in Hamburg guaranteed to take delivery of the Lafayettes and get them out of the imperial domain within twelve days, the prisoners would be released without further promises on their part. A somewhat hesitant Romeuf conveyed this to Lafayette with a fervent plea for acceptance. The general agreed, and on September 19, 1797, the prisoners of Olmütz were released. Lafayette was forty years old.

16
Exile

LAFAYETTE EMERGED FROM more than five years of prison physically changed but mentally unaltered. The world around him presented a similar picture: much had happened, but while his sworn enemies the despots of Europe still sat with apparent safety on their thrones, in France a government with aims and methods he could agree with, if not totally respect, had succeeded the constitutional fumblings and subsequent excuses of those who had ruled when he had last been free. Prison usually hardens rather than corrects its victims, especially if their crimes are political, and Lafayette emerged a very hard man indeed.

But for someone who had been at the very center of events, to come out with no active responsibilities was very galling. He loudly proclaimed that his only wish was to retire to the lands Adrienne had inherited east of Paris, but like Cincinnatus, and even more to the point, like Washington, he expected to hold himself in readiness until the call came. Imprisonment by the enemies of his country, and survival when so many of his political contemporaries had been cut down, should have brought an enhanced reputation and a mellow glow of forgiveness. But because he refused to regard himself as a spent force, the directors of France refused to allow him into the country. Lafayette blamed Bonaparte for insisting that he stay out of France, but certainly the directors had no wish to be bothered with a general likely to lecture the nation on principles they preferred to forget.

Although rarely a politic man, Lafayette hastened to thank Bonaparte for his deliverance, and then began to thank all those in America, England, and France who had helped, financially or otherwise, to get his friends and family released. Adrienne pledged a substantial sum to Bollmann, in return for the services he had tried in vain to render her husband, and even though the family was ruined, financial advances were made, with Adrienne's inheritance as security, to those even worse off than they, such as Lafayette's old "foster-father" the Comte de Lusignem. The group proceeded slowly, because of Adrienne's ill-health, toward Wittmold where the de Tessés, and one of Adrienne's two surviving sisters, Pauline de Montagu, awaited them. Wherever they were recognized they were surrounded by admirers, a state of affairs which boosted both Lafayette's morale and his belief that the spirit of liberty was alive and well. But it also made his inability to take up the sword on its behalf more galling.

There was always, of course, the pen. Once settled at Wittmold, where Adrienne's very devout sister found Lafayette's dogmatism as irritating as she found the endless talk of politics boring, he began to pour out letters and plans. His enthusiasm was natural to one who for five years had been restricted to a toothpick and soot or lemon juice. Shortly after coming out of prison, he had heard news of the coup of 18 Fructidor (September 4, 1797). The Constitution of the Year III (1795), which abolished universal suffrage and gave political power to the propertied classes, had brought about, among other things, a revival of salon life, of displays of wealth and ostentation, of inflation – and of the constitutional monarchists. It was to counter the influence of the last that the coup of 18 Fructidor took place: three of the five directors acted against the other two and brought Paris under a sudden military occupation such as it had not known since the days of the absolute monarchy. The legislature was purged and several hundred opponents of republicanism were deported to Guiana. Opposition papers were suppressed. It was just like old times.

Lafayette had approved of the Constitution of the Year III, with some reservations, doubtless because it was the nearest thing so far to the American system, most notably in its two-chamber arrangement. But he strongly disapproved of 18 Fructidor, as he always disapproved of coups by those in power and directed against representative institutions. The only time the consistent Lafayette justified violence against the established order was when that order itself violated the terms of its mandate. This, he maintained, was what the Assembly had done in 1792 under the malign influence of the Jacobins. The directors, however, used Fructidor merely to get rid of their opponents, which was not, in Lafayette's mind, calculated to advance the cause of liberty. He did not stint his criticisms, even when writing to the directors to thank them for their part in securing his release. It was not altogether surprising that they should have wanted to keep him out of the way.

If exile was, in Lafayette's words, like being dead, life at Wittmold was almost jolly. Mme de Simiane, who had also survived the Terror, was so anxious to see the prisoners and offer them comfort that she had herself smuggled out of France with a false passport, thanks to the help of an old Jacobin friend. She arrived expecting to find everybody mourning their lost relatives and their lost chances, and was amazed to find the air filled with talk of weddings and baptisms. Pauline de Montagu was about to give birth, but more important than that was the impending marriage of the Lafayettes' eldest daughter, Anastasie, to the shy Charles de Latour-Maubourg, brother of the general's fellow-prisoner. The apparently unshockable Mme de Tessé professed horror at this idea, partly because both bride and groom were virtually penniless, but mainly because she considered scandalous the informal way in which the matter was proposed and accepted, by Lafayette. Having stated that there had, in her opinion, been nothing like it since Adam and Eve, she soon took charge of the arrangements. Adrienne was still too ill, suffering from the results of her long confinement, to do much to help, but Pauline de Montagu was forever on the go, despite being so hugely pregnant that Mme de Simiane thought she might give birth in a closet. The marriage went off well (May 1798), and not long afterwards Mme de Montagu delivered. Mme de Tessé got so excited she sprinkled eau-de-cologne over the child's head instead of water, making a huge sign of the cross the while, agnostic old Voltairean though she was.

The Lafayettes had to find somewhere of their own until – assuming it might ever happen – the general was allowed back in France. For the next few months they wandered from one place to another, according to the successes or reverses of French arms, which might make where they were enemy territory and hence too dangerous to stay in. As Virginie de Lafayette put it, nowhere held them, and they thought only of moving. As soon as she was well enough, Adrienne, who was not proscribed in France and whose passport was still in order, set out to reorganize their lives once more. She had two principal objects: to get the Noailles' inheritance, which she shared with her sisters, straightened out; and to get Lafayette's name struck off the list of those proscribed. Failing that, she wanted to get official recognition of his right, as a French citizen, to stay in a country that was neutral or friendly to France.

The general himself was full of suggestions and orders, and as Adrienne was the sole person who might act on them, he poured them out only slightly diluted with that affectionate concern for her acquired in prison. On one occasion he went too far, and when she wrote back saying she had had enough of his carping and nagging, it took him several letters of injured tenderness before he returned to his old form. But all that was merely business, and politics were his real love. In a long letter of self-defense that is reminiscent of the correspondence with Mme de Simiane, he admits that "Doubtless I've made a lot of mistakes, but that's because I've done a lot." He stood on his principles when everyone else neglected theirs, he would never bend to a prevailing wind, and he would never and could never do something in which he didn't believe. As a result, he sadly concludes, "My political life is over. I shall be full of life for my friends, but for the public, a museum piece, or library book." And yet he felt as strongly about the future of liberty, and politics, as he had at nineteen. He decried "demi-amateurs," and concluded that there was too much cowardice and apathy about for the causes in which he believed to triumph. Only his instinct told him he was not destined solely for exile.

The trouble was that he stood for values which had been discredited before they had had a chance to be absorbed. The events of 1789 were not yet a decade behind them, but for most of the French people the watchword Lafayette used, "Liberty, Equality, and Public Order," was quite irrelevant. Such slogans had led to the Terror, which had become a bogey as frightening as "anarchy and chaos." Lafayette opposed the new order without having anything to put in its place except his version of the old, which had utterly collapsed, and whose other architects were all dead or silent in exile. He was not a monarchist; he was not a Jacobin; he approved the 1795 Constitution, yet attacked Fructidor; he talked incessantly about liberty, yet was remembered as the perpetrator of the Massacre of the Champ de Mars; he attacked the execution of the king yet proclaimed himself a republican. Who could make sense of such a man? Add to that the fact that the organized opposition to which he might have allied himself – the constitutional monarchists – distrusted him, and had besides been decimated by the Fructidor coup, and you have a situation in which someone with Lafayette's principles had no support or constituency. But then he'd been away a long time.

Meanwhile he was poor, unemployed, and uncertain of his prospects. He proposed to Bureaux de Pusy that they write a memoir defending their record and that of the victims of the Terror – a memoir that would rise above the pettiness of party and tell the truth. He prepared some notes, which appear in his own memoirs, but nothing came of them. He concocted a great scheme for editing a series of books about the old regimes' abuses in France, England, America and Germany, and urged Adrienne, when she was in Paris, to find a "good" writer (needless to say he gave her a few names). She did not do so, and another non-fiction moneyspinner was aborted.

There was always the possibility of going to America, where a welcome and the chance of earning a living farming awaited him. Washington had retired from the presidency, but although Lafayette often talked about following his example, the fact was his "father" was a full quarter of a century older than he was. Adrienne's health, besides, still wasn't quite up to crossing the Atlantic, and Lafayette was very reluctant to jeopardize his French citizenship by leaving for the United States while still on the proscribed list. Then there was the bad publicity that might result if the champion of liberty abandoned his country while it was menaced by the despotic forces of the coalition – even if the champion was given no opportunity to help his fellow-citizens. Nevertheless it was an idea, and a tempting one. Money was of course a problem, and a tentative approach was made, via the American minister at The Hague, to get some recompense for all the money Lafayette had spent during the American Revolution. But the matter had to be handled with great delicacy, not only because of the general's feelings on the subject – he believed the Americans had helped and honored him sufficiently for his services, and any further offer should come from them – but because, as a French citizen, Lafayette could not accept a pension from a foreign power. The possibility of compensation in land was mentioned, but this did not bear fruit for many years, when Lafayette was no longer in dire need. Meanwhile diplomatic relations between France and America became strained to breaking-point, over an American trade treaty concluded with England, and that long-disputed doctrine, the freedom of the seas. In July, 1798, America declared null all her treaties with France, and Washington was actually called out of retirement to head the army that would repel a possible French attack. In such circumstances Lafayette's dual patriotism caused him agonies. He hardly needed Washington's stern and fatherly advice against crossing the Atlantic until relations between the two countries were again normal.

So he settled in Holland, in a house in Vianen they could scarcely afford, and which, though beautiful, lacked even the bare essentials of housekeeping. Here, in the freezing spring of 1799, the three surviving Noailles sisters, Adrienne de Lafayette, Pauline de Montagu and Rosalie de Grammont, pooled their resources to make things as comfortable as possible. In the evenings, they shared their memories, sitting in a fireless room wrapped in as many garments as they could find. The prodigality of Lafayette's entertaining style did not diminish merely because of their poverty. When she found she had to provide something substantial for fifteen or so hungry people, Adrienne invariably fell back on *oeufs à la neige*, which made use of many eggs, much milk, and sugar, and which, though sickly, was certainly filling. Possibly it was seeing it appear again and again that made Pauline de Montagu's husband joke that he only had one good meal in Holland, and that was in Utrecht.

Adrienne went again to Paris to pursue the questions of the

Lagrange estate and her husband's status. England meanwhile threatened Holland, and thereby Lafayette. Adrienne was desperately worried and wished the way was clear to go to America; her husband was furious that there was nothing he could do to help the French, who were fighting alongside the Dutch. The sight of the tricolor moved him to tears. His son Georges, having returned from America to rejoin his family, actually went into battle as a volunteer. The English were repulsed and the Dutch patriots saved. Much moved by the successes of the French flag, Lafayette convinced himself that if he made a sudden appearance in Paris the government would either rally to his principles or kill him. But Bonaparte got there before him.

Twelve years Lafayette's junior (though Lafayette had become a general at an earlier age), Bonaparte had the charisma conferred by undisputed military success. He had the advantage of never having declared his political allegiance, which was more exciting than the eternal verities attached to Lafayette's name. Although the Caesar-like idea of conquering Egypt had been his own, Bonaparte prudently extricated himself and arrived in Paris in October 1799, to find Sieyès, the great survivor, contemplating a coup on Fructidorean lines. When a nation becomes as used as France had to coups and counter-coups, to constitution succeeding constitution, to the ins and outs of politicians, one more assault on their representative institutions, especially if made in the name of "the country in danger," makes sadly little difference. Sieyès commanded a considerable political following, Bonaparte commanded an army. If they allied, their opponents would either have to call on foreign troops or raise the masses – always a risky procedure, especially when Sieyès' enemies were more right-wing than left.

From Holland, Lafayette's analysis of the state of the nation showed he knew things had to change. Apart from himself as the symbol of unity, he thought that for a people alienated from the processes of government, the best solution would be to give them liberal institutions instead of a "tyrannical convention," so that the majority would not become counter-revolutionary out of sheer desperation. His alternative was a coup of his own. But he had no followers, no loyal soldiers, no program save the principles of a decade ago. Bonaparte was popular, unfettered by principles, and he had the army. Thus, thanks largely to the intervention of his brother Lucien when he lost his head in trying to get rid of the Council of Five Hundred, Bonaparte carried out the coup of 18 Brumaire, and became first consul for an initial period of ten years.

Adrienne de Lafayette, shrewd as ever, had paid a call on Bonaparte before the coup, ostensibly to thank him again for their deliverance. He received her graciously, and spoke kindly of her husband, though in fact neither he nor Sieyès (whom she also visited) wanted Lafayette back in France. She advised her husband to write Bonaparte a flattering note, and she told him to make it short. Lafayette did as he was told. When the coup took place, and the Bonapartes proclaimed all the principles of 1789, Adrienne saw this as an opportunity for Lafayette to return. Perhaps she thought that Bonaparte's (and Sieyès') success would make them confident enough not to regard Lafayette as a challenge, or that their victory would make them generous, even tolerant, toward a long-standing exponent of the principles they claimed to espouse. All she wanted was to get her husband to her château at Lagrange and hold him to his solemn promise of retiring from public life in order to become a farmer.

She dispatched Alexandre Romeuf, Louis Romeuf's brother and also one of Lafayette's aides-de-camp, to Vianen armed with a false passport for her husband, and she told Lafayette that he would have to decide quickly whether or not he wanted to take the chance. Within two hours, he was on the road to Paris. He would have liked to re-enter public life as a man above party, to heal the wounds of factional strife and to bring the revolution to a final end. But he held to the promise he had made to Adrienne: only if he should be called to "patriotic duty" would he re-enter the sordid political arena. Nevertheless he allowed himself to believe that Bonaparte actually wanted him back to take up his old job of commandant-general of the national guard of Paris. As soon as he reached Paris he wrote to Bonaparte and Sieyès – a very old friend – informing them of his presence. The first consul was furious. Talleyrand and others came to warn Lafayette of Bonaparte's wrath, and advised him to return to exile. Lafayette maintained that since France had again become "free," thanks to the coup, so had he. He pointed to the consuls' vow to re-establish the republic "on the bases of liberty and justice," and he said he was bound for retirement. He did, however, remind his friends that threats or menaces only made him more determined.

For the new rulers of France, Lafayette was an irritant rather than a threat, since he had no appreciable following among the new generation of activists. His principles appeared outmoded and his survival merely quaint. In the spirit of harmony that makers of coups always proclaim as soon as they have got their real enemies out of the way, Lafayette's presence was tolerated, its official recognition left till later. But Bonaparte showed his displeasure by treating Lafayette, at least to begin with, as if he didn't exist. He demonstrated this in the pettiest way, and the one most hurtful to the general, by refusing to invite him to the memorial service held at Les Invalides to commemorate the death of Washington (which had occurred on December 14, 1799) and moreover the first consul personally vetted the funeral oration to ensure that it contained no mention of Lafayette's name.

So the ex-hero of two worlds, after visiting his aged but unchanged aunt at Chavaniac, settled into the vast and dilapidated château of Lagrange and, being forbidden Paris, concentrated on cultivating his estates. He formulated grandiose plans, while Adrienne naturally took charge of the details. Vaudoyer, who had worked on Chavaniac, was called in to improve Lagrange, and the painter Robert was commissioned to lay out the park. The result was very pleasing and very expensive. One economic suggestion from Lafayette was that they buy cheap or second-hand furniture. The only income would be from the farms attached to the estate; the only capital from compensation for lands sequestered by the state. Lafayette threw himself into agriculture, leaving it to his wife to get him off the proscribed list. But as he wouldn't permit his own name to be removed before this had been done for all his friends, Adrienne, still suffering from the effects of prison, had her hands full.

As in most things, she was successful, and when, on March 1, 1800, the first consul restored full rights to those *émigrés* and other proscribed people who had voted for the abolition of privileges on August 4, 1789, Lafayette's name was included. It was a curious basis for amnesty, from the man who in due course took the title of emperor and invented a whole set of new privileges fully as self-important as the old, but Bonaparte was nothing if not supple. Having made Lafayette feel his displeasure, he was now cordial, even welcoming. Lafayette in turn, always ready to see merit in those who were pleasant to him, provided they did not flagrantly contravene his well-known principles, was flattered and flattering. Bonaparte, he said, reminded him of Frederick the Great.

The two men saw a lot of one another over the two-day festivities arranged by Joseph Bonaparte to celebrate the patching-up of relations with the United States. The first consul had been very impressed by the deep hatred shown toward Lafayette by the Austrians: getting him out of Olmütz, he said, was one of the most difficult parts of their negotiations. Relations between the pair were naturally quite formal, as was to be expected from two great egotists. Bonaparte told Lafayette that the French had "gone cold on the subject of liberty"; Lafayette replied that that may have been so, but "they were more than ever in a state to receive it" – from Bonaparte, of course. Only when Lafayette started talking about the American notion of appointing a president for life, and how it might work in France, did Bonaparte give him his full attention. Lafayette mentioned that in America the president went around without pomp or bodyguards. "You would agree," said Bonaparte with some force, "that in France that wouldn't do at all."

Yet for all the kindness shown by the first consul and his brother Joseph, it was obvious that no government job with real responsibility attached was going to be offered to Lafayette. If they wanted him at all, it was as window-dressing, and that was a role he was not prepared to accept. He said of himself that he wanted glory, not power. He would have liked to have been involved in politics, but only on his own terms. In the face of a power as immovable as Bonaparte, Lafayette contented, even consoled, himself with his past record and his rural retreat. In this last, he had the added pleasure of Mme de Simiane, of the Princesse d'Hénin, and of the acerbic company of Mme de Tessé, all of whom came to stay at Lagrange. Mme de Tessé not only lent the Lafayettes money, but furnished an apartment in the château at her own expense. Adrienne received everyone with perfect hospitality. They were all growing old.

Her husband's private life consisted of the dignified pursuit of agriculture, his public life of a dignified refusal to take high but ornamental office. For most people the relative calm that Adrienne at last enjoyed would have been enough. Not for Lafayette. A new enthusiasm was added to his armory of old ones. He plunged into farming with ideas (culled from books) as new and, in the opinion of his neighbors, as reckless as his first adventures in the cause of liberty. He gave his orders as if for battle, and his herds, his crops, and his yields were soon the best in the area, and his methods soon copied. In politics, far from accepting Bonaparte as everyone else had done, he remained intransigently opposed to "arbitrary government," and said so. When Talleyrand, as minister for foreign affairs, offered him the job of being ambassador to America, he replied that he was too American to play the role of a foreigner there. But the real reason was his reluctance to be Bonaparte's representative among those who had formed the principles on which he stood, and whose much-needed respect might diminish if he deviated from them. When he was pressed to accept a place in the French Senate, he refused because he felt that he would have to take up a position which "the government would regard as insurrectionary, and the opposition as timid." It was a matter of pride as well as principle. But he was of course flattered that the administration considered him sufficiently important to woo. And he fulfilled his civic duties by accepting the job of elector for the department of Seine-et-Marne, an office for life that was nevertheless put to the test of a vote.

On one occasion Bonaparte said affectionately to Lafayette, "Yours was a good way of doing things. To direct the affairs of one's country and then, when shipwrecked, to have nothing to do with one's enemies – that's the way things ought to be done!" But in a revealing conversation that took place in 1802, the first consul, in pleasant enough fashion, accused Lafayette of lending his name to his country's enemies. Lafayette protested that he was silent in his rural retreat, but that if anyone asked him if the regime corresponded with his ideas on liberty, he was forced to say it didn't: "I'd like to be prudent, but not a renegade." "What do you mean by your term 'arbitrary regime?'" said Bonaparte. "Yours wasn't, I agree, but you could always rely on disorder to cope with your enemies. I was only in the pit while you were on stage, but I was watching hard. Yes, to make those – see reason, you had to foment disorder." Lafayette of course hotly denied this, but whether Bonaparte was serious or just baiting him, he was always a shrewd observer.

"Don't you agree," Bonaparte went on, "that with France in the state in which I found it, I was forced to take irregular measures?" "That's not the question," replied Lafayette, "I'm not talking about this instant, nor of this or that action, it's the direction I complain about, and which affects me so." For that matter, the first consul returned, "I have plenty to complain about where you are concerned," but he concluded by saying that at least he recognized that Lafayette had always held a good opinion of him personally. "Yes," replied the general, "a free government with you at its head, that's what I require."

Lafayette, in his forties, had acquired dignity by being consistent (or stubborn or pig-headed, according to taste). But both by upbringing, with its code of *noblesse oblige*, and by temperament, he could not relinquish public service having once been so excited by its burdens. He would neither bend nor break, but when the final rupture with Bonaparte occurred because Lafayette voted against the consulate-for-life (May 1802), the active political life for which he not-so-secretly longed, despite his protestations that he was a mere rustic, must have seemed denied forever. For all that, he could not stop saying what he felt and calling for a government based on liberty. There were few who listened and many, around Bonaparte especially, who were very irritated. But since the only people with power and organization to change the government were the monarchists and other riff-raff with whom Lafayette would never have associated himself, it was safe, as far as the administration was concerned, to let him rant on. Like other retired generals who are frozen out of the central arena, he never ceased to believe that the call would come again. But in that belief he was virtually alone.

In February, 1802, Lafayette slipped and broke his femur. Typically for a man with his enthusiasm for novelty, he opted for a form of treatment that required him to have his leg imprisoned in a machine that constantly stretched it. The first treatment lasted for more than a fortnight, and though the pain was excruciating, Lafayette never once complained. He was consoled in his illness by a constant stream of inquiries and visitors, from members of the government and the general public, concerned about his progress. Joseph Bonaparte sent a messenger daily for bulletins, which was both kind and a flattering testament to his importance. When the machine was taken off – and with it a portion of Lafayette's thigh – it was discovered that the straps had cut into the muscles and tendons, causing the skin to turn gangrenous. The general took five weeks to recover from this "treatment," and was left with deep scars and a permanently stiff hip that forced him to limp. Yet he never criticized his doctors.

Bravery is somewhat baffling to those who lack it. Everyone hopes to be brave when necessary, but when one tries to understand the quality in others, one tends to oversimplify their predicament, to make it seem as if bravery were the only honorable course open. Lafayette was not a marble hero, a man who lacked human failings. Yet among his close friends, those who had shared his enthusiasm for 1776 and 1789, and lived to say so, none was as outspoken as he. His old mentor Ségur even became Napoleon's grand master of ceremonies when the latter declared himself emperor, and others lived as they had under the old regime, that is to say, accepting what benefits the system offered them and tut-tutting in private. Some went to America and lived in honorable style, and this choice was offered to Lafayette by his old friend Jefferson, now president. Having learned of the estrangement between Lafayette and the government, Jefferson offered him the governorship of Louisiana, which had just been purchased from France, Lafayette having played a part in the negotiations. Congress also granted him that portion of land – some 11,000 acres – to which his rank and service in the revolution entitled him. Originally in Ohio, these were transferred to Louisiana, which greatly increased their value. Lafayette was very proud that Congress, whose ever more bitter divisions on party lines he deplored, should come together in unanimous resolve where he was concerned. Yet he refused Jefferson's offer, even though the president pressed him to leave a "shaky" France for the "peace and future prosperity" of the promised land, where his qualities made him uniquely fitted to govern a Franco-American state.

Why didn't Lafayette accept? He and his wife were convalescent, but that was not sufficient reason. His Chavaniac aunt was eighty-three years old, but though her nephew's visits were a high spot in her life, they were rare enough for us to conclude that Lafayette regarded them as only an intermittent duty. The real reason was a combination of pride, honor, and obstinacy, which combined to produce the bravery for which Lafayette was famous. A certain General Moreau was implicated in a plot against Bonaparte, and arrested. Lafayette was warned that he would suffer the same fate, as Moreau was an old colleague of his. While neither Napoleon nor Joseph Bonaparte believed him capable of joining an aristocratic plot, Napoleon at least thought it politic to worry Lafayette a little. At this point, lacking a following and unable effectively to persuade the government to adopt his way of thinking, harassed and unwell, Lafayette received Jefferson's proposal. What stopped him accepting was the thought that it might seem as if Bonaparte had him on the run. Threats and menaces, he had often said, only made him more determined. His may have been a lone voice, but he believed it was more effective, and more honorable, to raise it inside his country, rather than from the safety of exile. He was, besides, very proud of being French, and he did not want to give Bonaparte the opportunity, or the satisfaction, of depriving him of his citizenship, or denying him the right to re-enter France.

So he replied to Jefferson that, whereas the cause of liberty in America had no need of him, he could not withdraw from France while it was "in the grip of despotism." To do so might discourage those (few though they were) who might call on him. And he then attempted to testify in court on Moreau's behalf, but was denied the opportunity. Lafayette deplored this "judicial tyranny" – but even his dangerously outspoken opposition did not prevent the government from still trying to woo him over. Lafayette persisted in refusing all offers, whether of the Legion of Honor or the efforts of Joseph – now Prince Joseph – to get him into the Senate. Lafayette supposed that Napoleon would have preferred the inconvenience of having him as a senator to the publicity given to his opposition. He stated that, while he was always ready to serve liberty, he could not express himself through the silent assent that would be expected in the Senate. No further offers were made.

If Lafayette was brave, he was not, at this stage, effective; but then he did not really expect to be. If he had had more of a following he would doubtless have been arrested: as it was the government obviously preferred to leave him alone, perhaps for fear of adverse publicity but also as proof of its "libertarian" principles. Napoleon no more wanted to give Lafayette the satisfaction of martyrdom than Lafayette wanted to satisfy him by accepting his regime. There was a sort of love-hate relationship between the two. Lafayette cited Napoleon, with approval, as combining four essential qualities – calculating, preparing, gambling and waiting. Himself a poor calculator, too impulsive to make thorough preparations, a long-standing opponent of gambling, Lafayette found, for the first time in his life (if we exclude his five years in jail), that he was capable of waiting for his principles to triumph.

Once his three children were married and he was a grand-father, Lafayette found increasing satisfaction in family life. He was, for the first time, often at home, seeing to the estate, and even when he went to Paris Adrienne knew that at least his life was not in danger.

Having cut himself off from physical contact with America, and saddened that the principles for which he had fought in France were washed out by the "counter-revolution" of the empire – and even more by the fact that a regime he genuinely regarded as despotic was tolerated by the vast majority of his countrymen – his family, his farm, and his optimism were his three chief supports.

Unlike most men who grow old Lafayette always believed things would get better, regardless of the number of times he was proved wrong. But the loss of Adrienne, for so long his chief prop, was extremely hard to bear. In a long letter to his ex-fellow-prisoner Latour-Maubourg, he movingly described his wife's last weeks, surrounded by family and friends, who included Mme de Simiane, no longer a threat, to whom Adrienne had even lent money. Even in her delirious moments Adrienne's first concerns were for his husband. Lafayette quotes her as saying, "It seems to me that the world is being remade from the beginning: there is no end to all these experiments. When on earth will it run smoothly on two wheels, as you want it to?"

"You're not a Christian, are you?" she asked him one day. When he didn't reply, she said, "I know what you are: a Fayettist." "You may think me arrogant," he returned, "but aren't you a bit of one yourself?" "I am, with all my soul," she said, "I feel I would give my life for that sect." She often said, "My children must put up with having a stupid mother, since their father is willing to put up with a stupid wife." Lafayette admitted to one pang of jealousy, after thirty-four years of marriage, when he was asked to give up his place by her death-bed to her pious sister Pauline de Montagu, in case Adrienne wished to make her religious devotions. But Adrienne sent her away, and died, on December 24, 1807, with her husband's hand in hers, whispering "I am all yours." She was buried in the cemetery of Picpus she and her sisters had founded, on the site of the mass grave where her executed relatives were laid. "Up to now," Lafayette told Latour-Maubourg, "you have found me stronger than my circumstances; today, the circumstance is stronger than I."

Adrienne had said that she wouldn't mind if Lafayette remarried after her death, but they had been together too long for that. The friends and mistresses of his youth were old: though he continued to show a lively interest in pretty girls, his relationships had none of the old permanence. Indeed his devotion to Adrienne's memory was such that every single morning he would dismiss his valet and shut himself in his room, holding a portrait of her that he carried round his neck (which had her last words engraved upon it), pressing it to his lips, and meditating for about a quarter of an hour. If disturbed in these devotions, he became extremely cross.

Lafayette sustained himself by continuing to champion his

principles. Napoleon had his measure when he remarked, "Everyone has been brought into line with one exception: Lafayette! He's never taken back a word. You see him quiet now; well, I'm telling you myself, he's all ready to begin again." Lafayette was careful to keep in touch with events in Europe and America; he was mortified to learn that his would-be rescuer Bollmann was implicated in the treasonable conspiracy of Aaron Burr, and considered it a triumph of American justice when Bollmann was released. If he now had time to go to the theater (he admired the pseudo-classical style of tragedians like Talma), he was always ready to speak his mind, to defend victims of persecution, and to entertain liberals from anywhere. He followed the successes of French arms with delight, but was not astonished at the reverses of the Russian campaign, which he attributed to Napoleonic grandeur. Bernadotte told him, before leaving to take up the throne of Sweden, that his "very existence was miraculous," but Lafayette always believed he was invulnerable. He had survived so much. Even the plots and counter-plots against the emperor, which Lafayette neither joined nor disapproved, failed to disquiet him, though his family must have had anxious moments.

When Napoleon's empire faced defeat, and the forces of the allies against France were about to attack Paris (February, 1814), Lafayette happened to be in the capital for the funeral of Mme de Tessé (whose death had followed her husband's and that of Lafayette's old guardian the Comte de Lusignem). Lafayette threw himself into action and tried to rally the national guard for the defense of the capital. He also proposed that Napoleon abdicate. No one, however, listened to such radical advice, and at the end of March the allies took Paris. Lafayette's reaction was to shut himself up in the apartment he had aquired, in tears.

The restoration of the Bourbons aroused mixed feelings in him. They appeared to be popular, even if Louis XVIII's corpulent waddle was an irresistible reminder of the king France had beheaded, but perhaps the family would bring the peace and stability for which France longed. Lafayette admitted he was moved by the sight of his old school friend the Comte d'Artois, brother of the late king, in the streets, and he dearly hoped that they had learned enough to become supporters of liberty. Unfortunately the Bourbons were famous for learning nothing and forgetting nothing. They believed in their divine right as a matter of principle, if not practice, and one of their first actions was to replace the revolutionary tricolor, whose parent Lafayette claimed to be, with the Bourbon white. Lafayette nevertheless got himself dressed in uniform and presented himself at the first royal audience. He was well received, which raised his hopes that the new era would fulfill the promises of the old.

For a cynic, things had come full circle, but Lafayette was still a romantic. Life under Napoleon had been possible because he knew it would not last; life under the Bourbons might be pleasurable because the lessons of 1789 could not simply be blotted out and ignored, and because there was a sense of familiarity in the old ways which the Napoleonic court had never mastered.

Lafayette might now hope for a re-entry into politics. Apart from his farms, there was little else for him to do, and he saw this as an opportunity to crown the promises of his early years. He was never content to regard himself as a museum piece. But the Bourbons trusted him no more than Napoleon had done. Talleyrand, a willow to Lafayette's oak, playing the same role for the king as he had for the emperor, made a tentative approach on behalf of the new regime, but Lafayette disapproved of Talleyrand's political conduct, especially since he had signed away the gains France had made through the Napoleonic wars. The Bourbons, far from healing and conciliating, chose to ignore the men of the previous twenty-five years, and their achievements. As a result their initial popularity rapidly vanished. The fact that they were restored to the throne on the points of foreign bayonets hardly endeared them to their defeated countrymen, and resentment was not slow in surfacing. Lafayette, meeting Tsar Alexander at Mme de Staël's salon, and finding him a liberal fellow, asked why he had permitted so "incorrigible" a family to be restored. The Tsar blamed his allies – as did all of France.

Nor were the Bourbon efforts at constitutional monarchy very inspiring. Lafayette told himself that a greater degree of liberty existed under Louis XVIII than under the emperor, and he approved of the two-chamber system of government. But in the end he was offered no post, and soon he began to reiterate his famous principles – the inevitable sign of his frustration. When the government attempted to issue updated equivalents of the notorious *lettres de cachet* (not, however, against himself) Lafayette offered his house as refuge to one of their intended victims. This was tantamount to a declaration of opposition, and royalist pamphlets began to appear attacking Lafayette's role in the revolution, referring especially to the days of October 1789 and the flight to Varennes. After forty years in public life Lafayette was well used to such things, and had prided himself on never bothering to rebut a slander. This time, however, the period between his hopes being raised and seeing them destroyed was too short to bear, and he prepared notes for a riposte. He was prevented from publishing them by news of Napoleon's escape from Elba and his landing in France, the period known as the Hundred Days.

Lafayette dashed to Paris from Lagrange to be at the center of affairs. He still mistrusted Napoleon, and felt that if only the Bourbons had offered the right guarantees of liberty, the French people would have remained loyal to them. His friends, and the public, strongly disagreed, and the popularity of Napoleon, and the dignified way in which he ordered no blood should be shed for his sake, impressed even Lafayette. Yet he noted rather sardonically that the emperor's vocabulary changed: when he first disembarked he addressed his audience as "citizens," but they soon became "Frenchmen" and, by the time he arrived in the capital, "subjects." Lafayette was convinced that the emperor would ruin the nation with further war for, unless some compromise were negotiated, the allied powers would not accept Napoleon any more than he would accept their dictation. Lafayette therefore tried to persuade the Bourbons to take a stand as Napoleon advanced across France. The court at last offered Lafayette his old job as commander of the national guard, but he had little chance to do anything. He recommended the summoning of all deputies who had been members of every representative assembly since 1789, to "oppose Napoleon's physical force with a moral one." But this rather impractical idea met with no support. The national guard, being members of the bourgeoisie who did better under a peaceful restoration than a war-like emperor, offered to guard the royal palace of the Tuileries. Arrangements to do so were being made when it was learned that the royal family had fled, so hurriedly that the king forgot his wallet. They managed, however, to stuff the crown jewels, which even Napoleon had regarded as state property, into their baggage. Yet Lafayette's sense of honor made him stay until the bitter end. "It would be strange," he wrote, "to be proscribed twice over for the house of Bourbon."

When Napoleon triumphantly entered Paris, Lafayette stayed three days to show he was not afraid, and then retired in disgust to his farms. The emperor was reported to have said that it wasn't the coalition of kings but the force of liberal ideas that overthrew him. But his apparent conversion wasn't nearly enough for Lafayette. Not that the emperor's first worry was the aging incorrigible. It was only when he was faced with internal collapse and external defeat that Napoleon determined to make concessions. In April 1815 Lafayette was summoned by Prince Joseph. One last attempt was made to bring Lafayette into the fold – this time not only to save the emperor, but the empire itself.

17
Full Circle

LAFAYETTE HAD ALWAYS liked Joseph Bonaparte, and the two were similar: both liberal, both well-intentioned, and both ineffective when it came to wielding power. No one could doubt that this time the country really was in danger, and that with an enemy force on its borders, summoned by the Bourbons themselves, France had need of every patriot. Certainly Lafayette was ready to answer such a call. But he made very clear his reservations, and insisted that what he did was on his own terms, not the emperor's.

Napoleon, he told Joseph, would never mend his ways, and he openly declared his part in having tried to rally opinion around the Bourbons. But with the threat of foreign invasion, Lafayette considered Napoleon to be the lesser of two evils. He was sure the emperor's government was going to be as bad as ever, and he wanted it to last for the shortest possible time. Joseph admitted that his brother had always been against a representative assembly, but said that for the new Chamber of Peers, Lafayette's name was first on the list about to be published. Lafayette replied that he had always been against the hereditary peerage, and he wasn't about to enter it at the emperor's bidding. "I am," he said, "a man of the people, and it is only by the choice of the people that I should emerge from my retreat." In May 1815 a new constitution, somewhat on the English model, was promulgated, and though Lafayette protested that it was decreed rather than discussed, he supported it, and was elected president of the electoral college of Seine-et-Marne and Melun, whose choice for deputy he became.

Joseph Bonaparte, entertaining Lafayette to dinner, wanted to bring him together with his brother the emperor, but Lafayette refused until his duties as deputy should officially renew their contact. Joseph then wanted him to accept nomination to the peerage: this Lafayette again refused, whereupon Joseph rather touchingly said there would be such an outcry if the list were published without Lafayette's name he wished the general would at least publicly explain his refusal. The general obliged.

When the Chamber met and proceeded to elect its president, Lafayette was heavily defeated for the post. He was, however, elected vice-president: his popularity among the elected representatives of the people was less than he hoped or imagined. But intransigence is not a quality that appeals to politicians.

The first thing Lafayette objected to in the Chamber was the terms of the oath of loyalty, which demanded the defence of the imperial dynasty to the exclusion of all others. When he heard this the emperor remarked, "There goes Lafayette, already declaring war on me!" The two met again at the formal opening of the session. Napoleon stopped in front of Lafayette and said, "It's twelve years since I've had the pleasure of seeing you." Doubtless he wasn't expecting much, for Lafayette replied dryly, "Yes, sire, it is that long." Napoleon later remarked that the country air was doing Lafayette good. "Very much so," was all the general would say.

Lafayette next objected to the deferential address of the deputies: as a result, it was slightly amended to prove, Lafayette said, that they weren't merely "Napoleon's club." The emperor went to the front in the middle of June and returned from Waterloo. As the familiar air of crisis settled on the capital, deputies discussed rumors that Napoleon was about to dissolve the Chamber and assume the mantle of dictatorship, which would, of course, have meant silencing dissenters like Lafayette. His worst fears again realized, the general exhorted his colleagues to rally around the tricolor, that old "standard of '89, of liberty, equality, and public order." He proposed that the Chamber declare itself in permanent session and that it invite the military leaders to report on the situation. The nation was again threatened by invasion, and there was always the chance of civil disturbance from within. The Chamber agreed.

In special conference, Lafayette next proposed that Napoleon abdicate for the sake of the country. This was one of the demands of the victorious allies, for they wanted to restore the Bourbons once more. Lafayette, however, dreamed of a return to 1789, and threatened that if the emperor did not step down he would move that the throne be declared forfeited. This was the maneuver that had deprived Louis XVI of power, to which Lafayette had at that time so strenuously objected. The emperor yielded, and abdicated in favor of his son, but the Chamber refused to do more than accept the fact that he had abdicated. Since the foreign powers were insulting enough to demand that the ex-emperor be handed over to them, his person was declared to be under the protection of the nation.

It was not like 1789, when no one knew quite what to do. France had had so many changes of government that the deputies were by now familiar with the form. They proceeded to elect a provisional government of three deputies and two peers. Lafayette stood for election and was furious at being unsuccessful. He blamed it on his old enemy "party intrigue," but it was merely proof that he had no real constituency – a fact that the Bonapartists had known all along, and which had kept him safe from arrest. He wasn't even named commander of the national guard: that job went to one of the greatest of Napoleon's marshals, Masséna. But Lafayette was made a member of the delegation sent to treat with the victorious allies. At least he spoke English.

The delegates tried to end the war on the basis that Napoleon was no longer emperor. The English delegate, Lord Stewart, demanded that Napoleon be handed over to them. Lafayette replied that he was amazed at such a request, particularly when made to an ex-prisoner of Olmütz. (When told of this Napoleon said, "I have never attacked M. de Lafayette's feelings or intentions; I only complain of their fatal results.") The allies demanded unconditional surrender, and prepared to enter Paris for a second time. The Chamber, on July 5th, passed both a Declaration of Rights and a manifesto containing all the demands Lafayette and others had made since 1789. Unfortunately he had no part in this, as he was away with his delegation. But his principles were once more the basis for a resounding proclamation of defiance.

The allies repeated their demand for unconditional surrender. Lafayette tried again to rally opposition, but the provisional government – in the hope, Lafayette thought, of avoiding the penalties of proscription – gave in. On July 7th Blücher entered Paris and the capital was once more under foreign military occupation. When the deputies presented themselves at the Chamber on the following day, the gates were shut against them. "Is this on the order of the English prince regent?" taunted Lafayette through the railings, and forthwith invited the deputies to gather at his house. There some of them signed a protest which was mere gesture. On the 15th Napoleon surrendered to the English, disappointing Lafayette who had wanted him to seek refuge in America. Louis XVIII sat himself on the throne. Lafayette wanted to retire to his farms and park at Lagrange, but he couldn't bear to do so as it was occupied by foreign troops billeted there.

By the end of 1815 he was deeper in retirement than ever. And the counter-revolution was in full swing: censorship was reimposed, heavy penalties were threatened for any who preached the overthrow of the government, and the franchise was severely restricted. The promises of Louis XVIII's Charter were not far removed from the reforms proposed by the Assembly of Notables, way back in

1787, and they incorporated some of the convenient bureaucratic improvements carried out under Napoleon. But they fell as short of the aspirations of old liberals like Lafayette as all the constitutions – save that of 1791, which hardly stood a chance – that had preceded them.

When history repeats itself within living memory, those who were there for the first time round are often content to sit wagging their heads. Not Lafayette. Under the consulate and the empire he had remained outside the political arena because no representative assembly existed and he disdained nomination by a despot. He nevertheless maintained that the most effective way of implementing his principles was through representative political institutions, assuming these existed. The restoration at least brought into being a two-chamber system, the lower of which was subject to election. True, the electorate consisted of 96,000 relatively wealthy men, paying at least 300 francs in direct taxation – the sort of money landowners could afford – and these were supposed to represent a population of some twenty-six million. True, to be a candidate you had to be over forty and pay at least a thousand francs in tax. True, the elections were "managed," which is to say government opponents sometimes had their taxes reduced to render them ineligible to vote, electoral meetings were forbidden, and the electoral colleges were presided over by government officials. But it was something to have even this degree of representative government, and besides, France was a little weary of change that only came about through violence. So Lafayette stood, as candidate of Paris, for the Chamber of Deputies in 1817, after two years of rustic isolation. He was heavily defeated: the capital was not yet ready to vote Left. But a year later, standing for La Sarthe, he was successful, by 569 votes out of 1055. The king was very upset by this, and when Lafayette came to take the oath the public galleries were crammed with the curious. Was the revolution about to renew itself?

Rhetorical questions often deserve the answer no, and this is no exception. Despite his long-held distrust of parties, Lafayette now realized that the only way he could hope to be effective was as a member of an identifiable group. Since French political parties have always been coalitions of various interests, this did not involve an intolerable amount of party discipline. Lafayette sat with the Left, as a liberal or "independent." In all the speeches he made as deputy, he showed the greatest respect for the forms of debate and the rules of the Chamber. Though he consistently attacked the erosion of liberty with which he accused the government, it might have seemed as if the man who, it was often remembered, had once pronounced that "insurrection was a sacred duty," was tamed. This was, however, an illusion.

Lafayette spoke with feeling on behalf of the liberty of the individual, against the censorship of the press, for the rights of political refugees, and against the death penalty. The assassination of the Duc de Berry (February 1820) led the administration to propose far harsher laws on arrest and detention. Lafayette argued that repression would never prevent violent crime, and called for the promised guarantees of liberty to be constitutionally established. This speech was regarded by many as revolutionary, primarily because it was so optimistic about the youth of France. Despite all the difficulties of opposition, Lafayette's faith still appeared undented: as he wrote to President Monroe (the fifth of his old American friends to achieve supreme office), "this new generation is enlightened, and generous, above both Jacobinism and Bonapartism. It will support, I am sure, the rights of pure liberty."

Yet he felt that those rights were being progressively gobbled by the government, and he had always maintained that observance of the law was a two-way matter. An illegal action by the administration, in his view, freed its opponents to act outside the law, in the law's defense. Lafayette had hoped that the revolution was over, but what he saw happening he termed the counter-revolution. As deputy he claimed to have received dozens of letters and petitions demanding that all the provisions of the 1814 Charter be carried out, and that the electoral law be reformed to widen the franchise. When he spoke on these matters he felt he was acting according to the wishes of his constituents. But the opposition in the Chamber, though vociferous and growing, was not effective. Never the most patient of men, Lafayette was attracted by what seemed a more effective champion of liberty, the secret society called the Charbonnerie. Secret societies enjoyed a vogue under the restoration as they had under the old regime, and Lafayette was an addict of long standing. The Right had their clandestine "Chevaliers de la Foi," to which the Left's answer was, as usual, a number of scattered and warring groups, of which the Charbonnerie was the largest.

If dabbling in secret societies might seem childish, let alone dangerous, for a man in his sixties, we have to consider both Lafayette's nature and the irresistible force of his reputation. He was impatient enough to prefer action to speeches, old enough to be reckless, and perhaps vain enough to respond to the overtures of radicals half his age. The fact is that, on the one hand, Lafayette was a respected member of the Chamber of Deputies, where he was a leader of the Left, and on the other, from 1821–1822, he joined a conspiracy whose aim was the violent overthrow of the Bourbons and the setting-up of a provisional government with himself as one of its members.

The Charbonnerie, which took its name from the Italian freedom-fighters, the Carbonari, was patterned on the masonic structure. It possibly owed its origins to the mining associations of the Franche-Comté, was devotedly egalitarian, and as ritualistic as the masons, who had by this time become upholders of the established order. As befitted a secret society, there were no archives, so our picture of the Charbonnerie is necessarily tentative. It was started by some students in 1821, and its leader emerged as a thirty-year-old named Bazard. It had a complex organization, based on *ventes* or secret cells in each zone or village. If there were many of these in an area a *vente centrale* coordinated their efforts. Next in the hierarchy of this guerrilla organization was an *haute vente,* which received the news and views of the grass-roots through representatives using codes, signs, and passwords, and which transmitted the orders of the *vente suprême*, of which both Lafayette and his son Georges were members. The members of the various *ventes* were not supposed to know each other, the cells had no contact with each other, and no one knew who his superior was, communication being maintained through "messengers." On top of all this there was a quasi-religious ritual, which included the swearing of oaths on a dagger.

The apparent strength of the Charbonnerie, as demonstrated by the clandestine complications of its organization, was the basis of its appeal. And not only to Lafayette, who had long ago discovered that a revolution needed strategy, organization, and money; many other opposition deputies were also involved, and financial backing was rumored to come from bankers hostile to the government (such as Laffitte). To embrace, in such company, the dangers of subversive plotting was almost a duty for Lafayette. For young radicals born under the republic, frustrated by the futility of protesting through the permitted channels against an aged and reactionary monarchy, the appeal of organized violence was obvious. The ritual, the grass-roots network of coordinated cells, the strategy (which, although sketchy, at least proposed something to take the place of the king), all in the sacred name of liberty, made the Charbonnerie irresistible to many, perhaps some 4,000 in Paris alone. Lafayette, flattered that a whole new generation should embrace his principles, and even be prepared to die for them, was never able to resist a call to put his body where his mouth was. As so often in the past, the initiative was not his, but he embraced it with all his heart.

Lafayette insisted that the various cells of the organization, while respecting the personal scruples of every member, swore to work only for a situation in which the French people would be able to choose their own form of government; not to make promises to any party or dynasty; and to re-establish the municipal and electoral administrations, the primary assemblies, the national guard nominating its own officers, and the procedures for convoking deputies, according to the law of 1791. These promises justified, in his eyes, taking up arms against the established regime. All power, when they took it, was to be regarded as provisional until the people made known their will. The trouble was that all these activities were known to the government through their spies. Stendhal, who met Lafayette often in the 1820s at the salon of Mme de Tracy, wrote that a M. Lavenelle had the job of reporting on Lafayette's activities to the Tuileries. The joke (according to Stendhal) was that Lafayette and his friends, like Benjamin Constant, took Lavenelle into their confidence because they considered him a partisan of their views. They were apparently convinced by his "terrorist" past, and the fact that he talked about nothing but advancing on the palace and "massacring all the Bourbons." Now while Lafayette was not known for his discretion, he was usually cautious of people who were consistently outspoken. Whether or not Stendhal was right, the government was certainly aware of what Lafayette and his accomplices were up to. And theirs was not the only revolutionary plot in existence.

The Charbonnerie's idea was that the provisional government, with Lafayette as a member, would be declared at Belfort, in Alsace. The plan, presumably, was to raise the standard of revolt and enlist the support of the national guard, thus engendering a mass uprising against the Bourbons. Lafayette, having passed the anniversary of Adrienne's death at Lagrange, set out with his son Georges for Belfort on December 20, 1821. On the first day of the new year, when they had nearly reached their destination, they were warned that the plot had been discovered. The Lafayettes went into hiding at the house of a liberal deputy nearby. They stayed a few days and then returned to Lagrange (which was of course under police surveillance). Four sergeants of La Rochelle, as well as other military figures, were tried, condemned and executed for their part in the conspiracy. Lafayette was implicated, along with Benjamin Constant, the banker Laffitte and other opposition deputies.

Lafayette demanded that any accusations against them be delivered in the Chamber of Deputies itself, so that they could be answered, with maximum publicity, in the face of the nation. Whether the solidarity of the Charbonnerie had prevented the government from obtaining direct evidence of Lafayette's complicity, or whether the administration wanted to avoid the publicity of bringing so redoubtable an opponent to trial, Lafayette was left alone. The death of the others naturally caused him grief, and he tried to finance their escape from the scaffold, but in vain. None of the plots to overthrow the Bourbons in the name of liberty succeeded. Hindsight makes it easy to say France was not ready, that she was sick of violence, determined on peace at any price. But while Lafayette bemoaned the apathy of his fellow-countrymen, it took only eight more years before the same people turned out their king. Certainly the failure of the conspiracies of 1821–1822 can be explained by the lack of effective support in the army, national guard, towns and villages, and most especially in Paris. But also much to blame was an organization that was more apparent than real, a lack of planning and a failure in timing, and perhaps most important, a program based, in Lafayette's case, on the principles of thirty years before, that simply did not inspire the necessary public confidence.

Not that Lafayette was solely involved in plotting and speechifying. Thanks to the meetings between him and Stendhal, and to his doctor Jules Cloquet (who worshiped him), we have much more personal detail about his old age, when his reputation was already firm, than about his youth, when he was creating it. Lafayette's six volumes of memoirs, the principal source for his biographers, spend little time on personal matters: a paragraph in his own draft saying that he would spare us "a confession concerning a scarcely edifying youth, and even the story of two passions for famous beauties," was excised, with filial piety, by his son Georges. His contemporaries were bitchy (like Bachaumont), politically hostile (like Bouillé), or more concerned with their own apologia (like Ségur). But Stendhal had no axe to grind. The two met when the writer was in his forties and the general in his late sixties. From almost every other account, one might imagine that Lafayette was always, as it were, on duty. For Stendhal, however, the general's chief social occupation appeared to be pulling at the skirts of pretty girls, "(vulgarly, grabbing)," not once but often, and without ever appearing embarrassed by it.

Stendhal found Lafayette a hero in the classical mode. The general was the top attraction at Mme de Tracy's (whose daughter was married to his son); he would limp in with his "badly-made clothes" and short wig, "giving away nothing, like an old family portrait," and sit, soon to be surrounded by an admiring, even sycophantic, crowd of liberal sympathizers. He was "polite in the manner of royalty," but he would scandalize his circle by abruptly leaving them to admire, at close range, the "pretty shoulders of a new arrival. . . . His abandoned fans were left with nothing to do but simper." Naturally this behavior also scandalized the "ladies of thirty-five years of age," but Lafayette cared nothing about that. When he wasn't grappling with young beauties, or performing some great historical action, he would expound the commonplaces of his principles. Stendhal thought him a great party leader, not only because of his past and present activities, but because he never upset anyone and he always flattered them by remembering their names. This was fine disinterestedness on Stendhal's part, considering that he and the general were rivals in passion for an eighteen-year-old Portuguese girl, the friend of one of Lafayette's daughters. "Lafayette imagined, as he did with any young woman, that she had picked him out . . . and, what is interesting, he was often right to imagine so. His European glory, the fundamental elegance of his speeches, despite their apparent simplicity, his eyes which lit up as soon as they chanced upon the base of a pretty bust, all this enabled him to spend his last years pleasurably. . . ." Such was Stendhal's judgment.

From his doctor, of course, we have a picture that is much more pious. He and Stendhal agreed that Lafayette was tall, and Dr. Cloquet reported that he was "noticeably stout, but not obese," but after that Cloquet's portrait is all principle and duty. At least we have Stendhal to prove that Lafayette was human.

He had, according to Cloquet, a fresh complexion, without wrinkles, and a low voice that grew loud when he was excited by his subject. He was a little deaf, suffered from gout, could only sit down slowly – because of his accident – but had excellent vision. He dressed simply in a long gray or dark frock-coat, trousers with gaiters, and a round hat. He was scrupulous about personal cleanliness, and in his last years, though he liked to dine at home surrounded by a mixed and numerous company, he ate only a piece of fish or wing of chicken and drank only water. One interesting indication of the strain his position made him suffer was that he had an almost constant nervous cough.

He had become a man of routine, natural to his age and necessary because of his commitments. He slept for about seven hours, dreaming only rarely, and he believed in early rising. He had himself woken at 5 A.M., and spent till 7 in bed, reading books on history, politics, or agriculture, and doing some of his huge correspondence. When he got up and had washed, he would pay his usual homage to Adrienne's memory and then work in his study. Overseeing the details and accounts of farm management was a regular task, and his manager would wait in the park below for orders which Lafayette would shout from the window through a megaphone. The manager had no need of such aids to reply.

He would breakfast around 10 and then skim through the French and foreign papers. At noon he went on a tour of the farms, returning around 3 to work in his study with his secretaries. At 6 a dinner bell would sound and his guests would assemble; after the meal he would stay chatting or, if it was only family, even his adored grandchildren, he would do another couple of hours' work. He usually retired at about 10.30.

The winters were spent in Paris, in his apartment on the Rue d'Anjou-St-Honoré. His rooms were on the first floor, and could be opened to form one long gallery for receptions, which always took place on Tuesdays. Liberality and equality were the rule, and anyone with a claim on his hospitality (any American for example) was welcome. One political guest once remarked that his salon was full of people with very suspicious reputations, to which Lafayette replied that their job was to find out what went on in his home. "Even if I lived in a house of crystal," he said, "I would allow their spies in my courtyard."

As lord of Lagrange, Lafayette was almost feudally generous. Every Monday 200 pounds of bread were baked for distribution to the poor, which went up to 600 pounds when times were bad. Soup and cash were available for those in need; the care of the sick was paid for, and often the fines of those caught poaching. The house had become a sort of museum of presents offered to him, and was full of precious souvenirs, such as Washington's eyeglasses. The famous sword of honor which Franklin had presented him in the name of the American people had been buried by Adrienne during the Terror; when Georges dug it up, its gold blade was eaten away, so Lafayette had grafted onto the handle the blade of the sword presented by the national guard of Paris on his retirement in 1791. Few men have spares for their honors.

Although, according to Stendhal, indecorous himself, Lafayette could not accept this in others. Cloquet relates how a young man was a little too forward with his host. The offender was treated with scrupulous politeness, but the chill of disapproval was such that he left the château the same evening. Although his guests were many, to visit Lagrange was to come under police surveillance, and therefore involved a certain risk. Lafayette sheltered political refugees, both French and foreign; with his close interest in the struggles for independence taking place in Belgium, Italy, Spain, Portugal, and above all Poland, casualties of these battles were often hidden by him. Had the police entered the château – which, as far as is known, they did only once – they would also have found a large cache of "subversive" literature, for Lafayette kept several copies of all the anti-government pamphlets.

His opinions were all very public. He told Cloquet he was opposed to all *coups d'état,* under whatever form of government, because he regarded them as contrary to justice. But this was some years after the failure of the Charbonnerie, and, though Lafayette rarely changed his opinions, he may not have wanted to shock his doctor. Force was only to be used to defend or demand one's rights, when reason or injustice had proved incapable of preserving them. Where there was injustice, Lafayette dropped all moderation and believed in outright resistance to it.

Government, he thought, should be an open, not a secret, affair. An hereditary nobility was as poor a thing as an aristocracy of money. And, on the subject of money, Lafayette strongly disapproved of gambling and of state lotteries. He was a great believer in education as a bulwark against tyranny, and as a force for social and moral improvement, especially at primary level: this was always part of his electoral manifestoes under the restoration. But he was modern enough to believe that studies should be directed toward "useful tasks," and he admired the old Chinese emperors who encouraged the manual workers by leading the plough once a year. Universal education for all would make better citizens, and allow each to choose the career he wanted and for which he was fitted. In this, as in so many of his ideas, Lafayette was echoing the old aims of the Enlightenment which, because he had survived for so long, were once again positively avant-garde.

But he was always more of an activist than a talker. In the spring of 1823 he was involved in the "Manuel Affair," concerning a deputy, M. Manuel, who was expelled from the Chamber on the insistence of the Right because of an attacking speech about the need for revolutionary France to defend herself by force. Despite the expulsion order, Manuel took his seat in the Chamber, and was surrounded by the deputies of the Left. The national guard was ordered to take Manuel away, but were stopped by the voice of their founder Lafayette, crying "What, the national guard used to carry out such an order? This dishonors them!" At which the guard withdrew in some confusion. One observer said that Lafayette had found himself to be thirty years old again. At the end of that year, the Chamber was dissolved. Following the usual pendulum swing of public opinion, the elections went badly for the Left. Lafayette, standing for Meaux, was defeated, a victim or a casualty of the limited French democracy. But any disappointment was more than compensated by the fulfillment of a long-considered plan: a final expedition to America.

An invitation had been issued by President Monroe shortly before the French election results were known (February 1824). Congress had resolved to offer the old hero a vessel of state to convey him to their shores, but this Lafayette refused, saying he preferred to go by ordinary packet-boat. In July, with Georges, his valet Bastien, and his secretary Levasseur, Lafayette embarked at Le Havre on an American merchant-ship. To warm his heart an enthusiastic crowd gathered, despite an intimidating number of police, to wish him *bon voyage*. His triumphant journey, which lasted for over a year and took him through all the states of the union, makes the modern manifestations of mass hero-worship pale into insignificance. Wherever he went, thousands lined the route, many of them having walked many miles for the privilege. He endured countless dinners, official speeches and functions, balls, formal tours, presentations, citations, addresses, visits and letters. His secretary once collapsed under the strain, shortly before meeting the aged Jefferson at Monticello, but for Lafayette this apotheosis was rejuvenating. So, of course, were the very many pretty girls assembled to do him honor. There was "nothing so beautiful," he said, "as in the appearance of the ladies who deigned to come over to meet an old soldier of their country."

When they went to the theater (of which Lafayette was quite fond), the play was interrupted as soon as they were recognized. Veterans of his campaigns tottered in, a military band vainly trying to keep pace with them, to salute the last general of the revolutionary war. Wherever he went he was the guest of the nation. Jefferson wrote that he hoped they would not kill him with their kindness. The one thing that worried Lafayette was that, so often forced to make impromptu replies to an oration recalling his glorious past, he fell back on the same phrases over and over again. His speeches referred to the splendid unity of the past, without mentioning the disillusion of the present. He went alone into Washington's tomb, while a funeral salvo was sounded; he emerged in tears and was presented with a ring containing a lock of his "father's" hair. He was received by Senate and Congress (among the foreign dignitaries he noted the absence of the French ambassador), and was pleased that those kept apart for years by party bitterness came together because of him. And Congress at last showed its pecuniary regard for the "hero of two worlds": it voted him $200,000 as an indemnity for the expenses he had incurred (in the form of stock redeemable in ten years, carrying a six percent rate of interest annually), and a township of 24,000 acres. There were a tiny handful of representatives who voted against these proposals, and they were so attacked in the papers that they presented themselves personally to Lafayette to explain. He said that if he had been a congressman he would have voted against the motion too. Everyone was pleased.

He was not too busy to ignore European politics, and especially the cause of the Greeks (to which Byron gave his life): he arranged a subscriptions for a small steamboat to be sent to them. In France the death of Louis XVIII meant that his old schoolfellow Charles X became king – and he offered concessions that revived Lafayette's hopes for liberalism. He was saddened by news of the death of the Princesse d'Hénin, and he began greatly to miss his family and grandchildren. He could do little to influence his adopted country, but his gout improved. He bravely pursued his life-long campaign against slavery, and in New Orleans received with great warmth the blacks who had fought in defense of the town. In the spring of 1825, while traveling up the Ohio, a great adventure occurred when his boat was shipwrecked. His only anxiety, which was great indeed, was for his son Georges, but once he was safe the general was quite pleased to have lost several hundred letters he should have been answering.

He retained, however, the French-English dictionary he always relied on – and within a month he had six hundred new letters demanding reply.

Lafayette found he could not refuse the offer of a forty-four gun frigate to take him home, which had been named "after a rivulet rather than a river, a defeat rather than a victory, solely to recall my first battle and my wound" – the *Brandywine*. Before he left, in an extraordinary tribute to his contribution to the founding of the republic, three ex-presidents – Jefferson, Madison, and Monroe – gathered to do him honor. The new president, John Quincy Adams, gave a dinner to celebrate the general's sixty-eighth birthday. The president broke with the etiquette forbidding toasts at his table to propose, "The twenty-second of February and the sixth of September, birthdays of Washington and Lafayette." Deeply moved, Lafayette proposed in turn, "The fourth of July, birthday of liberty in the two hemispheres." After a mammoth farewell reception and a final presidential address, the Lafayettes left in September 1825. The inhabitants of Le Havre, where they landed, were just as enthusiastic as they had been the year before. When the general and his entourage got to Rouen, on their way to Lagrange, riotous demonstrations in their favor took place, despite savage police repression. And when they finally arrived home a fête for more than four thousand was given in Lafayette's honor, its costs met from public subscription. Lafayette had recaptured his reputation.

Being a hero, however, has its obligations, and nowhere are these felt more pressingly than in the financial field. A public reputation attracts requests for help, all the more if the subject is renowned for philanthropy as Lafayette was. His memoirs show his generous response to political causes; his unpublished papers are full of pleas for money. In America, especially, while he was the triumphal guest of the nation, dozens of convoluted begging letters were showered on him among the hundreds of testimonials to his achievements. But Lafayette always had an aristocratic attitude to money, perhaps in reaction to the tightness of his childhood, perhaps because, as soon as he came into his fortune, there were always people managing it for him. He gave, even if he had nothing.

America's generous gift to Lafayette was much needed, especially as the earlier grant of 11,000 acres in Louisiana was involving the family in prolonged litigation. Adrienne had always been the best manager in the family, and after she died Lafayette ran up an enormous credit, paying no debts at all between 1802 and 1812. He borrowed money from all kinds of people, many of them wealthy Americans, and offered as security mortgages on Lagrange. Despite this, he also lent money in large quantities. Adrienne had always seen to the welfare of the family's servants and dependents; Lafayette carried on the tradition, and was even more generous than his wife had been to charity. His name was always to be found heading the subscription list of a good cause. Never an extravagant man personally, and very far from being a fashionable dresser, his own expenses were largely the costs of medical treatment to his leg, furnishing the house (which after his last American trip filled up with mementoes and presentations), and having his books leather-bound. Yet, when the time came for the *émigrés* who had suffered during the revolution to be compensated, Lafayette claimed his share. He had always, in fact, denied being an *émigré*, since they had been prepared to fight their own countrymen. He had been a proscribed exile, but however great the distinction, his property had been sold and the money had gone to the state. Adrienne had arranged for Chavaniac to be bought back, but the family had received nothing for the estates that had accompanied it. Lafayette was awarded 325,767 francs 90 centimes compensation. Such sums were always useful.

Lagrange became a comfortable retreat, full of friends and family as well as refugees. Mme de Simiane had retired to Cirey, but her old room was taken over by James Fenimore Cooper, who became so frequent a visitor he even kept his books there. The general was surrounded by grandchildren and great-grandchildren – and he enjoyed the almost constant attention of the attractive Princesse Christine de Belgiojoso. Privately, then, he led a life as full as ever; publicly, he was as active as he had always been. The liberal causes he espoused in old age – from his opposition to censorship to his concrete support for any nation fighting for its independence – mattered as much, if not more, to him as when he was young, and his championing them was more dangerous, and more honorable, because they weren't fashionable. Merely to list them is to downgrade their importance, to give a false impression that they were only routine at the end of a long and crowded life. The fact was that Lafayette remained a fighter at an age when men are supposed to grow moderate. As Charles X put it, "I know of only two men who have always professed the same principles, myself and Lafayette: him as defender of liberty, and me as king of the aristocracy." Both of them grew more uncompromising, the king in defense of his prerogatives, and Lafayette for the unfinished business of the old constituent Assembly. The general stood for the unfulfilled promises of 1789, and he survived long enough to see these become once more radical. His own reputation, enhanced by his energy and never-failing optimism, had been made sufficiently long ago for a new generation to forgive and forget his mistakes, as he had himself forgotten them.

He was ahead of public opinion, as shown by his poor performance when he again stood for election as deputy in June 1827. In fact, he only scraped in. But this did not stop him immediately taking the offensive, as for example when he delivered a rousing oration at the funeral of his old colleague Manuel. The printer, publisher, and bookseller of his speech were all prosecuted, whereupon Lafayette protested that he wasn't included in the accusation and took all responsibility for the speech and its publication. Those who had been held were acquitted and, despite Lafayette's pugnacity, the police said that there was no need to prosecute anyone. But if this might have looked like weakness, or even cowardice, the administration gave little away in response to the demands of the Left. When Charles X was reviewing the national guard he was greeted with cries of "Down with the Jesuits! Down with the ministers! Long live the liberty of the press!" This cocktail of protests resulted in the guard being dissolved, and shortly afterwards the Chamber went with it. Despite widespread ballot-rigging by the government, the new Chamber was more or less equally divided between Right and Left, except for a hard core of extremists on the Right. The new administration offered some concessions to the liberals, but far from enough to quieten their opposition. With the limited franchise and the power of the government to fix the results, the liberals and the Left could never hope to gain power through the ballot box. (Even a subscription dinner for Lafayette in his constituency was harassed by the police.) The opposition therefore demanded a complete reform of the electoral system, which alone would enable them to take office peaceably. Since the administration would not grant such a demand, the impossibility of effective opposition in the Chamber led to preparations for a tough struggle on both sides. There was no open declaration of war, but as the Left gathered support it also got itself organized. It was nearly fifteen years since the last bloody upheaval which had restored the Bourbons: long enough for the slogans of "liberty" and "equality" to have acquired a nostalgic and forgiving glow, rather like their champion Lafayette. In the interval the opposition had grown in strength and influence; while nobody would think of preparing for a showdown without being confident of the ability to win, a war between autocratic privilege and bourgeois importance was inevitable, with the prize being an effective say in government. It is difficult to blame the whole thing on the wooden-headed obstinacy of Charles X: possibly he and his favorite Jules Polignac really believed that a touch of "strong government" was what the people wanted. By one of those misjudgments common to paranoid administrations (which is to say, those who combine inflated feelings of their own rectitude with the conviction they are being persecuted), they underestimated the opposition's support, organization, and resources. Instead of neutralizing the opposition by the traditional method of co-opting them and extending their basis of power, they decided to reduce it and show the people who was really in charge.

The Left organized themselves through committees for electoral reform; one of those which used Lafayette's name as patron was called "Help youself and Heaven will help you." The general believed that the government was sowing the seeds of its own downfall. As he wrote to Dupont de l'Eure, "the French people, in fact, having become more industrialized and landowning than ever before, need a rest; but if one can prove to them that this rest is incompatible with the maintenance of indispensable rights, they will want to have all the rights that belong to them. This favor they can only enjoy through the bad conduct of the government." One of the rights the French workers wanted, incidentally, was that of free wage-bargaining, in order to combat the perennial inflation.

Lafayette was alternatively optimistic and pessimistic. Describing the political situation at the end of 1828 as "three steps forward and two back," he quoted Mme de Staël's remark that "in France one doesn't conspire, one encourages oneself," adding that "today she would have said 'one gives in'." As for conspiring, he may have learned something from his previous failures in that field. He was not, anyway, the Left's sole leader. If it had any cohesion as a movement, it was agreed only on opposition to unfettered royal rule and to an extension of the franchise. The majority wanted the king to change his ministers, who they claimed were misleading him; to them "revolution" was as bad as "republic," which summoned up dreadful memories of the Terror. Then there were those, of whom Lafayette was one, who were convinced that the king would not give way and that he would therefore have to be replaced. Lafayette himself would have preferred a republic, in view of the persistent failures of the Bourbon kings, but he had very few supporters among the deputies. The most powerful advocate of a change of monarch was the banker and opposition deputy Laffitte who was a partisan of the Duc d'Orléans. His money and contacts went into ensuring that, when they made their move, they would have this alternative to Charles X ready and willing, making the change as peaceful and inexpensive as possible. Lafayette was not a party to this: he was for acting first and then letting the people have their say. But as he would never have put himself forward for high office, and while he of course supported the most radical members of the opposition – those, that is, who wanted to do away with the ruling Bourbons if it should prove necessary – he was once more in the position of accepting the initiative, not taking it.

That he was personally popular as an opposition leader was proved by the immensely successful tour he took through the Auvergne, ending in Lyon. Although the government ordered the suppression of all popular demonstrations in his favor, towns were lit up for him, banquets prepared, parties, where lovely ladies abounded, thrown in his honor, and presentations and formal addresses showered on him. (A trip to the west of France planned by the king, on the other hand, was canceled for fear of hostile demonstrations.) For Lafayette it was like America, or, more to his taste, like the old days, before the massacre of the Champ de Mars. His personal survival, and the fact that the principles for which he stood represented the only chance his audience would have of gaining a say in their government, were responsible for his success. Nevertheless he still did not try to present himself as an alternative to the present administration. The political situation worried him, and the air was filled with sinister rumors. In a letter to an unnamed friend (for when the memoirs were published many of his correspondents were still alive, and might not have wished to run the risk of being associated with so notorious a rebel), Lafayette says that these rumors appeared to be worrying even some members of the court, who were warning the liberals not to be too rash. There was talk too of ministerial changes, which the general reckoned was just to distract the liberals from vigorously demanding guarantees of liberty. To his doctor he confided, "What can you do [about the Bourbons]? They are three centuries behind. They are lunatics: Charles X will get himself dismissed, and with a little bit of sense he could have been as happy as a mouse in a pâté."

New elections were held in June 1830: the opposition gained 274 seats, the government 143, with eleven uncommitted. Lafayette, undeterred by his past failures, grew even more uncompromising; after his own re-election he wrote to someone who had lost because he was thought too "emphatic," "the electors still don't realize that it's weakness and not vigor that has caused all the troubles they fear will return." The mood of the opposition was obviously buoyant. When the king was reputed to be about to offer concessions, Lafayette reckoned it was because he had gone to his foreign friends for help and they'd told him he was on his own. Far from there being concessions, however, the king and Polignac, on July 25th, promulgated the Four Ordinances. These dissolved the new Chamber, convoked the electoral colleges to choose a new one, restricted the vote to the richest quarter of the electorate, and banned the publication of any paper less than twenty-five pages long without official authorization. Lafayette happened to be at Lagrange; as soon as he heard the news he hurried to Paris. He again felt called upon to be where the action was.

No one who has not lived through the possibilities of a revolutionary situation, when ideas that were once dangerous and abstract tremble into reality, can understand what it is like to have a second chance. To feel, after years of frustration and despair, that electric mood, to try and shape it so as to avoid the mistakes and compromises of the last time, to sense the possibility of bringing the whole thing to an explosive climax as fulfilling for the nation as for oneself – this was the opportunity now given to Lafayette. It was summer, the students were on holiday, and the legal channels of protest had proved quite ineffective. The barricades went up in Paris, erected by artisans and students to whom Lafayette at once gave enthusiastic support. He was prepared to support violence because he believed the government had violated its charter by issuing the Four Ordinances. In the name of public order, he wanted the violence controlled. The authority and prestige of his support was flattering to the demonstrators, as he was flattered by the warm reception they gave him. The young had no one who could command public support outside their own ranks and generation. And Lafayette was free of any taint of compromise with the government, a rare quality indeed. For far too long the Chamber had been meeting royal fire with nothing but oil. Here in the streets were people prepared to do what Lafayette had always promised, to give their lives for liberty. To be old is to be denied many opportunities: Lafayette found that his youth was restored.

Fighting had already started when Lafayette arrived on the night of July 27th. The royal troops used real bullets against crowds armed only with cobbles, and many were killed on both sides. Those deputies of the Left who were in Paris held a series of meetings in each other's houses. The majority of them were for stopping the fighting, but they had no more control over what was going on in the streets than did the king. During July 28th, the first of the "Three Glorious Days," the City Hall changed hands several times. By that evening it was held, at some cost, by the insurgents. At a meeting of his colleagues that night, this success emboldened Lafayette to say that a revolution was taking place, and that it was no longer possible to observe "strict legality." The immediate reaction of the majority was to try and halt the revolution at once. Lafayette asked that they declare themselves in permanent session, as if they represented the Chamber before it had been dissolved, and that they discuss the formation of a provisional government. He of course shared his colleagues' concern that they take control over what was happening, but he also grew impatient with their indecisiveness. His name, he proclaimed, had, with his consent, been placed at the head of the insurrection, and while he wanted his fellow-deputies to endorse his actions, if by the following day they had decided nothing he said he would regard himself as free to act as an ordinary individual.

It is difficult to know how far Lafayette himself could have controlled events, for the Revolution of 1830, unlike that of 1789, was planned, organized, and well financed. Laffitte was already in touch with the Duc d'Orléans, and he also acted as intermediary in a vain attempt to bribe the military commander of Paris to join their side. The deputies showed themselves as anxious to control Lafayette as they were to control the people on the barricades, and the latter were only held together by the common threat of the royal troops. But the demonstrators would not disband unless the royal troops were withdrawn. As that appeared unlikely to happen, the deputies had to consider re-forming the national guard, the only force at their command capable of securing order. As this would have been counter to the royal decrees that had previously dissolved the guard, to set it up again was to assume a part of the royal prerogative – a revolutionary step, but necessary in case those manning the barricades were to turn against the deputies, as well as the crown. But calling up the guard would mean strengthening Lafayette's position, for he was not only the deputy hailed with most enthusiasm in the streets, but also the guard's revered founder. Many of his colleagues had no desire to add to his popularity.

The general spent the night of July 28th inspecting the barricades. As he clambered over all obstructions – at the age of 73 – he received an emotional welcome. A group of five deputies meanwhile saw the Duc de Raguse, the military commander of Paris, which had officially been declared under siege. The five asked for the repeal of the Ordinances; the duc asked that they recall the people to their duty. The deputies replied that they had no such control over the people, and that if the king didn't change his mind, they would have to support the resistance (as if, at that stage, there was much they could do about it). Raguse, by Lafayette's account (and he was not one of the deputation), asked if the deputies wished to see Polignac, who was apparently in the next room. They said they would have no objection; Raguse went out, but soon after returned and said talks would be "superfluous." With the administration obviously closed to compromise, the deputies, in order to control the initiative that had been taken in the streets, were forced to adopt Lafayette's suggestion and form a provisional government. The next step was to call up the national guard.

They could not do this without Lafayette, and on July 29th, at Laffitte's house, he was given the necessary authority by his fellow-deputies. Although he already felt the Orléanist faction to be busy, he refused a request to nominate a municipal commission to run the affairs of the capital, a task he left to his colleagues. Once more he turned down the chance to take the initiative because of the delicacy of his principles. He went at once to the City Hall and showed himself to an immensely enthusiastic crowd, at the same time as the Tuileries and the Louvre were taken by the "patriots." Unless the government was prepared to massacre enormous numbers of

Parisians, victory in the capital for their opponents appeared inevitable. This galvanized the king no less than the deputies, for neither wanted control to slip out of their hands. There were cries from the crowd around the City Hall for Lafayette to accept the post of commandant-general of the national guard – an exact repeat of July 1789. He accepted. He immediately took steps to organize the defense of the city, for "to do nothing would be a betrayal." "My conduct at 73 years of age shall be what it was at 32," he proclaimed, and his first official order of the day ended, "Liberty will triumph, or we shall die together."

The deputies, again at Laffitte's house, appointed five commissioners to consult with the Chamber of Peers, just as placards began to appear all over Paris calling for the Duc d'Orléans to be made king. With Lafayette fully occupied, Laffitte was free to maneuver on behalf of d'Orléans, and when a message came from the king offering to repeal the Ordinances and call new elections, it was Laffitte who persuaded the deputies not to accept. Obviously aware of what was afoot, for the king had sent him a message containing the same offer, Lafayette dispatched his colleague Odilon Barrot to the deputies from his headquarters at the City Hall. What most concerned him, he said, was that there would be divisions among the people of Paris as to what to do next, that the fate of the nation might be decided without the help of the Chambers, and that therefore it was surely better *not* to name a new head of government (for to name him without consultation smacked of divine right) before calling a general assembly and publicly stating the guarantees of liberty that were to surround the crown.

But this attempt to consult the general will, according to Lafayette's principles, was forestalled by the arrival at Laffitte's house of the deputation sent to the Peers, with the agreed idea of calling on the Duc d'Orléans to be lieutenant-general of the kingdom. The compromise title was to give Charles X a face-saving chance to abdicate of his own accord. D'Orléans himself was a little wary, and consulted Talleyrand, who urged him to accept. Amid the deputies, meanwhile, the most powerful argument swaying the group to accept d'Orléans – one which revealed remarkably little faith in Lafayette – was that Paris might fall apart at any moment. The future of France apparently had to be decided immediately. Benjamin Constant suggested going to the duc with a declaration containing their required guarantees for a new charter, and this was unanimously agreed.

On July 30th, with the worst of the fighting over (and some two thousand dead, the vast majority "patriots"), Lafayette was asked for an explicit reply to give to the royal troops who wanted to know the position of their master following his offer of concessions. Back came the answer that "any reconciliation is impossible, and that the royal family had ceased to reign."

According to fellow-deputy Odilon Barrot, Lafayette was now indisputable master of the situation. Certainly he was the idol of the crowds who were masters of the streets. His sympathies were for an American-style republic, in which case he would almost certainly have been provisional president. But the enthusiasm of a crowd is a fickle thing, as he knew better than anyone. To take on the problems of the nation, at his age, was no easy task, especially in the face of probable hostility from his fellow-deputies. Besides, rather than being hamstrung by the routines of political power he preferred gloriously to champion his principles.

There was a story that some of those surrounding him suggested that he take the crown. But whatever his feelings about the hereditary monarchy, he was a legitimist, and he had no dynastic claims whatever on the throne. So he dismissed the proposal in a joke, quoting the Maréchal Saxe's remark when offered membership of the *Académie Française*: "It would become me," he said, "as well as a ring would a cat."

If he were, as some of his admirers claimed, in a position to decide the fate of France, he was always a man for doing things the proper way. To declare that the king had ceased to reign was a fact; to announce a republic with only the crowds around the City Hall to back him up was a different matter. There was already a provisional government and a municipal authority; the future had to be decided, in Lafayette's view, by them. The alternative was to risk a divisive civil war among the opposition, and that would have been unthinkable. Uncertainty and prolonged disorder always led to some form of dictatorship, and he had had enough of that. He could have gone to the deputies and attempted to convince them that a republic was the only answer, but he did not. He sent messages instead, perhaps because he was too busy, or simply too resigned, to do otherwise. If he had any personal ambitions, which is doubtful, he deliberately forfeited them. On July 31st, he explained the summoning of the Duc d'Orléans to the people of Paris by saying it had been done by the deputies who were soon to meet in regular session, in conformity with the mandate of their constituents. He ended by saying, "Liberty, equality, and public order has always been my motto: I shall be faithful to it."

The Duc d'Orléans, however, knew on which side his bread was buttered, and as soon as he arrived at the Palais-Royal, he sent a message congratulating Lafayette on his role and asking if he could come and see him on the morrow. When the duc arrived, those around the City Hall were hostile: Orléanist placards had been torn down, and there were shouts of "No more Bourbons!" If ever Lafayette had wanted supreme power, this was his moment to take it. He did not. He received the duc and escorted him up the stairway, with the deputies and the duc's supporters following. The crowd outside continued to shout against d'Orléans and for Lafayette. He had to choose between accepting the wish of demonstrators with nothing but their enthusiasm to support him, and a claimant to the throne endorsed by his colleagues, whose democratic right to make such a choice Lafayette no longer bothered to dispute. He made a dramatic gesture reminiscent of his gallantry with Marie-Antoinette during the October days. Placing a tricolor in the arms of the duc – the standard that had not been seen in France for fifteen years, and which Lafayette had restored – he took him out onto the balcony and, in full view of the crowd, embraced him. The spectators applauded, and cries of "Long live the Duc d'Orléans" were followed by "Long live Lafayette!" As Chateaubriand put it, "Lafayette's republican kiss made a king."

But the shouting did not mean that everything was over. To appease the more critical of his supporters, Lafayette undertook to see the duc and obtain from him guarantees of liberty. The outcome of this meeting was described by the general as "a popular throne surrounded by republican institutions." "The constitutional monarchy," he is reported to have said, "is the best of republics." He regarded the duc as having made solemn promises about the future, embodying all the principles for which Lafayette was celebrated. The duc did not regard himself as so bound, though he was too prudent at this point to say so.

Lafayette still wanted to limit the functions of d'Orléans as lieutenant-general until a new constitution could be prepared, but the majority of deputies were against him, and in the interests of unity he dropped the matter. Then Charles X abdicated in favor of his grandson. The Duc d'Orléans convoked the Chambers in his new capacity, and announced the abdication, without mentioning the grandson. The throne was then offered to him, and he accepted. Lafayette could claim to have been responsible for the creation of Louis-Philippe, for he persuaded the "citizen-king" to adopt the name, instead of the more formal Philippe VII. The revolution appeared once more to be over.

Lafayette then accepted the post he had refused in 1790, that of commandant-general of all the national guards of France. A new government was appointed, and after one week Lafayette's ordinance that had opened the ranks of the guard to all citizens capable of bearing arms was annulled. History repeated itself with the utmost fidelity: the bourgeois citizens who had once more taken power no more wanted a possibly hostile armed force in their midst than they had wanted to court the old dangers of a republic. Some heated spirits tried to organize demonstrations around the Chamber of Deputies. Lafayette pledged his life to defend the deputies' freedom to debate. With obvious misgivings he wrote to a friend that, if everything were not perfect, liberty had made great gains, and would make still greater ones. It was, certainly, the first time the people's elected representatives had taken it upon themselves to strip the crown from one Bourbon and offer it to another. But success in revolutions goes to the best organized, not the most popular – and there had been no one as organized as Laffitte.

Having identified himself with the new administration, Lafayette felt that at least he could work from within to secure those principles of liberty for which he had so long fought. This was a new role for him, equivalent to abandoning the role of referee to take up that of goal-keeper. But no ministry was offered to him; he remained, as before, only in charge of the guard.

The transfer of power from elderly autocrat to pear-shaped "citizen-king" was almost deceptively easy, though one must not forget it had cost the lives of at least two thousand people in the capital alone. "I have done what my conscience dictated," wrote Lafayette, adding, "If I have made a mistake, it is in good faith." The honey-moon period allotted to all new regimes was enjoyed by no one more than he. At a municipal banquet in his honor Lafayette uttered his routine warning about the dangers of divisiveness and anarchy, but he went on in terms that reflected his own pride as well as his audience's: "You are no longer the descendants of the old regime, amazed to learn that you possess rights and duties; you are the children, the pupils of the revolution, and your conduct in these great days of glory and liberty has just shown the difference."

When Polignac and other former ministers of Charles X were arrested, disturbances broke out. Some wanted to execute their former governors as scapegoats; some, doubtless, used the occasion to protest at the neat way in which the transfer of power had been tied up, with precious little reference to the citizenry. Lafayette, as the living embodiment of law and order, asked his fellow-citizens "not only in the exercise of his public duty, but as a mark of personal friendship, not to give themselves over to these apparent disorders." Such was his prestige that his wishes were respected and his orders obeyed.

Amid the revival of the splendors of '89, which included a spectacular review of the national guard at the Champ de Mars, Lafayette did not omit to speak out, as a deputy, in favor of those liberal principles that had always sustained him. His energy una-bated, he argued for the abolition of the death penalty, the hereditary peerage, and the traffic in slaves. But the cause in which he was most active was that of the struggle for independence, wherever a nation

273

fought against tyranny. In this he clashed with the wishes of the new government.

The supporters of the "republican throne" were anxious for peace in order to secure their prosperity, and they were determined to remain neutral in foreign affairs. The European powers were satisfied because one Bourbon was much like another, and as long as France didn't start interfering with the "balance of power," which naturally supported despots rather than republicans, the nation would be safe from foreign intervention. The advent of the "citizen-king," who wisely relied on advice from the Rothschilds to increase his personal fortune (in return for which he granted them a monopoly over the raising of government loans) ushered in an age of un-paralleled speculation and corruption. Lafayette, in his aristocratic way, was indifferent to the management of money, a subject of which he was totally ignorant. But the cause of independence meant a lot to him, and it was only with difficulty that he restrained himself when he had to explain the official policy of "non-intervention" to those "patriots" in Belgium who declared their independence from Holland, or those fighting the throne of Spain, who looked to him for material support. He went some way toward easing his conscience by raising money on his own account for the Spanish patriots, but it was a far cry from the full-blooded support he would have liked to have given. He was told that if he refused to sanction measures of which he disapproved, he would lose his popularity. "I regard popularity," he cannily replied, "as the most precious of treasures, but as with all treasures, one must know how to enjoy it as well as how to get rid of it."

One of the past debts he did attempt to pay was to raise a monu-ment to the four sergeants of La Rochelle who had gone to the scaffold as victims of the abortive Charbonnerie plot. He also had presented to the king those who had been political prisoners since 1815. He cleverly managed all of this during the brief period when the king was being particularly nice to him. When Joseph Bona-parte wrote from his exile in America pressing the Napoleonic cause on Lafayette, the general replied reminding his friend that although Louis-Philippe carried the "distressing" name of Bourbon, it was at least a guarantee against war, and moreover four months of the new regime had convinced Lafayette that it conformed to the will of the majority. To an anonymous correspondent, in November 1830, he confided his unhappiness at having to quarrel with ministers, and his sadness that the new administration was not going in the direction he wanted it to. He complained at the way that they managed the Chamber, and, in another revealing letter, he wrote that many supporters of the present order had become irritated by him and were trying to discredit him in order to lessen the consequences of getting rid of him. "One was more at ease on the barricades," he noted ruefully. He hinted that Belgian patriots had made overtures to him to see if he would accept their crown; his reply was that he had done enough for republicanism by contributing to the foundation of the French throne. Plainly he was himself becoming disillusioned.

In December there were violent demonstrations over the trial of Charles X's ministers. Lafayette calmed the first of these simply by walking among the demonstrators, and afterwards delivering his old lecture on the dangers of liberty degenerating into licence and the terrors of anarchy. He preferred, at this stage, law and order to revolution, and he pressed for universal suffrage so that democratic expression would be given the widest play. Perhaps his experience of the machinations of power had reinforced his old repugnance for politics and the limits on conscience imposed by responsibility. Opposition was preferable, even though he recognized that power lay with the politicians. Though the support of the public sustained him, he was tired and saddened. And the king's new ministers, realizing that Lafayette's attitude held no danger for them, moved to get rid of him. His opposition within government circles was a nuisance, and his constant reference to principles interfered with the smooth running of business. At least in opposition he would be powerless, for although he undoubtedly had a large following he would surely never use it against the appointed government, and while he might attack them verbally, he could never claim to influence them, as he could from the inside.

Once the renewed outbreaks of violence around the ex-ministers' trial had been brought under control by the national guard, the government began to discuss its reorganization. The Chamber passed a motion abolishing the post of commandant-general of the national guards of the whole kingdom, which Lafayette held. It was thought that the ministry would at least give the general the Paris guard, but the most that Laffitte, then president of the council, would offer was the purely honorary post of commandant. This was a direct insult: Lafayette refused the offer and on December 25th handed in his resignation. Louis-Philippe sent three notes during the day, protesting his affection for Lafayette and maintaining his ignorance of what was happening (which could not have been true). That night king and general met. Lafayette said that by resigning he would "remove the screen between the king and the public which his [Lafayette's] mandate had erected," but added that he took the opportunity to retire from a "false position" that associated him with "deviations from the July Revolution." He went to the Chamber and explained that his resignation was not a matter of personalities, but that he would now be better able to express his opinions. With this renewed declaration of opposition he found himself once more back in private life. Resignations are sad, but his must have been something of a relief. His beloved guard was reorganized the following spring, limiting membership to those who paid direct taxes, and bringing its administration and finance under government control. The administration was pretty sure of itself, but it had to be certain.

Lafayette described the Chamber's conduct towards him as a *coup* mounted by those who had no wish to see the promises of the July Revolution fulfilled. In his farewell address to the guard, however, he emphasized that his opposition was not to be taken as the basis of a *coup* against the government. Never a man for sulking in his tent, he took an energetic part in the Chamber's debates, and became the most enthusiastic supporter of the Polish fight for independence then beginning in earnest. (He demanded from Laffitte a yes-or-no answer to his request for a government loan to the Polish patriots – and got the expected "no.") When the Italians attempted to rise against their foreign masters they asked Lafayette for support; he carefully explained to them the French non-intervention policy, but attacked in the Chamber the government's inaction in the face of other powers intervening in these struggles. His name was first on the list of subscribers for a new daily paper "representing the energetic opposition of the Left," and proposing to support "the rights of Poles, Spanish, Portuguese, Italians, Belgians, and all who cry out for national independence." He claimed to receive more than two hundred letters a day, many expressing opposition to the government, and he became involved in one more subversive organization that the administration regarded with the greatest mistrust: the "National Association," formed with the ostensible purpose of protecting France against foreign intervention and preventing a return of the elder branch of the Bourbon dynasty. The Poles made him an honorary member of their national guard in recognition of his support. When he attended the anniversary celebrations of the July Revolution at the Panthéon, at which the king appeared not to recognize him, he had the satisfaction of hearing the crowds shout his name coupled with that of Poland.

In June 1832 the opposition to the government made itself once more felt on the streets, after the funeral of the opposition deputy General Lamarque. That the French appeared peculiarly prone to periodic outbreaks of violence was perhaps less due to national character than the habit their governments had of loudly proclaiming their principles – following the precedent of 1789 – and then blatantly traducing them. Louis-Philippe's character had professed religious toleration, abolished censorship, prohibited the king from suspending the law, and preserved Lafayette's beloved two-chamber system. It also suppressed the hereditary peerage, but replaced it with a nominated upper chamber, swapping the old aristocracy for the new plutocracy.

The vote was given to all those who paid 200 francs in direct taxation – some three percent of the male population. Then strict control over the press was progressively introduced, and the opposition stringently policed. It did not seem, therefore, as if the "martyrs" of the "Three Glorious Days" had given their lives for very much and this explains the violence of the demonstrations around Lamarque's funeral.

Lafayette disapproved of the violence because it stood so little chance of success. When a crowd of young people surrounded his carriage and demanded that he give the order to advance, he said that his first order was to obey his own conscience and good sense. He then went home, but the presence of dragoons led to further excitement among the crowd that remained. The national guard was called, the king appeared on horseback and declared, quite unnecessarily according to Lafayette, a state of siege, and some eight hundred people were killed or wounded. Lafayette was accused of inciting the violence by putting a wreath on top of the old sans-culotte symbol, the red cap of liberty. He replied very tartly that he had always been against the violence symbolized by the red bonnet, but that he did protest against the counter-revolution then in progress, which reminded him of so many of the illegalities and immoralities of its predecessors. Tactically, what he most regretted was that if the demonstration had passed off peacefully, the king might not have been able to ignore the protests of some 30,000 citizens. The violence, however, for which Lafayette blamed his old enemies the "factions," gave the government an excuse for cracking down on the opposition.

The general most regretted the apathy of his fellow-citizens who were not engaged in street-fighting, and the "light-hearted way" in which they allowed themselves to be stripped of their liberties. He felt that the government was taking them back to the days of 1814, and in concert with the foreign powers was trying to crush the spirit of liberty at home and abroad. He believed it to be his duty and, more significant, his destiny, to speak out against these things, but he admitted that "luckily for my peace of mind, my personal position and my age exempt me from all agitation." One thing that delighted him, amid the encircling political gloom, was that he won, in the autumn of 1832, four prizes at the local agricultural show near Lagrange.

He was not left in peace even at Lagrange: a Polish refugee whom he was sheltering there, M. Lelewel, was arrested at the château by police and taken away. Lafayette protested in the Chamber, but was told that Lelewel was a troublemaker who had broken his promises not to visit Paris at a time when the government was anxious to keep all political refugees as far away from potential trouble-spots as possible. Lafayette of course continued to champion all victims of oppression, retaining that peculiar and complex combination of optimism and romanticism, of outspokenness and moderation, that characterized his years in opposition. One example of his sense of honor was his reminder to a colleague that they had to defend the liberty of the press for those papers hostile to their views, as well as for those they could call friendly. And a final example of his optimism was his letter to his colleague Dupont de l'Eure, following the death in a duel of their fellow member of the opposition, Dulong. Urging his friend not to despair or to resign, but to wait for better times, he went on confidently, "they will arrive, be certain of that, and it would be distressing for the future of our country to let ourselves be carried away by a perfectly natural feeling of disgust" – a serene comment for a man of seventy-six.

Despite his age, Lafayette insisted on attending Dulong's funeral, both as a friend and as a public gesture of opposition. During the long walk to the cemetry he caught a cold. He himself did not regard his illness as serious, even though it kept him in bed for more than two months. Apart from four doctors, he was attended by the lovely Princesse de Belgiojoso, for whom he had what Dr Cloquet described as "a pure love." (She was something of a necrophiliac, but perhaps Lafayette did not suspect this.) His illness did not prevent him from keeping up with political events, and one of the things which saddened him was to hear from President Andrew Jackson of the increasingly bitter party divisions of his adopted country, America. As he got better, he was allowed out, but on a carriage ride he was caught in an icy shower and his condition rapidly deteriorated. Reading of a report of his own death in the *Gazette de Suisse*, he warned his doctors to be wary of newspapers. His closest companion was a little white dog given him by another lady admirer: it never left his bed. Nor did his sense of humor. When one of his doctors referred to him as the father of the French people, he smiled and said, "Yes, to the extent that they don't do a thing I tell them." Bulletins on his progress were published by the liberal press. Two days before he died he sent his grandson to the Princesse de Belgiojoso to tell her he missed her. At 4 A.M. on May 20, 1834, he lapsed into a coma; by 4.30, clutching the medallion containing Adrienne's portrait, he was dead.

An all-party delegation of deputies was chosen to attend the funeral, a normal practice in mourning a dead member. The government took the strictest precautions against demonstrations of any sort, lining the funeral route with troops. So tight was their control that in all the vast procession the only incidents occurred when some young people tried vainly to break into the cortège. Lafayette was buried next to his wife in the cemetery of Picpus; sprinkled on his tomb was earth from the United States, which found enough unity to declare official mourning throughout the nation. This was more than his own country did for him.

Considering the length and diversity of Lafayette's life, as well as the amount that has been written about him, it is not easy to conclude with a remark that is adequate both as summary and tribute. I shall content myself with saying that he was a man reckless enough, stubborn enough, persistent enough, and finally, courageous enough, never to give up hope.

Notes on Sources

LAFAYETTE'S OWN *Mémoires, correspondence, et manuscrits,* 6 vols (Paris, 1837–1838) add up to some 3325 pages, and were edited by his family to show the great man's devotion to liberty and the domestic virtues. They are nevertheless overwhelmingly accurate in factual detail, when compared to other contemporary material, and every biographer must rely on them.

There is a considerable amount of unpublished manuscript material written by or to Lafayette. The Library of Congress's *Quarterly Journal* (April 1972) vol. 29, no. 2, performed an immensely valuable service by listing all the collections in America which contain papers on Lafayette, as well as publishing extracts from the most important. But the most dramatic find in recent years has been the rooms full of manuscripts discovered by the Comte and Comtesse de Chambrun in the château of Lagrange. René de Chambrun is in the process of sorting these out himself, and it will take several years. He allowed André Maurois to see some of the papers in order to write a life of Adrienne de Lafayette (which was published in 1960), but no one else will be permitted to examine the material until it has all been catalogued. M. de Chambrun was kind enough to talk to me about some of the papers he has sorted, and Maurois revealed more about Lafayette's father and a fair amount about the marquis's private life. If all this material makes little difference to the known facts about Lafayette, it certainly adds color to a picture that has too often been just black-and-white.

Of the general biographies of Lafayette, Brand Whitlock's is the most readable (2 vols, New York, 1929), and Etienne Charavay's the most painstaking (Paris, 1898). S. W. Jackson published a thorough study of the material written about him (*Lafayette: A Bibliography,* New York, 1930). But no one working in the field can avoid deep indebtedness to the labors of Professor Louis Gottschalk, who since the 1930s has been engaged in an exhaustive biography of Lafayette, of which four volumes have appeared to date, taking the general to the age of thirty-three. (There is also, among other related studies, Gottschalk's *Lady-in-Waiting* [Baltimore, 1939], which is about Aglaé d'Hunolstein.) The first of these definitive tomes is *Lafayette Comes to America* (Chicago, 1935), and I can best pay tribute to its scholarship by saying that I have relied on it when in doubt.

One of Lafayette's descendants, Edmond, allowed a "Fragment d'Autobiographie" to be published in *La Haute Loire* (September 6, 1883), in which the marquis writes briefly of the happiness of his years at Chavaniac, the beast of Gevaudan, and some incidents during his schooling. But even then the picture is sketchy. Local books and historical pamphlets, such as those in the libraries of Clermont-Ferrand and Le Puy, tell one little more than Lafayette did. A visit to the Auvergne itself is more useful, though the modern "improvements" made by the present owners of Chavaniac – The La Fayette Memorial Inc. – are, to say the least, controversial. The château still seems to me gloomy, but it does show Lafayette's (or his architect's) somewhat garish taste in decoration. On sale at the château (the village itself has now been renamed Chavaniac-Lafayette) is *Au Pays de La Fayette*, an inaccurate but useful pamphlet by Ulysse Rouchon, who also wrote a study of the general's neighbor La Colombe, *Un Ami de La Fayette: Le Chevalier de La Colombe* (Paris, 1924). A descriptive book on the château was written by Henri Mosnier, *Le Château de Chavaniac-Lafayette* (Le Puy, 1883). As to the family's winter mansion in Brioude, it is now a gray block of flats and a petrol station – only a plaque on the wall indicates its origins. The château of Vissac is in ruins. For some interesting information on the social habits of the local gentry, there is a booklet on the nearby Vivarois nobility, *Essai sur la noblesse vivaroise* (Aubenas, 1913) by Ch. du Besset.

It was the fashion for men and women of intellect to publish memoirs explaining or defending their conduct and paying homage to their ancestors. Adrienne de Lafayette's own *Notice sur la vie de sa mère Mme la Duchesse d'Ayen* was published with her daughter, Virginie de Lasteyrie's *Vie de Mme de Lafayette,* 2nd ed. (Paris, 1869), and both works are as unaffected as Adrienne herself. The Comte de Ségur published his *Mémoirs, ou souvenirs et anecdotes* in three volumes in 1825–1826: Lafayette read and approved them. The Marquis de Bouillé's *Mémoires* were edited by M. Berville and M. Barrière, 2nd ed. (Paris, 1821): Lafayette reviewed them (the note appears in the fourth volume of his own memoirs) very politely. As for life in Paris and at court before the revolution, far more interesting than the modern digests (such as the Hachette "Daily Life" series) are the observations of contemporaries. L. S. Mercier was one of the wittiest and most penetrating, *Tableau de Paris,* new ed. 12 vols (Amsterdam, 1782–8), while the bookseller S. P. Hardy gives a deadpan middle-class view in *Mes Loisirs,* tome 1 (1764–73); ed. MM. Tourneaux and Vitrac (Paris, 1912). There are also the disapproving observations of Marie-Antoinette's goings-on at court by her mother's ambassador: *Marie-Antoinette: Correspondence secrète entre Marie-Thérèse et le comte Mercy-Argenteau,* ed. A. d'Arneth and A. Geffroy, 2nd ed., 3 vols (Paris 1875).

More modern works I found useful were *La Noblesse de France et l'opinion publique au 18e siecle* by Henri Carré (Paris, 1920); on life in the army, *La Vie militaire sous l'Ancien Régime* by Albert Babeau, 2 vols (Paris, 1889–90); and on what people were reading and saying about liberty, *L'Esprit révolutionnaire en France et aux Etats-Unis* by Bernard Fäy (Paris, 1925). On Lafayette's contribution to the American cause, there is the mighty, if partisan, work of Henri Doniol, *Histoire de la participation de la France a l'établissement des Etats-Unis d'Amerique,* 5 vols (Paris, 1886–90).

The best source for Lafayette's actions and opinions during his first two trips to America is the *Letters* in volume one of his memoirs; they are more accurate than his commentaries, which were written later, at varying intervals, and which tend to put him in the best possible light. To compare his first impressions with the realities of the situation, I found Carl Bridenbaugh's *Cities in Revolt: Urban Life in America 1743–76* (New York, 1955) very helpful. Russel Blaine Nye's *The Cultural Life of the New Nation 1776–1830* (New York, 1960) was full of fascinating information. The ideological background is discussed in Bernard Bailyn's *The Ideological Origins of the American Revolution* (New York, 1968), as well as *The Life of the Mind in America* by Perry Miller (New York, 1965) and Staughton Lynd's *Intellectual Origins of American Radicalism* (New York, 1968: this is especially interesting on Jefferson and his views on property). Two collections of documents, though overlapping, told me more than volumes of commentary: *The American Revolution 1763–83,* edited by R. D. Morris (New York, 1970) and *The Revolution in America 1754–88,* edited by J. R. Pole (London, 1970). The most useful and succinct single-volume history of the period is, in my opinion, J. R. Alden's *The American Revolution* (New York, 1954).

I relied heavily on D. S. Freeman's *Washington* (a one-volume abridgment of the original seven was edited by Richard Harwell, New York, 1968) for a clear, thorough, and balanced picture of the situation from the commander-in-chief's point of view. And on military life, especially the difficulties, privations, misery, and exhilaration of being a soldier in the Continental army, I value *The Private Soldier under Washington* by Charles K. Bolton (New York, 1902), who was the first to sift through the contemporary records and journals and emerge with a clear, if sketchy, picture. It seems strange that there has not been more research among such records, so that the attitudes and actions of ordinary people involved in the fight for independence are more clearly revealed. This is being done for those involved in the French Revolution, but for the American, Jesse Lemisch's essay "The American Revolution seen from the bottom up," in *Towards a New Past,* edited by Barton J. Bernstein (New York, 1968) does not seem to me to augur well.

The American and French Revolutions are compared in Crane Brinton's once-provocative, but now I think outdated, book *The Anatomy of Revolution,* revised edition (New York, 1965). Then there is de Tocqueville's *The Ancien Régime and the French Revolution*

(Paris, 1865; New York, 1955). Finally there is Professor Gottschalk's volume on this period, *Lafayette Joins the American Army* (Chicago, 1937).

The second volume of Lafayette's memoirs runs from 1782 to 1790. Professor Gottschalk takes three volumes to cover almost the same interval: *Lafayette and the Close of the American Revolution* (Chicago, 1942); *Lafayette Between the American and the French Revolution* (Chicago, 1950); and, with M. Maddox, *Lafayette in the French Revolution: Through the October Days* (Chicago, 1969). One could argue, if one dared, with Professor Gottschalk's interpretation of events, but his thoroughness in tracking down every relevant fact is breath-taking. He demonstrates, interestingly, that Lafayette himself was rarely wrong on details, even though he naturally put his own gloss on things.

For the period immediately preceding the revolution, and during the revolution itself, court life was described by Mme de La Tour du Pin, who published her memoirs under the title *Journal d'une femme de cinquante ans*; they have been translated by Félice Harcourt (London, 1969). Restif de la Bretonne was a friend of L. S. Mercier, and as a social observer no less sharp. There is also the complete contrast between Gouverneur Morris's *Diary and Letters,* ed. A. C. Morris, 2 vols (London, 1889, and the English acidity of Arthur Young, *Travels in France during the years 1787, 1788 and 1789* (Suffolk, 1792; 4th ed., London, 1892). Among modern historians, Richard Cobb is unique, not only in the sources he examines, but in the way he writes about them: for Lafayette's period there is *The Police and the People: French Popular Protest 1789–1820* (London, 1970). I also found three books by George Rudé particularly helpful on the role of the crowd in contributing to the French Revolution: *Paris and London in the 18th Century* (London, 1952), *The Crowd in History 1730–1848* (New York, 1964), and *The Crowd in the French Revolution* (Oxford, 1959). As to the general books on the subject, I can only say that the three I enjoyed most amid the acres of print on the subject were Georges Lefebvre's *The Coming of the French Revolution* (first published in 1939, it was translated by R. R. Palmer and published by Princeton in 1947); J. M. Thompson's miraculously lucid *The French Revolution* (Oxford, 1943); and Alfred Cobban's *A History of Modern France,* 2 vols (Harmondsworth, Middlesex, 1957, 1961).

Once Lafayette took the position of commandant-general of the national guard, a shoal of pamphlets attacking and defending him appeared. Almost every one is listed in the *Catalogue de l'histoire de la Révolution Française,* 7 vols (Paris, 1936–69) by André Martin and Gérard Walter, or in Walter's *Répertoire de l'histoire de la révolution française* 2 vols (Paris, 1941, 1951). Nevertheless you come across ones that have been wrongly categorized, or wrongly replaced, if you are permitted to venture among the stacks at the Bibliothèque Nationale. The British Museum has an almost overlapping selection of pamphlets that is slightly easier to get at. Otherwise, I found useful Marcel Reinhard's *Nouvelle Histoire de Paris: La Révolution 1789–99* (Paris, 1971), which is full of details difficult to find elsewhere.

When Lafayette was in prison some of his letters naturally got mislaid: Jules Thomas published some of these in *Correspondence inédite de La Fayette 1793–1801* (Paris, n.d.). For the family's life in exile, A. Callet's memoir *A. P. D. de Noailles, Marquise de Montagu*, 5th ed. (Paris, 1866) is invaluable.

My information on the organization of the Charbonnerie I got from *Le "Complot" des Sergents de la Rochelle* (1969) by Jean Baylot.

Stendhal's picture of Lafayette appears in *Souvenirs d'Egotisme*, (new ed., Paris 1950); Jules Cloquet's in *Souvenirs sur la vie privée du Général Lafayette* (Paris, 1836). On the Princesse de Belgiojoso's peculiarities see Marro Praz, *The Romantic Agony* (2nd edition, London, 1951). Lafayette's secretary A. Levasseur (whom Stendhal found uncouth) published his account of their American trip, *Lafayette in America 1824 and 1825*; translated from the French, 2 vols (New York, 1829). Finally B. Sarrans, who became Lafayette's secretary during the Three Glorious Days of 1830, published his version of what happened in *Memoirs of General Lafayette and of the French Revolution of 1830*, translated, 2 vols (London, 1832). It is naturally partisan: only Lafayette himself, it seems, could maintain an equable tone when writing about those who wronged or disappointed him. His prose style is not elegant, as Ségur's was, nor exciting, nor free from confusion. But considering the millions of words he wrote, the picture his six volumes of memoirs give of his life and feelings is still the best starting-place for those in search of his personality.

Index

Names with the particle *de* or *d'* have been alphabetized under the main element of the name: e.g., for Vicomte de Noailles, *see* Noailles, Vicomte de. The Marquis de Lafayette has been abbreviated to "L." in the sub-headings.

DATE DUE

AP7 '80			
AP 9 '82			
AP 22'88			
MR 12'84			
GAYLORD			PRINTED IN U.S.A.